The Panic of 1857
and the Coming of the Civil War

The Panic of 1857
and the Coming of the Civil War

JAMES L. HUSTON

Louisiana State University Press
Baton Rouge and London

Designer: Laura Roubique Gleason
Typeface: Caledonia
Typesetter: G & S Typesetters, Inc.
Printer: Thomson-Shore, Inc.
Binder: John H. Dekker & Sons, Inc.

An earlier version of a portion of Chapter Two appeared in *Agricultural History*, LVII
(1983). Portions of Chapter Three appeared previously in *Mid-America*, LXV (1983).
Portions of Chapter Four appeared previously in *Historian*, XLVI (1984), *Journal of
American History*, LXX (1983), and *Mid-America*, LXV (1983). Earlier versions of
Chapter Eight appeared in *Agricultural History*, LVII (1983), and *Rhode Island
History*, XLI (1982).

10 9 8 7 6 5 4 3 2 1

Library of Congress Cataloging-in-Publication Data

Huston, James L., 1947–
    The panic of 1857 and the coming of the Civil War.

    Bibliography: p.
    Includes index.
    1. Depressions—1857—United States.   2. United
States—Economic conditions—To 1865.   3. United States—
Politics and government—1857–1861.   I. Title.
HB37171857.H87   1987   338.5'42   87-2705
ISBN 0-8071-1368-9

The Press gratefully acknowledges the support of the Dickerson Fund of
the history department at the University of Illinois, Urbana.

Lovingly dedicated to my mother, Esther May Huston, and to the memory of my father, Lawrence B. Huston

Contents

Tables

Preface

In a bibliographic essay appended to their masterful work *The Civil War and Reconstruction*, James G. Randall and David H. Donald noted that the one monograph that dealt with the Panic of 1857 was "inadequate." The problem from Randall and Donald's perspective was that although the economic aspects of the Panic of 1857 had received attention, the political ramifications had not. The only published works that have focused upon the relations between the monetary collapse and antebellum sectional tensions have been an article by Samuel Rezneck and a superb chapter by Allan Nevins in *The Emergence of Lincoln*. Despite the obvious need for a thorough study of the Panic's impact upon social and political developments, the scholars who have been attracted to the 1857 crash have continued to analyze its economic dimensions.[1] Within the last decade there has emerged an interest in discovering other facets of the Panic of 1857, but there has of yet been no extended treatment. This book is intended to remedy that deficiency.[2]

1. James G. Randall and David H. Donald, *The Civil War and Reconstruction*, (2nd ed.; Boston, 1969), 748; Samuel Rezneck, "The Influence of Depression Upon American Opinion, 1857–1859," *Journal of Economic History*, II (1942), 1–23, hereinafter cited as *JEH;* Allan Nevins, *The Emergence of Lincoln* (New York, 1950), I, 176–97; George Washington Van Vleck, *The Panic of 1857: An Analytical Study* (New York, 1943); Melvin W. Ecke, "The Fiscal Aspects of the Panic of 1857" (Ph.D. dissertation, Princeton University, 1951); Peter Temin, "The Panic of 1857," *Intermountain Economic Review*, VI (1975), 1–12.

2. William Gerald Shade, *Banks or No Banks: The Money Issue in Western Politics, 1832–1865* (Detroit, 1972); Bruce W. Collins, "The Politics of Particularism: Economic Issues in the Major Northern States of the U.S.A., 1857–1858" (Ph.D. dissertation, Cambridge University, England, 1975). The latest synthesis of the Civil War and Reconstruction era, James M. McPherson, *Ordeal by Fire: The Civil War and Reconstruction* (New York, 1982), has but minimal reference to the Panic of 1857.

There are a number of compelling reasons to investigate the financial collapse of 1857 besides the one of fitting the event properly into the chronology of escalating sectional animosities. In the early part of the twentieth century, progressive historians offered an economic explanation for the coming of the Civil War, which postulated that the conflict arose from a clash between southern plantation lords and northern industrial capitalists over the formulation of federal economic policy. This interpretation soon fell before the onslaught of new historiographical schools, but by the late 1960s the concept of economic forces in American history, if not explicit economic determinism, had been reinvigorated by a group of scholars known as the New Left. In the scholarly battles over the origins of the sectional conflict, however, few historians ever chose to investigate whether the Panic lent any pertinent evidence to the debate. That is ironic, for few episodes could be devised that would reveal more about sectional or class motivations in the antebellum era than a financial crash in the midst of the bitterest years of sectional recrimination.

Closely related to the subject of the contribution of the Panic of 1857 to sectional bitterness is the matter of how economic questions arising from the financial suspension influenced political thought and behavior. It is generally conceded that between 1854 and 1857 the slavery extension issue, in its many guises, dominated national politics. In this study I examine how the parties initially reacted to the Panic of 1857 and to the sudden appearance of economic issues, how the parties incorporated these issues into their platforms and campaign efforts, and how the issues were invested with the appropriate ideology. In particular, I scrutinize the Republican handling of economic policy in light of the mongrel character of the party's coalition: did Republicans simply represent born-again Whiggery, or were they able to engraft a "free labor" ideology on old Whig economic programs and make them acceptable to non-Whig elements in the party? Most secondary literature properly claims that the Republicans gained from the economic problems generated by the business recession. That affirmation rather begs the question of the political impotency of the Democracy—North and South—in the realm of economic affairs. Another matter that concerned me was whether a discernible, quantitative effect upon popular voting could be tied to the Panic. By selective quotation it is quite easy to paint a (false) picture of a nation in 1857 and 1858 seething with economic complaints. I hope to place the problem of economic issues in context and to locate specifically those areas that most probably reacted to the business downturn.

Two other themes have greatly informed the writing of this manuscript. One involves the subject of economic thought as it existed in the antebellum decade. When I began this project I decided that it would be necessary to determine how contemporaries understood the functioning of their economic system, partly out of a desire to discover whether any postbellum additions to economic theory drew their inspiration from the 1857 experience. What I found was an elaborate and rather logical way of thinking about people's behavior and business operations. These views explained what had often been a mystery to me: by what convolution of logic did nineteenth-century thinkers and politicians believe that high tariffs or a specie currency would cure depressions? I discovered that the realm of economic thought included other and more exciting discussions as well. Not only was it apparent that political leaders shaped their programs largely by the state of free trade and protectionist theory but also that the preachings of economists touched the most hotly contested subjects of the era: slavery, abolitionism, the fate of labor, and southern attitudes toward patriarchy. Economic thought does not, I believe, resolve the interpretative questions that engulf these subjects, but it does offer a different and rewarding perspective.

The last theme I pursue in the study is one that occurred to me when I finished reading Eric Foner's excellent study on early Republicanism.[3] If the Republicans had such a blatant, staunch free labor ideology, expressed in innumerable books, pamphlets, and speeches, how did it fit with the rising industrialization in the United States and the increasing number of industrial operatives? For the last two decades, labor history has been in ferment; the result has been an outpouring of monographs on the condition and culture of the American working class. But seldom have the authors of these studies connected working-class unrest with national political trends, especially in the antebellum decade.[4] One of my goals is to unearth whatever linkages there may have been between worker discontent, Republican free labor ideology, and the coming of the Civil War.

I have drawn largely upon traditional sources and methods in order to explore the impact of the Panic of 1857 upon political attitudes and behavior, although I have employed some quantitative techniques to

3. Eric Foner, *Free Soil, Free Labor, Free Men: The Ideology of the Republican Party before the Civil War* (New York, 1970).
4. See Ronald W. Schatz, "Review Essay: Labor Historians, Labor Economics, and the Question of Synthesis," *Journal of American History*, LXXI (1984), 93–95, hereinafter cited as *JAH*.

detect voting tendencies in certain elections. This monograph is a national and not a local study, and only those developments which entered national awareness are investigated. I have relied heavily upon newspapers, periodicals, and manuscript collections of national figures—the "elite" portion of American society and politics. The historiography of the past twenty-five years has emphatically revealed the limitations of the traditional approach: local developments may have been, and in some ways undoubtedly were, more important to nineteenth-century Americans than congressional law making; and editorialists and politicians usually occupied a different social position than the mass of voters and therefore did not necessarily articulate the sentiments of the citizenry. I recognize those shortcomings but have decided to live with them. The Civil War was a national event, and it seems rather dubious to me to argue that this cataclysm arose from idiosyncratic local affairs. It may certainly be true that national political leaders did not reflect the concerns of their constituents; nonetheless, I find history without reference to contemporary opinion to be unintelligible or at least truncated. There is danger in imputing the attitudes and sentiments of some for others, but I shall risk making the assumption.[5]

This book approaches the Panic of 1857 and its aftermath in a narrative fashion. Chapter 1 provides the economic and political background necessary to understand the state of economic issues in the United States and the essential machinery of finance. In Chapter 2 the chronology of the Panic is presented, for the timing of business dislocation in the various regions conditioned the manner of public response. This chapter also provides the story of the bread riots of 1857, a by-product of the collapse that heightened dialogue over the question of the fate of labor, and the market reporters' explanation of the banking failure. The varied reactions to the Panic are given in Chapter 3, with emphasis on the Democratic and Republican struggle to decide how to wield the crash to their advantage. Attention is also given to the general public's discussion of the reasons for the failure and to the deliberations of sectional agitators. The topics of the free trade versus protectionist framework of economic thought, the southern paradox over free trade

5. The charge that "elite" political opinion was unrepresentative of the public has never been actually proven. Several studies have shown that political figures have had vastly different socioeconomic profiles than their constituents, but no investigation has yet demonstrated systematically and quantitatively that the opinions of the elite differed appreciably from the views of the citizenry.

economics and patriarchal slavery, and the rising concern over the fate of the industrial worker are discussed in Chapter 4. These themes are integrated with the growing strength of economic issues in the political arena for the remainder of the book. Chapter 5 portrays the rise of the economic issues after the Lecompton Constitution was disposed, and Chapter 6 evaluates the role the Panic played in the northern congressional "revolution" of 1858. These electoral effects are followed in Chapter 7, when the Democrats were given the opportunity to respond to the altered electoral conditions. Chapter 8 completes the story of the nation's recovery from the Panic, demonstrates how southerners began to use the Panic to attract northern conservatives to their cause, and stresses the prominence of worker unrest in 1859 and 1860, symbolized by the massive shoemakers' strike in Lynn, Massachusetts. Chapter 9 examines Republican, northern Democratic, southern Democratic, and conservative campaign goals in 1860 and how the Panic helped shape each party's strategy. The conclusion, Chapter 10, offers a summary and a consideration of how the Panic of 1857 fits into the historiography of Civil War causation.

Acknowledgments

In the long and arduous process of putting this manuscript into finished form, I have incurred a great number of intellectual and personal debts. Winton U. Solberg, Walter L. Arnstein, Clark C. Spence, Richard C. Rohrs, LeRoy H. Fischer, H. James Henderson, and Kenneth M. Stampp read the manuscript in various stages of completion and offered useful suggestions (frequently, it must be confessed, concerning length). A number of anonymous reviewers perused these pages, and though I found many of their criticisms exasperating, on the whole they raised fair questions and aided immensely in improving the presentation and analysis. Librarians at the Historical Society of Pennsylvania, the Library of Congress, Duke University, the Virginia Historical Society, and the Illinois Historical Survey were always courteous and accommodating. I would like especially to praise a system and a group of librarians without which I suspect most historical endeavors would never be completed. The system is Interlibrary Loan and the librarians are those overworked and underpaid souls who staff it. Without their diligence, this book could never have been written; the system and the people in it are altogether admirable. Most of the early drafts of this book were typed by myself, but Dawn Carr and Jean Stiemke, secretaries for the Oklahoma State University History Department, graciously volunteered to "process" the final copy. I have been the recipient of much sound advice and courtesy from the staff of the Louisiana State University Press, and I would especially like to thank Editor Elizabeth L. Carpelan for her skillful editing, and Senior Editor Margaret Fisher Dalrymple and Managing Editor Catherine F. Barton for their enthusiasm toward my work. In the years I labored on this monograph, I received constant encouragement and inspiration from my wife, Kathy. Besides buoying up my sometimes flagging spirits, she also performed the unrewarding task of putting up with me through the time-consuming process of revising and retyping. Finally, my greatest thanks and appreciation goes to my mentor, Robert W. Johannsen. His discussions with me sharpened my focus and forced me to defend my ideas more precisely and circumspectly; his advice was indispensable. Although I have benefited from numerous criticisms and suggestions from many individuals, all errors of fact and interpretation are, unfortunately, my own.

The Panic of 1857
and the Coming of the Civil War

ONE / A Pensive Nation

The course of political, social, and economic developments in the United States for the three decades prior to 1860 largely determined the effects that the Panic of 1857 had upon sectional attitudes. The economic conditions that the Panic exposed, and which became the justification for certain sectional appeals, were in large part the results of an economic growth based increasingly upon regional specialization. Likewise, the many-faceted political response to the 1857 monetary failure was a product of the attitudes that individuals had formed during previous banking crises. The financial crash evoked fears about the future stability of society that had troubled numerous Americans ever since the country had set upon the path of industrialization in the 1820s. In many respects, then, the Panic of 1857 did not originate new sectional viewpoints or economic theories; instead, it most often reinforced and intensified prevailing ones.

Several circumstances helped to generate the Panic of 1857 and the depression that followed. Of these, the one that captured the most immediate attention was the banking system. As a result of banking troubles in the first half of the nineteenth century, the public perceived of and treated financial institutions differently from other business pursuits. Whereas ironmongers, textile owners, and farmers were generally left to their own devices with regard to labor policies and production techniques, state governments attempted to goad bankers into prudent behavior. Few Americans heeded the arguments of economic theorists that the law of supply and demand would regulate the issuance of currency just as surely as it determined the price of textile products. Banking operations seemed altogether mysterious to many citizens, and not a little sinister, and numerous Americans demanded that the financial community be regulated.

By the 1850s the states and not the federal government controlled the activities of the banks. Under the leadership of Andrew Jackson, the Democratic party in the 1830s had terminated the Second Bank of the United States, the one federal financial institution that exercised some measure of restraint over the rest of the nation's banks. In its place the Democrats established the financially impotent Independent Treasury, whose sole function was to hold the government's revenue. Although the federal government, at least when in the hands of the Democratic party, found ample justification for divorcing the national government from the monetary system, the state governments never questioned either their right or their duty to supervise the banks within their boundaries. The difficulty for the state authorities was producing the appropriate legislation.

After the Panic of 1837, most state legislators concurred that their principal objective was to stop the reckless emission of paper money. This desire to curb the proliferation of bank note currency had by the 1850s produced a startling diversity of banking practices. Several states created state banking systems in which a central agency ensured that the institutions did not stray from prudent currency emissions. Other states continued to grant special charters to banks, following the custom established at the founding of the republic. New York had perfected a system known as free banking that was first pioneered in Michigan. Free banking laws permitted unhindered entry into the field without special permission from the state legislature. This did not mean, however, that the government relinquished all its regulatory capabilities. The authorities required prospective financiers to amass a certain amount of capital, to deposit stocks and bonds with a state comptroller to ensure the integrity of bank note issues, and to maintain a specie reserve. The free banking system became popular in the 1850s but did not displace the chartered or state banks. Indeed, much of the confusion in monetary affairs in the antebellum years arose from the circumstance that various states, like Virginia, had all three systems operating simultaneously.[1]

1. Bray Hammond, *Banks and Politics in America from the Revolution to the Civil War* (Princeton, N.J., 1957), 556–63; Paul B. Trescott, *Financing American Enterprise: The Story of Commercial Banking* (New York, 1963), 30–34; Leonard C. Helderman, *National and State Banks: A Study of Their Origins* (Boston, 1931), 11–34, 42–66, 96–97, 109–10, 117, 120; John Jay Knox, *A History of Banking in the United States* (New York, 1900), 457–58, 528–34, 699, 732–36, 782–85.

There were other arrangements, some taken by the bankers themselves, to impose stability upon American finance. Since 1818 the banks in New England operated under the auspices of the Suffolk system in which member institutions maintained a stated amount of specie at Boston's Suffolk Bank in order that their notes would be received at par. Louisiana legislators took a different approach; in 1842 they revised their banking statutes and required banks to maintain a 33-1/3 percent specie reserve ratio between assets (bullion) and liabilities (bank notes plus deposits). New York bankers developed another institutional safeguard. They created a clearinghouse association in 1853 by which the member banks could clear accounts with other city banks at the close of the week. If any establishment had acted irresponsibly, the excess notes would be immediately detected because the culprit bank would not be able to settle its affairs. Regardless of local arrangements, New York's banks supplied the only centralizing influence in American finance. Those banks had grown with the city's commerce, and since the city was the focal point of American trade, the city's banks became the center of American finance. By presenting bank notes from other areas of the country for redemption, New Yorkers acted as a brake on the irresponsible expansion of paper money.[2]

Americans in the 1850s believed that they had solved most of the ills to which the financial community was prone. They failed to notice, however, the appearance of new banking practices that created dangers different from those faced in the 1830s. For example, the development of demand deposits largely went uninvestigated. Depositors placed funds in a bank which they could withdraw at their pleasure, but bankers tended to use deposits as a source to expand their loans. The peril was that during a period of uncertainty depositors would withdraw their money and leave the banks without the specie needed to meet their other obligations, thus causing a liquidity crisis.[3]

One of the peculiarities that would play an important role in the nation's adjustment to the Panic of 1857 was regional economic specialization. The southern slave states concentrated their business efforts on the agricultural staples of cotton, tobacco, rice, and sugar. In the

2. August C. Bolino, *The Development of the American Economy* (2nd ed.; Columbus, Ohio, 1966), 193–95; Stephen A. Caldwell, *A Banking History of Louisiana* (Baton Rouge, 1935), 66–86; Hammond, *Banks and Politics*, 549–56.

3. Fritz Redlich, *The Molding of American Banking: Men and Ideas* (2nd ed.; 1947; rpr. New York, 1968), II, 1–7.

West and the Great Lakes region, the population generally engaged in the cultivation of wheat and corn and the processing of pork. New England and the Middle Atlantic states of Pennsylvania, New Jersey, and New York housed the nation's industrial plant and also provided the mercantile and financial services needed to run the economy. None of these regions were wholly devoted to one pursuit, and most areas had a considerable degree of diversification. But the patterns of trade that had developed for each section were of great importance. The South relied on the Northeast for financial and mercantile operations, but since its principal market was England, the South's prosperity was more dependent upon England's economic health than upon any other circumstance. The West and the Northeast, however, were being tied together by a railroad network, and trade between the two regions was brisk. One result of this commerce was that easterners who invested in western railroads or who sold manufactured goods to the region's inhabitants would be subject to any misfortune that befell that area. In 1857 that fact had not yet impressed many individuals because for nine years the West had undergone rapid economic expansion.[4]

An important element of the American economy in the 1850s was the abdication of all levels of government from responsibility for supervising the business system. In the years following the War of 1812 local and state governments along with the national administration had tried to push the country into the machine age by granting tax exemptions to desirable types of enterprises, subscribing to stock issues, and adjusting tariff rates. The disasters that overtook many state and county governments after the Panic of 1837 disabused local legislators of their designs of fostering economic progress by governmental fiat. The federal government also participated in this resolve to allow the private economy to function without legislative interference. Only in the areas of tariff rates and public land prices could the federal government influence the economy. Yet even in these instances the national government was sacrificing its powers: the Walker tariff of 1846 materially reduced the high customs duties of the tariff of 1842, and many individuals hoped to see the tariff duties either lowered to an absolute minimum or abolished entirely. Public sentiment in the 1850s looked favorably

4. Van Vleck, *The Panic of 1857*, 6–7, 17–19, 24–25; George Rogers Taylor, *The Transportation Revolution, 1815–1860* (New York, 1951), 80–94, 166–67, 169–70; Allan Nevins, *Ordeal of the Union* (New York, 1947), II, 194–201.

upon the idea of allowing actual settlers to obtain without charge portions of the public domain. The only exception to the gradual adoption of a laissez faire policy by the federal government was the call for government aid in the construction of a railroad to the Pacific.[5]

There were many indications in the 1850s that all was not right with the economy. Throughout the decade imports had been greater than exports, and consequently the country had suffered a continuous drain of precious metals.[6] In addition to the difficulties associated with foreign trade, Americans had experienced some abrupt business gyrations between 1850 and 1855. There had been a sharp contraction at the start of the decade and an even steeper one in 1854. The nation witnessed with foreboding a frenzy of land speculation in the middle of the decade, a circumstance that reminded many citizens of the events that had preceded the Panic of 1837. Although the nation remained in a prosperous condition until 1857, stock prices, railroad investment, land sales, and immigrant arrivals had all peaked between 1853 and 1855. After 1855 the indices began a downward movement.

One feature that generally escaped notice and calculation was the effect of the Crimean War upon the American economy. Westward expansion had resulted in the peopling of the Great Lakes region and the construction of a railroad system to connect the east coast with the western states. But the occupation of the majority of the inhabitants was agriculture, and their productivity was so great that it threatened to overwhelm the domestic market. Just when it appeared that the western boom was going to collapse, however, Europe went to war. The Crimean conflict upset Europe's normal agricultural markets and permitted Americans to supply the foodstuffs once provided by Russia and various central European states. This unexpected demand for

5. Herman E. Krooss and Paul Studenski, *Financial History of the United States* (2nd ed.; New York, 1963), 122–23, 132–35; Oscar Handlin and Mary Flug Handlin, *Commonwealth: A Study of the Role of Government in the American Economy: Massachusetts, 1774–1861* (Rev. ed.; Cambridge, Mass., 1969), 182–202, 224; Henry N. Broude, "The Role of the State in American Economic Development," in Harry N. Scheiber (ed.), *United States Economic History: Selected Readings* (New York, 1964), 116–30; Carter Goodrich, *Government Promotion of American Canals and Railroads, 1800–1890* (New York, 1960), 171 and *passim*.

6. Joseph C. G. Kennedy (comp.), *Preliminary Report on the Eighth Census* (Washington, D.C., 1862), 192–93, 234–35; U.S. Department of Commerce, Bureau of the Census, *Historical Statistics of the United States: Colonial Times to 1970* (Washington, D.C., 1975), 1020.

American western grains buoyed the economy between 1854 and 1856. But in March 1856 the Crimean War ended, and few Americans foresaw what peace in Europe would entail for the economy.[7]

Many facets of the American reaction to the Panic of 1857 were governed by the fact that the economic endeavors of the different sections had produced different social arrangements. Southern prosperity depended on the use of slave labor, and that institution had permitted unique customs and ideas to evolve there. The population of the North was subject to influences that more or less failed to penetrate the slave states. The advent of industrialization, with its creation of new social classes, and the impact of large-scale immigration gave northern society, particularly the Northeast, problems with which the South had little acquaintance. The Panic of 1857 would highlight these contrasting social characteristics and advance them to the forefront of the sectional controversy.

The outstanding feature of southern civilization was the presence of the institution of slavery. In 1860, approximately four and a half million persons of African descent dwelt in the United States, of whom nearly four million were slaves. Although slaves were used in numerous types of activities, they generally labored in the Deep South cultivating the staples that brought the region its prosperity—cotton, rice, sugar, and tobacco. Not only did the slaves constitute about one-third of the South's total population, they also represented an investment of roughly three billion dollars. That southern slavery stood for such a large portion of the South's inhabitants, involved such huge amounts of capital, and accounted for so much of the region's income, were more than ample reasons for southerners to defend the institution.[8]

7. Those writing about the business cycle in the 1850s have erected various breaking points in the downturn of the economy. I have followed largely the analysis of Albert Fishlow, *American Railroads and the Transformation of the Ante-Bellum Economy* (Cambridge, Mass., 1965), 114–15. See also Douglass C. North, *The Economic Growth of the United States, 1790–1860* (Englewood Cliffs, N.J., 1961), 70–71, 105, 137–40, 213; Jeffrey G. Williamson, *American Growth and the Balance of Payments, 1820–1913: A Study of the Long Swing* (Chapel Hill, 1964), 111–20.

8. Kennedy (comp.), *Preliminary Report on the Eighth Census*, 134–35; Clement Eaton, *A History of the Old South*, (2nd ed.; New York, 1966), 212–26, 402–403; Paul Wallace Gates, *The Farmer's Age: Agriculture, 1815–1860* (New York, 1960), 118–22, 138; Gerald Gunderson, "The Origin of the American Civil War," *JEH*, XXXIV (1974), 916–17; Gavin Wright, *The Political Economy of the Cotton South: Households, Markets, and Wealth in the Nineteenth Century* (New York, 1978), 10–43, 90–91, 139–44.

Exactly what effect slavery had on the South's social structure re-
mains a matter of controversy. It would appear that the institution
produced a more stratified, class-conscious society than that in the
North. There was greater inequality in the distribution of wealth in
the South than elsewhere in the nation, and the southern upper class
seemed more disposed to assume the trappings of an aristocracy. But
slavery did not create a monolithic region in which only one class and
one interest prevailed. Southern society had its share of complexities
and internal conflicts as did every section in the country. On one topic,
however, the South did act as a monolith: the necessity of preserving
the peculiar institution.[9]

Two aspects of southern society owed their existence distinctly to
the presence of slavery and became prime subjects of discussion in the
aftermath of the Panic of 1857. One was the development of an argument to justify slavery. Since the late 1820s various southerners had
been promoting the idea that southern slavery was not a necessary evil
but a positive good. Several rationales were given in defense of slavery: Africans were a naturally inferior people, the bondage of the African promoted white equality, slavery was the only means by which
cotton could be produced, the scriptures sanctioned the institution,
and slavery was a means of controlling a vengeful and barbaric people.
In the 1850s another idea grew in strength: slavery was a far more hu-
mane means of ensuring an adequate material existence for the laborer
than the wage system practiced in the North.[10]

The other unique characteristic of southern society that slavery promoted was a virtual unanimity on the part of southerners in the 1850s
that the power of the federal government remain weak. This convic-

9. Eugene D. Genovese, *The Political Economy of Slavery: Studies in the Economy
& Society of the Slave South* (New York, 1965), 247–58; Ralph A. Wooster, *The People in
Power: Courthouse and Statehouse in the Lower South, 1850–1860* (Knoxville, 1969),
4–15, 105–13; Fletcher M. Green, *Constitutional Development in the South Atlantic
States, 1776–1860: A Study in the Evolution of Democracy* (Chapel Hill, 1930), 149–64;
Stephen Hahn, *The Roots of Southern Populism: Yeoman Farmers and the Transforma-
tion of the Georgia Upcountry, 1850–1890* (New York, 1983), 16–49; J. Mills Thornton,
III, *Politics and Power in the Slave Society: Alabama, 1800–1860* (Baton Rouge, 1978),
20–58, 204–27.

10. William Summer Jenkins, *Pro-Slavery Thought in the Old South* (Chapel Hill,
1935), *passim;* Richard Hofstadter, *The American Political Tradition and the Men Who
Made It* (New York, 1948), 79–90; Wilfred Carsel, "The Slaveholders' Indictment of
Northern Wage Slavery," *Journal of Southern History,* VI (1940), 504–20, hereinafter
cited as *JSH.*

tion came naturally to southern Democrats who had always espoused the national creed of states' rights and a restricted national government. By the 1850s the Democrats had become the dominant party of the Deep South, despite a persistent albeit faltering Whig opposition, and thus their view of federal relations became the region's view. Moreover, the accretion of Whigs into the Democracy in the early part of the 1850s—for example, Alexander H. Stephens and Robert Toombs—did not alter the party's general demand for a strict interpretation of the Constitution. Only the border state Whigs kept alive the ideal of an energetic government. Behind the South's generally unified stand on the observance of states' rights was a fear prevalent among political leaders that an increasingly powerful federal government could affect the health of the peculiar institution. Thus most southern representatives and senators opposed free land for western settlers, protective tariffs, bounties for manufacturers, river and harbor improvements, and aid to education. Sometimes southerners perceived that these programs directly threatened the existence of slavery by damaging its profitability; at other times they felt that these schemes endangered the peculiar institution by enlarging the scope of the federal government's powers. The result was that southern political figures were the most vocal proponents of laissez faire policies in the nation.[11]

Northerners did not have the single dominating economic and social institution that southerners had, but they were heavily influenced by two mighty forces: industrialization and immigration. Of the many alterations the advance of the machine age made in the United States, one of the most important was the creation of a class of factory workers. In the late 1820s the industrial workers had noisily announced their appearance in economic life by forming unions, which usually enjoyed only a fleeting existence. Another wave of unionism struck the North in the 1840s, but the movement fell prey to the dreams of middle-class reformers. By the 1850s labor leaders had refined their goals and focused union activities upon higher wages, shorter hours, and better working conditions. An indication of the growth and success

11. Roy M. Robbins, *Our Landed Heritage: The Public Domain, 1776–1936* (Princeton, N.J., 1942), 169–72; Robert Royal Russel, *Economic Aspects of Southern Sectionalism, 1840–1861* (Urbana, Ill., 1923), 151–72; David M. Potter, *The Impending Crisis, 1848–1861*, ed. Don E. Fehrenbacher (New York, 1976), 234–40; William J. Cooper, Jr., *The South and the Politics of Slavery, 1828–1856* (Baton Rouge, 1978), xi–xv, and *passim*; Allen Kaufman, *Capitalism, Slavery, and Republican Values: Antebellum Political Economists, 1819–1848* (Austin, Tex., 1982), xxvi, 82–84.

of the union organization effort was the establishment of three permanent national craft unions in the 1850s: the Typographical Association (1852), the Hat Finishers' Association (1854), and the Stonecutters' Association (1854). But the surge of worker unrest was a troubling phenomenon for the rest of northern society. By the antebellum decade, northerners realized that the number of factory laborers was destined to grow until the operatives became a major element in society. But northerners feared that the workers might demand—and possibly obtain through the nation's democratic political machinery—a restructuring of the economic system. Thus by 1857 northerners were pondering the question of providing for the welfare of the free laborer without sacrificing the practices of free enterprise capitalism.[12]

The other unsettling factor in northern society was the infusion of vast numbers of immigrants. Nearly three million foreigners came to the United States in the 1850s, principally from Germany, Ireland, and England. While the new arrivals brought with them needed skills and muscle, they posed a major problem for the natives. Often the customs of the newcomers clashed with the practices of American citizens. This was particularly true in regard to religion. Many of the new arrivals belonged to the Catholic church, which prior to 1845 had not been a major part of American religious life. Protestants often reacted to the increased Catholic numbers with bigotry and prejudice. In addition to the religious problem, the immigrants often vied with American workers for jobs, which heightened ethnic animosities. One indication of the intensity of ill will the natives held for the newcomers was the formation of the American, or Know-Nothing, party in the early and middle years of the decade. Members of this party sought to eliminate the influence of immigrants in American politics by changing the naturalization laws. Although the American party enjoyed national support, immigration was transforming northern society, not the slaveholding South.[13]

The Panic of 1857 occurred when the principal topic of political debate was the extension of slavery into the territories. The issue had become

12. Philip Taft, *Organized Labor in American History* (New York, 1964), 34–58; Joseph G. Rayback, *A History of American Labor* (Rev. ed.; New York, 1966), 92–105.

13. Kennedy (comp.), *Preliminary Report on the Eighth Census*, 18–19; Ray Allen Billington, *The Protestant Crusade, 1800–1860: A Study of the Origins of American Nativism* (New York, 1952), 262, 288–314, 322–44; Michael F. Holt, "The Politics of Impatience: The Origins of Know Nothingism," *JAH*, LX (1973), 309–31.

the center of attention in 1846 when David Wilmot, Democratic representative from Pennsylvania, proposed that slavery be prohibited in all land acquired from Mexico. Although a compromise on the subject was achieved in 1850, the problem refused to disappear. Stephen A. Douglas reignited the furor over the expansion of slavery when he introduced the Kansas-Nebraska Act in 1854, which afforded southerners the opportunity to take their slaves above the sacrosanct Missouri Compromise line. This deed brought the Republican party into existence, the party's members uniting behind the demand that the federal government should exclude slavery from the territories. After 1854 the Republicans' insistence that slavery be confined to its former boundaries became the cornerstone of the party's platform. Prior to 1857 Republicans attacked slavery and its extension on legal and moral grounds, and revealed as well a deep-seated fear that the continued growth of the peculiar institution would erode northern freedom and prosperity. Although Republicans often criticized slavery's economic backwardness and its stranglehold on beneficial federal legislation, they seldom used concrete economic issues as a means to attract voters, for the health of the economy from 1854 to early 1857 operated against such a strategy.

The decade of the 1850s was unkind to the Democratic party. In local and state contests the Democracy confronted a host of moral and ethnic issues—prohibition, moral reform laws, immigration—that siphoned off popular support for the party among Protestant natives. On the national level, the party was wracked by the territorial problem. Northern Democrats generally adhered to the ideas of Stephen A. Douglas, who advocated a policy of noninterference on the part of the federal government. He insisted that western settlers be allowed to determine the question of slavery for themselves. But southern Democrats desired greater assurances that the peculiar institution would be allowed to expand and that it would be treated in the territories the same as any northern institution. The struggle between northern and southern Democrats for the proper stance on the territorial issue ultimately drove many out of the party. Despite other issues that weakened (or strengthened) the party, the Democracy never could shake the death grip the issue of slavery extension had on national leaders, and hence could never escape the hold the controversy had on the future well-being of the party.[14]

14. The political events of the 1850s have been related in a number of good histories. For general works see Randall and Donald, *The Civil War and Reconstruction;* Nevins,

The Republican party, in contrast to the Democrats, had several characteristics that the 1857 monetary collapse would accentuate. The essential Republican argument about slavery derived from the teachings of abolitionists. Although the abolitionists exhibited a concern for the plight of the slave and testified against racial prejudice, they had also concocted a theory postulating that slaveholders ultimately sought to seize control of the federal government, extinguish civil liberties, spread slavery throughout the nation, and lower the condition of the free white worker to that of the slave. This became known as the Slave Power conspiracy. The Republicans seized the idea and based their campaigns upon it—although the Republicans more strongly emphasized the benefits that would accrue to white northerners from curtailing slavery than the justice that would be rendered to the slave. This concept easily accommodated economic issues.[15]

Another facet of the Republican party that would clearly emerge from the financial crash of 1857 was its coalition nature. To some extent political abolitionists, free soilers, ex-Democrats, Whigs, and nativists had coalesced by 1857 to ward off what they felt were the aggressions of the Slave Power. Whereas the territorial issue was divisive for the Democrats, it was the sole unifying factor for the Republicans. But Republican unity only extended to the question of slavery in the territories; on nearly all other matters the party members followed the dictates of their political heritages.[16]

Electoral results revealed two important attributes of the political world before the Panic of 1857 became a topic of discussion. In the election of 1856 James Buchanan was elevated to the presidency because he had carried the solid South plus California and four crucial northern states—Pennsylvania, Indiana, Illinois, and New Jersey. Democrats knew that future successes depended upon keeping these

The Emergence of Lincoln, and Ordeal of the Union; Potter, The Impending Crisis; McPherson, Ordeal by Fire. For a novel interpretation of the rise of the slavery question because of the disintegration of the second party system, see Michael F. Holt, The Political Crisis of the 1850s (New York, 1978), 40–118, 151–52.

15. James Brewer Stewart, Holy Warriors: The Abolitionists and American Slavery (New York, 1976), 75–86; Larry Gara, "Slavery and the Slave Power: A Crucial Distinction," Civil War History, XV (1969), 5–18, hereinafter cited as CWH; Russel Blaine Nye, Fettered Freedom: Civil Liberties and the Slavery Controversy, 1830–1860 (Urbana, Ill., 1972), 316–17; David Brion Davis, The Slave Power Conspiracy and the Paranoid Style (Baton Rouge, 1969), 64–65, 72–81.

16. Foner, Free Soil, Free Labor, Free Men, 103–225; Richard H. Sewell, Ballots for Freedom: Antislavery Politics in the United States, 1837–1860 (New York, 1976), 304–10.

northern states in the Democratic fold, while Republicans realized that the capture of these states was the indispensable prerequisite for their rise to national dominance. Thus the states of Pennsylvania, Indiana, Illinois, and New Jersey became the focal point of political strategy. The second factor influencing American politics was the strength of the nativists. In the crucial states the Know-Nothings held the balance of power but refused to coalesce with either the Republicans or the Democrats, the Know-Nothings believing both parties guilty of extremism and sectionalism. Yet a majority of the American party members had a Whig background; they were, in short, vulnerable to an appeal based on economic issues.[17]

The United States entered the year 1857 with a considerable amount of wariness and foreboding. Franklin Pierce in his last annual message to Congress warned the nation of the growing rift between the sections, naming specifically the Republican party as the agent of discord. Congress engaged in an extensive debate over the message, members of the respective parties flinging accusations and aspersions at one another. The Congress, however, found sufficient time to pass a new tariff. Imports into the United States had been so great that treasury coffers were overflowing and taking precious metals out of circulation. Nearly everyone agreed that to reduce the treasury surplus the tariff had to be lowered. Certain manufacturers saw this as an opportunity to remove the import tax on raw materials and thereby lower production costs. But instead of becoming an enactment to protect American industrial interests, the measure which Congress finally passed instituted a general reduction of all import duties.

When James Buchanan took the oath of office on March 4, 1857, he promised the citizenry prosperity and an end to the strife over slavery. Buchanan's hopes for prosperity arose mainly from the experience of the last few years, but as to sectional wrangling he counted on a definitive ruling by the Supreme Court on a case involving the slave Dred Scott. The new chief of state, however, relied on more than simple faith, for he had contacted members of the tribunal to express his desire to bring the territorial issue to a close. A few days later the court

17. Potter, *The Impending Crisis*, 255–65; Roy Franklin Nichols and Philip S. Klein, "The Election of 1856," in Arthur M. Schlesinger, Jr., Fred L. Israel, and William P. Hansen (eds.), *The Coming to Power: Critical Presidential Elections in American History* (New York, 1972), 91–117.

rendered its decision: Dred Scott could not plead in federal courts because Negroes were not citizens and had virtually no rights under the Constitution. Chief Justice Taney, who delivered the majority opinion, further declared that the Missouri Compromise was unconstitutional and the Congress had no authority to exclude certain types of property from the territories. The Republicans were furious. The rationale for their party's existence consisted of halting the spread of slavery, and with this decision the Supreme Court had barred Republicans from legally fulfilling their mission.

During the spring months of 1857, two important movements surfaced. New York City banks greatly increased their lines of discounts. This development, plus the extent of foreign goods pouring into the nation, raised fears of an economic collapse among some jittery commentators. Meanwhile, a showdown approached in Kansas. Buchanan had sent Robert J. Walker, career Democrat and ardent land speculator, to Kansas as territorial governor. The free-soil faction felt oppressed by those favoring slavery and hence refused, for various reasons, to vote in a June election to determine delegates to a constitutional convention. Proslavery advocates thus won the battle for delegates. For tactical reasons the proslavery constitutional electors chose to wait to draft a constitution until the territorial legislative elections were held in October. Walker had already determined that the majority of the people residing in Kansas did not desire slavery but could nonetheless be enticed into the Democratic party. Unfortunately the Kansas proslavery faction decided upon a desperate bid to make Kansas a slave state. A breach over the form and content of the constitution of Kansas between the governor and proslavery advocates began to widen.[18]

As events in Kansas were reaching a climax, news from New York City created a stir. On August 24, 1857, one of the largest of the New York financial institutions, the important and highly esteemed Ohio Life Insurance and Trust Company, failed. The Panic of 1857 had begun.

18. For Kansas and Lecompton, see Potter, *The Impending Crisis*, Chaps. 11, 12; for the tariff of 1857, consult Thomas Monroe Pitkin, "The Tariff and the Early Republican Party" (Ph.D. dissertation, Western Reserve University, 1935), 29–57, and Frank W. Taussig, *The Tariff History of the United States* (7th ed.; New York, 1923), 112–15. For movements of loans and discounts, see Temin, "The Panic of 1857," 1–12. The ramifications of the Dred Scott decision are presented by Don E. Fehrenbacher, *The Dred Scott Case: Its Significance in American Law and Politics* (New York, 1978).

TWO / Panic Stalks Wall Street

The course the Panic took between late August and mid-October had a significant bearing upon the manner in which Americans reacted to the crisis. Due to a bountiful harvest, most Americans anticipated a rewarding fall trade and expected any monetary difficulty to remain isolated in New York City. When the financial problems overwhelmed commerce and industry, few were disposed to look at any group other than New York bankers as the agent of their troubles. Moreover, it was during the height and the immediate aftermath of the Panic that two phenomena were noted: the commercial might of southern cotton and the marginal existence of northern wage earners. These observations became a vital part of sectional arguments long after the banking turmoil itself had disappeared.

New York's financial community trembled at the news of the failure of the Ohio Life Insurance and Trust Company, the largest and most respected bank in Ohio. The institution engaged primarily in currency exchange operations and was a major outlet of eastern credit to the financially starved West. To attract more business the Ohio Life had established a branch in New York City, but the manager of the New York office, Edwin C. Ludlow, embezzled funds and loaned credit too freely. Ludlow's operations resulted in the inability of the bank to pay its notes, forcing the bank president, Charles Stetson, to announce suspension of specie payment. The suspension "acted as a clap of thunder in a clear sky" and struck financiers like a "cannon shot." New York's money men, already worried about a possible specie drain because of an imbalance in America's foreign trade, now feared that the public might lose confidence in banks and demand immediate redemption of their notes.[1]

1. Quotes from Cincinnati *Daily Gazette*, August 25, 1857; James S. Gibbons, *The Banks of New-York, Their Dealers, The Clearing House, and the Panic of 1857* (New

The initial impact of investor uneasiness over the collapse of the Ohio Life was confined almost entirely to the New York Stock Exchange. Stocks of all kinds, but especially railroad shares, experienced a sharp decline. Four days after the Ohio Life's suspension, the price for a share of Illinois Central Railroad stock fell from 113 to 92; the Chicago and Rock Island Line registered a loss of ten points, while the Reading Railroad plunged from 68 to 60¼ per share. The stock market continued to falter for the next three weeks. Accompanying the unwelcome reports of falling stock prices were the melancholy announcements of bankrupt companies. Speculators and "a host of smaller brokers" also collapsed under the strained financial conditions.[2]

While many citizens felt little sympathy for stockbrokers and speculators, they were quite apprehensive about the reactions of bankers. The financiers cut their loans and discounts from $120,100,000 to $116,600,000, a curtailment one editor called "very sharp." At the same time bankers pared down their liabilities, they increased their supply of gold. The amount of specie in New York banks rose from $9,200,000 on August 29 to $13,500,000 three weeks later. Even though bankers hoarded their specie, they faced a danger from demand deposits. On August 8, the New York banks had $94,500,000 in deposits, but the fear that suspension might occur had driven depositors to reclaim their funds. By the middle of September these trepidations were starting to be realized as the amount of deposits dwindled to $75,800,000.[3]

Few people believed in the first few days following the suspension of the Ohio Life that New York's ills would involve anyone other than speculators. But the mechanism that would spread financial chaos elsewhere quickly emerged. New Yorkers desired to augment their specie holdings so as to meet any sudden demand; to do so, they pressed others to redeem the bank notes that they possessed, and these notes originated in smaller banks throughout the nation. These interior banks were eventually forced to redeem their notes; many were unable

---

York, 1864), 344–51. For background on the Ohio Life Insurance and Trust Company, see Van Vleck, *The Panic of 1857*, 64–65; Mortimer Spiegelman, "The Failure of the Ohio Life Insurance and Trust Company, 1857," *Ohio State Archeological and Historical Quarterly*, LVII (1948), 247–65.

2. *Bankers' Magazine*, XII (September, 1857), 254–55, XII (October, 1857), 334–35; New York *Herald*, August 25, 26, 27, 1857; *Frank Leslie's Illustrated Newspaper*, September 5, 1857, p. 215.

3. For the New York weekly bank statement see *Hunt's Merchants' Magazine*, XXXVIII (February, 1858), 197, XL (February, 1859), 215, hereinafter cited as *Hunt's*; quote from New York *Daily Tribune*, September 1, 1857.

to do so. Thus by September reports of bank failures began to fill the press. So common were bank closings that the Cleveland *Plain Dealer* satirically listed the broken banks under the caption of "List of Late bustified Banks. (Corrected Hourly)."[4]

But the rest of the nation initially failed to appreciate how dangerous the situation in New York was. Westerners were quite sure that no financial disruption could reach them, for their economy was based on "grain and beef, and hogs, and produce that cannot be so far depreciated in value as bank or railroad stocks." Southerners maintained that only speculators would be ruined in the wake of the suspension of the Ohio Life, and they added that such an event would be a benefit to the nation. The editor of the Louisville *Courier* wrote for many when he belittled the New York stock market: "Their houses are dens of iniquity. Their aim is financial ruin. Their code of laws is that of the gambler, the sharper, the imposter, the cheat, and the swindler." Reporters along the Atlantic coast also denied that the troubles of New York would amount to much. Washington journalists held that the nation had too much wealth in the form of grains and cotton to be affected by paper issuances in the Empire City.[5]

Bankers had two sources of gold upon which to call if the financial system failed to function properly: the California gold mines and the United States government. Unfortunately, neither of these altered the course of events. Bankers counted heavily upon a gold shipment from California to relieve the pressure to redeem notes. But on September 12 they learned that the *Central America,* a vessel carrying $1,500,000 in bullion, had sunk off the coast of South America.[6] The secretary of the treasury, Howell Cobb, aided New York's distressed financial community by buying back some of the national debt, thereby injecting a portion of the government's gold into the economy. Although Cobb's

4. Cleveland *Daily Plain Dealer,* September 2, 1857; Scull Camblos & Co. to James Martin Bell, September 11, 1857, in James Martin Bell Papers, Manuscript Department, William R. Perkins Library, Duke University, hereinafter cited as *DU.* For the financial hold the New York bankers had over the rest of the nation, consult Thomas Senior Berry, *Western Prices Before 1861: A Study of the Cincinnati Market* (Cambridge, Mass., 1943), 522; Walter Buckingham Smith and Arthur Harrison Cole, *Fluctuations in American Business, 1790–1860* (Cambridge, Mass., 1935), 130–33.

5. Chicago *Daily Tribune,* August 27, 1857; Louisville *Daily Courier,* August 29, 1857; Providence *Daily Tribune,* August 31, 1857; Washington (D.C.) *Union,* August 28, 1857.

6. *Harper's Weekly,* September 26, 1857, pp. 611, 615; Van Vleck, *The Panic of 1857,* 68.

action was economically correct and well-intentioned, it did not persuade noteholders that the banks were sound. The pressure mounted.[7]

The last week of September brought more bad news. Not only did bank statements continue to exhibit the worsening credit situation, but there was also an important bank failure in Pennsylvania. On September 25, Philadelphia's Bank of Pennsylvania announced suspension of specie payment. The news raced around the city and soon Chestnut Street was packed with frenzied noteholders and depositors demanding specie payment. One of Philadelphia's bankers, Jay Cooke, had been warned that the city's banks could not long continue to pay out gold and silver; if they did, "they will certainly suspend before long." This was precisely what the noteholders accomplished. To stave off total failure the bankers declared suspension of specie payment. The suspension was not unexpected; Pitt Cooke wrote his brother that "the bolt at last has fallen that for weeks had impended over you."[8]

Philadelphia's suspension immediately produced a banking run throughout the nation, and now the panic that had been contained to a limited number of noteholders and financiers was elevated to the Panic. In the days following the crash in Philadelphia, news of banking failures throughout the country filled the newspapers. While some state banking systems, such as that in Rhode Island, quickly folded, the two most important centers of American finance, New York and Boston, held firm. Observers confidently predicted that the Panic would not topple these pillars of American banking integrity.[9]

Some individuals were not so sanguine about New York's position, for they perceived dangerous tendencies in the city's money market. Henry J. Raymond, owner and chief editor of the New York *Times,* fretted over the inability of the bankers to act in concert; the bankers seemed to be concerned only about their own welfare and not the community's. Edward Clark told Jay Cooke that he was also disturbed about the policies that the Wall Street financiers pursued. He was attempting to secure a loan to keep his banking operations afloat and

7. Ecke, "The Fiscal Aspects of the Panic of 1857," 145–50; David Kinley, *The History, Organization and Influence of the Independent Treasury of the United States* (New York, 1893), 61–62.

8. F. C. Harris to Jay Cooke, September 22, 1857, Pitt Cooke to Jay Cooke, October 3, 1857, both in Jay Cooke Papers, Historical Society of Pennsylvania, Philadelphia, Pa., hereinafter cited as HSP; New York *Daily Tribune,* September 22, 26, 1857.

9. New York *Daily Tribune,* September 28, 29, 30, 1857; Boston *Post,* September 28, 29, 30, 1857; Providence *Daily Tribune,* October 2, 3, 1857.

could not locate a creditor. He wrote that "money is *not tight*—it is *not to be had at all*. No money, no confidence and no value to anything." Then Clark exploded at the activities of his fellow financiers: "The N.Y.C. banks are in a more precarious position than I supposed. There is no concert of action and they don't willingly help the weaker brethren. The Continental was thrown out in the Exchange yesterday or this morning & some parties among the Bks. favored each Bank taking care of itself. If that policy had ruled they would all have suspended before 3 o'clock today."[10]

By late September it became clear, much to the dismay of the public, that the financial problems would not be confined to speculators and stock jobbers. The Panic in New York was affecting every sector of the economy. When New York called for specie, the ability of interior banks to offer credit and loans to merchants and industrialists was reduced because the amount of loans granted depended partly upon the amount of gold and silver the banks had amassed. Contemporaries called this state of affairs a "financial stringency." Around the country the result was the same: transportation halted, industrial production ceased, and construction stopped.

Many individuals believed a "revulsion" in monetary affairs impossible because of the size of the southern and western harvest. But in September the prices of western staples began a precipitous decline because produce was being neither shipped nor demanded in other markets because of the credit problem. Superfine wheat flour on the New York market fell from an average of $6.35 per barrel in July, 1857, to $5.65 in September, to $4.55 in October. In a like manner the price of western white wheat fell from an average of $1.92 per bushel in July, to $1.60 in September, to $1.37 in October. Cotton, the great southern staple, resisted the downward turn in prices longer than other goods, but nonetheless its monthly average price also dropped, from 15-5/8 cents per pound in September to 12-1/2 cents per pound in October.[11]

For western farmers the fall in crop prices was a horrible shock. Some business observers, such as the journalists of *Hunt's Merchants' Magazine* and *Bankers' Magazine*, had been concerned about the small spring trade and the possible economic effects of the new peace in Europe. The early days of fall revealed that these reporters were correct,

10. New York *Times*, September 29, 1857; Edward W. Clark to Jay Cooke, September 29, 1857, in Cooke Papers.
11. *Senate Executive Documents*, 35th Cong., 2nd Sess., No. 1, p. 58.

for Europeans did not order western foodstuffs in the usual quantities. The "advices" on European market conditions, transmitted by trading vessels, uniformly stated that American grains were unneeded. As one editor in Indianapolis explained to his readers, prices would stay low because although the United States had a full harvest, so did England, France, and Russia. Even though Russia struggled with the aftereffects of the Crimean War, she would still "have millions of bushels [of wheat] for exportation" and thus be able to sell at a lower price than American shippers.[12]

Many easterners maintained that if western farmers would sell their crops, the financial strain would disappear. The cycle of credit, they believed, ultimately ended with the farmer. Bankers loaned money to merchants who in turn extended credit to farmers; if westerners sold their crop, they could repay the merchants who could then retire their debts to the banks. But western farmers were evidently unconvinced that they had lost their position in the European market. They refused to sell their crops because they felt the price was too low. As financial conditions in the East deteriorated, many individuals, like the editor of the Milwaukee *Daily Free Democrat*, exhorted the farmers to "sell your Grain and pay your Debts" in order to revive the economy.[13]

The first week of October found the financial structure crumbling and trade at a standstill. Noteholders and depositors jammed into banks demanding payment in coin. Between September 26 and October 10 banks reduced loans and discounts from $107,800,000 to $101,900,000, while deposits fell from $73,300,000 to $63,300,000. The failures that attended this contraction of credit were "massive." In the West previously unquestioned securities and bank paper were rejected. St. Louis bankers, for example, at first refused to accept Illinois paper currency until persuaded otherwise by the Illinois bank commissioner.[14]

As the seriousness of the situation increased, various individuals pleaded for calm, rational thinking. But by early October the Panic of 1857 was earning its nomenclature; men, especially in banking circles,

12. Indianapolis *Daily Journal*, September 28, 1857; *Hunt's*, XXXVI (June, 1857), 709, XXXVII (September, 1857), 335; *Bankers' Magazine*, XII (July, 1857), 86, XII (September, 1857), 254.

13. Milwaukee *Daily Free Democrat*, October 5, 1857.

14. Bank statements in *Hunt's*, XXXVIII (February, 1858), 197, XL (February, 1859), 215; *Frank Leslie's Illustrated Newspaper*, October 3, 1857, p. 279; New York *Times*, October 5, 7, 8, 1857; Chicago *Daily Tribune*, September 28, October 5, 7, 9, 1857.

seemed utterly possessed by some demonic force. The psychology of the Panic was recorded and analyzed. George T. Strong, a conservative New York businessman, wrote of the scramble to avoid collapse: "The remedy for this crisis must be psychological rather than financial. It is an epidemic of fear and distrust that every one admits to be without real ground *except* the very sufficient ground that everyone else is known to share them." Newspaper editors told depositors and financial leaders to fight "FEAR" and "unreasoning panic." One Rhode Islander even advised against publishing lists of broken companies: "The rule is, build up and not pull down."[15]

Journalists demanded a stop to the credit contraction—to the reduction of loans and discounts—because this policy was destroying "legitimate" industry and commerce. No one complained about the havoc the Panic wreaked upon speculators in August and early September, but many cries were raised when the Panic started to bankrupt reputable firms in October. Merchants in the large cities held meetings to demand that the banks open lines of credit and end the pressure on the business community. In New York the middlemen tried to obtain a pledge for an increase of six to ten million dollars in discounts from the bankers, but the hard-pressed financiers were unable to comply.[16]

Americans also became aware by the end of September that the financial turmoil was affecting another segment of the economy. Not only did the credit stringency halt mercantile activity, it also hindered manufacturers. The newspaper notices of suspended operations provided ample testimony to the dire straits of American industry. And each announcement added to the growing number of unemployed who roamed the streets. In New York it was estimated that two-thirds to three-fourths of the shipbuilders had been laid off. Providence once had 1,494 employees manufacturing jewelry; by the middle of October only 314 were still working.[17]

Financiers faced a dilemma that made it virtually impossible for

15. Allan Nevins and Milton Halsey Thomas (eds.), *The Diary of George Templeton Strong* (New York, 1952), II, 359; Newark *Daily Advertiser*, October 6, 9, 1857; Providence *Daily Tribune*, September 18, 1857.

16. Boston *Post*, October 3, 1857; New York *Times*, October 8, 9, 10, 1857; Philadelphia *Evening Bulletin*, October 9, 1857.

17. Harrisburg (Pa.) *Daily Telegraph*, September 3, 21, 29, 1857; Boston *Post*, September 9, 14, 30, 1857; *Daily True American* (Trenton, N.J.), October 9, 12, 1857; Rhode Island Society for the Encouragement of Domestic Industry, *Transactions for the Year 1857* (Providence, 1858), 77–88.

them to meet the credit demands of the public. The development of deposit banking during the decade had created a generally unrecognized danger to the system. Bankers enticed customers to their institutions by offering interest on deposits. In order to profit from this practice, the financiers used the deposits as a basis upon which they could offer short-term loans, referred to as call loans. These loans were most commonly made to stockbrokers and were to be repaid immediately upon request by the bank. In addition, the loans usually took the form of discounts or bank notes, and as a result the issuing agency might be called upon to redeem the notes in specie. The hazardous element in the process was that depositors could withdraw their money in gold and silver at their own caprice. A sudden withdrawal of deposits left the bank with large liabilities in the form of bank notes, which had to be paid in gold when brought to the bank for redemption. In order to protect their specie holdings, bankers curtailed their loans and discounts and demanded payment of call loans. If the individuals who contracted the call loans were unable to pay, then the bank's position became more precarious. In the Panic of 1857 this situation was compounded by a general fear that the banks were unsafe, which induced large numbers of depositors to reclaim their money. Bankers thus had no other resource than to refuse credit to merchants and others if they expected to keep enough gold to maintain specie payment.[18]

That deposits and call loans were indeed contributing to credit contraction was revealed in the correspondence of a Tennessee banker, William B. Campbell. Laboring under the monetary strain, William Campbell wrote his uncle to obtain advice about meeting the emergency. He admitted a mistake in one regard: "Our error has been in discounting too much for the last six months, and discounting on our deposits." The reply of his uncle confirmed the younger Campbell's fears concerning deposits. He told his nephew "to be on your guard against depositors,—and you will find it a bad business to pay interest on general deposits." William Campbell's uncle continued to offer suggestions and on one occasion outlined the course of action bankers throughout the Union were following, but which made merchants and the general public scream in anger: "There may be a respite—and there is no sort of doubt that the safest and best course for you and your

18. *Hunt's*, XXXVII (October, 1857), 452–53; *Bankers' Magazine*, XII (October, 1857), 334; Gibbons, *The Banks of New-York*, 354–60; Redlich, *The Molding of American Banking*, II, 1–3.

partners, is to reduce your discounts as fast as you prudently can and pay off your deposits. Then come what may you are safe." This safety for the bankers, many people believed, meant ruin for everyone else.[19]

The second week of October brought the Panic of 1857 to a climax. The banks of New York mightily resisted a general suspension of specie payment. Massive runs on the banks occurred on Friday and Saturday, the ninth and tenth, resulting in the failure of several important banks. Sunday gave the financiers a needed respite, but on Monday the note-holding mob packed Wall Street and demanded redemption of their notes. Again the New York banks weathered the storm, but again with reduced numbers and decreased assets. The bank presidents met that evening at the clearinghouse to declare their resolution to uphold financial integrity, to redeem all notes in specie, and to argue that the financial peril had passed.

On Tuesday morning the bankers found out that the public believed that the integrity of New York's financial institutions was as low as the level of specie in their vaults. A mob of twenty to thirty thousand frenzied New Yorkers "thronged the sidewalks and choked the entrances to the banks, demanding specie for notes and checks." When the business day ended at 3:30 P.M., eighteen more banks had announced suspension. The beleaguered bank presidents met twice that evening. Three days before the banks had $11,476,000 in specie; they estimated their reserves on Monday night to be only $5,800,000. One more day and all the banks would fall before the noteholders. There was really no choice, so the financiers resolved that "it is expedient that the banks of this city suspend specie payments tomorrow."[20]

The reaction of the rest of the country's financial institutions to New York's suspension was immediate and predictable. Other bankers correctly surmised that if they attempted to continue specie payment, New Yorkers would purchase their bank notes and quickly demand redemption so as to stockpile specie in the city. As virtually all the other bankers of the country refused to ruin themselves for the benefit of the New Yorkers, they suspended specie payment as well. The other financial systems in the nation did not resist casting aspersions upon the quality of New York's banking fraternity. As the Boston *Post* taunted,

19. William B. Campbell to David Campbell, October 12, 27, 1857, David Campbell to William A. Campbell, October 1, November 1, 1857, all in Campbell Family Papers, DU.

20. New York *Times*, October 12, 13, 14, 1857; quote from *Harper's Weekly*, October 24, 1857, p. 678; *Bankers' Magazine*, XII (November, 1857), 412–13.

"our banks held up manfully, until *after the New York banks with all their bluster and boasting, had fallen.*"[21]

Not all of the states were engulfed in the specie suspension, although most contemporaries considered it a general banking collapse. The four states of Ohio, Indiana, Kentucky, and Louisiana maintained specie payment. The only true banking failure in Ohio was, oddly enough, the Ohio Life. Otherwise in both Ohio and Indiana a regional panic in 1855 had already destroyed weaker banks and had placed the financial systems on a more prudent basis. Kentucky and Louisiana escaped suspension primarily because they allowed the credit stringency to drive merchants, manufacturers, and planters to ruin. Kentucky and Louisiana therefore maintained banking integrity at the cost of other economic activities. They did not escape from the Panic unscathed, however, as was later claimed.[22]

The suspension of specie payment created an awkward financial condition, but one to which the country quickly adjusted. Howell Cobb ceased his efforts to inject gold into the economy and directed his attention to the probable effect the "revulsion" would have on government revenue. Although most states, in particular New York and Pennsylvania, had laws making it illegal for their banks to suspend specie payment, legislators quickly yielded to the undeniable needs of the economy and passed laws that momentarily permitted the banks to forgo redemption of their notes. New York bankers also made peace with their country cousins and established a formula by which the notes of the interior would be allowed to float in the city before being presented for redemption. In the West, however, there were complications because of wildcat banking in Nebraska; bank notes from that territory flooded Illinois, Wisconsin, and Iowa. The notes were virtually worthless, and bankers would not honor them.[23]

The financial world actually recovered quite rapidly from the sus-

---

21. Boston *Post*, October 15, 1857; Richmond (Va.) *Enquirer*, October 16, 1857; Mobile *Daily Register*, October 17, 1857.

22. For Ohio and Indiana see Indianapolis *Daily Journal*, October 16, 19, 21, November 5, December 2, 22, 1857, January 13, 1858; Ernest Ludlow Bogart, *Financial History of Ohio* (Urbana-Champaign, Ill., 1912), 286–87. For Louisiana and Kentucky, see *Daily Picayune* (New Orleans), October 15–28, November 3, 7, 1857; Louisville *Daily Courier*, October 15–19, 27, November 18, December 2, 22, 1857; George D. Green, *Finance and Economic Development in the Old South: Louisiana Banking, 1804–1861* (Stanford, Calif., 1972), 56–57, 119–21, 161.

23. *Hunt's*, XXXVII (November, 1857), 582–83, XXXVII (December, 1857), 711; F. Cyril James, *The Growth of Chicago Banks* (New York, 1938), I, 267–71; J. Sterling Mor-

pension. Loans, discounts, deposits, and the amount of bank notes in circulation slowly and cautiously rose, although by January, 1858, they were still far below the levels attained during the summer of 1857. Specie, on the other hand, rapidly accumulated in New York. Less than one month after the suspension the amount of specie in the city's banks rose to $16,500,000, and on December 12 the banks possessed $26,100,000 in gold and silver. As bankers obtained a more favorable specie to liabilities ratio, they considered a resumption of specie payment. Two months after the suspension the New York banks declared that "on and after tomorrow we will resume specie payments in full on all liabilities." Not long afterward most of the nation's other banking systems returned to a hard money standard. North Carolina editor William W. Holden, contemplating the brevity of the monetary crisis and the speed with which it passed, wrote that "it was a *fast* panic, and therefore in entire keeping with this fast age."[24]

Certainly the Panic of 1857 generated widespread anger over the unexpected and sudden demise of national prosperity, which was quickly translated into political rhetoric. The financial debacle also left a social legacy that would haunt many individuals for several years. Although banks righted themselves quickly after the October suspension, commerce and industry required more time to resume pre-Panic levels of activity.[25] The consequence of slow recovery for industrial and commercial pursuits was unemployment. In the fall of 1857 poverty-stricken people remonstrated against their harsh fate by instigating strikes and conducting rallies for public relief. These activities became a centerpiece for the next three years in sectional debates concerning the fate of the free laborers of the North.

As the numbers of jobless swelled in October and November an uneasy wariness permeated the larger cities. Various individuals, like the editor of the Louisville *Courier*, began to fear that the state of the

---

ton, Albert Watkins, and George L. Miller, *Illustrated History of Nebraska* (3rd ed.; Lincoln, Neb., 1911), II, 304–23.

24. Bank statements in *Hunt's*, XXXVIII (February, 1858), 197, XL (February, 1859), 215; clearinghouse resolution in New York *Times*, December 12, 1857; Holden quote in *Semi-Weekly Standard* (Raleigh, N.C.), January 23, 1858.

25. Harrisburg *Daily Telegraph*, October 16, 1857; Lowell *Courier* quoted by Chicago *Daily Tribune*, October 28, 1857; *Cambria Tribune* (Johnstown, Pa.), October 28, 1857. By newspaper accounts, it seems that unemployment peaked in late October and early November.

economy foretold a "terrible suffering to the poor." The unfortunate jobless were facing the approaching winter with no means to acquire shelter, food, or clothing. In Philadelphia, Peter Lesley, a statistician for the American Iron Association, wrote to the abolitionist Lydia Maria Child about social conditions in the City of Brotherly Love: "A nightmare broods over society. The City is as still as a Sabbath day. The oldest, wealthiest houses are crashing down day by day, as their heaviest days come round. Scores of thousands are out of work. Bread riots are dreaded. Winter is coming. God alone foresees the history of the next six months."[26]

New York City, with unemployment estimates ranging from 30,000 to 100,000, was the urban area with the greatest number of jobless and the most volatile social conditions. The mayor of New York in 1857, Fernando Wood, did not have the temperament or perhaps the wisdom to handle the crisis. Born in 1812, Wood hailed from a moderately prosperous family and became a well-to-do merchant. Politics, however, not commerce, was the love of his life, and he quickly sided with the Jacksonians and joined Tammany Hall. He acquired more stature over the years until he finally became mayor in 1854. But Wood's tenure in office was marred by controversy; he fought with Republicans over patronage in the city, and in the summer of 1857 he had a serious, albeit ludicrous, confrontation with the governor over control of the city's police force.[27]

Wood planned to aid the jobless by increasing employment on public works, which included the new Central Park, and to pay the men in cornmeal, potatoes, and flour. The mayor expected to finance this scheme by issuing bonds redeemable in fifty years and bearing 7 percent interest. Critics dubbed the proposal the "bread and potatoes" message, but the attention of most journalists fastened onto one passage in which Wood seemed to sanction the robbery of the rich by the poor:

> In the days of general prosperity they [the poor] labor for a mere subsistence, whilst other classes accumulate wealth, and in the days of general

26. Louisville *Daily Courier*, October 17, 1857; Peter Lesley to Lydia M. Child, October 11, 1857, in Mary Lesley Ames (ed.), *Life and Letters of Peter and Susan Lesley* (New York, 1909), I, 351.

27. For background on Fernando Wood, consult Samuel Augustus Pleasants, *Fernando Wood of New York City* (New York, 1948), 11–26, 50–83; Leonard Chalmers, "Tammany Hall, Fernando Wood, and the Struggle to Control New York City, 1857–1859," *New-York Historical Society Quarterly*, LIII (1969), 7–12.

depression, they are the first to feel the change, without the means to avoid or endure reverses. Truly may it be said that in New-York those who produce everything get nothing, and those who produce nothing get everything. They labor without income whilst surrounded by thousands living in affluence and splendor who have income without labor. But now, even this resource, with its poor pittance, is to be taken from them.

To Henry J. Raymond, Wood's communication was an invitation to class warfare; the "demagogue" Wood had raised "the banner of the most fiery communism."[28]

Notices announcing unemployment rallies at Tompkins Square first appeared in early November. Nearly two thousand persons crowded the square at the first meeting to hear orators extol the virtues of Mayor Wood's plan. Prejudiced observers believed Wood designed the entire affair to capture the votes of the lower class for the mayoral election later in the month. But more was involved than just political manipulations. One speaker told the workers to buy weapons and prepare to take what the wealthy would not give. At another gathering, one individual led the unemployed to Wall Street and spoke of relieving the bankers of the specie in their vaults if the plight of the jobless went unheeded.[29]

At first those who lauded Wood's bread and potatoes message controlled the crowds at Tompkins Square, but soon the gatherings acquired a more radical character. Wood was compelled at one point to address the unemployed, and he stressed the need for all citizens to obey the law. As the days wore on and the city council failed to provide relief, the crowds became more difficult to pacify. On November 10 a splinter group left Tompkins Square and marched on City Hall. Wood had the municipal building surrounded by police; the state militia was also called up, and the federal government sent troops to guard the customhouse. At the continuing Tompkins Square demonstrations, Wood was denounced and his name hooted. "Who is this Fernando Wood to whom we are told to put our trust?" asked one George Camphill. "He is a politician—he is a selfish, scheming politician." Camphill exhorted his audience to "*organize*," and then, after they had prepared for the worst, "we must not beg, but *demand* work; and if we do not get it *we can do* what we please." The rhetoric of the workers' demonstra-

28. New York *Times*, October 23, 27, 1857.

29. New York *Herald*, November 3, 1857; New York *Daily Tribune*, November 3, 6, 7, 1857.

tions gave credence to Horace Greeley's editorial remark in the *Tribune;* the people were "incensed" with the mayor and lived "in serious dread of what his message may led to."[30]

The workers' demonstrations lasted for two weeks and then simply disintegrated. Job openings at various public enterprises drew many away from Tompkins Square, as a scramble erupted for the positions at the Croton aqueduct and Central Park projects. But the collapse of the meetings probably owed a great deal to the perceived strength of the established authorities. After two weeks of rhetoric, the unemployed evidently realized that they could not force a capitulation from the city government.

Other northern cities shared New York's experience with the unemployed, although only in the Empire City did the distressed engage in such threatening actions. Philadelphia, Harrisburg, Chicago, Newark, Trenton, St. Louis, and Louisville contended with demonstrations of the jobless. Some speakers voiced radical sentiments, but the basic tone of the gatherings was moderate. A few of the orators at these meetings called for the workingmen to form unions and force their employers to grant decent wages. The main focus of attention at the demonstrations was to pressure local governments into funding public work projects for the unemployed; in most cases, but not all, the authorities failed to act upon these suggestions.[31]

If labor spokesmen did not obtain the aid they felt was the workers' due in the winter of 1857–1858, they at least witnessed a strong response to their advocacy of organizing unions. When the economy faltered because of the tight credit policies of the banks, not only were workers dismissed from their jobs, but wages for those who remained were cut roughly 15 to 20 percent. In most cases the real wage did not change because of the price depression that accompanied the Panic, but workingmen throughout the nation were incensed at the reduction of nominal wages. Moreover, in the last months of 1857 innumerable strikes plagued the already sinking economy. Irish workers at the

---

30. Camphill quote in New York *Daily Tribune*, November 12, 1857; Greeley quote, *ibid.*, November 10, 1857.

31. Philadelphia *Evening Bulletin*, November 10–14, 20, 1857; Newark *Daily Advertiser*, November 9, 11, 12, 1857; *Daily True American* (Trenton, N.J.), November 9, 10, 1857; Harrisburg *Daily Telegraph*, November 3, 5, 1857; Chicago *Daily Tribune*, November 14, 16, 1857; Lynn (Mass.) *News*, November 10, 24, 1857; Louisville *Daily Courier*, November 2, 9, 13, 1857; Benjamin J. Klebaner, "Poor Relief and Public Works During the Depression of 1857," *Historian*, XXII (1960), 264–79.

Bergen Tunnel, female employees at textile mills in Lancaster, Pennsylvania, dock workers at the Cunard Line in New Jersey, laborers for the Marietta Railroad in Ohio, and machine operatives of the Southern Michigan Railroad were just a few of the groups that staged walkouts. Besides wage cuts and layoffs, laborers complained about a peculiar condition the Panic had created; business firms, and railroads in particular, could not pay the workers their back wages. The Panic had destroyed so much bank note circulation that many enterprises were left with worthless paper that no one would accept.[32]

The year 1858 brought no respite from strikes. Pennsylvania's iron foundries suffered sporadic work stoppages and the state's coal fields endured continual labor unrest; there were strikes against New England's textile plants and railroad companies.[33] Accompanying the wave of turnouts in 1858 were fresh demands for labor unions. At Ashland, Pennsylvania, miners formed a union in May, 1858, and declared that "a general strike, and nothing less than a general strike by all persons employed in and about the anthracite collieries of Pennsylvania, will give to us remunerating wages for our hard labor." Shoemakers in Lynn, Massachusetts, also established a union and started collecting money for a strike fund. While the laborers were usually unsuccessful in their organizing attempts in 1858, they emphatically demonstrated that the establishment of unions was the means by which they intended to contest the policies of employers.[34]

The characteristics of the recession that followed the Panic of 1857 had much to do with the way politicians and firebrands used the financial collapse in their rhetorical tirades and electoral appeals. The economic downturn indicated which states would be most susceptible to an appeal based on economic issues. Many contemporaries thought that the Panic had revealed the true economic relationships between

32. Harrisburg *Daily Telegraph*, September 3, 4, 1857; New York *Times*, October 10, 12, 1857; New York *Daily Tribune*, November 4, 17, 1857; Hartford (Conn.) *Daily Times*, November 7, 13, 1857; Chicago *Daily Tribune*, December 8, 1857, January 13, 1858.

33. *Miner's Journal* (Pottsville, Pa.), May 15, 22, June 12, 19, 26, July 3, 1858; *Cambria Tribune*, (Johnstown, Pa.), April 10, 17, May 1, 1858; Hartford (Conn.) *Daily Times*, April 8, 1858; New York *Daily Tribune*, April 3, 6, 1858.

34. *Miner's Journal* (Pottsville, Pa.), May 29, 1858; *Bay State* (Lynn, Mass.), October 14, 1858; Lynn (Mass.) *News*, July 27, 1858; Paul Gustaf Faler, "Workingmen, Mechanics and Social Change: Lynn, Massachusetts, 1800–1860" (Ph.D. dissertation, University of Wisconsin, 1971), 457–59.

the nation's regions—that is, which areas were actually dependent upon others for prosperity. And the behavior of the economy in 1858 also lent strength to the argument that the South's business system operated on a more secure foundation than enterprise in the East or West.

Many Americans hoped that the brevity of the financial crash would mean that business activity would soon resume a hectic and productive pace. These hopes were dashed. The nadir of the depression associated with the Panic most likely occurred in late October and early November, but the return to full employment production was delayed for nearly two years. Although banks had reestablished specie payment, eastern financiers were loath to grant loans to industrial enterprises and were particularly reluctant to accommodate the currency needs of the West.[35]

Pennsylvania's iron industry perhaps suffered the most from the depression. From October, 1857, through March, 1858, the furnaces of Pennsylvania were silent and cold. One correspondent of the New York *Tribune* estimated that one-third to one-half of all the state's furnaces, bloomaries, and forges were out of operation. By late spring increased activity in the iron districts was noted by newspaper correspondents, but the loss of production in 1857 and 1858 was significant. In 1856 the iron industry produced 883,000 tons of all types of iron; in 1857 and 1858 the totals were 798,000 and 705,000 tons respectively.[36]

Coal operators also endured hard times in 1858. Although the tonnage of anthracite sent to market for 1858 was slightly above that of 1857 (1857—7,693,000 tons; 1858–7,772,000 tons) the chronicler of the Pennsylvania coal industry, Henry Bannan of Pottsville, complained that insufficient demand from "iron works, factories and steamers" reduced coal's profitability. Few orders were placed for the lump and broken coal required for industrial purposes. Instead, Bannan believed, an unexpected rise for prepared coal (used for heating homes) in the last three months of 1858 saved the coal operators from disaster.[37]

35. On currency problems of the West, see Indianapolis *Daily Journal*, March 2, 17, May 8, 26, 1858; Chicago *Daily Tribune*, December 31, 1857, January 6, 8, 9, 22, May 4, 1858.

36. New York *Daily Tribune*, April 6, 1858; James M. Swank, *History of the Manufacture of Iron in All Ages, and Particularly in the United States from Colonial Times to 1891* (Philadelphia, 1892), 376.

37. Quotes from *Miner's Journal* (Pottsville, Pa.), July 17, 1858, January 12, 1861.

New England's manufacturers also found 1858 to be a poor year. The shoe industry had a trade as well as could be "reasonably expected," but the producers were afraid that the western market had collapsed. The West lacked credit and could not sell their crops—and the West was one of the shoemakers' principal markets. Nor did New England's textile industry fare well. Besides the generally depressed economic conditions, many observers felt that cotton manufacturing had internal problems that further hindered profitability; too many firms had entered the field, and the increased competition had resulted in abnormally low prices. Whatever the reasons for the woes of the textile producers, most contemporaries agreed that 1858 was one of the worst years in memory for the industry.[38]

Shipbuilding was another endeavor decimated by the Panic of 1857. Henry J. Raymond expressed his dismay at the decay of the industry: "We are building no new ships, and the shipyards from Maine to Maryland are being dismantled and broken up; and this great business, which has been our boast for fifty years, will soon be nearly extinct." American shipbuilders had their own problems, however, and the Panic merely accelerated an already obvious trend. Americans continued to construct the beautiful but obsolescent wooden clipper ships while the merchants of the world turned to iron hulls. The large decline in ship tonnage produced by Americans was a testament to that industry's technological backwardness.[39]

Most journalists and business reporters at the close of 1857 agreed that economic recovery depended upon a resurgence in western activity. Unfortunately, the West did not recover in 1858. Prices for western breadstuffs remained low and farmers faced problems with the weather in the summer. The dilemma for the rest of the economy was that the West was the debtor section of the nation. Only when westerners finally paid their debts could the economy return to full production.

38. New York *Daily Tribune*, September 17, 23, 1858; Boston Board of Trade, *Fifth Annual Report* (Boston, 1859), 163–65, 176–78; Paul F. McGouldrick, *New England Textiles in the Nineteenth Century: Profits and Investment* (Cambridge, Mass., 1968), 81–82, 108, 119; Lance E. Davis and H. Louis Stettler, III, "The New England Textile Industry, 1825–60: Trends and Fluctuations," in *Output, Employment, and Productivity in the United States after 1800* (New York, 1966), 221. Vol. XXX of Conference on Research in Income and Wealth, *Studies in Income and Wealth*.

39. New York *Times*, November 24, 1858, January 6, 1859; W. H. Bunting (comp. and annotator), *Portrait of a Port: Boston, 1852–1914* (Cambridge, Mass., 1971), 9.

The difficulty facing westerners, which became increasingly apparent, was their inability to find a market for their crops. Spectacular western population growth for the last two decades had resulted in equally spectacular growth in western agricultural production. By the 1850s much of the West's prosperity depended upon shipping surplus grains to Europe. During the Panic, however, it was obvious that Europe no longer required western staples. Indeed, newspaper reports throughout 1858 emphasized the effect of the European market upon American grain prices. One paper stated that "the aspect of our general markets for produce today, was unfavorable under the discouraging advices from abroad." Another reporter on economic affairs announced that the "latest advices from Europe represent the growing crops to be promising well, and this, with the large supply of wheat now in the country, and the absence of all urgent demand for flour except the present temporary one at home, will tend to diminish, rather than advance, prices."[40]

Whether the farmers had a good or poor crop made little difference in the breadstuffs market. Shipments of western produce to the East, minimal as they were in 1858, went unsold; the grains were simply warehoused. The inability of westerners to sell their grains overseas prompted inquiries as to European, especially British, intentions. One letter fell into the possession of the Detroit *Free Press* in which an Englishman explained competition and the laws of supply and demand to the Americans: "Much stress is laid by friends on your side on the small export trade your shippers are doing, but we have so many ways in which we are supplied with grain and flour as to make us almost independent of the United States; and we are sorry that some of our friends should imagine that high prices ruling with you should produce a corresponding advance here, such not being the case." Government figures demonstrated that the European demand for American foodstuffs had almost vanished. In the fiscal year ending June 30, 1857, England had purchased 8,560,000 bushels of wheat and 1,027,000 barrels of flour; by the next fiscal year the totals had fallen to 5,121,000 bushels and 893,000 barrels respectively; and for the year ending June 30, 1859, the amounts were a meager 984,000 bushels of wheat and 166,000

40. Cincinnati *Daily Gazette*, November 24, December 1, 1857; Indianapolis *Daily Journal*, June 23, 1858; Percy Wells Bidwell and John I. Falconer, *History of Agriculture in the Northern United States, 1620–1860* (Washington, D.C., 1925), 336.

barrels of flour. The West had lost a primary market and prosperity would not return until by some circumstance demand for the region's products rose.[41]

The effect of the West's inability to sell its staples was immediately reflected in the railroad industry. The mileage of railroad track laid down in the West during the 1850s was nothing short of phenomenal. The speed with which railroads were built had elicited many detractions, however, and when so many railroads collapsed so quickly under the stringent credit conditions of 1857 many commentators decided that the overly rapid construction of lines had caused the Panic.[42]

Americans thus rigorously investigated the railroads and reported all the malpractices they found. According to one source, American roads "were made upon the cheap principle," while others charged that many lines were conceived in fraud and nurtured with corruption. Railroads indulged in ruinous competition, and efforts to control freight rates never succeeded. The leading advocate of responsible railroad expansion, Henry Varnum Poor, was particularly distressed at American railway practices. Corporation managers underestimated expenses, overestimated revenues, and then lied to the public in their annual reports. The existence of incompetent railroad managers, according to Poor, was a result of the corporate form of business; it absolved the manager from "those moral responsibilities" that would naturally arise from personal ownership of the firm.[43]

Poor soon realized, as did others, that the problems of the western railroads did not all stem from ignorant and corrupt management. In the various reports of western roads a constant refrain of the directors was that their difficulties originated in "the small amount of produce in the State, to be moved previous to the last harvest, and the general depression in business since then." By the end of 1858 Poor admitted that the reason for the abject earning records of the railroads was "the low price of breadstuffs." Freeman Hunt also believed that it "is in this question of the grain crops that the future of the railroads in this coun-

41. Detroit *Daily Free Press*, October 10, 1858; unnumbered reports entitled "Commerce and Navigation," in *Senate Executive Documents*, 35th Cong., 1st Sess., 20–23, 26–27, 46–49; *Senate Executive Documents*, 35th Cong., 2nd Sess., 16–17, 24–25, 46–49; *Senate Executive Documents*, 36th Cong., 1st Sess., 16–17, 24–25, 46–49.

42. *Harper's Weekly*, December 19, 1857, p. 802, January 23, 1858, p. 50; *American Railroad Journal*, October 17, 1857, p. 660, November 7, 1857, pp. 705, 712.

43. Quotes from *Frank Leslie's Illustrated Newspaper*, January 8, 1859, p. 86; *American Railroad Journal*, March 6, 1858, p. 152.

try is so completely involved." While noting that presently many investors shunned railroads, Hunt predicted that demand for western
crops would again rise, thus stimulating the business of western railroads: "Those who have [the] patience to wait for that day will find the
investments, now so much sneered at, among the most profitable in
the world." [44]

In vibrant contrast to the North was the smooth and profitable functioning of the southern economy. Southerners were, of course, ap-
palled at the price drop of their staples that accompanied New York's
financial distress. One market reporter estimated that planters would
lose "from *sixty to one hundred millions of dollars* on the present crop
of cotton." Tobacco suffered the same price decline, and for a time the
tobacco market was "utterly depressed." [45]

In 1858, however, both cotton and tobacco fared well in the marts of
the world. Although prices for the staples did not return to the heights
of the summer of 1857, southerners encountered no difficulty in securing a market for their produce. The growth and prosperity of southern
railroads particularly demonstrated the effects of the continued sal-
ability of cotton and tobacco. Unlike northern lines, southern roads did
not lose revenue from a decline in the amount of freight transported,
and southern lines consistently issued respectable dividends to their
stockholders. Cotton was specifically mentioned in many railroad reports as being the chief article of freight and the principal reason for
continued prosperity. Some southern railroads tried to lure investors
by pointing out that the seemingly insatiable demand for cotton ensured that southern railroads would never lack a product to ship. [46]

Throughout 1858 businessmen and journalists were aware that the
"South pays up its bills well and promptly, while it is almost impossible
to get a dollar from the West." The great West, to which all the eastern
capital had flowed, now proved incapable of rescuing the economy. "It
seems now that the cotton crop is going to be the means of setting the
trade of the country on its legs again," admitted the editor of *Harper's*

44. Quotes from *American Railroad Journal*, May 15, 1858, p. 305, October 30,
1858, p. 696; *Hunt's*, XXXVIII (April, 1858), 464.

45. *Southern Recorder* (Milledgeville, Ga.), October 20, 1857; Richmond (Va.)
Whig, September 15, October 13, November 27, December 18, 25, 1857.

46. *American Railroad Journal*, January 2, 1858, p. 5, January 9, 1858, p. 18, February 6, 1858, p. 88, March 13, 1858, p. 165, May 15, 1858, pp. 306, 309, 315, August 28,
1858, p. 549; Merl E. Reed, *New Orleans and the Railroads: The Struggle for Commercial Empire, 1830–1860* (Baton Rouge, 1966), 100–101, 124–25.

Weekly. "Our other great staple—breadstuffs—is in an unpromising condition." As the editor of the *Scientific American* perceptively observed, the economic effects of the Panic of 1857 proved that "'cotton is King,' and rules in the marts and cabinets of nations."[47]

In the aftermath of New York's suspension of specie payments, Americans offered a myriad of explanations for the financial collapse. But business journalists correctly understood the cause of the Panic, and subsequent developments in 1859 and 1860 did not alter their conclusions. The Panic of 1857 originated, they properly claimed, in the termination of the Crimean War, which enabled Europeans to redirect their energies to normal economic pursuits. In particular, Britain, France, the central European states, and Russia rehabilitated their agricultural endeavors and so competed with Americans in the European breadstuffs market. The result was that the western farmer lost a market, and this loss subjected the West to economic stagnation.[48] But the general public exploded in frustration and wrath over the monetary failure, and that outcry utterly buried the accurate conclusions of market reporters. Instead, the Panic of 1857 reminded most Americans of a traditional explanation for business reverses and of a traditional enemy as well. The 1857 crash reignited the political passions that had surrounded Andrew Jackson's war on the Second Bank of the United States. Once again the politicians were to fight over the role of banks in American economic life.

47. New York *Economist* quoted by Richmond (Va.) *Enquirer*, October 26, 1858; *Harper's Weekly*, November 13, 1858, pp. 722–23; *Scientific American*, September 25, 1858, p. 21.

48. Economic historians have offered various explanations for the Panic of 1857. George W. Van Vleck, in *The Panic of 1857*, 53–58, argued that the conclusion of the Crimean War created a specie flow from Britain to France; to protect herself, Britain raised her discount rate and drew gold out of the United States. Albert Fishlow, in *American Railroads and the Transformation of the Ante-Bellum Economy*, 114–15, posits that the economy peaked in 1853–54, and only the intervention of the Crimean War kept the country from experiencing the Panic at an earlier date. Fritz Redlich, in *The Molding of American Banking*, II, 1–3, maintains that the Panic of 1857 was the product of a liquidity crisis created by deposit banking. Peter Temin, in "The Panic of 1857," 9–11, believes that the monetary collapse was a minor event in American economic history and that miscalculations by bankers brought about the episode. The strength of the contemporary business chroniclers' interpretation that the fall in European demand for American foodstuffs produced the Panic is that this analysis can explain both the monetary failure and the depression that followed. For an elaboration of the views of contemporary market reporters, see James L. Huston, "Western Grains and the Panic of 1857," *Agricultural History*, LVII (1983), 14–32.

THREE / Public and Political Reactions

The financial turmoil of 1857 instigated a wide-ranging and angry debate over economic policy. This discussion surprisingly did not influence the sectional controversy over slavery, at least for the time being. Although many southerners and a few abolitionists pressed the financial crash into service for their pro- and antislavery causes, the general public's reaction, as well as the political one in the fall 1857 elections, was usually void of sectional bitterness. Most Americans, politically interested or otherwise, treated the Panic solely as an economic problem, not a sectional one. One particular circumstance about the financial suspension accounted for this unusual response. The experience of the months of financial stringency led nearly everyone to conclude that the banking community brought economic chaos down upon the nation because of its poor judgment and greed. Thus not only did southerners and northern Democrats caluminate against bankers but so did Republicans, old-line Whigs, merchants, and industrialists.

Americans in the immediate aftermath of the banking failure did not generally believe that their business woes originated in the readjustment of the Atlantic economy to the termination of the Crimean War. Instead, they lashed out at whatever national idiosyncracy seemed to harbor a dangerous tendency. Thus, the onslaught of the Panic was due to nothing more than a lack of confidence in the banks. Or, for many others, the financial trouble stemmed from the poor character traits of the people—the "inordinate greed for money," the pursuit of wealth with "ravenous intensity," the indulgence in "fast liv[ing]." Americans forgot about frugality and bought vast quantities of consumer goods on credit. Many people agreed with the famed Massachusetts orator Edward Everett when he wrote, "I believe that it [the Panic] was caused by a mountain load of DEBT." Others maintained that American youth turned away from productive labor and entered the professions, which created an "ill apportionment of industry"—that is, there were too many lawyers and not enough farmers.[1]

After venting their spleen on diverse elements of the national character, commentators turned to what they felt were some of the unhealthy developments in business life that had occurred over the past decade. Many blamed the depression on the rise of corporations in economic activity, because corporations released managers from personal responsibility. Others located the source of the nation's financial ills in the gold mines of California. Far from aiding the growth of the economy, California gold hindered real progress because it induced unnecessary imports and an expansion of paper money. Another favorite target of newspaper editors and economic crusaders was the railroad industry. James Gordon Bennett, proprietor of the New York *Herald*, was particularly vitriolic in his denunciation of the enterprise. According to Bennett, the Ohio Life collapsed because of the concern's "operating in railroad bonds and stocks," and the lesson to be learned from the financial stringency was to "have nothing to do with railroad securities." Popular wrath also fell upon western land speculators and town builders. Many agreed with the young Ohio school teacher James A. Garfield that "land speculation and the over drug[g]ing of the financial machinery in every department had made the explosion."[2]

But most Americans did not hold individuals responsible for their personal misfortunes during the economic downturn. Instead, they blamed the economic system for plunging vast numbers into poverty. An example of most commentators' ability to overlook the peccadilloes of their fellowmen was the manner in which editors, politicians, and other observers treated the unemployed. Virtually no one, regardless of political affiliation, argued that the desperate condition of the jobless

1. Philadelphia *Southern Monitor*, quoted by Richmond (Va.) *Enquirer*, October 20, 1857; *Harper's New Monthly Magazine*, XVI (April, 1858), 694; Cleveland *Daily Plain Dealer*, October 24, 1857; Edward Everett, *The Mount Vernon Papers* (New York, 1860), 167, 177; *American Railway Times*, October 15, 1857; *Democratic Press* (York, Pa.), December 1, 1857.

2. For remarks on corporations, see E. B. Bigelow, *Remarks of the Depressed Condition of Manufacturers in Massachusetts* (Boston, 1858), 4–14. The role of California gold can be found in Wm. Worthington Fowler, *Ten Years in Wall Street* (Hartford, Conn., 1870), 109–10. Contemporary attitudes toward railroads are reflected in New York *Herald*, August 25, September 5, October 15, 1857. For Garfield, see Harry James Brown and Frederick D. Williams (eds.), *The Diary of James A. Garfield* (East Lansing, Mich., 1967), I, 298.

was the result of their own character flaws. As one Democratic editor sermonized, "If the world owes any man a living, it owes it to him who produces the means of living for all others." The Republican Horace Greeley agreed; he felt that "society, through its political organization or framework should make adequate provision against involuntary idleness and consequent need on the part of its members."[3]

In judging whether individual vices or a defective commercial system created the Panic, Americans relied upon some well-defined expectations as to how an economy should distribute its rewards. The business affairs of the nation were governed by certain institutions, rules, and regulations. If the system accorded with natural laws, then indeed individuals brought on their own misfortunes. An economy governed by the appropriate laws and procedures invariably provided the highest possible standard of living, ample opportunities, and a just recompense to all who labored. An improperly constructed economy resulted in depressions, an unfair distribution of wealth, and few outlets for talent. Under an "oppressive" system, individuals could not be held accountable for their private fates, for the system warped the true path of economic pursuit and erected blockades to material and moral improvement. Because the optimistic multitude considered depressions aberrations, they believed that the origin of the Panic lay somewhere in the economic system. In the fall of 1857, virtually the entire nation proclaimed that bankers were guilty of causing the collapse. Through their policy of credit contraction bankers had managed to alienate nearly everyone in the country, even those whom the financiers had once counted as friends.

The business chroniclers of the day had little praise for the policies of the bankers during the fall of 1857. J. Smith Homans, who edited *Bankers' Magazine,* charged that the collapse was due to the "injudicious curtailment of loans—the want of harmony and consistency in the movements of the banks." Freeman Hunt, who edited the other major journal of business affairs, *Hunt's Merchants' Magazine,* excoriated the financial practices concerning demand deposits and call loans. The railroad publicist Henry Varnum Poor lashed out at the bankers'

3. *Democratic Press* (York, Pa.), October 27, 1857; New York *Daily Tribune,* November 7, 1857. This interpretation differs from that of Eric Foner, *Free Soil, Free Labor, Free Men,* 24–25, who believes that Republicans blamed the miseries of the poor upon their character faults rather than finding the trouble in the economic system. In the instance of the Panic of 1857, however, Republicans as well as Democrats had a more complex view of economic troubles. More is developed on the labor problem in Chap. 4.

habits of granting long-term loans based on stockholdings instead of capital or business paper. Bankers themselves were not happy with their performance in the Panic of 1857. The chief clerk of the New York clearinghouse, James S. Gibbons, found that the banks had contracted credit too quickly. Basing his charge on the weekly accounts published by the clearinghouse, Gibbons later wrote that the figures demonstrated "beyond cavil, that the *banks*, not the depositors, took the lead in forcing liquidation."[4]

The individuals who most used the banks to conduct their businesses, the merchants, showed an animosity toward the financiers. Middlemen in New York and Boston had held meetings during the Panic to demand increased loans and discounts. After specie suspension, a committee of New York hardware merchants offered to a gathering of their number a report that attributed "a great deal of our trouble to the action of the Banks," because the banks had encouraged "overtrading" by granting credit too easily. At board of trade and chamber of commerce meetings, merchants continued to attack credit policies, usually calling for higher specie reserve ratios, shorter credit terms, and the elimination of small-denomination bank notes.[5]

To the extent that industrialists talked about banking matters, they also revealed a certain hostility toward financiers. Nathan Appleton, an old Whig war-horse and preeminent Massachusetts textile manufacturer, demonstrated his dislike of banks when he wrote that he felt "no hesitation" at all in affixing the blame for the Panic upon "the continued contraction of the New York banks since the 5th of September, without the slightest necessity." Other manufacturers spoke of tariffs and unfair foreign competition at their meetings, yet most also demanded a reform of the credit system.[6]

If the business community complained about the behavior of the nation's financiers, their cries of anger were barely audible compared to

4. *Banker's Magazine*, XII (November, 1857), 390, 413, 429–34; *Hunt's*, XXXVII (November, 1857), 582–85, XXXVII (October, 1857), 452–53; *American Railroad Journal*, October 10, 1857, pp. 648–49; Gibbons, *The Banks of New-York*, 354, 365–75.

5. Report of hardware merchants in New York *Times*, October 26, November 7, 1857; Boston merchants in Boston *Post*, October 3, 1857; Philadelphia *Evening Bulletin*, October 9, November 24, 1857; Charleston *Daily Courier*, November 13, 1857.

6. Quote from letter of Nathan Appleton, October 12, 1857, in *Hunt's*, XXXVII (November, 1857), 595; Francis W. Gregory, *Nathan Appleton: Merchant and Entrepreneur, 1779–1861* (Charlottesville, Va., 1975), 212; Glenn Porter and Harold C. Livesay, *Merchants and Manufacturers: Studies in the Changing Structure of Nineteenth-Century Marketing* (Baltimore, 1971), 63–77.

the avalanche of vituperation that emanated from press and rostrum. Railing against the policies of bankers was not the monopoly of any particular region, political party, or occupational group. Southerners were furious at the actions of both their state banks and the New York City banks. Democrats below the Mason-Dixon Line decried the "tyranny" of banks and the "manner in which these vampyres ply their trade of drawing aliment from the pores of the business community—in which they generate moral pestilence with its accompaniment of horrors." Southern Whigs, while not following their political opponents in proposed reforms or in the violence of their rhetoric, nonetheless pointed to the "vast expansion of the currency" and to financial speculation as the chief agents of the crash.[7]

Northern Democrats matched the furor of their southern compeers. The excitable editor of the Cleveland *Daily Plain Dealer* exulted that "public opinion is getting to be almost universal, that Banks are the bane of our steady prosperity." Other Democratic organs denounced the "giant monopolies" of finance that engaged in illegitimate stock market activities, issued worthless "rag money," and ignored the welfare of merchants and industrialists. Democrats also sneered at the attempts of bankers to obtain legislative sanction for the specie suspension. The banker's argument that a legalized suspension was "*relief for the people*," argued the editor of the *Daily Illinois State Register*, stretched "credulity beyond parallel." He then asked, "Do suspended banks stop the collection of outstanding claims? Do they permit, without pretext, the day of payment of notes of their customers to pass by?—We all know that they do no such thing."[8]

The peculiar circumstances of the Panic of 1857, especially the policy of contraction, enabled many Republicans to join the Democrats in disparaging financiers. Henry J. Raymond believed the collapse was the result of "the lack of integrity on the part of the managers of certain great money corporations on both sides of the Atlantic," while other Republicans noted with disgust the intimate connections between banks and "that nest of gamblers, the Brokers' Board." Resolutions of Rhode Island Democrats against banks were concurred with by

7. *Mississippian* (Jackson), January 8, 1858; *Mississippi Free Trader* (Natchez), October 23, 1857; Richmond (Va.) *Whig*, October 6, 1857.

8. Cleveland *Daily Plain Dealer*, November 2, 1857; New York *Herald*, September 2, 1857; Detroit *Daily Free Press*, October 13, 1857; *Daily True American* (Trenton, N.J.), November 4, 5, 1857; Boston *Post*, September 19, 1857; *Daily Illinois State Register* (Springfield), October 13, 1857.

one Providence Republican editor who stated that the views expressed by the Democrats were "entertained by men in all parties." A correspondent of Ohio congressman John Sherman reported that the "great majority of our intelligent business men—Whigs as well as others—attribute our present financial trouble, in a great measure, to the action of the banks themselves," and the banks "by their recent conduct, are without the pale of the sympathy of nine tenths of the voters, (*Whig* and Democratic) of the Union." And few Democratic journals could match the bitterness of the Chicago *Tribune:* "The bank presidents met regularly, and resolved to expand. They adjourned and proceeded to contract with all their might. They put merchants and manufacturers into liquidation, and cast laborers into the street. They took new turns on the screw every discount day and reduced the community to the extremity of desperation. Exasperated beyond bounds, the people exercised their prerogative of demanding their money from these wreckers. . . . It does not become the bank presidents to cry out against the 'lack of confidence.' The lack of confidence began with themselves."[9]

The reason for the uniformity in the angry response of most Americans to the behavior of bankers in 1857 was the bankers' seeming willingness to crush the rest of the business community in order to save themselves. The financiers earned more enmity when, seeing that suspension was unavoidable, they begged state legislatures to legalize the suspension so that creditors could not force them into bankruptcy. This momentary congruence of political opinion was not destined to last, but the immediate general reaction to the Panic tended to one point: virtually everybody blamed the crash upon the nation's financiers.

The political parties soon divided over the questions of banks and the cause of the Panic of 1857. Despite the consensus that bankers had misbehaved during the crisis, the politicians soon fell to bickering over appropriate punishments and remedies. As the political battle concerning the Panic heated up, the most obvious trend was the division of the participants into the groups that had fought over the rechartering of the Second Bank of the United States. The Panic of 1857 was for many individuals simply a revisitation of the Panic of 1837, and hence

9. New York *Times*, December 7, 1857; New York *Daily Tribune*, October 1, 1857; Providence *Daily Tribune*, October 26, 1857; Henry D. Cooke to John Sherman, November 17, 1857, in John Sherman Papers, Manuscripts Division, Library of Congress, Washington, D.C., hereinafter cited as LC; Chicago *Daily Tribune*, October 16, 1857.

they invoked the arguments and party divisions of that earlier period. The reaction of the majority of Americans to the Panic of 1857 was often an unthinking reflex to the banking issue.

From the moment the Ohio Life failed, Democrats laid responsibility for the financial derangement upon the bankers. "De-cenially, and sometimes annually," thundered the Cleveland *Daily Plain Dealer*, "we are called upon to warn the farmer, mechanic, and laboring man, against the Rag Barrons, Charter Mongers and Privileged Orders, who are after a division of their hard earnings in the way of burst up banks and repudiated promises to pay." Prominent Democrats published letters and delivered speeches in which they denounced banks for creating a paper money; almost without exception they demanded a specie currency. Some individuals also used the Panic as a means to bind the party together. John Van Buren hoped to lure his father out of retirement and thus heal the breach in the New York Democracy over the slavery question by stressing the need for currency reform.[10]

The Democrats' hostility toward banks during the Panic of 1857 stemmed from the nature of American banking. Financial institutions were often the ill-conceived creations of state legislatures, which bestowed upon the banks special privileges and powers. But bankers pursued their own selfish goals and forgot or ignored the welfare of the community. Thus in 1857 the banks, which had been established for the sole purpose of managing credit and providing financial stability, had miscalculated the needs of the country because of their "insatiable" thirst for profits. The end result of this behavior was unemployment for the masses; the Democrats believed that the unemployed were thus "swindled out of an honest livelihood by the base conduct of a band of heartless money changers."[11]

Of all the economic sins listed by nineteenth-century Democrats, the greatest was the emission of an unbacked paper currency. "Banks were originally instituted to keep and pay out deposits entrusted to their care, and not to make money," observed one Mississippi editor, "but among the many inventions of modern civilization to cheat nature out of the great primordial curse [*i.e.*, labor], that of paper-issuing Banks stand[s] foremost." Democrats blamed the inflation of the 1850s

10. Cleveland *Daily Plain Dealer*, August 28, 1857; John D. Van Buren to Martin Van Buren, October 22, 1857, in Martin Van Buren Papers, LC; Thomas Hart Benton, "Col. Benton on Banks and Currency," *Banker's Magazine*, XII (January, 1858), 559–65; James Guthrie, "Address on the Currency," *Bankers' Magazine*, XII (February, 1858), 596–97.

11. *Allegheny Mountain Echo* (Johnstown, Pa.), November 18, 1857.

on excessive note issues and held that the only safe system was one in which all bank notes could be immediately redeemed in specie. Gold and silver were the only proper mediums of exchange for the nation. The administration organ, the Washington *Union*, probably gave the most typical and exhaustive—and redundant and boring—Democratic analysis of the causes of the Panic. No reader of the paper was taken by surprise to find that the *Union* leveled its political cannons at the role of banks in issuing an unsecured currency.[12]

The Democrats' cure for the financial malaise followed logically from their analysis of the origins of the monetary failure. As soon as the financial troubles grew into a Panic, Democrats called for stiffer specie reserve ratios, a bankruptcy law for moneyed corporations, the establishment of state independent treasuries, and the curtailment of paper money emissions. Some Democrats advocated the abolition of banks, but this was not common. Democrats generally agreed that the most important reform was to eliminate paper money of small denominations. One correspondent of James Buchanan revealed how this Democratic solution for the currency would operate: "If Congress has lost control over it [the currency], they should reacquire it—by an amendment of the Constitution any Bank note of less than $5 should not be allowed to circulate after a certain period—nothing less than $10 after another period and nothing less than $20 after another period. When we get to that point, we shall be safe." The reduction of bank notes of small denominations became the most widely accepted Democratic reform of the financial system during the Panic.[13]

Republicans failed to duplicate the Democrats' ability to achieve a near-monolithic stand on the causes of and the remedies for the crash. Indeed, the Republican party's attempt to handle the issue of banking legislation demonstrated that the only common bond among Republicans was hostility to slavery's expansion. The recently established organization contained individuals from a wide array of political backgrounds—abolitionists, Democrats, Whigs, nativists, and free soilers. While Republicans agreed on halting the spread of slavery into the territories, there was no party consensus on economic questions. As a

12. Quote from *Mississippi Free Trader* (Natchez), October 30, 1857; Washington (D.C.) *Union*, August 28, October 7, 8, 10, 13, 21, 24, 31, 1857.

13. Charles Macalester to James Buchanan, October 20, 1857, in James Buchanan Papers, HSP; Rezneck, "The Influence of Depression Upon American Opinion," 10–12; Bruce W. Collins, "Economic Issues in Ohio's Politics During the Recession of 1857–1858," *Ohio History*, LXXXIX (1980), 51–53.

consequence the economic ideas of any individual Republican depended almost solely on his past political affiliation. The Panic of 1857,
therefore, exposed the disorganization of the Republicans on issues
other than that of slavery.

Those individuals who once identified with Henry Clay and Daniel
Webster quickly resurrected the old Whig doctrines and applied them
to the Panic. Whether or not they belonged to the Republican party, or
whether they hailed from the North or the South, former Whigs proclaimed with the Washington *Daily National Intelligencer* that the solution to the Panic was "a National Bank and a Protective Tariff." As
one journalist wrote, "The principles of the Whig party must again become the controlling policy of the nation."[14]

The idea of protectionism in particular sparked a considerable
amount of enthusiasm. Former Whigs blamed the Panic on the low
Democratic tariff of 1857 that caused a trade imbalance in favor of Europe, which then produced a drain of American specie to that continent. Pennsylvanians more than any others welcomed the resurgence
of protectionism. One editor in the state wrote, "'Protection to American Labor' should most certainly be, and is, more sensible than the
motto—'our country, right or wrong.'" Even some southern Whigs
blamed the Panic on the "Free Trade Tariff." The leading South Carolina industrialist, the textile manufacturer William Gregg, wrote to
Rhode Island Senator James F. Simmons expressing his approval of a
higher tariff: "You are right about a moderate Tariff, if all the Eastern
people had entertained your views the South never would have become so hostile to the measure."[15]

Many former Whigs also desired a new national bank and hoped
that the experience of 1857 would make the public understand the necessity of having such a guardian over the states. The reason a new national bank was needed, according to the *Daily National Intelligencer*,
was that such an institution would act as "a regulator which shall correct the unsteady motion and restrain the unsafe velocity of each cog
and wheel in the complex machine of public credit and business life."
Conservatives praised the power of the Bank of England and ap-

14. *Daily National Intelligencer* (Washington, D.C.), October 31, 1857; Lebanon
(Pa.) *Courier*, October 23, 1857.
15. Letter of N. P. Tallmadge in *Daily National Intelligencer* (Washington, D.C.),
November 5, 1858; *Cambria Tribune* (Johnstown, Pa.), January 20, 1858; Richmond (Va.)
Whig, October 6, 1857; William Gregg to James F. Simmons, December 29, 1857, in
James Fowler Simmons Papers, LC.

plauded that institution's performance. Southern Whigs were more pleased, generally speaking, with the idea of a new national bank than with a higher tariff. The southern opposition believed a bank was a "useful institution, and that a properly conducted bank would be of great benefit."[16]

But in the autumn of 1857 Republicans hesitated to accept the old Whig economic cures of a high tariff and a national bank. Many Republicans who once swore allegiance to Henry Clay had no desire to see a new national bank. One editor referred to such an institution as "a powerful engine for mischief." Many Whiggish Republicans had become enamored with the free banking system, which was, in the phrase of the Indianapolis *Daily Journal*, "the best that human wisdom has yet devised to supply the defects of an inevitable credit system." These Republicans were even amenable to a reform of the banking laws, but they refused to countenance the "reckless anti-bank tirades" of the Democrats.[17]

The real difficulty the Republican party faced in regard to economic issues was the presence of a significant number of former Democrats and free soilers in positions of leadership in the party. These included Ohio Governor Salmon P. Chase, New Hampshire Senator John P. Hale, Massachusetts representatives George S. Boutwell and Nathaniel P. Banks, New York *Evening Post* editor William Cullen Bryant, Pennsylvania congressman Galusha A. Grow, the Keystone State's Judge David Wilmot, Illinois Senator Lyman Trumbull, and the occasional mayor of Chicago, John Wentworth. The Republicans of Democratic antecedents, hereinafter denoted as Democrat-Republicans, usually were ardent Jacksonian economists, believers in free trade, specie currency, and laissez faire government. The Panic of 1857 did not alter their economic convictions.[18]

Democrat-Republicans attacked banks and paper money with as

16. *Daily National Intelligencer* (Washington, D.C.), October 22, 1857; John Crosby Brown, *A Hundred Years of Merchant Banking: A History of Brown Brothers and Company, Brown, Shipley & Company and the Allied Firms* (New York, 1909), 218; Vicksburg *Daily Whig*, November 12, 1858. The importance of the banking issue to southern Whigs is addressed by Charles Grier Sellers, Jr., "Who Were the Southern Whigs?" *American Historical Review*, LIX (1954), 335–46, hereinafter cited as *AHR*.

17. *Miner's Journal* (Pottsville, Pa.), November 14, 1857; Indianapolis *Daily Journal*, October 14, 1857; Cincinnati *Daily Gazette*, September 29, 1857.

18. For Democrats in the Republican party, see Foner, *Free Soil, Free Labor, Free Men*, 149–85; Judah B. Ginsberg, "Barnburners, Free Soilers, and the New York Republican Party," *New York History*, LVII (1976), 478–500.

much vehemence as the regular Democracy. Jesse K. Dubois wrote Lyman Trumbull to thank the senator for his views on the banking problems and then added that "I shall not *ever consent* that the Bank companies shall cease in doing their duty. It is better for us at once to know the end, of all the *Bogus* Banking than to be tampering with a set of Insolent Banks and in the end get fooled by them." Nathaniel P. Banks, who won the Massachusetts governorship in the elections of 1857, recommended that the state legislature suppress small bank notes and impose a high specie reserve ratio, which were typical Democratic demands. Governor Salmon P. Chase suggested that Ohio implement another Democratic program, a state independent treasury.[19]

Nor did the Democrat-Republicans evince any desire to see the country return to protectionism. John Wentworth in Chicago noticed how "some editors with Whig proclivities" were expounding upon the need for a higher tariff, but he argued that instead the country should follow the rest of the world "in a direction favorable to free trade principles." Only in Pennsylvania did the tariff attract the Democrat-Republicans, and that was due to the nature of the state's iron interests. Otherwise the Democrat-Republicans refused to heed the siren call of the tariff—at least momentarily.[20]

Republican reformer-editor Horace Greeley caught the dissension in the Republican party over the economic issues raised by the Panic. Greeley preferred the doctrines of the defunct Whig party and longed to push the Republicans into an advocacy of economic nationalism. Yet New York City was a perfect example of the troubles that beset the Republican party in regard to economic matters: the Democratic barn-burner element of the party had already declared hostility to a resurrection of the Whig program and one of the important Republican newspapers, the *Evening Post,* was violently Jacksonian on economic questions. Greeley understood that if the party tried to erect some standard on economic issues it would disintegrate. The chief editor of the *Tribune* tried to sum up the Republican position on the Panic, and in so doing he illustrated the weakness of the Republicans on issues not

19. Jesse K. DuBois to Lyman Trumbull, October 5, 1857, in Lyman Trumbull Papers, LC; Boston *Post,* January 8, 1858; Bogart, *Financial History of Ohio,* 89–91, 165, 288–89.

20. Chicago *Daily Democrat,* October 7, 1857; Erwin Stanley Bradley, *Simon Cameron, Lincoln's Secretary of War: A Political Biography* (Philadelphia, 1966), 59–61; Malcolm Rogers Eiselen, *The Rise of Pennsylvania Protectionism* (Philadelphia, 1932), 237–41, 247.

directly linked to slavery: "The party in power is about to make an attack on the Banks, in the hope of distracting attention from the great issue of Slavery Extension. The Republicans must not allow themselves to be thus distracted and divided. Some of us are Bank men, others for Hard Money; but neither Banks nor Hard Money have any place in our platform, and any Republican is at perfect liberty to cherish and maintain his own theory with regard to the Currency." Greeley was correct. The Republicans issued a silent truce on economic questions and allowed members of the party to advocate whatever course of action seemed proper. If this had not been done, the Republicans would have faced the difficult, if not impossible, task of keeping their coalition together.[21]

Despite this acrimonious, partisan debate over banks following the Panic of 1857, there was in reality a general agreement among contemporaries about financial operations. Americans of all political persuasions viewed banks as abnormal economic enterprises. Farmers, laborers, mechanics, industrialists, and merchants all contributed something tangible to the economy; such individuals either produced wealth or moved goods to markets. Under these circumstances the imperial law of supply and demand ruled, and Americans believed, in accordance with the doctrines of Adam Smith, that businessmen who sought to maximize their earnings did the public a great service. By seeking more profits, these businessmen expanded markets, increased employment, and generated more national wealth. But contemporaries doubted that the profit motive produced the same beneficial results in finance as it did in industry, agriculture, and commerce. Bankers, in the public mind, did not create physical wealth; their function was to safeguard the currency, protect deposits, loan capital to entrepreneurs, and extend short-term credit to merchants. Financiers, when left to their own devices, tried to increase bank earnings through currency manipulations, and this activity, in the popular view, was a redistribution of existing wealth rather than the creation of new wealth. Americans characterized this means of profit-making as inequitable, and therefore they demanded that legislators enact laws that would adequately prevent currency manipulations.[22]

The Panic of 1837 was a valuable lesson to those who lived to see the

21. New York *Daily Tribune*, November 16, 1857.
22. Providence *Daily Tribune*, October 13, 1857; New York *Daily Tribune*, September 10, 1857; Milwaukee *Daily Free Democrat*, September 21, 1857; Detroit *Daily Free Press*, October 13, 1857.

financial disaster of 1857. Republicans adopted the warning of Jacksonian Democrats that central banks could be utilized by individuals to wreak havoc on the economy. "Banks should not be monopolies—accommodating the few, and turning a cold shoulder to the many," commented a Whiggish editor. Conversely, Democrats tacitly acknowledged the necessity of banks to aid commerce. In 1857, the party of Jackson attacked currency, not the existence of banks. Democrats, too, had learned from the crash of 1837.[23]

Democratic and Republican ideas on banking began to converge. Although they differed on the not unimportant question of a national bank, both parties desired to erect barriers to irresponsible currency emission. Banking theory and the desires of the banking community itself tended to push everyone along the lines of higher specie reserve ratios and an extension of the free banking system. Thus demand for change was channeled into strengthening the laws already upon the statute books. What legislators needed to do was to find the correct specie reserve ratio and the proper amount of securities that banks had to hold. Republicans and Democrats clashed over questions of small note issues and the use of paper money generally, but on the proper system of banking their dissimilarities tended to narrow.[24]

Important state elections in the fall of 1857—especially in Pennsylvania, New York, Massachusetts, and Ohio—allowed political leaders to exaggerate the banking policy differences between the parties. Rather quickly the Panic was pressed into electioneering service. Massachusetts Democrats blamed their state's difficulties on Republican banking legislation and called for retrenchment and reform. The Ohio Democracy sought to unseat the Republican incumbent Salmon P.

23. Providence *Daily Tribune*, October 12, 1857; Cincinnati *Daily Gazette*, August 28, 1857; Mobile *Daily Register*, November 8, 1857; Detroit *Daily Free Press*, October 13, 1857.

24. William G. Shade, *Banks or No Banks*, 207–23, generally interprets the political reactions in the Old Northwest as a continuation of the pattern begun in Andrew Jackson's presidency and notes the political difficulties of the Republicans. He does not emphasize, however, many of the similarities in bank policy that the two parties came to advocate. Bruce W. Collins, in "The Politics of Particularism," contests the view that the Republicans believed in intervention in the economy and that the Democrats were adherents of laissez faire principles. He believes the reverse was the case. The thesis offered here is that differences between the parties by the 1850s on banking questions have been somewhat exaggerated, and that the Republicans were indeed interventionist and the Democrats decidedly laissez faire.

Chase by charging the Republicans with malfeasance and ineptitude in office. The basis for their claims was that the failure of the Ohio Life jeopardized the credit of the state, and the state treasurer had, it was discovered, embezzled funds. New York Democrats attempted to discredit the Kansas issue now that the more "practical" matter of bank suspensions had arisen.[25]

The Republican response to the Democratic challenge on banking programs during the campaign revealed the unusual coalition problems of the party. The Republican gubernatorial candidates in Ohio, New York, and Massachusetts offered Democratic solutions to the banking dilemma; Nathaniel P. Banks even complimented the economic ideas of Democrat James Guthrie, former secretary of the treasury. Ex-Democrat David Dudley Field authored a series of resolutions by which New York Republicans hoped to capture the state's voters. The banking resolution stated that Republicans were opposed to "all partial and monopoly favoring legislation, holding that the State shall abstain from appropriating the public moneys for private or legal purposes."[26]

Much of the nation's political interest centered on the Pennsylvania gubernatorial contest. Political analysts realized that the Keystone State had guaranteed James Buchanan the Presidency in 1856 when the state had given the Democracy a meager but definite majority. Pennsylvania was the one northern state in which the Democracy controlled virtually all political offices, and it was also the one state that made possible the election of Democratic Presidents. If Frémont had carried Pennsylvania and one other state—such as New Jersey— Buchanan would not have become the chief executive. Most Pennsylvania elections therefore stimulated considerable political speculation.

The Democrats nominated William F. Packer, and they had little doubt as to his eventual victory. A goodly amount of the Democrats' optimism arose from the gubernatorial nominee chosen by the Republicans, David Wilmot. Wilmot belonged to the small, vociferous, and largely unpopular antislavery wing of the party. Moreover, the Pennsylvania Americans retained their separate identity and refused to co-

25. Boston *Post*, October 17, 24, 31, 1857; Cleveland *Daily Plain Dealer*, September 2, 7, 11, 18, 1857; quote from New York *Herald*, September 18, 1857; Collins, "The Politics of Particularism," 15–28, 45–58, 131–48.

26. Boston *Post*, October 16, 1857; *Daily Ohio State Journal* (Columbus), September 1, 1857; Bogart, *Financial History of Ohio*, 288–89; "Republican Address to the Citizens of New York" in New York *Daily Tribune*, September 25, 1857.

alesce with the Republicans. Democrats saw a divided opposition and accurately reasoned that theirs would be the stronger party at the October poll.

During the campaign the Pennsylvania Democrats reiterated their standard arguments against the Republicans: Republicans were rabid sectionalists who desired to promote racial equality. When the Panic of 1857 destroyed commerce and industry in the state, the Democrats proclaimed their fidelity to the interests of the workingman and their animosity to the banks. But the Democrats made one tactical error: they berated Wilmot because of his well-known free trade proclivities. This manuever was not without its merits, for Pennsylvania's citizens were most noted politically for their zealous support of high tariffs. However, the use of this tactic implied that if national tariff policy proved inimical to the state's important iron and coal interests, then the party would move to revise tariff rates upward. Time would prove that such was not to be the case.[27]

The Republicans labored under the knowledge that a Wilmot victory was improbable due to the inability, and unwillingness, of their party to fuse with the American party. They had not calculated, however, upon the additional burden which the Panic of 1857 imposed. Wilmot had intended to campaign on the sole issue of halting the spread of slavery into the territories. When the Panic of 1857 crippled the iron industry, the party eagerly turned to an advocacy of protectionism.[28] But at the same time that they unfurled the protectionist banner, they realized that they had nominated a notorious advocate of free trade.

David Wilmot understood his peculiar, unexpected, and awkward position, but he also demonstrated that the Republicans who had once been devotees of Jacksonian economics could momentarily relax their economic doctrines if the action promised a victory over the Slave Power. Thus Wilmot wrote a public letter to David S. Brown, a New

27. *Luzerne Union* (Wilkes-Barre), September 16, 1857; Erie (Pa.) *Weekly Observer*, September 26, 1857; *Allegheny Mountain Echo* (Johnstown, Pa.), September 30, 1857.
28. Alexander K. McClure, *Old Time Notes of Pennsylvania* (Philadelphia, 1905), I, 297–318; Charles Buxton Going, *David Wilmot, Free-Soiler: A Biography of the Great Advocate of the Wilmot Proviso* (New York, 1924), 498–501. Pennsylvania Republicans were usually a fusion party, and in 1857 they called themselves the American-Republican party, despite the fact that the American party still maintained its old organization. The term *Republican* has been used instead of contemporary nomenclature in order to prevent confusion.

York merchant, discussing the Panic. Wilmot deplored the soaring unemployment and the destitution that the financial collapse would ultimately bring to thousands of families. This economic reversal, he said, had generated a new interest in the "tariff policy of the country." Wilmot, like all Pennsylvania Republicans, blamed the low tariff of 1857 for the Panic. He then advocated a tariff that would provide "incidental protection, without a gross violation of the revenue principle"—still the standard Democratic position on the tariff—but would ensure that "American enterprise and labor" would be shielded from unfair foreign competition. In his summary of the principles at stake in the election, Wilmot constructed an important bridge that allowed the free-soil element of the party to acquiesce to Whig economics: "The great struggle in which we are now engaged, and in which my feelings are so deeply embarked, is a struggle to maintain the dignity and rights of free labor against the degrading competition of the labor of the slave; and I am equally in favor of protecting our American labor against a ruinous competition with the cheap labor of the old world." Wilmot, of course, did not stray too far from Democratic economic principles, nor was he the only Pennsylvanian to bind together the fate of the free worker, antislavery, and high tariffs. That a former Democrat could do so, however, was a portentous event for the Republican party.[29]

To what extent the Panic of 1857 affected the local contests of 1857 is debatable, for there were few surprises in the election results. The Democrats were victorious in Pennsylvania and New York, made strong inroads in Ohio (nearly defeating Chase), and were routed in Massachusetts. The election totals revealed Democratic percentage gains, although these probably arose from a lower voter turnout; the only significant change from the voting in 1856 was the virtual disappearance of the American party (see Table 1). Other issues in 1857—Kansas, Dred Scott, and local matters—probably had as much impact upon voters as the Panic. The electoral weight of the Panic would not be felt for another year.[30]

The results of the northern elections in 1857 encouraged Democrats everywhere and gave them an optimistic view of the political future. "The revolution is tremendous," declared William F. Storey, proprietor of the Detroit *Free Press*. "Niggerism is prostate. No broken

---

29. David Wilmot to David S. Brown, September 28, 1857, in New York *Daily Tribune*, October 2, 1857; for the election of 1857 in Pennsylvania, consult Eiselen, *The Rise of Pennsylvania Protectionism*, 241–46; Collins, "The Politics of Particularism," 88–94.

30. Collins, "The Politics of Particularism," 53–57, 93, 134–36, 142–45.

Table 1

Party Performance in Selected Northern State Elections, 1856 and 1857

State	Year	Office	Republican %	Democrat %	American %	Total Vote
Maine	1856	president	61.30	35.66	3.04	109,584
	1857	governor	56.11	43.89	0.0	96,943
New Hampshire	1856	president	53.59	45.82	0.59	71,556
	1857	governor	52.39	47.26	0.35	66,344
Vermont	1856	president	78.07	20.86	1.07	50,675
	1857	governor	66.13	32.21	0.66	40,315
Massachusetts	1856	president	64.76	23.49	11.75	167,056
	1857	governor	46.67	24.07	29.26	128,329
Rhode Island	1856	president	57.85	33.70	8.45	19,822
	1857	governor	65.25	34.75	0.0	14,744
Connecticut	1856	president	53.18	43.57	3.25	80,325
	1857	governor	50.43	49.57	0.0	62,860
New York	1856	president	46.29	32.84	20.87	596,486
	1857	sec. of state	40.34	44.45	15.21	439,789
Pennsylvania	1856	president	32.10	50.07	17.83	460,937
	1857	governor	40.24	52.01	7.75	363,155
Ohio	1856	president	48.51	44.21	7.28	386,492
	1857	governor	48.69	48.24	3.07	329,745
Iowa	1856	president	49.22	40.50	10.28	89,304
	1857	governor	51.85	48.15	0.0	58,135
Wisconsin	1856	president	55.30	44.22	0.48	119,513
	1857	governor	50.07	49.93	0.0	90,000

SOURCE: Computations made from *Tribune Almanac*, 1858

bank is so low. It is dead." A common theme among the Democrats was the demise of the Republican party. Southerners did not fail to notice the immense majority in Buchanan's home state. A Georgia reporter wrote, "Pennsylvania, the old Keystone State, takes her position by her more Southern sisters, and comes with such a majority as to entitle her a special demonstration of joy at her entire and we hope, eternal delivery from fanaticism and treason."[31]

Republicans had a less joyful task in explaining the voting results of the autumnal elections. Wisconsin's Carl Schurz, the showcase German immigrant who sided with the Republicans, believed the Panic had kept responsible, industrious party members from going to the polls. Know-Nothings, complained other Republicans, obdurately refused coalition and allowed Democrats to grab victory from the divided opposition. Others relied upon the usual sour grapes explanation: the Democracy corrupted the people with money, machine tactics, and aliens. But no amount of rationalizing could disguise the fact that the Republicans had suffered a setback in the 1857 elections.[32]

Democrats only had a few days of jubilation, satisfaction, and complacency. For just as the Panic ended and the election results were tallied, news arrived that Kansans had voted in favor of a proslavery state constitution and were applying for entrance into the Union. Circumstances surrounding the election of delegates to the constitutional convention, the decision not to allow the inhabitants to vote on the whole constitution but merely on its clause concerning slavery, and the seemingly fraudulent manner in which ratification took place, aroused the fears and hostilities that had haunted the country in 1856. When Nathaniel P. Banks congratulated Salmon P. Chase on his narrow victory in Ohio, the Massachusetts governor-elect did not bewail the effects of the Panic of 1857, nor the frauds in the Ohio treasury, nor the shifting allegiances of old Whigs and Know-Nothings; instead he concentrated solely on Kansas, the Lecompton Constitution, and the power of slavery in national affairs.[33] Whatever impact the Panic had

31. Detroit *Daily Free Press*, October 18, 1857; *Federal Union* (Milledgeville, Ga.), October 27, 1857.

32. Carl Schurz to Henry Meyer, November 25, 1857, in Joseph Schafer (trans. and ed.), *Intimate Letters of Carl Schurz, 1841–1869* (1928; rpr. New York, 1970), 180; Philadelphia *Evening Bulletin*, October 14, 1857; Providence *Daily Tribune*, October 26, 1857; Chicago *Daily Tribune*, November 4, 1857.

33. Nathaniel P. Banks to Salmon P. Chase, December 10, 1857, in Salmon Portland Chase Papers, HSP.

on Republican and Democratic leaders, it soon faded in the growing recognition that Congress faced a new struggle over slavery in the territories.

The elections of 1857 did not terminate political debate in the states over the appropriate means of adjusting laws to meet the lingering financial exigency. Indeed, political wars over banking legislation consumed local politics throughout 1858, especially in Virginia, Georgia, South Carolina, New York, Ohio, and Wisconsin. The Panic of 1857 created numerous conflicts between suspended banks and the requirements of state statutes, crippled the abilities of many states to continue internal improvement programs, and inspired a number of reforms that exacerbated antagonisms between urban and rural residents. Most of the legislative discussion on banking reform was intensely partisan. Democrats argued for punishment and stringent credit restrictions, while the opposition, although not unappreciative of reform efforts, sought to protect banks from liquidation or further embarrassment. Yet this debate never achieved national recognition. Bank policy was left to the states. The national legislators, as it turned out, only took cognizance of the northern economic depression, not the financial suspension.

Most state administrations and legislatures faced an immediate dilemma because of their existing statutes on banking. In order to reduce speculation and to coerce financiers into cautious credit practices, most states had passed laws punishing banks if ever they suspended specie payment. South Carolina fined banks 5 percent of their circulation if the institutions failed to provide specie payment; laws in New York and Pennsylvania decreed death to those corporations that suspended. Because of these laws, state legislatures had to choose between enforcement or leniency. Virtually all states passed relief measures delaying the time at which penalties would be inflicted.[34]

34. Harrisburg (Pa.) *Daily Telegraph*, October 5–14, 1857; *Harper's New Monthly Magazine*, XVI (December, 1857), 113; *House Executive Documents*, 35th Cong., 1st Sess., No. 107, pp. 181–83, 193–95, 214–15, 229, 241–43; *House Executive Documents*, 35th Cong., 2nd Sess.., No. 112, p. 172; Claude A. Campbell, *The Development of Banking in Tennessee* (Nashville, 1932), 133–53; Charleston *Mercury*, November 10, 1857; J. Mauldin Lesesne, *The Bank of the State of South Carolina: A General and Political History* (Columbia, S.C., 1970), 109–14; Milton Sidney Heath, *Constructive Liberalism: The Role of the State in Economic Development in Georgia to 1860* (Cambridge, Mass., 1954), 224–27; Bogart, *Financial History of Ohio*, 290–94.

Partisan tempers flared throughout the land over the passage of legislation giving the financiers extra time to arrange their affairs and reestablish specie payment. The laws infuriated the Democrats, North and South, because such enactments were "relief laws" or "stay laws" for banks, the idea of which bankers railed at if ever any other portion of the community sought legislative suspension of contracted debt. In Mississippi, the Democracy succeeded in destroying the two "monster" banks (the total capital of the two being, as of January 1, 1858, $1,450,000) within its boundaries. Governor Joseph Brown of Georgia vetoed a measure delaying penalties for Georgia banks; in South Carolina the comptroller general of the currency, J. D. Ashmore, said the "banks are in the hands of mere speculators," and he attacked them as "hucksters." Ohio Democrats attempted to levy a punitive tax on bank property because of the credit stringency of 1857, and in Nebraska, where so much wildcat banking had thrived, the territorial legislature finally made banking a criminal offense.[35]

Opposition leaders—Whigs and nativists in the South; Republicans, nativists, and Whigs in the North—defended the system of banking even though they were slightly less ready to do battle for individual bankers. One North Carolina Whig editor demanded to know why the Democracy made such a ruckus about the suspension and the banking system, for if the system were "vicious, who, we pray to know, is responsible for the mischief inflicted by it, the party who made the system, or the party that did not make it?" In Pennsylvania, the Whiggish proprietor of the Lebanon *Courier* indicated disaffection with Governor Pollack's call for a special assembly to provide relief to bankers. "We do not at all feel like endorsing the call," he wrote; "The policy of the thing may be good, but we dislike the principle." But once the editor witnessed the mounting Democratic outcry against the banks, he was, it seemed, forced to their defense. He lashed out at "Locofoco leaders" playing the "Jacobian and demagogue" about banks: "Democratic leaders have long been crying out against Banks, yet all that time they have been controlling two-thirds, at least, of the Banking capital of the country."[36]

35. Charleston *Daily Courier*, November 26, 1857; Charleston *Mercury*, November 10, 26, 1857; on Mississippi banks see *House Executive Documents*, 38th Cong., 1st Sess., No. 20, p. 216; *House Executive Documents*, 35th Cong., 1st Sess., No. 107, pp. 214–15; Joseph Howard Parks, *Joseph E. Brown of Georgia* (Baton Rouge, 1977), 43–50, 69–75; Bogart, *Financial History of Ohio*, 290–94; William E. Kuhn, *History of Nebraska Banking: A Centennial Retrospect* (Lincoln, Neb., 1908), 5–8.

36. Raleigh *Weekly Register*, October 28, 1857; Lebanon (Pa.) *Courier*, October 2, 9, 1857.

Opposition leaders took the position that if the banks were punished, then all other economic endeavors would be punished as well.
By threatening reprisals, legislators only made bankers press their
claims on businessmen and farmers with more desperation. In South
Carolina, the textile industrialist William Gregg warned that cotton
planters would be ruined if bankers failed to receive relief. A Georgia
Whig editor argued that Governor Brown in his fight against the banks
would end up wounding "the very class of his fellow-citizens . . . whom
the Governor no doubt is anxious to protect." An opposition editor in
Pennsylvania disliked relief for banks, but if a reprieve from existing
statutes were not afforded, the race to collect debts "will close up nine
out of every ten of the manufacturing establishments of the State, and
suspend all mining operations."[37] In the states, party lines over banking issues were fairly rigidly drawn: Democrats sought penalties, and
the opposition insisted upon preservation.

The Panic of 1857 accidently incited further partisan divisions over
the role of state governments in funding internal improvements. A
number of states either had extensive state-owned or state-financed
transportation systems in operation or were in the process of creating
them. The Panic of 1857 diminished state revenues, and legislatures
and localities were forced to reconsider their projects. Missourians had
committed their state banking system to finance an extensive railroad
network. The Panic caused a momentary crisis, but government officials managed to uphold the bank's financial integrity and to keep the
state's railroad plans intact. Such was not the case in Virginia. There
the economic disruption persuaded Governor Henry A. Wise to delay
his schemes for internal improvements in the western part of the state
and to advocate a tax on state bonds, a move which many feared would
kill improvement schemes altogether. Perhaps the greatest furor over
government-backed railroad expansion occurred in Minnesota, at that
time a territory, and Wisconsin. Minnesota passed a five million dollar
loan in 1858 for railroad construction, but western economic problems
continued into 1859 and the roads could not repay the loan. Wisconsin
raised funds for railroad growth by allowing farmers to mortgage their
lands in order to invest in railroad ventures. When Wisconsin railroads
ran into difficult times in 1858 and 1859, eastern creditors tried to reclaim their loans by foreclosing on Wisconsin farmers. That activity

37. Lesesne, *The Bank of the State of South Carolina*, 109–14; Broadus Mitchell,
William Gregg: Factory Master of the Old South (Chapel Hill, 1928), 184–96; *Southern
Recorder* (Milledgeville, Ga.), November 9, 1858; Harrisburg *Daily Telegraph*, Octo-
ber 5, 1857.

elicited a popular howl of protest, and the legislature responded by passing a "stay" law—that is, a law stopping creditors from collecting on obligations.[38] Westerners may have continued to believe that government subsidization of internal improvements was a practical necessity, but easterners were less sure. The Panic of 1857, because of internal revenue problems, powerfully aided a conviction that government should not be engaged in economic pursuits of any kind. In New York the problem took the form of whether the Erie Canal should be enlarged and tolls increased; in Pennsylvania it involved whether the state should sell its Mainline Canal and feeder canals to private companies. The New York legislature finally did pass legislation for the widening of the Erie Canal, and Pennsylvania by 1860 had successfully transferred state enterprises to private hands.

Local politics over these questions at times took some unusual forms. The opposition often desired to end government involvement in the economy, while Democrats often sought to preserve state control of certain activities. However, a host of factors were involved in state politics over internal improvements besides commitment to an economic philosophy. The counties that benefited from government schemes were loath to sacrifice their advantages; representatives from these locales, regardless of party identification, tried to sustain state control. And frequently embedded in these disputes was an East-West struggle or one that pitted developed areas against developing ones. Perhaps as significant as anything else, government enterprises also meant government patronage for the party in power. In Pennsylvania opposition leaders referred to the Democrats as the "canal Democracy"; one of the major reasons for their desire to sell the Mainline Canal was to deprive the Democrats of that source of political strength.[39]

Of the many reforms proposed to prevent future banking suspension, the most widely advocated by state administrators was to make

38. *House Executive Documents*, 35th Cong., 1st Sess., No. 107, pp. 254–56; James Neal Primm, *Economic Policy in the Development of a Western State: Missouri, 1820–1860* (Cambridge, Mass., 1954), 105–10; Richmond (Va.) *Enquirer*, December 8, 1857, April 6, 20, 1858; William Watts Folwell, "The Five Million Loan," *Collections of the Minnesota Historical Society*, XV (1915), 189–203; Richard N. Current, *The Civil War Era, 1848–1873* (Madison, Wisc., 1976), 243–50. Vol. II of William F. Thompson (ed.), *The History of Wisconsin*, 6 vols. projected.

39. Louis Hartz, *Economic Policy and Democratic Thought: Pennsylvania, 1776–1860* (Cambridge, Mass., 1948), 20–21, 161; Collins, "The Politics of Particularism," 52–60, 63–77, 101–13; Lewistown (Pa.) *Gazette*, July 12, 1854.

banks hold, by law, a higher ratio of specie reserves to circulation (or to capital or to deposits). The governors of New York, Pennsylvania, Louisiana, Tennessee, Virginia, Vermont, Connecticut, and Massachusetts, as well as other state spokesmen, advocated this remedy.[40] However, when legislatures enacted such new requirements, the laws provoked a fight between settled communities with established financial institutions and areas that wanted a less stringent credit system. Massachusetts passed a specie reserve law (15 percent specie reserve to amount of capital) in 1858. Country banks immediately saw this as a move to favor Boston banks under the Suffolk system of redemption. Country banks brought the same complaint toward urban banks in New York. The drive to ensure credit stability in the banking system by means of specie reserve requirements had the effect of withholding credit from developing areas. This defect, seen in state activities following the Panic of 1857, would also become a feature of the national banking system established during the Civil War; the specie reserve requirements brought credit stability to the settled states of the East, but credit stringency to the South and West.[41]

Yet for all this state activity and partisan struggle over legislation, the question of banking practices never became a national issue, never grabbed the serious, constant attention of the United States Congress. This was not due to a reluctance on the part of Democrats or the Buchanan administration to utilize the banking issue; Buchanan in fact wanted it to become the principal topic of debate. The Democracy expected electoral victories and enlarged majorities if banks became the focus of party strife. Yet reform of financial institutions never evolved into an important national issue, and the reason for this circumstance is clear: by the middle of 1858 virtually all banking systems in the United States had resumed specie payment, and there was no longer any perceived difficulties with finance. Banking problems simply disappeared before the Democrats could make political capital out of paper money

40. *House Executive Documents*, 35th Cong., 2nd Sess., No. 112, pp. 25, 31, 70–71; *House Executive Documents*, 35th Cong., 1st Sess., No. 107, pp. 123–24, 159, 181–83, 200–208, 241–43.

41. Redlich, *The Molding of American Banking*, II, 8–9; Wilfred S. Lake, "The End of the Suffolk System," *JEH*, VII (1947), 193–207; Collins, "The Politics of Particularism," 28–35, 59–62, 96–100; New York *Times*, October 23, 1858; John A. James, *Money and Capital Markets in Postbellum America* (Princeton, N.J., 1978), Chaps. 1–3; Roger L. Ransom and Richard Sutch, *One Kind of Freedom: The Economic Consequences of Emancipation* (London, 1977), 110–13.

woes.[42] What remained was not advantageous to the Democracy: a recession in the North. Banking convulsions elicited political responses favorable to the Democrats, but business stagnation brought forth a popular set of solutions that usually operated advantageously for the opposition. Hence the banking issue was not destined to aid the Democracy, which party leaders would agonizingly come to understand in the fall of 1858.

There were various groups in the United States who had few formal bonds to political parties but who reacted strongly to the Panic of 1857. Clergymen, literary figures, reformers, and communitarians all contributed in some measure to the public inquiry into the financial crash. Of these nonpolitical groups who discussed the Panic of 1857, the two most important were the northern abolitionists and the southern fire-eaters. But the fire-eaters and abolitionists interjected a new dimension to the debate over the Panic of 1857 that had largely been absent: sectional rancor.

Abolitionism had its own peculiar problems in the 1850s. When the crusade against slavery started in earnest during the 1830s, the abolitionists hoped to destroy southern bondage by gathering those who were morally outraged at the institution and by agitating the question before the public; they intended to achieve their goal through peaceful, nonviolent means. By the 1850s, however, the question of slavery had become the central issue of politics. The result was that the lofty concern of the abolitionists for the welfare of the slave was being replaced by a northern fear of the power and designs of the slaveholders. Some abolitionists, impatient at the lack of success of the movement, began to reject pacifist means.

The abolitionists were convinced that the two pillars upholding chattel slavery in the United States were the federal government and organized religion. If these two institutions were pulled down, then slavery would perish. In accordance with this analysis abolitionists had scheduled a "Disunion Convention" to meet at Cleveland on October 28, 1857. At this gathering abolitionists would discuss ways to effect the separation of the slaveholding states from the nonslaveholding states and deprive slavery of the sustaining power of the federal government. The Panic of 1857 suddenly intervened and the most famous of the abolitionists, William Lloyd Garrison, proposed that the con-

42. This conclusion was also reached by Bruce W. Collins, "The Democrats' Electoral Fortunes During the Lecompton Crisis," *CWH*, XXIV (1978), 328.

vention be postponed because of the financial derangement. In fact, the Panic made Garrison cancel all of his speaking engagements.

In one of his letters expressing his regrets at being unable to attend an antislavery meeting, Garrison presented the abolitionist interpretation of the Panic of 1857. He did not use either economic theory or banking practices to explain the cause of the financial failure. Instead he maintained that slavery inculcated the vices of selfishness, dishonesty, and speculation, which naturally produced an erratic economy. "Let others talk of the immediate causes of the present chaotic state of things as they may," Garrison summarized; "for one, I believe it is owing to the existence, growth, extension and supremacy of slavery, in a preëminent degree."[43]

Other abolitionists quickly confirmed Garrison's opinions. At the Cleveland disunion convention, held despite Garrison's absence, the delegates repeated the sentiments in Garrison's letter. The *Radical Abolitionist* believed that all slaveholding nations were "subject to financial revulsions" because of the immorality of slavery. The focus of the abolitionists in regard to the Panic, then, was to detail the individual faults that the practices of slavery encouraged and how these shortcomings then led to commercial disaster.[44]

The abolitionists did not consider the Panic in an economic light, preferring rather to use it for propaganda. Whatever thoughts the abolitionists entertained about the functioning of the economy were undisclosed, and later developments ensured that their attention turned elsewhere. The outbreak of religious revivalism consumed the intellectual efforts of the antislavery crusaders. Economic questions, with the possible exceptions of free land and free trade, received scant consideration from them. Indeed, to the extent such a mentality was possible, abolitionists displayed on the whole an amazing nonchalance about economic affairs.[45]

43. William Lloyd Garrison to Samuel J. May, October 18, 1857, Garrision to Pennsylvania Anti-Slavery Society, October 20, 1857, both in Louis Ruchames and Walter M. Merrill (eds.), *The Letters of William Lloyd Garrison* (Cambridge, Mass., 1971–81), IV, 490, 491–94; *Liberator*, October 23, 1857.

44. *Radical Abolitionist* quoted by *Liberator* (Boston), October 23, 1857; letter of Gerrit Smith in New York *Daily Tribune*, January 5, 1858; Parker Pillsbury to William Lloyd Garrison, October 26, 1857, in *National Anti-Slavery Standard* (New York), November 14, 1857; speech of Abbey Kelley Foster at Cleveland in *National Anti-Slavery Standard* (New York), November 21, 1857; speech of William Furness in *National Anti-Slavery Standard* (New York), November 14, 1857.

45. See the reports on the reform meetings contained in Philadelphia *Evening Bulletin*, October 26, 1857; *Anti-Slavery Bugle* (Salem, Ohio), November 7, 1857; New York

The southern counterparts of the abolitionists also seized the opportunities offered by the Panic to press their sectional goals. Southern partisans used the collapse to demonstrate the burdens and injustices the South suffered while a part of the Union. There was one important difference, however, between the northern and southern agitators; northerners largely ignored the conclusions of the abolitionists, but the analysis of the southern fire-eaters had a wide and appreciative audience below the Mason-Dixon Line.

The general southern response to the Panic was conditioned by the region's high expectations with regard to the sale of the cotton and tobacco crops. The dismal effect of the Panic on the prime southern staples was all too certain—prices fell disastrously. Cotton declined over five cents a pound in the fall months of 1857. The planters endured the greatest losses, for they had made consumption purchases on the premise that cotton prices would remain high. The suffering of the planters was unjust because the "planters are not the cause of this terrible monetary convulsion."[46]

The South's troubles, so southerners thought, originated in the irresponsible actions of the New York financiers. New York bankers had acted like "charlatans in commerce" during the crisis and had discharged their duties "unfaithfully, recklessly, [and] ruinously." Southerners everywhere raised the cry that "causes entirely foreign to the operations of our Banks" created the suspension. All the pressure upon southern lending institutions came wholly from the North, and particularly from New York City.[47]

As southern businessmen watched their hopes for great profits go awry, and as southern politicians saw their banks crumble into the ignominy of suspension, they increasingly found the source of their misfortunes in the deficient character traits of northerners. The basis of northern wealth was ephemeral. In the free states "all is wild speculation and consequent disaster." Southerners believed the cause of the Panic was "the wild speculations of Northern and Western corporations

---

Daily Tribune, May 12, June 29, September 11, 1858; James L. Huston, "Abolitionists and an Errant Economy: The Panic of 1857 and Abolitionist Economic Ideas," *Mid-America*, LXV (1983), 15–27.

46. *Mississippi Free Trader* (Natchez), October 16, 1857; *Southern Recorder* (Milledgeville, Ga.), October 20, 1857.

47. *De Bow's Review*, XXV (November, 1858), 561; editorial comment in *Russell's Magazine*, II (November, 1857), 177; Charleston *Mercury*, October 12, 1857; Nevins, *The Emergence of Lincoln*, I, 195–97.

and individuals in waste lands, internal improvements, palatial buildings, together with every species of stock jobbing and wild adventure." In contrast, the slaveholding states had "not overtraded, or hazarded [themselves] in unprofitable speculations." Whereas the North indulged in every possible excess, the South had conducted its business upon "wholesome principles" and had lived within its means.[48]

Many ties bound the separate states together in a union, and not the least of them were economic. With the destruction of trade and finance in the autumn of 1857, these economic ties appeared to southerners to be more like a noose than a web of beneficial interdependence. The products of the South, so crucial to the world economy, moved only because of the credit facilities of New York. Southerners, incensed by their mercantile dilemma, pointed to New York as the "unnatural intervening agency" that created such economic hardship for their section. Tobacco planters were especially angry at the manner in which New Yorkers speculated with their crop.[49]

If southerners conducted their businesses on sound principles and engaged in truly productive enterprises instead of speculative ones, the solution to the depressions they endured came to one point: southerners required their own credit facilities and direct trade with Europe. Only then would they be safe from the mismanagement and folly that characterized northern enterprise. In Herschel V. Johnson's words, the Panic of 1857 gave an "emphatic illustration of the vast importance to the South, of direct trade between her own and foreign ports, and in her own bottomry."[50]

Although southerners viewed the Panic of 1857 through eyes of self-interest, their initial reaction hardly differed from the rest of the nation. As in the political questions concerning banks and paper money, the South engaged in the same type of debates and uttered the same sentiments as did the entire nation. Decrying the influence of New York and striking at the business ethics of the American Babylon was a

48. *Southern Advocate* (Huntsville, Ala.), September 24, 1857; *States* (Washington, D.C.), October 16, 1857; Raleigh (N.C.) *Weekly Register*, November 4, 1857; "Mercator" in Charleston *Daily Courier*, December 1, 1857.

49. Quote from Charleston *Mercury*, October 13, 1857; "Who Profits by Our Commerce," *De Bow's Review*, XXIV (May 1858), 449–50; Russel, *Economic Aspects of Southern Sectionalism*, 94–100; Joseph Clarke Robert, *The Tobacco Kingdom: Plantation, Market, and Factory in Virginia and North Carolina, 1800–1860* (Durham, N.C., 1938), 155–57, 227–33.

50. Herschel V. Johnson to Robert Habersham, October 19, 1857, in *Southern Recorder* (Milledgeville, Ga.), October 27, 1857.

national pastime, not a southern innovation. The southern deprecation of speculation and extravagance was hardly more acerbic than the northern one. Nor were northerners especially joyous over New York City's control over credit facilities. As the Republican editor of the Philadelphia *Evening Bulletin* lamented, "Every one knows that every particle of distress in the country is owing to New York . . . and that we are suffering wholly from the state of affairs in New York." Few Americans outside the Empire State doubted the stability of their own financial systems; it was the wreckers of New York City who plunged the nation into the abyss.[51]

Yet there was a harshness and a bitterness in southern voices that was not reflected elsewhere, and the solutions the slaveholding states sought were not duplicated in any other area of the nation. The call for direct trade with Europe had more implications than merely economic safety; in the words of one writer, such direct trade would be "the most prominently legitimate phase of the independence of the Southern States." An Alabama editor spoke of the necessity of southern independence, though qualifying his statement by disowning secessionist intentions, when he considered the economic relations between the sections that the Panic had exposed. The South needed independence even within the Union because the "South and the North are as diverse in all that constitutes national identity, as any two races of people within the pale of civilization." During the first days of financial stringency, a series of articles on sectional questions by an author using the pseudonym of "Cassandra" appeared in the Charleston *Mercury*. This individual tied the business problems of the South to the policies of the national government, which, he claimed, transferred southern wealth to northern merchants and industrialists. Cassandra concluded his articles by calling the United States Congress a "foreign government."[52]

Although southerners lashed out at northern activities that brought hard times to the South, they realized that their section escaped much of the social turmoil visited upon northern cities. One peculiar aspect of the Panic of 1857 was that it fortified the southern belief in the permanence of southern prosperity because it demonstrated the indispensability of cotton to world commerce. The Richmond *South* boasted,

51. Philadelphia *Evening Bulletin*, September 26, 1857; Indianapolis *Daily Journal*, October 24, 1857; Detroit *Daily Free Press*, November 14, 1857.

52. *States* (Washington, D.C.), November 20, 1857; Mobile *Daily Register*, October 11, 1857; letters of "Cassandra" in Charleston *Mercury*, September 8, 10, 12, 14, 16, 19, 1857; Nevins, *The Emergence of Lincoln*, I, 217.

correctly as it turned out, that the "present crisis will show that the *slave labor staples of the South* will furnish the means of extrication from commercial indebtedness."[53]

For several years, at least since David Christy of Cincinnati had coined the phrase in 1853, southerners had either suspected or declared that cotton was king. Cotton had regularly accounted for over one-half the dollar value of American exports. But southerners did not have to mention the fact; northerners and Englishmen recognized the circumstance and substantiated the claim with more precision—if with less propaganda—than the defenders of slavery ever did.

Britishers who were anxious about their country's sole reliance upon the United States for cotton formed a Cotton Supply Association in 1857, whose purpose was to foster cotton cultivation in India, Egypt, and Africa. Manufacturers fretted that the continued high price of the raw product would make cotton manufacturing unprofitable. That cotton was a necessary and important item of trade none would deny; the unimpeachable London *Times* stated that "this plant is now considered, and with perfect reason, as one of the chief elements in the wealth of nations." Although abolitionist sentiments were expressed in the meetings of the Cotton Supply Association, the true goal was never forgotten. In the society's tracts and in parliamentary debates, Englishmen detailed the depths of the depression into which the country would be plunged if ever the American cotton crop failed. The debate in England over the power southern slaveholders exerted on the British economy was followed closely in the northern United States press, and the value the English placed on cotton was duly noted by all, including Republicans and abolitionists.[54]

Southerners displayed no outward alarm at the activities of the Cotton Supply Association. Although well-informed of British intentions, southerners maintained that their region was more than capable of handling increases in the demand for cotton and that no other region of the world could displace them. They held this opinion for two rea-

53. Richmond (Va.) *South* quoted by *Mississippi Free Trader* (Natchez), November 6, 1857.

54. London *Times*, October 12, 1857, quoted by *Daily National Intelligencer* (Washington, D.C.), November 4, 1857; London *Times* quoted by *Frank Leslie's Illustrated Newspaper*, July 18, 1857, p. 103; *Liberator* (Boston), November 19, 1858; New York *Daily Tribune*, June 28, 1858, March 25, August 16, 1859; Frank Lawrence Owsley, *King Cotton Diplomacy: Foreign Relations of the Confederate States of America* (Chicago, 1931), 2–17.

sons: American cotton was better suited to British textile machinery, and cotton could not be grown profitably without slave labor. It was this last point in particular that southerners wanted to impress on all those interested in the supply of cotton. Southerners therefore believed that they occupied a remarkable economic position: the demand for cotton grew faster than the supply, and the demand was almost wholly for American cotton. One result of the Panic of 1857 was to offer irrefutable proof that slave-grown cotton was king and destined to remain so.[55]

The political reaction to the Panic of 1857 did not initially add to the growing sectional rift over the question of slavery and its extension. Republicans, Democrats, and Americans responded to the financial crash in a most predictable manner, generally relying on the economic ideas and solutions that had prevailed in Jackson's day. When politicians in 1857 debated the origins of and the remedies for the Panic, they usually avoided entangling economic policy matters with those involving slavery. Outside of the political arena, the general public concerned itself with banking difficulties, not with any alleged connection between banks and slavery. Even abolitionists failed to utilize the monetary collapse to their advantage; after one brief attempt to blame the slaveholders for the banking failure, they lapsed into their more customary and comfortable mode of criticizing slavery as a sinful institution. Only the southern reaction to the Panic contained elements of bitter sectional rancor. But in an odd fashion, the economic turmoil, instead of frightening southerners, reassured them. The Panic produced unmistakable evidence that the South's prosperity was secure and growing, while that of the North's was artificial and failing.

There was, however, a dynamic quality about the popular response to the Panic of 1857 that needed time to mature. From the moment that the Ohio Life failed, certain individuals linked together banks, tariffs, paper money, slavery, and free labor. The relations between these subjects became further entwined as the depression continued

55. Holt Wilson, "Cotton, Steam and Machinery," *Southern Literary Messenger*, XXVII (September, 1858), 161–76; *Mississippi Free Trader* (Natchez), September 18, 1857; "English Opinion, Cotton, Slave Trade, etc.," *De Bow's Review*, XXIII (September, 1857), 282–84; John M. Cardoza, "Supply and Consumption of Cotton, Present and Prospective," *De Bow's Review*, XXII (April 1857), 343–45; Ronald T. Takaki, *A Pro-Slavery Crusade: The Agitation to Reopen the African Slave Trade* (New York, 1971), 11, 33–43.

and as politicians sought solutions for business stagnation. Heavily involved in these topics was the state of economic knowledge, for economic theory often defined the way various problems would be understood. A lasting effect of the Panic of 1857 was that it activated a heated debate over the economic status of banks, tariffs, slaves, and free laborers. This debate would ultimately intensify the discord between the North and the South.

F O U R / Economic Thought
and the Panic of 1857

The financial crisis of 1857 reinvigorated a long-standing controversy over appropriate national economic policy—that is, whether the nation should establish free trade in its international dealings with the world or erect high tariff barriers to protect certain types of business activities. For much of the 1850s the quarrel over free trade or protectionism had lain dormant, but its reawakening in 1857 had distinct repercussions for the sectional conflict over slavery. Since 1846 the question of slavery extension had been one of the focal points of national politics. The Panic of 1857 started to force discussion of concrete economic questions into the heated debates over slavery's expansion. This development increased the bitterness between the North and the South because the economic issues, besides affecting paramount propertied interests, emphasized the question of which section would establish dominance in the creation and implementation of federal policies, economic or otherwise.

Out of the struggle between free traders and protectionists for control of the nation's commercial regulations arose two other themes that slowly entered the sectional debate. One involved the particular ideas southerners used to justify their social institutions. By drawing attention to certain aspects of the Panic of 1857, southerners presented themselves as devotees of a patriarchal society. Yet the Panic also revealed that southerners maintained free trade economic views that sharply conflicted with their proslavery attitudes. This paradox in southern economic thought persisted until 1861, and southerners in these years continued to point to the Panic of 1857 as the final proof for both their incompatible contentions that slavery promoted a contented working class and that free trade principles were the only true guides for governmental policies.

The other debate that emerged out of the rivalry between free trade and protectionism was over the future of the American laborer and what governmental action could most secure him adequate material rewards so that he would not become a threat to the nation's political and social institutions. This problem became entangled with the specific remedies that free traders and protectionists proposed to cure the nation of monetary revulsions. Hence the economic issues raised by the Panic easily became enmeshed with sectional attitudes because the policies involved the future security of the established social orders of both regions. In particular, the subject of the workers' status lent itself admirably to the Republicans' insistence that slavery endangered the material condition and moral elevation of the free laborer.

In the antebellum United States, economic thought divided into two major camps, free trade and protectionist. The essential difference between the two groups centered on governmental policy toward international commerce; free traders desired unhindered business exchanges between the United States and the rest of the world, while protectionists favored a drastic curtailment of foreign imports. During the Panic of 1857, each school offered a remedy for the depressed economy. Free traders claimed that the collapse proved that the nation required stronger restrictions on banks and currency emissions. Protectionists argued for a high tariff to stop the outflow of precious metals upon which the American banking system was based.

The two positions were reflected in the stands taken by the political parties in 1857. Democrats—in North and South—had been expositors of free trade principles since the days of Jackson, while the party in opposition, whatever its name, had usually adhered to some form of protectionism. In 1857, however, the diverse backgrounds of the members of the Republican party precluded that organization's hearty endorsement of a prohibitive tariff. But the analyses and logic employed by protectionists and free traders to derive their conclusions had considerable ramifications for sectional attitudes. The body of theory that each school possessed was repeated endlessly in politicians' reactions to the Panic of 1857 and was the foundation they used to discuss all subjects relating to the economy.

American free traders traced their ancestry to the Scottish philosopher Adam Smith, whose 1776 treatise, *An Inquiry into the Nature and Causes of the Wealth of Nations*, inaugurated serious discussion of economic principles. A host of Europeans developed and extended

Smith's ideas until they became collectively known as free trade economic theory. Americans quickly adopted the concepts Smith and his followers had delineated, and by the 1830s various Americans, such as Francis Wayland, a minister who later became president of Brown University, began publishing treatises on the subject. By the 1850s, the American proponents of the ideas of Adam Smith had obtained a considerable following, all of whom shared a common analytical framework by which they judged economic phenomena.[1]

Several key concepts underlay the theory of free trade and from them most of the philosophy's conclusions were derived. The two most important were man's individuality and his need to labor in order to survive. Through his individual effort man added a value to natural objects that was not originally there. Since only the exertions of one individual created something useful, that person had "a right to the exclusive possession of that value."[2] Thus the right of private property was established as both an economic and a moral principle.

In a barbarous state, men labored only to fulfill their immediate physical needs. The evolution of society from a primitive state to a civilized one was accompanied by a disposition to save certain goods for future use. This was the process of capital formation, for capital "was nothing less than the labor of the *past*." The accumulation of capital stock allowed a diversity of products to be manufactured, which in turn permitted the laborer to specialize in specific tasks. This was the principle of the "division of labor."[3]

In this new social environment, men exchanged the surpluses of their work for the surpluses of others' efforts. Civilization, in short, created a market. Consumers demanded goods and suppliers manufactured them. Free traders insisted that sooner or later supply would equal demand, that the market would achieve an equilibrium between consumers and producers. This was Adam Smith's law of supply and demand. In order to achieve this result, free traders maintained that the producing units had to compete with each other for customers. Competition forced the producer to lower his expectations of gain so

1. Joseph Dorfman, *The Economic Mind in American Civilization* (1946; rpr. New York, 1966), II, 512–26, 749–864; Carl William Kaiser, Jr., *History of the Academic Protectionist-Free Trade Controversy in America Before 1860* (Philadelphia, 1939), 92–97; Francis Wayland, *Elements of Political Economy* (4th ed.; Boston, 1856).

2. Wayland, *Elements of Political Economy*, 19.

3. Amasa Walker, *The Science of Wealth: A Manual of Political Economy* (Philadelphia, 1872), 32; Wayland, *Elements of Political Economy*, 30–41, 75–82.

that the consumer would not buy elsewhere, but the producer in return would never allow his profits to be lowered to the point at which he was sacrificing his welfare for the benefit of others. Competition thus permitted mutual benefits to those who supplied goods and to those who consumed them, while ensuring that no particular group obtained an unfair advantage.[4]

Individuality, property rights, competition, and supply and demand theorems engendered no conflict among the free traders. This did not hold true in the matter of exchange values and currency. Most free traders believed objects had an "intrinsic value," a worth originating in the object itself, that made it desirable. When man transformed natural materials and invested his labor in them, a new value was added. The labor used in this operation became the basis of what free traders called the "exchange value." When men traded their goods, they actually exchanged the amount of labor they had put into the product's creation.[5] Therefore any standard devised to measure values between different items had to reflect the different amounts of labor used in producing the goods. Although natural disasters or technological progress could cause exchange values to vacillate, most free traders believed that the standard chosen to represent exchange values should be made as stable as humanly possible. If the standard fluctuated, labor might be deprived of its just reward. For this reason free traders favored gold and silver for a nation's currency because the precious metals had an intrinsic value that governments could not alter.[6]

American free traders felt that two institutions were capable of deflecting a nation from its true economic path—the government and the banks. Free traders believed the functions of government were to establish weights and measures, protect private property, enforce contracts, and maintain law and order. Governments had no responsibilities beyond these; free traders insisted that for "an intelligent people, the sagacity of individuals will suggest far better schemes for their interest than any sovereign or legislature is likely to do." Banks represented a different type of danger. In the United States bankers had acquired the ability to emit a paper currency in place of specie. This immediately drew the ire of free traders because paper money had no

4. Wayland, *Elements of Political Economy*, 95–103.

5. *Ibid.*, 16–22; Amasa Walker, *The Nature and Uses of Money and Mixed Currency, with a History of the Wickaboag Bank* (Boston, 1857), 5.

6. Wayland, *Elements of Political Economy*, 196–99; George Opdyke, *A Treatise on Political Economy* (New York, 1851), 292–98.

intrinsic value and bankers could print the notes at their own caprice. This state of affairs inevitably produced inflation, because the money supply increased without any concomitant rise in physical output. Thus free traders lambasted paper money because it violated their cardinal rule that labor could only be securely rewarded if there was a nonfluctuating standard of value.[7]

Free traders explained international commerce by simply applying to nations the same set of laws they had developed for individuals. In the process of doing so, they gave an explanation for the existence of panics and depressions. Each country had certain natural advantages in the production of various goods. If no trade barriers were erected or subsidies granted, each nation would specialize in the areas that nature had best suited it for, and free exchanges among all nations would result in material advancement for all. American free traders, however, feared that the United States' love of paper money could undermine the functioning of the international system and produce an economic "revulsion." In their analysis, paper money under no restrictions generated inflation, which meant higher prices, and higher prices enticed foreign producers into the domestic market. But the imports had to be paid in gold, which caused a specie drain. Sooner or later the lack of precious metals in bank vaults frightened the financiers into a massive contraction of loans, which then forced the economy into depression. Free traders insisted that only a gold currency in the United States could ensure equilibrium in international trade and circumvent economic disasters.[8]

Free traders in the 1850s portrayed the economy as nothing less than a self-regulating machine that created wealth. All that men had to do to reap the benefits of this machine was to exercise personal freedom and try to satisfy their material desires. Any human tinkering with the mechanism by legislation or private monopoly only upset its delicate components and brought the machine to a halt. But this economic automaton supposedly could never break down, for instead of being made of metal and wood the gears that powered the free trade economy were natural laws, and natural laws, like gravity, never ceased functioning. As New York Republican George Opdyke phrased it,

7. Quote from George Tucker, *Political Economy for the People* (Philadelphia, 1859), 32; A Merchant of Boston [Samuel Hooper], *Currency or Money: Its Nature and Uses, and the Effects of the Circulation of Bank-Notes for Currency* (Boston, 1855), 19–21, 37–41.

8. Walker, *The Science of Wealth*, 90–97; Hooper, *Currency or Money*, 50, 62–63.

"Free trade permits the all-wise, benevolent and just laws, which the Creator has established to govern the production and distribution of wealth, to move on in uninterrupted harmony to the accomplishment of their appropriate ends."[9]

Free trade theory thus led its American practitioners immediately to the realm of finance in order to explain any perturbation in the economic system. During and after the Panic of 1857, they became the scrutinizers and critics of American banking practices. The ablest expositors of the free trade view of the origins of the crash were Amasa Walker, Samuel Hooper, Charles H. Carroll, and George Opdyke. Walker and Hooper were wealthy Bostonians and Massachusetts Republican state legislators; Opdyke and Carroll were representatives of the New York banking and commercial community. Although these individuals, as well as other contributors to the business press, advanced different remedies for the financial collapse and focused upon different aspects of American banking, they all concluded that the roots of the country's economic disorders lay in an undue expansion of the money supply.[10]

The basic flaw the free traders discovered in the United States' banking system was that current practices allowed loans and deposits to be transformed into a circulating medium of exchange. Most free traders felt that restrictions on paper money issuance—that is, circulation—were adequate, but that bankers had found a new means to increase the money supply. Whenever a bank granted a loan to an individual, the institution created a deposit in the name of the person who received it. But when the individual drew upon his account, he was paid either in the form of a discount or a bank note. By this route financiers transformed loans into circulation and thereby increased the money supply. Walker called this mixture of paper money and discounts based upon loans a "mixed currency" and faulted the banks for lacking sufficient specie reserves to cover these obligations. Samuel Hooper adhered to Walker's diagnosis, although he emphasized the role deposits played in expanding circulation. Opdyke felt that the "great outstanding defect in our banking system is its undue conversion of its own credit [loans and deposits] into currency." Carroll postu-

9. Opdyke, *A Treatise on Political Economy*, 260.

10. For biographical material on these individuals, consult Dorfman, *The Economic Mind in American Civilization*, II, 749–52; Redlich, *The Molding of American Banking*, II, 8–10; Lloyd W. Mints, *A History of Banking Theory in Great Britain and the United States* (Chicago, 1945), 155–56.

lated that loans and deposits actually represented debts; he thus characterized American finance as *"bank debt organized into currency."* [11]

Free traders offered various solutions for the currency dilemma. Walker desired a totally specie-based currency, although as a matter of practicality he settled for the elimination of bank notes of small denominations. His friend Samuel Hooper, however, was not so opposed to a paper currency. Instead, he hoped to enact laws that tied each bank's specie reserves to the amount of its loans. Both Opdyke and Carroll felt that the federal government should install a national gold certificate system in which all issues could be instantly redeemed in gold from the government. [12] Other free traders urged the abolition of the usury laws or favored a national Suffolk system based in New York. [13] Regardless of the concrete remedy proposed, all free traders favored securing a nonfluctuating standard of value.

Protectionists offered a somewhat different analysis of the functioning of the economy and a very different remedy for financial derangements. Protectionism, the economic philosophy that advocated prohibitive trade barriers, was the American offspring of seventeenth- and eighteenth-century European mercantilism. The two most significant early expositors of American trade restrictions were Alexander Hamilton and Henry Clay, both of whom stressed the necessity of developing an industrial base for the economy by promoting the expansion of the domestic market. Unlike free trade theory, however, protectionism originated in the nationalist concerns of politicians. In the 1820s certain writers started to gird protectionism with a stronger theoretical foundation. By the 1850s protectionism had attracted a wide following and offered a fairly coherent set of economic principles to justify its conclusions. The leading advocates of high tariff ideals in the ante-

11. Walker, *The Nature and Uses of Money*, 26–28, 32–37, 52; Samuel Hooper, *An Examination of the Theory and the Effect of Laws Regulating the Amount of Specie in Banks* (Boston, 1860), 14–16, 35–37, 40; George Opdyke, *et al.*, "A Report on the Currency," *Bankers' Magazine*, XIII (December, 1858), 484; Charles H. Carroll, "Organization of Debt into Currency," *Bankers' Magazine*, XIII (August, 1858), 137.

12. Amasa Walker, "The Commercial Crisis of 1857," *Hunt's*, XXXVII (November, 1857), 533; Hooper, *An Examination of the Theory*, 6–7, 8–12, 38–39, 46–49; Opdyke, *et al.*, "A Report on the Currency," *Bankers' Magazine*, XIII (December, 1858), 485–86; Charles H. Carroll, "Interest and Cheap Currency," *Hunt's*, XXXVIII (January, 1858), 42.

13. Editorial of Henry Varnum Poor in *American Railroad Journal*, January 2, 1858, p. 8; Edmund Dwight, "The Financial Revulsion and the New York Banking System," *Hunt's*, XXXVIII (February, 1858), 158, 160–63.

bellum period were Calvin Colton, a lay evangelist and professor of public economy at Trinity College; Stephen Colwell, a religious Pennsylvania ironmaster; Francis Bowen, a Harvard philosopher; E. Peshine Smith, a New York lawyer and adviser to Senator William H. Seward; the omnipresent Horace Greeley; and above all, the high priest of protectionism, Henry Charles Carey.[14]

Henry C. Carey was the individual most responsible for transforming protectionism from a political program to a theory of national wealth. He was born in Philadelphia in 1793, the son of Mathew Carey, an ardent supporter of Henry Clay and owner of an important publishing house. Henry extended the family's wealth into other enterprises during his business career, but he soon retired from active management of those pursuits to devote his time to the study of economics in particular and society in general. At first Carey posed as a champion of free trade, but the impact of the tariff of 1842 upon the economy altered his allegiances. By the end of the 1840s Carey was advancing the claims of protectionism with far more logic and consistency than they had been presented with before. His formulations tended to be a strong mixture of the ideas of Hamilton and Clay intermingled with his own concerns and discoveries. Carey was probably the most imaginative protectionist theorist in antebellum America.[15]

To discover the relationships that constituted the science of economics Carey began with an investigation of man. Carey believed that man's most important attributes were individuality and "ASSOCIATION with his fellowmen." The object of any social science therefore had to be to secure for each man the highest degree of individuality and the greatest power of association. In Carey's theory man by himself had to bend all his energies against nature in order to survive; any mechanical, musical, or scientific talents he might possess had to be shunted aside in order to procure food, shelter, and clothing. Only when men

14. Kaiser, *History of the Protectionist-Free Trade Controversy*, 27, 41–42; Dorfman, *The Economic Mind in American Civilization*, II, 567–97, 771–844; Arnold W. Green, *Henry Charles Carey: Nineteenth Century Sociologist* (Philadelphia, 1951), 6–10.

15. Dorfman, *The Economic Mind in American Civilization*, II, 789, 797–99. Carey has inspired both admiration and castigation. An unfavorable assessment of his contributions can be found in Irwin Unger, *The Greenback Era: A Social and Political History of American Finance, 1865–1879* (Princeton, N.J., 1964), 33–34, 50–58. A more positive view is presented by Paul K. Conkin, *Prophets of Prosperity: America's First Political Economists* (Bloomington, Ind., 1980), 261–307. A good work on general protectionist doctrines is Michael Hudson, *Economics and Technology in 19th Century American Thought: The Neglected American Economists* (New York, 1975).

gathered together could they focus on their God-given abilities and perfect their individual geniuses.[16] Carey therefore argued strenuously against dispersing the population over vast areas where individuals would live in isolation. Only from a populous settlement could there arise a demand for a multitude of products and services; this demand allowed workers to choose among a wide range of possible enployments. Carey believed that the process of association produced a diversity of employments, and diversity was the mark of an advanced civilization.[17]

The Philadelphia economist did not stray too far from basic free trade tenets on the production of goods and the acquisition of wealth. Carey assumed that one of the principal forces that motivated people was the desire for wealth, although Carey let wealth assume both physical and intangible forms. To explain how wealth was created, he divided economic functions into production and consumption, as did all antebellum economists. According to Carey, production and consumption were always equal as long as the members of society resided in close proximity to each other. With a cohesive group, demand was immediately known so that producers never manufactured more than was necessary. Population growth and individual tastes evoked a wide variety of desires provided that the people did not disperse, and hence the productions increasingly diversified and required more skill. As the urban centers manufactured more finished goods, the market for agricultural goods also grew, maintaining an equilibrium between the products of the plow, the loom, and the anvil. Carey explained that economic growth occurred in this perfectly balanced system because of additions to capital stock. He defined capital as the exertions of the past that had not been squandered in immediate consumption but saved to help produce future goods. He added an important criterion, however; the type of capital needed to promote greater wealth had to be fixed capital—homes, factories, fences, machinery, plows—and not "circulating" capital, or goods in transit.[18]

One of the major features of Carey's system (and indeed a prominent

16. Henry C. Carey, *Manual of Social Science: Being a Condensation of the "Principles of Social Science" by H. C. Carey*, ed. Kate McKean (Philadelphia, 1866), 37–47, 54–56; George Winston Smith, *Henry C. Carey and American Sectional Conflict* (Albuquerque, 1951), 18–19. The association that Carey spoke of is not to be confused with communitarian socialist experiments in the 1840s, many of which were termed "associationist" enterprises.

17. Carey, *Manual of Social Science*, 43–58, 107; Smith, *Henry C. Carey and American Sectional Conflict*, 18–19.

18. Carey, *Manual of Social Science*, 101–105, 109–11, 364–75, 392.

aspect of all protectionist literature) was a fervent denunciation of merchants. When association occurred, the farmer, because he lived near the cities, took his produce directly to the market. A merchant class might do some distributing but there was no transportation cost. The result was that the labor one put into his productions was instantly and fully realized. This process Carey termed "commerce."[19]

On the other hand, exchanges could be dominated by "trade," Carey's term for mercantile activities. Carey found the economic function as well as the social results of mercantile activity totally repugnant. Carey's ideal society required association, which brought all producers, and therefore all consumers, into close contact. Trade kept producers apart by positioning middlemen between those who labored for a living. The merchants decided what was needed and by whom; their orders issued forth and men were reduced "to the condition of a mere instrument to be used by the trader; or, in other words, to that of a slave."[20] Traders further tended to force production to specialize, which meant the neglect of all other economic possibilities. This, wrote Carey, was "centralization." He demanded diversity, and trade, especially free trade, turned entire nations into vast machines pouring forth only two or three products. Under the system of free trade the United States was degenerating into a monstrous robot that ignored all other pursuits in order to grow cotton, wheat, and corn. Carey insisted that the only beneficiary of this type of economic activity was Great Britain, and he found it no accident that the philosophy of free trade originated in that nation. For Carey, the different social results of free trade and protectionism were plain: free trade promoted singular economic endeavors that abetted monopolies, which then created class distinctions and inequality; in contrast, protectionism advanced diversity, which fostered equality and republican government.[21]

Like the free traders, Carey faced the problems of defining value and erecting a standard to facilitate exchanges. Although Carey maintained that the value of an object resulted from the interaction of men and machines and altered with the acquisition of capital stock—he called this the "cost of reproduction"—he basically adhered to the

19. *Ibid.*, 110–15.

20. *Ibid.*, 115; quote found in Henry C. Carey, *Letters to the President, on the Foreign and Domestic Policy of the Union*, in *Miscellaneous Works of Henry C. Carey* (Philadelphia, 1865), I, 43.

21. Carey, *Letters to the President*, 17, 144–47; Carey, *Manual of Social Science*, 113–15, 249–56, 291–95.

principle that labor was the essential criterion of value. He also felt the best standard of exchange value was gold and silver bullion, the currency for his economy of association. Carey compared currency to blood circulating in a body; the more blood, the more circulation, the better the health of the body. Money, or circulation, ought ever to expand in order to effect a salutary economy. The key was the rapidity of money going through the economy. To Carey it was obvious that the smaller the amount of money, the more slowly it traveled. Therefore the more gold and silver a nation had, the smoother the economy operated.[22]

Unlike the free traders, Carey held that because of the functions it fulfilled money was not just another commodity. Under the system of free trade, gold traveled to the area most in need of it, industrial England. This drained the United States of its gold supply, thereby halting the circulation of money in the American economy, and lowered the ability of the people to consume. The result was depression. Hard money and free trade were incompatible. Furthermore, Carey did not despise paper notes, for any addition to the supply of currency—as long as the base of gold and silver did not deteriorate—resulted in quicker circulation, which increased demand and thus boosted production.[23]

Carey accepted banks as the proper agents to hold gold and silver and dispense notes, although he usually did not enter into detail on the subjects of deposits, circulation, loans, and discounts. For Carey banks represented the general ideal of holding capital for future investments. He desired a stable currency, one that matched the money supply to the commodities produced, but he had no desire to witness monster banks in the republic. The Bank of England was an agent of trade and centralization, an "oppressive monopoly." He favored a system of many banks that catered to regional needs; he found the Suffolk system of New England to be the appropriate model.[24]

All parts of the economic structure devised by Carey—financiers, laborers, farmers, manufacturers—were locked in a web of interdependence, brought together by the principle of association. If one seg-

22. Carey, *Manual of Social Science*, 82–83, 113; A. D. H. Kaplan, *Henry Charles Carey: A Study in American Economic Thought* (Baltimore, 1931), 46.

23. Carey, *Manual of Social Science*, 280–87, 291–97, 300–309; Robert P. Sharkey, *Money, Class, and Party: An Economic Study of Civil War and Reconstruction* (Baltimore, 1959), 166–67.

24. Carey, *Manual of Social Science*, 315–16, 324–29; Smith, *Henry C. Carey and American Sectional Conflict*, 16–18.

ment of the economy suffered, the rest suffered to the same degree. Likewise, if aid were extended to one portion, all the other areas benefited accordingly. Within the confines of this associated society, free trade and competition operated to the betterment of mankind. Carey termed this process the "Harmony of Interests." He emphasized, however, that association could be only a regional phenomenon and not an international one, for international exchanges meant shipping goods over long distances, creating burdensome taxes on producers, and allowing merchants to dominate the economy.[25]

Government was to be limited so as not to interfere with individual desires. As did most mid-nineteenth-century Americans, Carey held that the main purposes of government were to protect life and property, to maintain contractual obligations, and to ensure an equitable system of justice. He also added one other function. Since individuality through association presented the greatest opportunities for human advancement in the arts, sciences, and professions, the government had to adopt the policy that would most enhance association— the tariff. A high wall of import duties halted the flow of foreign goods into the United States, making the nation rely on its own resources and creating a diversified economy. Diversification then led to a multitude of opportunities that allowed individual talents a full field in which to be employed. The tariff eliminated the need for merchants as now consumer and producer could bargain directly. Just as important, economic decisions were no longer dictated by the merchant class for an unsure, vacillating foreign demand. And finally, the tariff ended a disastrous outflow of specie to Great Britain.[26]

The protectionists' analysis of economic events led them during the Panic of 1857 to blame the financial crash upon the low-tariff policy of the Democrats. The most elaborate statement of the tariff origins of the Panic came from the pen of Carey. In his *Letters to the President* (1858), Carey once more presented his vision of economic progress to the nation. Like most protectionists, he argued that international revulsions originated in the free trade policies of England. Not only did that system drain the United States of specie, which therefore weakened the country's banking structure, but it also upset the normal equilibrium between supply and demand. Because nations devoted all

25. Carey, *Manual of Social Science*, 426–29; Kaplan, *Henry Charles Carey*, 36.
26. Carey, *Manual of Social Science*, 256–78; Carey, *Letters to the President*, 20, 79–81.

their energies to a few pursuits, they glutted the markets; this miscalculation on their part arose from the separation of consumers and producers by the merchant class.[27]

Other protectionists agreed. Horace Greeley called *Letters to the President* "by far the fullest discussion of the recent financial catastrophe, and of the present condition of the country, which has yet appeared." Ezra Seaman of Ann Arbor, Michigan, who helped to found some of the principles of national income accounting, also believed that the low tariff was responsible for the monetary collapse. Although Seaman noted several questionable features in the domestic economy, he emphasized the role of foreign debts: "Can any one doubt that the excessive importations of foreign goods, and the large exports of specie, operated as causes more potent than all others in producing the panic and revulsion of 1857?" Numerous contributors to the daily press also argued that the nation's low tariff policy promoted a specie outflow that had generated the Panic.[28]

Free trade and protectionist theorists freely criticized each other in their writings, although they seldom engaged in a verbal debate. Free traders charged that tariffs created inefficiencies in the economy by building up industries in which the nation had no competence, by deflecting investment away from more profitable employments, and by extinguishing the incentive to innovate. Free traders additionally maintained that tariffs not only created monopolies but also were a form of class legislation by which the farmers, merchants, and laborers paid tribute to the wealthy industrialists. Amasa Walker, among others, also felt that the protectionist remedy was inconsistent. Without a check on currency emission, prices would rise so much as to undo the work of a prohibitive tariff; eventually inflated prices would lure foreign manufacturers back into the domestic market.[29]

Protectionists angrily rejected the free trade critique of their ideas. They belittled the free traders' attack on paper money by noting that countries that relied on paper money, like England, were spared much of the turmoil of the Panic, whereas regions like the principality of Hamburg, whose economy rested on specie, suffered inordinately.

27. Carey, *Letters to the President*, 16, 79–92, 105–109.

28. New York *Daily Tribune*, April 29, 1858; Ezra Seaman, "Currency, Commerce, and Debts of the United States," *Hunt's*, XXXVIII (May, 1858), 536, 546.

29. Richard Sulley, "Free Trade and Protection: Or, A Partial Review of Mr. Carey's Letters to the President," *Hunt's*, XL (May, 1859), 532; Opdyke, *A Treatise on Political Economy*, 227–28, 231; Walker, *The Nature and Uses of Money*, 39.

Protectionists were particularly sensitive to the charges of monopoly and class favoritism. They rejoined, incorrectly, that the greatest disparity in wealth and the largest monopolies in the world occurred in the free trade country of Great Britain. Protectionists finally insisted that their program did not cultivate monopolies because one of the pillars of their theory was the establishment of internal competition.[30]

It was not, however, in the business press or in the pamphlets that the important debate between free traders and protectionists over the Panic of 1857 took place. This more bitter controversy occurred in the halls of Congress. Not only did congressmen and administration officials reiterate the nostrums that the economic theorists had devised, they also recited in significant detail the analysis by which the protectionists and free traders had arrived at their conclusions. The political debate over the Panic of 1857 manifested a concern that was not evident in the academic one: the question of high or low tariffs awoke the instincts of sectional self-interest among the congressmen, and that in its turn thrust the question of slavery into the controversy. The Panic of 1857 reawakened the economic question of free trade or protectionism at a time when the furor over the extension of slavery was reaching its climax.

There was an odd quality to the southern reaction to the Panic of 1857, particularly in regard to the concepts by which southerners evaluated economic phenomena. Much of their response was limited to complaining about the price drop their staples had suffered due to the Panic, and then later to exulting over the South's swift return to prosperity while the North was mired in the swamp of unemployment and business failure. But one event associated with the financial collapse drew considerable southern comment: the northern bread riots. Southerners did not, in general, engage in the national debate over banking policies and tariff rates. They did, however, see in the workers' demonstrations a means of justifying slavery. They therefore thrust into the debate over the Panic of 1857 the subject of the relative merits of a slave labor system as compared to a free labor system.

30. Carey, *Letters to the President*, 89–90; Henry C. Carey, *Financial Crises: Their Causes and Effects*, in *Miscellaneous Works of Henry C. Carey*, I, 9; Seaman, "Currency, Commerce, and Debts of the United States," *Hunt's*, XXXVIII (May, 1858), 537, 539, 545; Francis Bowen, *The Principles of Political Economy* (Boston, 1856), 129; Stephen Colwell, *The Claims of Labor, and Their Precedence to the Claims of Free Trade* (Philadelphia, 1861), 40–41.

Southerners gleefully contrasted the fate of the slave in the South with that of the free white worker in the North. While northern laborers were shaking the pillars of northern civilization, related the Richmond *South*, the southern laboring class was "content and quiet, because secure against want and suffering." The old-line Whig editor of Tennessee, "Parson" William G. Brownlow, caustically commented that northern philanthropists would have to cease sermonizing about the fate of slaves and attend to the "ragged starving poor, and devise ways and means for furnishing them bread." Upon receiving news of the northern labor riots, William W. Holden of North Carolina exclaimed, "How eagerly would these poor wretches devour what our well fed slaves waste!"[31]

Southerners did not halt at simply comparing the present needs of northern and southern workers. They extended their remarks to include the nature of northern society. The system of free labor was on trial, and some southerners offered the verdict that the system in the North was a "false" one. The essential weakness of northern institutions was revealed by the growing number of pauperized laborers who scarcely earned enough to maintain their physical existence. Sooner or later, the editor of the Charleston *Daily Courier* predicted, the impoverished masses would overturn northern society; the cataclysm might not occur in the immediate future, but "that it will come at last there can be no room for doubt."[32]

Southern society faced no such uprising from the laboring masses, partisans claimed, because in the South the workers were adequately provided for. The institution that guaranteed workers food, raiment, and shelter was slavery. According to numerous southern writers, northerners made a grave mistake when they separated capital and labor into two distinct entities; capital and labor then waged war on each other and produced the conditions that would finally lead to social disaster. This antagonism between labor and capital was not permitted under the slavery system, many southerners argued, because slavery transformed the laborer into a capital asset. In the words of the Mobile *Daily Register*, "Labor is capital in the South, and therefore, while

31. Richmond (Va.) *South* quoted by *Semi-Weekly Standard* (Raleigh, N.C.), October 21, 1857; Knoxville *Whig*, November 21, 1857; *Semi-Weekly Standard* (Raleigh, N.C.), November 11, 1857.
32. Mobile *Daily Register*, November 18, 1857; Charleston *Daily Courier*, November 10, 1857.

paying the cost of government, it is as carefully and tenderly guarded as the humanity and the avarice of its owners can induce."[33] The southern analysis of the northern labor riots indicated that southerners held economic principles widely at variance with those of northern economists. Whereas protectionists and free traders lauded individual freedom, the mobility of resources, and a classless society, southerners in their discussion of the workers' demonstrations seemed to uphold the principles of caste, inequality, and immobility. They appeared to sanction abandonment of market efficiency in order to preserve social stability. Southerners lumped all these characteristics under the title of the "patriarchal principle" and advocated an economics based on paternalism.[34]

The economic ideas expressed by southerners in response to the Panic of 1857 had a distinguished lineage. Over the decades, the proslavery argument had developed several rationales for the existence of slavery: biblical, historical, political, and ethnological. One prominent element in this defense of slavery was a comparison of the material well-being of the slave with the degraded condition of the northern factory operative. Since the 1820s, proslavery advocates had propounded the view that slavery ensured the worker a decent standard of living. Hence southerners in 1857 merely reiterated a proslavery labor doctrine that agitators had used for the past thirty years. The Panic of 1857 did not stimulate southerners to create new justifications for slavery; rather, it confirmed their old ones. Southerners saw the Panic of 1857 as concrete proof of the cruelty and chaos of northern free labor society and the humanity and stability of southern slave society.[35] What the Panic of 1857 revealed about southern thought was how surprisingly widespread these views of free and slave labor had become.

33. Mobile *Daily Register*, November 18, 1857.

34. See, for example, editorial in *Russell's Magazine*, III (December, 1857), 262; R. E. C., "The Problem of Free Society," *Southern Literary Messenger*, XXVI (June, 1858), 402; John Johnson, "Drudgery and Leisure, as Social Conditions," *Virginia University Magazine*, June, 1858, quoted by Charleston *Daily Courier*, July 28, 1858.

35. For the proslavery argument, consult Jenkins, *Pro-Slavery Thought in the Old South*, *passim*; Drew Gilpin Faust, *A Sacred Circle: The Dilemma of the Intellectual in the Old South, 1840–1860* (Baltimore, 1977), 114–43. On the proslavery critique of capitalism and free labor values, see James C. Hite and Ellen J. Hall, "The Reactionary Evolution of Economic Thought in Antebellum Virginia," *Virginia Magazine of History and Biography*, LXXX (1972), 476–88; Carsel, "The Slaveholders' Indictment of Northern Wage Slavery," 504–20.

The leading exponent of the patriarchal principle during and after the Panic of 1857 was the eccentric, self-taught, Virginian intellectual George Fitzhugh. Fitzhugh, who rose to notoriety in the antebellum decade, focused his criticisms upon the social results of the free labor system, or, more specifically, upon the economic doctrines of capitalism. He maintained that the boasted freedoms of the North were illusions and that the only freedom that northerners practiced was freedom from responsibility for the fate of their fellowmen. In capitalist societies, so Fitzhugh believed, the reigning ideal was the pursuit of avarice. No governmental or social authority was permitted to impede the gratification of material desires. The emphasis upon greed was the reason Fitzhugh found capitalistic economics immoral, because the practical result was that the intelligent took advantage of and oppressed the many. Capitalists, who had all the power of slaveholders but none of their social obligations, ground down the wages of the laborers for no worthier purpose than to add to their own material riches.[36]

Slavery, according to Fitzhugh, provided a comfortable existence for all members of society. Instead of pretending that all men were equals, the system of slavery recognized the natural distinctions that separated men, and the institution placed individuals in economic positions commensurate with their abilities. Slavery did not allow one class to take advantage of another; slavery taught the masters their obligations to the lower orders. By making the slave a part of the slaveholders' capital stock, slavery forced the masters, for pecuniary reasons if for no other, to care for the welfare of their laborers. Fitzhugh held that the sluggishness of southern economic growth, especially when compared to that of the North, occurred because of the treatment of the slaves; because slaves were better rewarded than free laborers, southerners had fewer funds to invest than did northern capitalists.[37]

Fitzhugh hailed the Panic of 1857 as a confirmation of proslavery doctrines. He averred that the crash was due to the "outgrowth of excessive trade," a feature peculiar to capitalist societies. But the South was spared the turmoil of its northern neighbors because slavery in-

36. For background on Fitzhugh see Harvey Wish, *George Fitzhugh: Propagandist of the Old South* (Baton Rouge, 1943), *passim;* C. Vann Woodward, "George Fitzhugh, *Sui Generis,*" introduction to George Fitzhugh, *Cannibals All! or Slaves Without Masters,* ed. C. Vann Woodward (Cambridge, Mass., 1960), xii–xx; Eugene D. Genovese, *The World the Slaveholders Made: Two Essays in Interpretation* (New York, 1969), 119–244.
37. Fitzhugh, *Cannibals All,* 8, 17, 19, 21–22, 25.

duced southerners to build their economy on the solid foundations of "land and negroes" which were "*national wealth* because they produce the necessaries of life." Fitzhugh claimed that the appropriate remedy for financial disturbances was the reestablishment of a system of entails. He also maintained that the bread riots demonstrated the tendency of free labor societies to produce social revolution, for in capitalist nations "the ruin of families, and the turning out of employment and starving of operatives, are daily occurrences." One novel idea that Fitzhugh added to the proslavery critique of the Panic of 1857 was the slightly veiled suggestion that free workers required some form of institutional arrangement, like slavery, to safeguard them from starvation and poverty.[38]

Fitzhugh extended the proslavery analysis of the Panic of 1857 in another regard. Southerners had deservedly earned the reputation of being the nation's premier advocates of free trade in international commerce and of laissez faire in regard to relations between the federal and state governments. Fitzhugh claimed that this was true only in regard to policy. Southerners benefited materially from low tariffs, and they required a weak, noninterventionist federal government to thwart northern attempts to abolish slavery. But Fitzhugh insisted that there was a vast difference between southern acceptance of the policy of free trade and southern allegiance to the theory's principles. He categorically denied that free trade doctrines, or capitalistic values, governed the southern business system. Instead, the southern economy embodied the antithesis of freedom, the patriarchal principle. Although southerners commonly testified about their adherence to free trade ideals, Fitzhugh maintained that the South had become "the most thoroughly anti-free trade [region] of any portion of civilized Christendom." He called upon his contemporaries to acknowledge "the exclusive and protective policy" they followed in state affairs and "to throw Adam Smith, Say, Ricardo & Co. in the fire."[39]

In their reaction to the northern bread riots, southerners appeared

---

38. [George Fitzhugh], "The Character and Causes of the Crisis," *De Bow's Review*, XXIV (January, 1858), 28, 29–34; Fitzhugh, "Wealth of the North and South," *De Bow's Review*, XXIII (December, 1857), 590–91; Fitzhugh, "Entails and Primogeniture," *De Bow's Review*, XXVII (August, 1859), 173–75; Fitzhugh, "Origin of Civilization—What is Property—Which is the Best Slave Race?" *De Bow's Review*, XXV (December, 1858), 654, 663.

39. George Fitzhugh, "Reaction and the Administration," *De Bow's Review*, XXV (October, 1858), 416; Fitzhugh, *Cannibals All*, 59.

to hold economic doctrines significantly different from those in the North. They pictured their society as following the patriarchal principle and avoiding the crass, selfish materialism of the North. Coupled with their own self-congratulatory comments on their region's social stability was a bitter denunciation of the economic ideals of northern society and of the chaos toward which those ideals were tending. These southern perceptions of the differences between the northern and southern economic orders obtained continual expression for the next three years. Many northerners concluded that southerners had left the mainstream of American culture.[40]

But there was a grave paradox in southern economic ideas, especially those of the proslavery school. Southerners did use the proslavery labor argument in their analysis of northern labor turmoil in 1857, but these were not the only economic views they expressed during the months of the Panic. The financial collapse presented southerners with a great array of banking and business problems that required legislative action. When southerners discussed the appropriate solutions to be applied, they used the concepts of free trade economics. Although Fitzhugh published reams of material in an attempt to persuade his compatriots to abandon free trade precepts, southerners demonstrated in their own local business affairs that they supported not only the policy of free trade but its theoretical foundations as well.

In numerous statements southerners showed their affinity for free trade economics. Like northerners, they believed that "political Economy partakes of the nature of a demonstrative science" and that market activities were governed by the "laws of nature."[41] In order to ensure prosperity, economic decisions must be left to "the control of enlightened self-interest rather than to that of theorizing politicians." There was also the matter of individual rights, for no man "can be said to enjoy his full right in his own property, in the proceeds of his industry, unless he is at liberty to exchange it at the highest price he can get, in the best market he can find for the commodities of his choice." This attitude inevitably led to an advocacy of the noninterventionist state

40. This particular reaction to the Panic was one of the phenomena that Nevins, in *The Emergence of Lincoln*, I, 176, 196–202, used to validate his interpretation that the North and South represented different civilizations.

41. Letter of "Cassandra" in Charleston *Mercury*, September 8, 1857; Richmond (Va.) *Enquirer*, October 16, 1857. On the southern exposition of free trade ideals, see Kaufman, *Capitalism, Slavery, and Republican Values*, 82–120.

and the principle of laissez faire. Governor Herschel V. Johnson of Georgia, in discussing that state's banking problems, admonished the legislature that "as a general rule, it is safest to meddle as little as possible with the currency of the country. The laws of trade regulate it best."[42]

If the individual had an absolute right to dispose of his property without governmental interference, the institution that determined his actions was the marketplace. "The maxim of buying in the cheapest market and selling in the dearest, which regulates every merchant in his individual dealings, is strictly applicable as the best rule to the trade of the whole country," commented one editor. Moreover, the "general laws of demand and supply" could operate for the international slave trade "as it does [for] every other, and the moment that home production was sufficient, it would banish from the market all foreign competition." One Arkansas editor explained that when the economy was not hampered by a false monetary system and impediments to trade, fluctuations in the values of products arose from "changes in the relations of supply and demand." Southerners also realized that extensive trade promoted economic growth and efficiency in production. An Alabama editor stated, "We honestly believe in the doctrine of a division of labor. Upon it depends the theory of free trade."[43]

Perhaps in no other debate connected with the Panic of 1857 was southern adherence to the doctrines of free trade so strikingly revealed as in a minor flurry of activity against southern usury laws. This argument took place wholly within the context of southern society and was not influenced by particular sectional concerns regarding federal economic policy. Practically every state in the Union had statutes governing usury, and southerners, like northern free traders, attacked these restrictions on the use of money as a violation of economic laws. Governor John A. Winston of Alabama urged a "modification" of the usury laws, arguing that such an alteration was "demanded by the more enlightened spirit of the times in which we live." Money would follow the laws of supply and demand like any other commodity but "legal tram-

42. Editorial, *De Bow's Review*, XXIII (December, 1857), 655; letter of "Cassandra" in Charleston *Mercury*, September 8, 1857; message of Herschel V. Johnson in *Federal Union* (Milledgeville, Ga.), November 5, 1857.

43. *Mississippi Free Trader* (Natchez), May 30, 1859; letter to the editor, Charleston *Mercury*, September 11, 1858; *Arkansas True Democrat* quoted in *Mississippian* (Jackson), January 5, 1859; Mobile *Daily Register*, October 11, 1857.

mels are thrown around the free operations of every citizen, greatly to the detriment of all parties." One contributor to the Charleston *Daily Courier* believed that money moved from one state to another when higher interest rates were available; the laws that limited interest rates in the original state thus deprived its own citizens of capital. He argued that interest rates would not become oppressive if left to natural devices because they would follow the basic law of all commodities, becoming "cheapest when left to themselves" because "freedom in commerce" produced an "equilibrium between the supply and demand in such a manner as to make the *natural* or *remunerative* price nearly the same as the *current*." William Brownlow attacked Tennessee's usury law and pontificated that the "great principle of supply and demand will regulate the money market; and we are in favor of free trade in the sale and purchase of money."[44]

In the debates over banking laws that arose in most southern states after the Panic of 1857, political leaders and editors commonly voiced their approval of competition and abhorrence of privileged, aristocratic groups or corporations, ideals that squared well with the dicta of free trade capitalist theory.[45] Although these views were more congenial to Democrats, party cleavage over banking in the South was largely a matter of policy, not philosophy; Whigs, Democrats, and other opposition forces did not stray far from basic capitalist dogmas. In the South Carolina legislature, a Mr. Whately attacked the banks for controlling capital: "It destroys all competition, and absorbs the entire floating capital of the country, and places it in the hands of the few." Fear of a privileged elite who achieved position via legislation was a common theme. In his excruciatingly long address to the Virginia legislature, Governor Henry A. Wise admonished his peers that a "moneyed aristocracy is the most dangerous enemy of this republic." Georgia's governor, Joseph Brown, after a year of struggling with his state's bank officers, warned the legislature that if "moneyed monopo-

44. Message of Gov. John A. Winston in Mobile *Daily Register*, November 12, 1858; Charleston *Daily Courier*, November 5, 1857; Knoxville *Whig*, December 5, 1857. An example of opposition to the repeal of the usury laws is M. C. Givens, "Should Our Usury Laws Be Repealed," *De Bow's Review*, XXVI (April, 1859), 445–47.

45. On southern banking during the Panic of 1857, see Chap. 3 above and Campbell, *The Development of Banking in Tennessee*, 135–53; Parks, *Joseph E. Brown of Georgia*, 43–50, 69–75; Alfred Glaze Smith, Jr., *Economic Readjustment of an Old Cotton State: South Carolina, 1820–1860* (Columbia, S.C., 1958), 209–16.

lies" were not checked in their usurpation of authority, those corporations would soon "make the people the subjects of their power." Similar pronouncements came from politicians in Tennessee, Alabama, Kentucky, and Mississippi.[46]

When discussing the banking problem, southerners frequently fell back upon the Jacksonian rhetoric of evaluating institutions in terms of their impact upon the common man. The editor of the *Mississippi Free Trader* exploded in wrath over the bankers' suspension of specie payment and fretted about the results this would have on "the hard working classes"; he counseled "the laboring and producing classes [to] refuse to touch" paper money in the future. When Democrat Joseph Brown lambasted the banks for injuring the state's "laboring classes," Whig editors promptly responded in the same "common people" idiom, declaimed the Democratic rhetoric as "this old song," and warned that banks were necessary for the well-being of the governor's "moderate, hard-working class."[47]

Contrary to Fitzhugh's hopes, southerners invariably employed free trade concepts in their discussion of southern business difficulties following the Panic of 1857. Rejection of those doctrines was extremely rare—indeed, it was Fitzhugh's theories, rather than those of Adam Smith, that most commonly met with southern repudiation. In response to the publication of several of Fitzhugh's articles in the Richmond *Enquirer,* a Professor R. Rapps of Randolph Macon College complimented the editors for not endorsing Fitzhugh's "erroneous, and I would say hurtful doctrines." The academician specifically reprobated Fitzhugh's assertion "that slavery (of course African) was irreconcilable with the principles of Political Economy." An author in the *Southern Literary Messenger* followed a line of argument that closely paralleled Fitzhugh's criticism of free society. Yet the writer specifically stated that he found Fitzhugh unacceptable because of the latter's dismissal of free trade principles.[48]

An additional aspect of southern economic thinking emerged during

46. Charleston *Daily Courier,* December 15, 1857; Richmond (Va.) *Enquirer,* December 8, 1857; *Federal Union* (Milledgeville, Ga.), November 9, 1858.

47. *Mississippi Free Trader* (Natchez), October 30, November 3, 1857; *Southern Recorder* (Milledgeville, Ga.), November 9, 1858; *Constitutionalist* (Augusta, Ga.) quoted by *Southern Recorder* (Milledgeville, Ga.), February 2, 1858.

48. Letter of R. Rapps in Richmond (Va.) *Enquirer,* November 19, 1858; R. E. C., "The Problem of Free Society," *Southern Literary Messenger,* XXVII (July, 1858), 12.

the Panic of 1857 that proved to be violently inconsistent with proslavery concepts. Southerners lavished praise upon the role free labor played in the economy. The free labor ideal had supposedly found a snug home in the Republican party, which based its appeal to the northern electorate upon free labor principles. Republicans defined a free labor society as one that welcomed progress in science and technology, allowed all men free scope to their talents, and elevated no group to an exalted position over others.[49]

During and after the Panic of 1857, southerners of all political backgrounds sang the praises of free labor with the same fervor as northerners. All men had to obey "the divine announcement" that "in the sweat of thy face, shalt thou eat bread." William W. Holden said that the biblical commandment to labor was not a malediction but "a blessing in disguise." Other southerners stated that northerners mistakenly believed that in the South labor was despised and degraded, but it was not so, for labor "is a badge of honor, and more active, more industrious, more laborious white men, do not exist in any section of the Union than at the South." Nor was "honest labor" limited to any particular occupation because "*all useful labor is honorable.*" No "poor man—no matter what his calling," added another editor, was better treated, "aided and abetted in all his honorable undertakings than in the South, or slaveholding States."[50]

Southerners postulated that, in Holden's words, labor was "the motive power of civilization" and that in order to secure the most benefits, individuals had only to form appropriate habits. Holden believed that "hardly any thing is impossible to a young man who is temperate, economical, and honorable, and who *labors* constantly and perseveringly." Some of the mercantile maxims of *Hunt's Merchants' Magazine* were brought before the southern public to point out the road to wealth. Others believed that Benjamin Franklin's advice of one hundred years

---

The opposition of southern intellectuals toward Fitzhugh is developed in Faust, *A Sacred Circle*, 127–31. See also Neal C. Gillespie, *The Collapse of Orthodoxy: The Intellectual Ordeal of George Frederick Holmes* (Charlottesville, Va., 1972), 157–58, 163, 173.

49. For a further discussion of the free labor ideology, see Foner, *Free Soil, Free Labor, Free Men*, 11–27.

50. *Southern Planter*, XVIII (August, 1858), 497; address of William W. Holden in *Semi-Weekly Standard* (Raleigh, N.C.), December 9, 1857; *Daily Picayune* (New Orleans) quoted by *Mississippi Free Trader* (Natchez), November 22, 1858; *Southern Watchman* quoted by *Southern Recorder* (Milledgeville, Ga.), June 29, 1858; Samuel M. Wolfe, *Helper's Impending Crisis Dissected* (Philadelphia, 1860), 58.

before still applied: "We are taxed twice as much by our idleness, three times as much by our pride, and four times as much by our folly."[51]

Southerners readily acceded to the necessity of cultivating the middle-class virtues of thrift, industriousness, temperance, and ambition. A North Carolina editor was pleased that the Panic of 1857 would have the effect of making men more "frugal." Another paper in 1860 offered its readers the advice New York Mayor Fernando Wood gave to some city cartmen; the Mayor told the men that the "highest position is as open to you as it is to other men," and all that was required of them was "determination, vigor, and indomitable perseverance." Few northerners matched the awesome Protestant ethic of the Texas firebrand, Senator Louis T. Wigfall. In an 1860 debate over the homestead proposal, Wigfall proclaimed, "I know it is popular to talk about poor men, but I tell you that poverty is a crime. A man who is poor has sinned . . . there is a screw loose in his head somewhere."[52]

The cultivation of fine character traits were vital to southerners, of course, because theirs was a society of mobility and opportunity. As in the North, the "very wealthy man of to-day may be the very poor man of tomorrow. The very poor man of this year, may be the millionaire of ten years hence." Southerners did have classes, but they were the eternal two classes—"the respectable and the loafing." An example of the praise heaped upon the self-made man came from George Prentis of the Louisville *Courier* in his remarks about Democratic vice-presidential nominee Joseph Lane: "Alone and unaided, poor and comparatively uneducated, he began the struggle of life"; he reached political heights "thanks to our republican institutions." Partial legislation and the lack of aristocratic castes permitted men to rise in the world. And if there were those in the South who longed for titled distinctions, there were also many who gloried in the ideal of republican simplicity. So Senator John J. Crittenden wrote his daughter to be leery of aristocratic wiles and to practice republican manners: "It behooves you to remember that you belong to a plain, free country, where there are neither nobles nor princes. I am afraid you will find it a little difficult to 'shuffle off the coil' of notions, tastes, and habits

51. *Semi-Weekly Standard* (Raleigh, N.C.), December 2, 9, 1857; *Southern Planter,* XIX (January, 1859), 6.

52. Raleigh (N.C.) *Weekly Register,* October 7, 1857; *Mississippi Free Trader* (Natchez), March 26, 1860; speech of Senator Wigfall, April 4, 1860, *Congressional Globe,* 36th Cong., 1st Sess., 1534; Alvy L. King, *Louis T. Wigfall: Southern Fire-eater* (Baton Rouge, 1970), 87–92.

which the artificial state of European society so cunningly and so pleasantly wraps around those who come within its splendid circles. Set not too much value on those things; they are but pageants, unreal, and fleeting."[53]

In their declarations about the Panic of 1857 southerners revealed their support for the scientific and material advances of the nineteenth century. During a debate in the Virginia assembly over state aid to a railroad company, one legislator declared, "on the one hand, it is a question of progress; a queston of advancement," of making Virginia "the most energetic of all the States in this Union." The editor of the Charleston *Daily Courier*, when reviewing the governor's annual message, maintained that South Carolinians must not "shrink from the sacrifices necessary to effect great public improvements, and to keep pace with the progress of the age." William Brownlow demanded that Tennesseans remember that "we live in an age of progress, and of improvements, in every thing" and that men in the mid-1850s knew what was better for themselves than "the antideluvians who lived before us."[54]

During the Panic of 1857, southerners demonstrated a full understanding of and a commitment to free trade economics. Certainly southern Democrats exhibited a passion for both the policy of free trade and the concepts that undergirded the theory. But southern Whigs and members of the American party were no less supportive of free trade doctrines, if not quite so enthusiastic about lower tariff rates. The tenets of free trade economics were those of capitalist economics, and virtually all shades of political opinion in the South rallied about the ideas of individualism, social mobility, and free choice in the marketplace— the hallmarks of capitalist theory.

Yet the embrace of capitalist ideals by southerners clashed terribly with the "patriarchal principle" they expounded regarding slavery and the fate of the northern wage earner. The basic dilemma was simply that capitalism rested on unrestricted freedom for all members of soci-

53. Richmond (Va.) *Whig*, December 29, 1857; Louisville *Courier*, October 31, 1860; John J. Crittenden to Mrs. A. M. Coleman, February 20, 1858, in Mrs. Chapman [Ann Mary Butler Crittenden] Coleman, *The Life of John J. Crittenden, with Selections from his Correspondence and Speeches* (Philadelphia, 1871), II, 143.

54. Richmond (Va.) *Enquirer*, March 5, 1858; Charleston *Daily Courier*, November 30, 1859; Knoxville *Whig*, December 5, 1857. A free labor philosophy in southern society is implied in both Thornton, *Power and Politics in a Slave Society*, 204–21, and Hahn, *The Roots of Southern Populism*, 52–85.

ety, whereas the slave system called for the curtailment of freedom for certain individuals and the imposition of social responsibilities upon others. George Fitzhugh probably understood better than any other southerner the incompatibility between capitalism and slavery. In late 1858 Fitzhugh wrote: "Political economy, or free trade, resulted as a fact from the abolition of feudal slavery several centuries before Adam Smith promulgated it as a system of philosophy. It is wholly at war with all systems of slavery, and most especially with the despotic slavery at the South. To be a free-trade man in its scientific sense is to be an abolitionist." Fitzhugh's assertion that abolitionists were free traders struck others as well. In writing to South Carolina Senator James H. Hammond, Henry C. Carey tried to prove that the senator's proslavery views did not fit with his advocacy of free trade. "Had I desired to find a correspondent who would be still more radical upon the free trade side [than William Cullen Bryant], I should have taken a thorough abolitionist."[55]

According to the state of economic knowledge that prevailed at the time, the inherent antagonism between slaveholding precepts and free trade economics arose out of the labor theory of value. Slavery was incompatible with capitalist economics for two important reasons: first, the most efficient means of rapid economic growth was by free labor; second, man had an absolute right to do anything he wished with the values (or products) created by his labor. At its core, the entire philosophy of free trade was based on individual decisions in the marketplace, on the premise that each man knew what was best for himself. If a man felt that his actions did not personally benefit himself, the incentive to work harder and to exercise his intelligence to increase his productivity vanished. Deprived of the fruits of his labor, the worker turned to slothful ways and unremunerative production.

This perception of the manner in which individuals improved their lot was the essential criticism northern free traders had of southern slavery. George Opdyke investigated slavery and found the institution to be a gross violation of natural laws. Opdyke summarized that slavery ultimately robbed "its victims of their dearest rights, and [sunk] them almost to a level with the brute creation." Frederick Law Olm-

55. *Daily National Intelligencer* (Washington, D.C.), December 22, 1858; Henry C. Carey to James H. Hammond, March 17, 1860, in Edward Carey Gardiner Collection, HSP.

sted also believed the imprudent work habits of the slave—laziness, indifference, inefficiency—arose because slavery denied the worker the benefits of his labor.[56]

Both Carey's and Fitzhugh's observation that abolitionists belonged to the free trade circle had a measure of validity. During and after the Panic of 1857, various abolitionists sang the praises of unfettered individual freedom. The abolitionist editor of the *National Era*, Gamaliel Bailey, proclaimed that "what we want from a Government is, *security to the rights of each citizen,* and then, generally, *to be let alone.*" The abolitionist press often criticized Carey's protectionist broadsides, and various reform meetings passed resolutions favoring the abolition of trade restrictions. Moreover, when abolitionists criticized slavery on economic grounds, they usually did so on the basis that slavery denied the worker the fruits of his labor. Hence William Lloyd Garrison would not believe that emancipation in the West Indies was an economic failure because to admit that emancipation had failed to rejuvenate the West Indian economy meant that slavery, with its "blood-reeking lash" and bestial treatment of labor, was "pecuniarily more profitable than the system of mutual compact and the stimulus of the hope of reward."[57]

The fact that the ideals of free trade were fundamentally opposed to slavery does not imply that the peculiar institution obtained a justification in the ideas of protectionists, who, after all, were entirely in the mainstream of capitalist thought. Although protectionist theorists were probably less likely to be in the abolitionist camp, they nevertheless indicated that they believed the institution would and should die a natural death.[58] The basic reason for protectionists' distaste of slavery was the same as the free traders': they adhered to the labor theory of value. Francis Bowen, for example, wrote that a sound economy required that "the laborer shall be sure of receiving the full amount of his wages, or shall be protected in the ownership of the values he has produced."[59] As long as protectionists accepted the premise that the

56. Opdyke, *A Treatise on Political Economy,* 327–33, 337; Laura Wood Roper, *FLO: A Biography of Frederick Law Olmstead* (Baltimore, 1973), 87–89.

57. *National Era* (Washington, D.C.), October 29, 1857; William L. Garrison to Ezra Hervey Heywood, July 30, 1860, in Ruchames and Merrill (eds.), *The Letters of William Lloyd Garrison,* 677; James L. Huston, "Abolitionists and an Errant Economy," 15–27.

58. Consult the hostile attitude protectionists harbored toward slavery in Carey, *Manual of Social Science,* 252–55, 268; Stephen Colwell, *The South: A Letter from a Friend in the North* (Philadelphia, 1856), 10–13, 18–19; E. Peshine Smith to Henry C. Carey, February 6, 1859, in Gardiner Collection.

59. Francis Bowen, *The Principles of Political Economy,* 76–77.

worker had a natural right to the objects he created, they could not condone slavery.

No school of economic thought in antebellum America could justify the South's peculiar institution. Some free traders and protectionists might have supported slavery for racial or social reasons, but an economic rationale did not exist as long as Americans believed that every man had a natural right to the products of his labor. In the first half of the nineteenth century, most Americans believed that economic and natural laws could never be in conflict. This attitude doubly ensured that slavery would never receive approval from northerners. One of the editors of the *North American Review* succintly expressed this common sentiment: "On a field of open competition, if free labor does not demonstrate its superiority, and win the reluctant and in time the hearty suffrage of its opponents, we are content to take issue on the side of slavery; for we do not believe that economical and moral laws can work otherwise than harmoniously."[60]

There were several ways that southerners could resolve their paradox over slavery and economic thought. George Fitzhugh hoped to persuade his compatriots to embrace entirely the patriarchal principle, to agree upon the social need to eliminate the personal freedoms of certain groups. But he wanted to avoid exonerating slavery on the grounds that the enslaved were of a different race than the masters. Most southerners did not follow Fitzhugh. The racial justification of slavery proved to be the means by which southerners could continue to espouse free trade sentiments while extolling the patriarchal ideal.[61]

Southern writers insisted that northerners be aware that the race of the enslaved altered economic theory. Africans were not intellectually fit for freedom; blacks, according to one commentator, had an "inherent intellectual imbecility." The mental inferiority of blacks, however, was coupled with an ability to withstand the tropical climate. Thus Africans could labor where whites could not. In particular, blacks could grow cotton, tobacco, rice, and sugar because of their natural talents for surviving tropical conditions. White southerners used these natural abilities of blacks to grow the goods the world craved. Southern slavery thus promoted the advance of civilization by producing crops the world desperately needed and by teaching Africans the rudiments of Chris-

60. "The Financial Crisis," *North America Review*, LXXXVI (January, 1858), 181–82.
61. Fitzhugh, *Cannibals All*, 199. It should be noted that as the Civil War approached, Fitzhugh himself came more and more to rely upon the racial justification of slavery; see Wish, *George Fitzhugh*, 298–301.

tian living. But the essential element in the system of slavery, as the proslavery agricultural reformer Edmund Ruffin claimed, was that blacks were only made useful because white southerners supplied "one directing mind, and one controlling will."[62]

A common method southerners employed after the Panic of 1857 to ensure that the ideals of free trade and patriarchy were not commingled was to argue earnestly that the South had two labor systems, one free, the other slave. One contributor to *Russell's Magazine* wrote that "Negroes only, with us, are slaves. Hired men are whites." The slave system was despotic and patriarchal, but whites competed in a free labor economy. Each was in its "proper sphere," stated the editor of the Richmond *Enquirer;* thus, he continued, "Let us hear no more of a contest between free and slave labor." The essential point was simple: the free white southern labor system had different governing principles (free trade) than the black slave labor system (patriarchy).[63]

Under the cover of racial doctrines the South could sneak out of the theoretical dilemmas posed by the peculiar institution. Southerners could honestly present themselves as believers in free labor. Capitalist notions were accepted because the concepts applied to Caucasians. Slavery was merely an aberration of economic laws because of the inherent mental backwardness of Africans and because the southern climate prohibited white men from using their superior intellects to grow the crops the manufacturers of the globe demanded. Nor did the southern veneration of egalitarian principles and republican government reveal hypocritical attitudes. The white South was egalitarian and republican; only the black South was caste-ridden and despotic.[64]

The free trade notions of many proslavery southerners could conceivably be explained in other ways, and thus the patriarchal quality of

62. George S. Sawyer, *Southern Institutes; or, An Inquiry into the Origin and Early Prevalence of Slavery and the Slave-Trade* (Philadelphia, 1859), 198–99; Edmund Ruffin, *The Political Economy of Slavery; or, The Institution Considered in regard to its Influence on Public Wealth and the General Welfare* (N.p., [1857]), 6–7, 9; on the slaves' abilities to labor in a tropical clime, see Richmond (Va.) *Enquirer,* November 27, 1857; *Daily Constitutionalist* (Augusta, Ga.), October 18, 1860.

63. "The Dual Form of Labour," *Russell's Magazine,* VI (October, 1859), 2; Richmond (Va.) *Enquirer,* May 28, 1858. However, see the awkward and uncertain comments made by Charles Bruce in Richmond (Va.) *Enquirer,* April 9, 1858, and by the editor of Charleston *Daily Courier,* July 2, 1858.

64. On the racial views of southerners see Stephen A. Channing, *Crisis of Fear: Secession in South Carolina* (New York, 1970), *passim;* George M. Fredrickson, *The Black Image in the White Mind: The Debate on Afro-American Character and Destiny, 1817–1914* (New York, 1971), 43–70; James Oakes, *The Ruling Race: A History of American Slaveholders* (New York, 1982), 130–36.

southern life be preserved without contradiction. Southerners obviously espoused the policy of free trade out of self-interest—their prosperity relied on a flourishing foreign trade. Moreover, the negative state, the laissez faire axiom, had important ramifications for southerners. By insisting upon an emasculated federal government, southerners would not have to fear northerners controlling the national legislature for their own aggrandizement, and a weak central government would pose no danger to the stability of the peculiar institution. It may also be argued that the clamor over banks, usury laws, and internal improvement schemes within the states was a reflection of the fears of the plantation masters that some new power might enter southern politics and erode their hegemony. There also exists the possibility that the advocacy of free trade was essentially an urban phenomenon, not reflective of the true rural nature of southern society.[65]

But a number of factors indicate that southerners imbibed heavily of the economics of free trade, and their pronouncements on the subject were no more deceptive than any other society's affirmation of a distinctive set of ideals. Current research has rather consistently emphasized that democratic ideas and social mobility throve among small slaveholders and nonslaveholders.[66] However, adherence to the idea of free trade by southerners makes sense when one accepts the division of economic activity they pointed to: a competitive egalitarian world for whites; a restrictive hierarchical world for blacks. In light of the large numbers of small slaveholders and nonslaveholders, it would seem more likely that southerners would describe themselves economically as adherents of capitalist values rather than patriarchal ones. Even the proslavery attack on the free labor society of the North had some of its origins, oddly enough, in free trade doctrines. Much of the proslavery criticism of northern economic problems stemmed from a belief that an increasing population would only enlarge the size of the poorer classes and plunge them into misery. Eventually this misery would take the form of a social cataclysm. But these views, so frequently aired by southerners in the 1850s, were descendants of Revolutionary republican ideas on society. Those ideas were part of a larger free trade perspective.[67]

65. For example, Thornton, *Politics and Power in a Slave Society*, 293–98, 337–39; Genovese, *The Political Economy of Slavery*, 13–34.
66. Thornton, *Politics and Power in a Slave Society*, 204–27; Hahn, *The Roots of Southern Populism*, 52–85; Oakes, *The Ruling Race*, 52–59, 127, 140–41, 147–49, 227.
67. Drew R. McCoy, *The Elusive Republic: Political Economy in Jeffersonian America* (Chapel Hill, 1980), 14–15, 50–52, 76–103, 126–29, 185–206.

There is one other reason to suspect that southerners were sincere in their arguments for free trade. The patriarchal principle and proslavery ruminations were little more than opinions and value judgments; outside of an axiom postulating capital's ownership of labor, proslavery writings offered little detail as to how an economy functioned. Nowhere in the proslavery argument was there an explanation of prices and price variations, interest rates, banking practices, technological advance, and international commerce. When economic problems arose, southerners of course turned to capitalist formulations because those concepts could aid them in finding solutions for concrete, daily economic vexations. Proslavery writings on economic matters were very often little more than glib, abstract generalizations. Southerners had yet to define the economic details of a patriarchal society.

Despite southerners' reliance on race to explain away the dilemma of a society that prized both proslavery and free labor doctrines, there was still an inconsistency between free trade and proslavery ideals that never could be resolved. The comparison southerners made between the fate of northern free workers and southern slaves in the autumn of 1857, and their glorification of the patriarchal ideal, had no foundation in free trade theory. Indeed, southern thought on economic matters became considerably muddled prior to secession. It was not uncommon for editors and commentators to adopt the extreme proslavery stand on the future dissolution of free labor society while at almost the same time applauding the middle-class virtues of thrift, honesty, hard work, ambition, and rugged individualism.[68] Southerners before 1860 largely stayed in the mainstream of American thought with regard to economic and social values. But the South's growing acceptance of some of the tenets of proslavery thought revealed that southerners had a tendency to adopt different cultural standards than did northerners. In 1860 free trade ideals dominated, but there was a discernible movement toward the patriarchal principle.[69]

One of the results of the Panic of 1857 was that it starkly revealed

68. See, for example, "The Dual Form of Labor," *Russell's Magazine*, VI (October, 1859), 1–16; Richmond (Va.) *Whig*, December 29, 1857, May 11, 1858; Richmond (Va.) *Enquirer*, November 24, 1857, May 24, 1859.

69. Two recent articles on the nature of southern society define the boundary over the debate of the old South's unique status: James M. McPherson, "Antebellum Southern Exceptionalism: A New Look at an Old Question," *CWH*, XXIX (1983), 230–44; and Edward Pessen, "How Different from Each Other Were the Antebellum North and South?" *AHR*, LXXXV (1980), 1119–49.

these two strands of incompatible southern thought. At various times southerners would erupt in proslavery fury and use the experience of the Panic as proof of their contention that slavery produced a more stable and equitable society than did the system of free labor. At other times they would advance capitalist concepts and clamor for the absolute sovereignty of the individual in economic affairs, using the Panic to substantiate this claim as well. In the debate over national economic policies that took place between 1858 and 1860 southerners would continually exhibit this paradox in their economic thought.[70]

The urban labor demonstrations following the suspension of specie payment in 1857 generated considerable discussion among northerners as well as among southerners. Northerners, unlike the proslavery advocates, did not immediately press the question of the fate of the free wage earner into the sectional controversy. Yet the difficulties experienced by an ill-fed and ill-clad working class presented many northerners with as many dilemmas as the question of slavery, for the matter involved the equity and stability of a society based on free enterprise. And the bread riots raised the subject in a most frightening manner. Orators at the labor demonstrations often threatened violence if their plight went unheeded. These activities produced shocked responses from the northern middle class. Henry Raymond wrote in an editorial on the New York tumult that the "tenor of the addresses" was "not Black Republican, but *Red* Republican,—the oratory of 1848, in the most oppressed communities of Europe, verging even to the terrible oratory of the time of ROBESPIERRE, sixty years before." The conservative editor of the Lynn, Massachusetts, *Weekly Reporter* perhaps best captured the fear that the Panic of 1857 brought to northerners: "For when the artisans lift their arms, nations totter and empires sink to decay. 'Bread or Blood!' is a terrible cry, and heaven grant that we may never hear it echoed through our streets."[71]

Northerners were genuinely perplexed at the outbreak of labor unrest following the Panic of 1857, and they struggled to understand its origins. Not a few commentators proposed that the riotous element among the unemployed were of foreign descent and were naturally

70. For a fuller elaboration of this section, see James L. Huston, "The Panic of 1857, Southern Economic Thought, and the Patriarchal Defense of Slavery," *Historian*, XLVI (1984), 163–86.

71. New York *Times*, November 6, 1857; Lynn (Mass.) *Weekly Reporter*, November 14, 1857.

given, in their opinion, to irrational behavior. Some, like one editor of the Chicago *Daily Tribune*, argued that the jobless were the authors of their own misfortune because of their improvident habits; the complaints of the unemployed were an "old and favorite dodge of the lazy, shiftless, worthless and drunken who infest every city." But most northerners did not react in this fashion since it was obvious that the majority of the participants in the labor demonstrations were honest but poor men who could not find work. The editor of the Indianapolis *Daily Journal* represented this attitude; he deprecated the lawless spirit of some of the gatherings, but he believed it was "idle [to repeat] the stale truisms that 'the law gives to every man his own,' and 'if a man starve in this country it is his own fault.'" The writer noted that the problem was simply that there were no jobs. He finally revealed his bewilderment at the situation by asking whether "anything [could] be more appalling in itself" than unemployment in a nation with a broad expanse of land and a "government that interferes with no white man's labor."[72]

Northern middle-class society entertained the nebulous ideas that in a free enterprise economy all participants would receive ample benefits, according to their natural endowments, and that the distribution of wealth would be roughly equal for all of society's members. During the aftermath of the Panic of 1857, northerners discussed and rejected the paternalism that infected the European systems of monarchy and socialism. They believed that these doctrines invariably produced inequalities in wealth because of the favoritism granted to various social groups.[73] Northerners reasoned that an economy based on freedom should produce a society different from one based on favoritism. Thus, they felt that the American economy, being free and open to all, would result in full employment, adequate remuneration of all workers, and an equal distribution of wealth. In short, they believed that the working class should prosper. But in the fall of 1857 it was evident that the workers were not prosperous. That circumstance required an explanation.

An answer to the northerners' dilemma over labor came from the South. The proslavery contingent had long argued that the working

72. Chicago *Daily Tribune*, November 13, 1857; Indianapolis *Daily Journal*, November 12, 1857.
73. For the contemporary discussion of the merits of socialism, see New York *Herald*, November 16, 1857; New York *Times*, October 21, 27, November 6, 10, 13, 1857; Chicago *Daily Tribune*, November 16, 1857.

class in free society posed a threat to stability and that sooner or later
the northern social edifice would collapse in a war between capitalists
and workers. Edmund Ruffin disclosed the means by which the northern economy drove the laborer to poverty and finally to desperate action. A dense population, Ruffin said, forced down wages because the
laborers competed among themselves for a limited number of jobs.
Eventually this process of competition reduced wages to the subsistence level—that is, to renumeration only sufficient to allow life to continue. The danger to northern society, the Richmond *South* added,
was that democratic institutions allowed the miserable workers "to
avenge their wrongs and gratify their passions" by wielding their numerical superiority at the ballot box, grabbing the reins of government,
and finally expropriating the wealth of the propertied classes.[74]

Ruffin, as well as numerous other southerners, emphasized that a
social cataclysm had not yet occurred in the North because of the existence of unpopulated western lands. Because laborers could migrate to
the West, they could, and did, reduce the labor supply in the East.
This resulted in the current condition of "fair and unusually higher
than fair" wages for the industrial worker. But the supply of unsettled
western lands, as southerners somewhat gloatingly pointed out, was
not inexhaustible. At some time in the future there would be no westward escape for the northern worker, and then the trap of subsistence
wages could not be avoided. Thus many southern commentators on the
northern bread riots felt that the demonstrations were not "abnormal"
for a free labor society but were "merely the ripples which agitate the
surface." The editor of the Charleston *Daily Courier* predicted that
sooner or later class warfare would erupt in the North. "That it will
come at last there can be no room for doubt," he warned.[75]

The proslavery analysis of northern labor relations had a solid basis
in contemporary free trade economic thought. The belief that the
worker would fall into abject poverty was a hypothesis devised by two
Englishmen, Thomas Malthus and David Ricardo. Adam Smith had

74. Ruffin, *The Political Economy of Slavery*, 6–7; Edmund Ruffin, "Slavery and
Free Labor Defined and Compared," *Southern Planter*, XIX (December, 1859), 730–31;
Richmond (Va.) *South* quoted by *Semi-Weekly Standard* (Raleigh, N.C.), October 21,
1857. For the widespread southern belief in the power of overpopulation, see Joseph J.
Spengler, "Population Theory in the Ante-Bellum South," *JSH*, II (1936), 365–85.

75. Ruffin, "Slavery and Free Labor Defined and Compared," *Southern Planter*, XIX
(December, 1859), 730–31; Mobile *Daily Register*, November 18, 1857; Charleston
Daily Courier, November 10, 1857. See also Kaufman, *Capitalism, Slavery, and Repub-
lican Values*, 90–91, 101–103, 111, 118–19.

been optimistic about the gradual improvement of life through increased productivity, but in 1798 Malthus published a short pamphlet in which he concluded that society could never improve the lot of the poor because of the pressure that population growth put upon resources. Malthus pointed out what seemed to be an unalterable fact: population doubled every few decades but the amount of land that produced the grains to sustain life remained constant. Malthus conceded that the law of supply and demand determined wages, but he insisted that the crucial factor was the supply of and not the demand for labor. Because the procreative instincts of the lower classes constantly augmented their numbers, the competition among them for occupations reduced wages to the lowest possible standard. If for some reason the demand for labor outstripped the supply, wages would rise. But the increased allowance merely fueled the animal instincts and in turn led to an increase of the laboring population. The cycle would once again depress the price of labor to the subsistence level.

In his *Principles of Political Economy* (1817), David Ricardo added a theory of rent to the Malthusian population crisis. Not only did the laborers multiply themselves into subsistence wages, they also put pressure on landlords to extend their operations to the furthest limit. As the agricultural segment already utilized the best farming lands— the best lands grew the most products and thus gave the most profits— the only areas left were those of marginal value, or those soils that rendered a smaller yield. The result was that prices for bread rose. Wages also increased to enable the worker to maintain his physical existence, but only the landlord reaped the benefits. Together, the Smithian relation of supply and demand, the Malthusian tenet of population growth, and the Ricardian theory of rent sealed the worker into an inescapable prison of misery and hunger.[76]

The most unsettling fact for Americans about the British theory of wages was that the men who developed the concept were the men who also created free trade economics (although Malthus was opposed to the repeal of the corn laws). Americans living in the northern states who espoused free trade principles therefore inherited the philosophy's prediction about the laborers' ultimate condition. In Europe such theories about the masses might be entertained in light of institutional

76. Robert L. Heilbroner, *The Worldly Philosophers: The Lives, Times, and Ideas of the Great Economic Thinkers* (New York, 1961), 49–78. This was the American understanding of Ricardo and Malthus in the antebellum decade, and it was a considerable oversimplification of their ideas.

checks on the abilities of the lower orders to alter their fate, but in the United States these checks were nonexistent. Nothing barred the workers from grasping control of the government and extinguishing property rights. Northern free traders could not allow this possibility.

Although northern free traders embraced the philosophy of free trade enthusiastically, they handled the axiom of poverty wages with difficulty. They certainly could not condone the limiting of competition by tariffs or trade unions, for that would be a violation of the principles of individual rights and a free marketplace. Francis Wayland offered one theoretical means by which the worker could avoid pauperization. He pointed out that if the demand for labor outstripped population growth, wages would rise; the only way to increase the demand for labor was by augmenting the amount of capital stock, which required greater investment by the capitalist. "And hence," Wayland triumphantly concluded, "there seems no need of any other means to prevent the too rapid increase of population, than to secure a correspondent increase of capital by which that population may be supported." Amasa Walker concurred with Wayland that the British doctrine of wages was in error, and he promoted a revision of Ricardo's rent theory.[77]

A number of northern free traders accepted the hypothesis that wages for industrial laborers were destined to fall to the subsistence level. This did not dismay them, however, because they believed the United States should not become a manufacturing nation but remain an agricultural one. They argued that competition with England in industrial wares was a useless task because of that country's superior advantages in labor costs and technological knowledge. The United States had a competitive edge over other nations in agriculture, not in industry. The quantity of arable land ensured that wages in other occupations would remain high. An Indiana free trader, Richard Sulley, accepted the premise that labor "gets no more than the necessary *rate* of wages for its own continuance," but he also explained that wages in the nation were high because "we have possessed an almost *unlimited* amount of *virgin* soil."[78]

77. Wayland, *Elements of Political Economy*, 292, 298, 305; Amasa Walker, "Rent," *Hunt's*, XLII (April, 1860), 302–10; Walker, *The Science of Wealth*, 95–96.

78. Richard Sulley, "Free Trade and Protection: or, A Partial Review of Mr. Carey's Letters to the President," *Hunt's*, XLI (September, 1859), 296; Richard Sulley, "Free Trade and Protection, or, A Partial Review of Mr. Carey's Letters to the President," *Hunt's*, XL (May, 1859), 532, 533, 540; Dorfman, *The Economic Mind in American Civilization*, II, 737, 754, 764–76; Leo Troy, *Organized Labor in New Jersey* (Princeton, N.J., 1965), 35.

American free traders proposed three solutions for the woes of the industrial worker. One was to increase investment and capital stock so that labor would always be fully employed. The second was to remove all tariff barriers so that the price of commodities would fall and the laborer would have more purchasing power. But the third became the most popular means of alleviating the workers' distress: relocating the unemployed to the West. The free trade analysis of labor naturally favored an immigration policy because the Malthusian-Ricardian theory was founded upon the interplay of land and wages. American free traders argued that the removal of labor to the West would reduce the supply of labor in the East and thereby allow wages to rise. Thus the northern free trade explanation for the high wages of the worker was ultimately no different than that of the proslavery advocates.

The idea of western migration gathered numerous adherents in 1857. Upon the appearance of labor turmoil the general public touted the migration policy as the cure for unemployment. All kinds of organizations proclaimed the necessity of transporting the jobless to the West. The moribund Land Reform Association under the direction of John Commerford recaptured some of its former energy and began petitioning Congress for a homestead act that would allow the actual settler to obtain land without charge. Charles Loring Brace of New York's famed Children's Aid Society published letters suggesting that all persons interested in aiding the poor should pool their funds and use the money to direct the jobless "into one great channel—that of EMIGRATION." Various industrial associations were also founded, the purpose of which, as one Jared Arnold of New York said, was to remove "the surplus labor out of our large cities."[79]

Abolitionists forwarded their own particular solutions to the labor crisis, but they also revealed their strong connections with the laissez faire school of economic philosophy by enlisting in the war to make a homestead policy a reality. Antislavery proponents believed that the

79. On the Land Reform Association, see New York *Daily Tribune*, November 25, 1858, July 21, 1859; for the other associations, see New York *Daily Tribune*, October 26, November 11, 1857, May 5, December 27, 1858. Historians have generally dismissed the idea that western lands propped up eastern wage rates; see Henry Nash Smith, *Virgin Land: The American West as Symbol and Myth* (Cambridge, Mass., 1950), 169–73, 204; Fred A. Shannon, "A Post Mortem on the Labor-Safety-Valve Theory," *Agricultural History*, XIX (1945), 31–38; Henry M. Littlefield, "Has the Safety Valve Come Back to Life?" *Agricultural History*, XXXVIII (1964), 47–49. However, in terms of the state of economic knowledge at the time, making land in the West free was a legitimate means to raise wage levels—at least in theory.

material status of the laborer might be advanced through education; they also argued, not unsurprisingly, that the abolition of slavery would benefit the free worker by removing the disastrous competition of the slave. The greatest reform the abolitionists advocated for the laborer was the establishment of a free land policy that would allow the unemployed to migrate to the West. Gamaliel Bailey, editor of the antislavery paper the *National Era,* was shocked by the New York labor demonstrations and feared that they might produce a class war. He immediately held aloft the homestead ideal as the means to avoid a social cataclysm because the enactment of the free land scheme would "secure to all our large cities a safety-drain—a means for drawing off excess labor—and thus contribut[e] to the sobriety, order, and elevation, of the laboring classes left behind." In the aftermath of the Panic of 1857, most abolitionists agreed with him.[80]

Whereas free trade doctrines inevitably led to an embrace of the homestead principle in order to secure material well-being for the laborer, protectionism offered a different analysis and a different solution. The Panic of 1857 did not spark any new theoretical thrusts on the labor question from protectionists. But the economic debacle did allow them to refocus public attention on the drawbacks of free trade theory vis-à-vis the working class. For the protectionists, the social disorder attending the Panic proved their claim that free trade practices inevitably resulted in discontented and impoverished laborers.

By the 1850s protectionism had metamorphosed from an economic philosophy designed to promote industrial growth to one that sought the well-being of the laborer. This transformation evidently began in the 1830s when the social tumults following the Panic of 1837 and the rise of trade unionism frightened many socially conservative protectionists.[81] They thus came to believe that the treatment of labor was, in Stephen Colwell's words, "the great social question not only of our day, but of all time to come." Holding that society must somehow make provisions for the comfort of the industrial workers, protectionists agreed that the predictions of Ricardo and Malthus had to be averted. Francis

80. *Anti-Slavery Bugle* (Salem, Ohio), November 7, 1857; George M. Weston, *Southern Slavery Reduces Northern Wages* (Washington, D.C., 1856), 5; letter of Gerrit Smith in New York *Daily Tribune,* January 5, 1858; *National Era* (Washington, D.C.), November 12, 1857.

81. George Benjamin Mangold, *The Labor Argument in the American Protective Tariff Discussion* (1908; rpr. New York, 1971), 84–96. The concern of protectionists over the fate of labor has also recently been emphasized by Allen Kaufman in his discussion of the works of Daniel Raymond, in *Capitalism, Slavery, and Republican Values,* 37–45.

Bowen captured the fear that stalked many protectionists: low wages could not be permitted to become the rule in the United States, for the "class of laborers, who must always form the majority in any community, and who, with us, also have the control in politics, will not be satisfied without organic changes in the laws, which will endanger at once our political and social system." And although protectionists rejected the Malthusian-Ricardian doctrines pertaining to wages, they also spurned the American free traders' elevation of westward migration as the appropriate solution for labor's inadequate remuneration. For protectionists, this remedy merely postponed the day of class judgment.[82]

The complete refutation of Malthusian and Ricardian wage doctrines fell to Henry C. Carey. He believed that the two Englishmen had reversed the natural laws concerning population and rent. Because of Carey's infatuation with his dream of an associated economic empire, increased population could never be injurious to society. More people in close proximity to each other generated an expansion of the market, which created a demand for more labor, which diversified possible occupations, which meant higher-paying jobs. Using this logic, he was able to reject the Malthusian fear of unrestrained population growth.[83]

Carey then repudiated the Ricardian rent theory by demonstrating that agricultural production could easily match population increases. He insisted that Ricardo inverted the true mode of agricultural expansion. The American experience revealed that settlers cultivated marginal lands first and then moved to more fertile soils, a reversal of the Ricardian process. This peculiar circumstance arose because the less productive lands were easier to clear and prepare for farming than the fecund ones. Nor did Ricardo err merely on the stages of agricultural operations; he also misconceived how yields were increased. After the rudimentary era of pioneering had ended and people entered into civilization by living close together, the farmer had to produce more crops and be less wasteful. The result of a nearby market transformed the farmer into a scientist who applied intensive agricultural methods. Aided by science and technology, the agrarians produced more from the same earth.[84]

Undermining the validity of Malthus' and Ricardo's labor formula-

---

82. Colwell, *The Claims of Labor*, 9; Bowen, *The Principles of Political Economy*, 18, 204; Calvin Colton, *The Rights of Labor* (3rd ed.; New York, 1847), 5.

83. Carey, *Manual of Social Science*, 436–65.

84. *Ibid.*, 92–93, 273–78, 401–12.

tions was only Carey's initial step, for their labor doctrines also constituted a general theory of the distribution of wealth. Their model left
landlords with most of the wealth, workers with a pittance, and industrialists with sufficient profits to continue production but not enough to
challenge the power of the landlords. Carey substituted his version of
wealth distribution for the one postulated by Ricardo and Malthus. In
the early stages of civilization economic power was concentrated in
the hands of the few, but as science and technology progressed, the laborer substituted "mental for merely physical force." The more the
laborer specialized, the more he was rewarded. Through time the laboring element in society received proportionately more than the employers, which indicated that the country tended toward an equal distribution of wealth. But in order to achieve this state, the nation had to
enjoy a variety of employments, which only the system of association
fostered. Carey proclaimed, therefore, that his protectionist ideals
produced weak governments and an equal distribution of wealth,
whereas free trade tenets brought about centralized governments and
an unjust distribution of wealth.[85]

Other protectionists accepted in one form or another Carey's ideas
on labor economics, and they also mirrored his concern about the distribution of wealth and the status of the laborer in American society.
While there was some disagreement as to how to achieve a better distribution of wealth, most high tariff proponents relied upon social mobility to ensure the laborer a fair proportion of the rewards of production. Hence Francis Bowen wrote that "it is the *fixedness*, and not the
inequality, of fortunes which is to be dreaded." The process of elevation was simply the conversion of the laborer to a capitalist; high wages
allowed the worker to save a portion of his earnings and eventually
open a small shop of his own. The protectionist analysis of the economic ills of England indicated that the root problem in that country
was the failure of British society to provide for social mobility; English
institutions trapped the laborer into a caste instead of allowing him the
opportunity to advance.[86]

There was, however, one additional argument employed by the protectionists that made their economics appealing to laborers, and it was
perhaps the one great revision of classical economics that they offered.

85. *Ibid.*, 392–95; Conkin, *Prophets of Prosperity*, 269–73, 282–87, 292–94.
86. Bowen, *The Principles of Political Economy*, 11–12, 16–17, 125, 196–99;
E. Peshine Smith, *A Manual of Political Economy* (New York, 1853), 83; Horace Greeley,
Essays Designed to Elucidate the Science of Political Economy (Boston, 1870), 160.

Advocates of a high tariff disputed the notion of beneficial competition and the application of the scientific mode of thought to human behavior. One of Carey's major complaints was that British economists forever "excluded all those parts of the ordinary man that are common to him and the angels, retaining carefully all those common to him and the beasts of the forests." Stephen Colwell bitterly denounced a political economy that in the garb of science "sternly rejects moral considerations." This unchristian attitude resulted in treating the laborer "as that mass of labor from which we are to obtain the largest quantity of products at the least possible expense." Free traders had reversed the true order of human concerns in economic behavior. Colwell insisted that "the first consideration is the man who labors, next the product, next the value of the product, next the mode of exchanging it for what the laborer wants, and then of markets, merchants, and trade, domestic and foreign." [87]

Protectionists complained that the free trade analysis required that men be treated like objects and commodities. The protectionists tried to convince the public that commodities could be abstracted into price levels determined by supply and demand without any grievous damage to reality, but that reducing a human being to a lump of flesh bartered away in the marketplace was both immoral and foolish. And if the moral argument convinced no one, then the protectionists could remind readers that inanimate objects could not yell "Bread or Blood" and overthrow civilizations—but human beings could.

The particular alteration protectionists wished to make in the marketplace in order to advance the welfare of the laborer was to direct competition into areas that did not result in the lowering of wage rates. They believed that competition with English manufacturers could only occur if American industrialists reduced wages to the English level of subsistence. This was, of course, the ancient "pauper labor" argument of the protectionists. Thus in the aftermath of the Panic of 1857 protectionist theorists reiterated their claim that competition with foreign nations should be banned by a tariff if it resulted in the degradation of the American worker. This policy intended to make certain that the enjoyable standard of living among American laborers would not be eroded by foreign competitors who paid miserly wages in order to undercut American manufacturers. With the American laborer's position secured by the tariff, the nation's industrialists could only advance by inventing

87. Carey, *Manual of Social Science*, 103–104; Colwell, *The Claims of Labor*, 38, 43.

new machines and increasing their capital stock. The effect of protectionist policy, so its promoters hoped, was to force competition wholly into the technological side of production and to forbid advancement that depended upon the lowering of the laborers' remuneration.[88]

Protectionist theorists therefore had a distinct answer to the labor problems the Panic of 1857 exposed, that of erecting a high tariff. In all their debates with free traders, they insisted that their advocacy of a tariff was intended to assist the worker and not the capitalist. Francis Bowen maintained that American manufacturers could easily compete with English ones. "Cheap labor," he wrote, "is the only requisite for placing them on the same level." But the protectionists realized the social dangers low wages entailed for the republic. Thus Bowen honestly stated that it was "not, then, for the sake of capital" that he desired a high tariff, but rather for the benefit of the American worker. Symbolic of the protectionist change in attitude was a banner that waved at an honorary banquet for Henry C. Carey in Philadelphia in 1859. Its inscription did not advocate protection to American manufacturers but instead "Protection to American Labor."[89]

During the Panic of 1857 and the labor riots that followed, protectionist labor views found quick acceptance from many public officials. In the midst of the gubernatorial race in Pennsylvania, the American-Republicans issued a resolution stating that "the very agony of the financial crisis in our midst, has been chiefly provoked by the policy of the so-called Democratic party, which has incessantly warred upon our domestic industry, and persistently encouraged the cheap labor of Europe." In New York an old-line Whig wrote to the *Daily Tribune* that he

88. Colwell, *The Claims of Labor*, 45; Greeley, *Essays Designed to Elucidate the Science of Political Economy*, 150–51; Carey, *Financial Crises*, 43–45.

89. Bowen, *The Principles of Political Economy*, 215; story on dinner for Carey in Philadelphia *Evening Bulletin*, April 28, 1859. Another topic generating controversy between free traders and protectionists was whether the interests of capital and labor were antagonistic (the free trade position) or harmonious (the protectionist viewpoint). Between 1857 and 1860, however, the debate over the welfare of the worker revolved more around the questions of population, labor supply, availability of land, and foreign competition than the matter of the relations of capital and labor. American protectionists and free traders were perhaps less at odds over the question than the secondary literature would suggest; protectionists assumed a measure of conflict whereas free traders adopted a harmony of interests theory of their own. See James L. Huston, "Facing an Angry Labor: The American Public Interprets the Shoemakers' Strike of 1860," *CWH*, XXVIII (1982), 206–207; remarks of Senator James F. Simmons in Philadelphia *Evening Bulletin*, June 16, 1858.

expected to participate in a convention on labor and wages in manufacturing. He cautioned that he was "wholly and strongly opposed to making the European standard of wages the guide or point to which to bring the wages of the laborers of the country," and that he favored protectionism.[90]

The bread riots of 1857 focused the attention of Americans upon the fate of the nation's wage earner. An editor of the *Scientific American* posed the dilemma accurately: "We should never willingly see the mechanics, artizans and laborers of our country compelled to receive the same wages that are paid abroad. How shall this contingency be avoided?"[91] Free trade and protectionist economic theories provided these answers: a high protective tariff to eliminate unfair labor competition from abroad; free land in the West so the worker might migrate there and reduce the labor supply in the East; and education, by which the mechanic might advance to more rewarding occupations. In the Panic of 1857 these three proposals reflected the general thinking of the northern public as to what measures designed to mitigate the lot of the worker would be legally and socially acceptable. The strength of the program of tariffs, free land, and education was that it required little change in the rest of society. No reordering of classes was needed, nor any modification of the work ethic. Capitalism, individualism, and the moral values associated with economic advancement did not suffer one whit from the policies of high tariffs, free land, and education. Yet by enacting these proposals, the Malthusian and Ricardian catastrophe was avoided. The three remedies constituted the most active program that a middle-class nation saddled with a limited government could concoct to take care of the lower classes.

The artisans for whom this program was designed had other ideas, however. There were elements in these programs that did appeal to them. They supported the antimonopoly position of the free traders, agreed with the desire of protectionists to curb unfair wage competition, and believed, as did the general public, that education was the true path to material and spiritual riches. But the workers harbored a suspicion of the free traders' emphasis on competition and worried that the benefits of protection might accrue only to the industrialist. By the 1850s the nation's operatives sought to better their condition by

90. Philadelphia *Evening Bulletin*, October 10, 1857; letter of H. D. Maxwell in New York *Daily Tribune*, November 3, 1857.

91. *Scientific American*, n.s., August 20, 1859, p. 121.

more direct action—by forming trade unions.[92] In 1857 few middle-class Americans were willing to sanction such gross violations of natural laws as trade unions. They were willing to offer only tariffs, free land, and education as palliatives for the workers' hard existence. This was not the labor program the artisan wanted, but ultimately it was the one he got.

National politics witnessed a number of divisions over the appropriate means of aiding the working class, and these divisions were not altogether sectional. In particular, northern Democrats retained their faith in free trade theory, arguing for "equal rights," laissez faire government, and low tariffs, although they were indeed more susceptible to bending economic principles than their southern comrades. Northern Democrats believed antimonopoly policies, equal rights, low taxation, and free western land would create an economy that would produce favorable opportunities for laborers.[93] Yet the altered state of the northern economy called for a more energetic policy than the northern Democracy could offer. Increasingly the protectionist vision of safeguarding the position of American workers became the vision of the political opposition, the Republicans. To the extent that Republicans represented the majority opinion of the North, it can be cautiously stated that northerners sanctioned meddling in the economy in order to create conditions that would dull the edge of worker unrest. But when any northerner sought to institute the program of high tariffs, free western land, and education, he found southerners—assisted at times by the northern Democracy—in adamant opposition. Thus the political fight over tariffs and western lands after 1857 was not merely a clash of material desires between the North and South; it became, in general, a sectional battle over the enactment of laws that would most benefit and preserve a particular social order. In the political cauldron of sectionalism, the issues of a high tariff, free western land, and edu-

92. John Pickering, *The Working Man's Political Economy, founded upon the Principle of Immutable Justice, and the Inalienable Rights of Man* (Cincinnati, 1847), 3–5, 34–38; William Dealtry, *The Laborer: A Remedy for His Wrongs: Or, a Disquisition on the Usages of Society* (Cincinnati, 1869), 12–13, 368; Henry Pelling, *American Labor* (Chicago, 1960), 38–39; James L. Huston, "A Political Response to Industrialism: The Republican Embrace of Protectionist Labor Doctrines," *JAH*, LXX (1983), 35–57.

93. On the northern Democrats, see Rush Welter, *The Mind of America, 1820–1860* (New York, 1975), 77–102, 129–37, 372–75. Northern Democrats had one other means of avoiding a pauperized laboring class: like southerners, they believed the country should remain agricultural.

cation as a means of assisting the worker became more and more parts of an antislavery program.

The Panic of 1857 gave birth to several concerns that would soon enter the political arena and heighten sectional tensions. The economic troubles produced by the Panic required attention from national leaders, and their understanding of the appropriate remedial actions was largely informed by the state of economic theory. All the available tools to influence the economy, however, involved issues that stirred sectional passions—public lands, the tariff, and, to some extent, banking regulations. Behind these economic questions lay more basic and crucial matters involving the protection of established social and economic relations. Among southerners, the Panic created two inharmonious, distinct, and strident attitudes: that the thrust of the nation toward laissez faire free trade be retained, and that slavery be prominently justified as a patriarchal institution affording security for its workers. Among northerners, the Panic instilled a fear of an aroused and desperate working class. This threat, however, could be circumvented by utilizing high tariffs, western lands, and education. The next two years saw these impulses imbedded in the sectional contest over slavery.

FIVE / Two Panics in Congress

The process of converting the economic issues produced by the Panic of 1857 into topics of sectional acrimony began with the convening of the first session of the Thirty-fifth Congress on December 7, 1857. At the same time that legislators pondered appropriate remedies for the business depression, they also struggled with the treacherous question of admitting Kansas into the Union as a slave state under the Lecompton Constitution. The congressional debate over the Panic did not differ from the public one that had occurred in October and November; the participants in both cases made constant reference to the subjects of the southern adherence to proslavery principles, the fate of the northern wage earner, and the merits of free trade versus protectionist commercial policy. Eventually these concerns invaded the fight over the Lecompton Constitution as well. The tie that bound together the two political problems of the Lecompton Constitution and the Panic of 1857 was the general question of what would be the future of the nation's two labor systems, free and slave.

The individuals who composed the first session of the Thirty-fifth Congress were a mixed lot who harbored more divisions than just those of party. The Democrats had many luminaries in the Senate who guarded their party's and their section's interests. From the South came the contemplative Robert M. T. Hunter of Virginia, the combative Robert Toombs of Georgia, the assertive Jefferson Davis of Mississippi, the vindictive James Slidell of Louisiana, and the intellectual James H. Hammond of South Carolina. Together these leading lights of the South zealously defended the doctrine of states' rights and the policies of free trade. Stephen A. Douglas of Illinois and William Bigler of Pennsylvania were the only noteworthy Democratic senators from the North; Douglas because he had captured the backing of the North-

western Democracy, and Bigler because he hailed from the same state
as the president. Although the Democrats maintained party unity on
most questions, the problem of the expansion of slavery into the territories was slowly separating them into northern and southern wings.
The focus of this split was Douglas and his principle of popular sovereignty, a doctrine southerners increasingly believed was inimical to the
spread of the peculiar institution.[1]

Senate Republicans matched their Democratic counterparts in wit,
vitality, and earnestness—and at times in divisiveness. Leading the
Republican entourage was the hawk-nosed New Yorker William H.
Seward, the strong man of the party. Seward's preeminence, however,
did not overshadow the contributions of other senate Republicans. A
number of former Democrats filled the Republicans' senatorial ranks:
Lyman Trumbull of Illinois, John P. Hale of New Hampshire, Hannibal
Hamlin of Maine, and Simon Cameron of Pennsylvania. From the
nearly defunct Whig party came antislavery radicals such as Benjamin
Franklin Wade of Ohio and Henry Wilson of Massachusetts. More conservative Republicans of Whig antecedents included William Pitt Fessenden of Maine and James F. Simmons of Rhode Island. Although
these Republicans often had serious disagreements among themselves
over economic and social issues, they suppressed these differences in
order to combat the extension of slavery into the territories.[2]

The members of the House usually reflected the attitudes of their
more illustrious colleagues in the Senate. Southerners provided the
corps of the states' rights Democracy in the House, including William
Boyce of South Carolina and Roger A. Pryor of Virginia. Northern
Democrats were somewhat undistinguished, the one exception being

1. *Mississippi Free Trader* (Natchez), March 1, 1858; William Y. Thompson, *Robert Toombs of Georgia* (Baton Rouge, 1966), 125–29; Samuel S. Cox, *Eight Years in Congress, from 1857–1865* (New York, 1865), 19–22; Hudson Strode, *Jefferson Davis: American Patriot, 1808–1861* (New York, 1955), xviii–xx; Elizabeth Merritt, *James Henry Hammond, 1807–1864* (Baltimore, 1923), 19–21, 103–104, 109–12; Robert W. Johannsen, *Stephen A. Douglas* (New York, 1973), vii–viii, 683–84.

2. Glyndon G. Van Deusen, *William Henry Seward* (New York, 1967), 183–88; Richard H. Sewell, *John P. Hale and the Politics of Abolition* (Cambridge, Mass., 1965), vii, 21–22, 27–42; H. Draper Hunt, *Hannibal Hamlin of Maine: Lincoln's First Vice-President* (Syracuse, N.Y., 1969), 26, 31, 35, 47; Mark M. Krug, *Lyman Trumbull: Conservative Radical* (New York, 1965), 28, 42, 61–65, 96–98; Bradley, *Simon Cameron*, 30, 33, 76–108; Charles A. Jellison, *Fessenden of Maine: Civil War Senator* (Syracuse, N.Y., 1962), 112–13; Richard H. Abbott, *Cobbler in Congress: The Life of Henry Wilson, 1812–1875* (Lexington, Ky., 1972), 4–17.

Pennsylvania's J. Glancy Jones. As chairman of the Ways and Means Committee and personal friend of the president, Jones wielded significant power. Republicans, however, had several individuals who exhibited independent action and who had earned national reputations: the venerable Joshua Giddings of Ohio, the abolitionist Owen Lovejoy of Illinois, the moderate but skilled parliamentarian John Sherman of Ohio, the Pennsylvania advocate of homesteads, Galusha A. Grow, and the sponsor of federal legislation to encourage the establishment of agricultural colleges, Justin S. Morrill of Vermont.[3]

President James Buchanan hoped to extract beneficial legislation from this willful and assertive group of congressmen. In particular, he hoped to achieve sectional harmony by bringing the debate over slavery in the territories to a close. The Democracy's control of both houses of Congress (39–25 in the Senate, 130–104 in the House) buoyed his hopes of doing so. Assisting Buchanan in his endeavors was a loyal but unremarkable cabinet: Attorney General Jeremiah S. Black, Secretary of the Navy Isaac Toucey, Postmaster Aaron V. Brown, Secretary of the Interior Jacob Thompson, Secretary of State Lewis Cass, and Secretary of War John B. Floyd. Buchanan's most trusted adviser, and the one who would deal most directly with the difficulties the Panic created, was a chestnut-haired, wealthy Georgian, Howell Cobb. The men who led the administration exhibited no brilliance and were indeed conservative, loyal Democrats who usually favored the southern states' rights interpretation of the Constitution.[4]

The first order of business for Congress was to consider the pro-

3. On congressional members, see: Cox, *Eight Years In Congress*, 22–23; *Harper's Weekly*, March 3, 1860, p. 132, April 14, 1860, p. 228; F. N. Boney, *John Letcher of Virginia: The Story of Virginia's Civil War Governor* (University, Ala., 1966), 14–15, 21–23; James Brewer Stewart, *Joshua R. Giddings and the Tactics of Radical Politics* (Cleveland, 1970), 25–27, 43–46, 85, 248; Patrick W. Riddleberger, *George Washington Julian: Radical Republican* (Indianapolis, 1966), 22–24, 34–36, 63–66, 77–78, 99–113; James T. DuBois and Gertrude S. Mathews, *Galusha A. Grow: Father of the Homestead Law* (Boston, 1917), 34–37, 46, 50–51, 70–71, 94–95; Edward Magdol, *Owen Lovejoy: Abolitionist in Congress* (New Brunswick, N.J., 1967), 25–27, 110–24.

4. Nevins, *The Emergence of Lincoln*, I, 61–65, makes Buchanan the tool of southern interests. Philip Shriver Klein, *President James Buchanan: A Biography* (University Park, Pa., 1962), 275–77, 308, depicts Buchanan more accurately as a strong-willed President who already favored the southern viewpoint. According to Horace Greeley (and eliminating the future Minnesota Delegation), the slaveholding states sent 25 Democrats and 5 Americans to the Senate, and 74 Democrats, 15 Americans, and 1 Republican (Blair) to the House. The North elected 14 Democrats and 20 Republicans to the Senate, and 56 Democrats and 88 Republicans to the House. There was confusion,

posals the president made in his annual message. Two topics in the communication were critical—the effects of the Panic and the admission of Kansas into the Union. The president first handled the matter of the financial collapse. Like most Americans, Buchanan was perplexed at this economic upheaval because it had arrived in the "midst of unsurpassed plenty" in agriculture and manufacturing. The president recorded the financial problems the revulsion threw upon the treasury, for government revenue primarily came from import duties, and the Panic had drastically reduced the normal volume of trade. Funds from that source had fallen below expectations. Buchanan therefore told Congress that some form of loan probably would be required to keep the government solvent. He also warned that although the members of the administration deeply sympathized with those out of work, the national government was "without the power to extend relief."

Passing beyond the general influences of the Panic, Buchanan then offered his analysis of the financial collapse. In so doing Buchanan stayed wholly within the established moderate free trade doctrines of the Democratic party: "It is apparent that our existing misfortunes have proceeded solely from our extravagant and vicious system of paper currency and bank credits, exciting the people to wild speculations and gambling in stocks." Buchanan advised state governments to establish a specie currency and to enact special laws to safeguard note issues by requiring a pledge of government securities. Unfortunately, the national government could do little; remedial action remained in the hands of the states. Buchanan only recommended that Congress should pass "a uniform bankrupt law applicable to all banking institutions throughout the United States," with provisions that suspension of specie payment would produce "civil death."[5]

Howell Cobb's report probed deeper into the effects of the Panic upon governmental finances, and he was emphatic in warning the public against expecting aid from the national government. Cobb felt that government receipts from customhouses would fall and place the government in a monetary stringency, but he thought the effects of the revulsion would quickly pass and by the middle of 1858 government

---

however, as to party identity, especially in regard to the Americans (*Tribune Almanac*, 1858, 16–18).

5. *Senate Executive Documents*, 35th Cong., 1st Sess., No. 11, pp. 3–9; Collins, "The Democrats' Electoral Fortunes During the Lecompton Crisis," 321–22.

revenue would again attain its normal level. To ensure that the national government would not face a shortage of funds to pay its debts, Cobb urged Congress to empower the treasury to float twenty million dollars of treasury notes, to be retired within one year. As to measures needed to prevent future monetary collapses, Cobb resorted to the teachings of free trade economists: the "true cause" of all such occurrences could be found in "the undue expansion of the credit system." To enforce financial prudence on the nation's financiers, Cobb seconded Buchanan's recommendation for a national bankruptcy law, but unlike the president, the secretary desired to include railroads in its provisions. Cobb also urged the states to copy the independent treasury system of the federal government, to outlaw all bank notes under twenty dollars, and to reestablish a metallic circulation.[6]

The Georgian referred again to the teachings of the free traders in order to dispel what he felt were dangerous notions that had infected selected portions of the population: relief and protection. The cries for aid had become strident because "there are many persons who seem to think it is the duty of the government to provide relief in all cases of trouble and distress." Some citizens had expressed hopes that the government would increase expenditures on public projects to "furnish employment to large numbers of worthy citizens." But, Cobb asked, "where shall we look for the power to do this in the Constitution? What provision of that instrument authorizes such a policy? The absence of a satisfactory reply to these inquiries is an unanswerable argument to the suggestion." Public works in progress would be completed, but the administration would not permit additional undertakings.[7]

On the topic of protection the secretary of the treasury was quite inflexible. Noting that the Panic had created a new wave of sentiment favoring protective tariffs, Cobb responded that to adopt such a policy would be "unwise and improper." Americans must consider the welfare of consumers as well as manufacturers. High tariffs, he continued, not only fostered monopolies but also transferred wealth from one class to another; therefore a protective tariff was "partial and unjust" in its operation.[8]

The financial views of the president and the secretary of the treasury were clearly derived from free trade doctrines, and the warm re-

6. *Senate Executive Documents*, 35th Cong., 1st Sess., No. 1, pp. 3–9, 18–23.
7. *Ibid.*, 11–12.
8. *Ibid.*, 13–16.

ception most Democratic journals gave to the administration's ideas on the Panic confirmed the basic free trade posture of the party. The Republican reaction demonstrated once more the dissension of that party on economic affairs. Editors of a Whig persuasion immediately attacked Cobb's calculations and called for a higher tariff. Other Republicans, however, expressed approval of the course outlined by the administration. The chief complaint that James Russell Lowell lodged against Buchanan's financial views, in consideration of the lengthy diatribe the president leveled at the banks, was that "it is a lamentably impotent conclusion to say, 'After all, we can't do much to help it!'"[9]

As important as the president's recommendations on financial matters were, the attention of the nation focused instantly on the admission of Kansas to the Union under the Lecompton Constitution. Buchanan and his advisers decided to press Congress to pass the enabling act which would make Kansas the thirty-fourth state. Buchanan was personally miffed at the decision of the Kansas constitutional convention not to submit the entire constitution to the vote of the people. Yet, as he argued to others, the legal forms were all proper and the letter of the law had been carried out by the territorial officials; therefore the enabling legislation ought to be passed. In so deciding Buchanan knew a defection from the Democracy would occur, but the president and his advisers had counted votes and decided the bill would pass if strong executive leadership bore down on the wavering. Editors instantly proclaimed that "the great question of the session of Congress that has just commenced is to be the Kansas question."[10]

As congressional battle lines over the Lecompton Constitution formed, the more practical matter of governmental finances forced its way into legislative awareness. A few days after the opening of Congress, Howell Cobb wrote to J. Glancy Jones that the condition of the treasury was precarious and required immediate action. He recommended legislation to enable the treasury to emit twenty million dollars of notes to meet the nation's liabilities. The Georgian believed that

9. For examples of the Democratic view of the administration's economic proposals, see Richmond (Va.) *Enquirer,* December 11, 1857; Boston *Post,* December 10, 1857; "President Buchanan's First Message," *United States Democratic Review,* n.s., XLI (January, 1858), 26. For Whig attitudes, see *Daily National Intelligencer* (Washington), December 15, 18, 28, 1857. For Republicans favorable to free trade solutions, see James Russell Lowell, "The President's Message," *Atlantic Monthly,* I (January, 1858), 372; New York *Evening Post,* December 9, 1857; Chicago *Daily Tribune,* December 12, 1857.

10. Potter, *The Impending Crisis,* 318–19; Klein, *President James Buchanan,* 308, 310–11; Philadelphia *Evening Bulletin,* December 7, 1857.

the government really did not require the total sum proposed, but he desired a margin of safety to guard against the unforeseen.[11]

The House and Senate acted quickly upon the proposals, and a general debate emerged over the origins of the Panic, the duration of the depression, and appropriate remedies. Senators indulged in more speculation over the various ways of analyzing the Panic than did the more practical members of the House. Hunter of Virginia initiated discussion of the treasury notes measure and reiterated the views of Cobb; he insisted especially that the legislation was only temporary and that soon income from customhouses would balance government expenditures. William Seward doubted that the effects of the Panic would endure and thought that recovery was imminent. Unlike the president, Seward excused the banks from culpability; he agreed that the treasury momentarily needed aid but that the amount legislated ought to be lowered.[12]

Seward's analysis found little support from his Republican colleagues. The newly elected senator from Rhode Island, James F. Simmons, rebuked Seward for dismissing the Panic as a minor business fluctuation: "I have seen many revulsions; but I have seen none so wide sweeping and destructive as that through which we are now passing." He placed the guilt for the Panic upon the tariff of 1857 and profligate government spending. Simmons' objections found favor with other Republicans and southern opposition leaders. The old-line Whigs John J. Crittenden of Kentucky and John Bell of Tennessee stressed the need for a new tariff, as did Henry Wilson, William Pitt Fessenden, and James Dixon.[13]

One aspect of the treasury notes proposal elicited a considerable debate. The treasury notes were intended to enable the government to meet its liabilities, but was the issuance of the notes designed to increase the monetary circulation of the nation? Republicans fastened upon the oddity of a president who, while attacking banks and an unsecured currency, asked Congress to allow the government to issue a paper money. Republican editors acidly commented on the hypocrisy of the Democrats for agitating against banks and then requesting the power to issue "*twenty millions* of 'Treasury Shinplasters.'"[14]

In the House, the question of whether the treasury notes would act

11. *House Miscellaneous Documents*, 35th Cong., 1st Sess., No. 8, pp. 1–2.

12. *Congressional Globe*, 35th Cong., 1st Sess., 67–68, 89, hereinafter cited as *Cong. Globe*.

13. *Ibid.*, 68–70, 72–74, 75–76, 85–86, 94.

14. *Ibid.*, 88–89, 95; quote from *Daily Illinois State Journal* (Springfield), December 28, 1857.

as a medium of exchange revealed once more the fissures among the Republicans over economic programs. The Democrat-Republicans attacked the proposal as a Democratic paper money scheme, while some Whig-Republicans saw in the administration measure an attempt to salvage the faltering independent treasury. Galusha A. Grow of Pennsylvania sparred with William Smith of Virginia over the bill. In their debate the Pennsylvanian reminded Congress that he only preached the old Democratic doctrines, and on the question of paper money, he said, "I will be considered as a sound, reliable Democrat."[15]

Despite the partisan recriminations against paper money, the independent treasury, New York bankers, low tariffs, and extravagance, the treasury notes legislation was passed quickly into law. Probably the immediate requirements of the treasury overrode any theoretical objections to Cobb's proposal, and the allegedly temporary nature of the exigency allowed many to bend their hard-currency scruples. Nonetheless, Grow's declaration of his allegiance to the old Democratic doctrines regarding the currency held true for those schooled in Jacksonian economics; Democratic converts to the Republican cause espoused the hard-money theories of the Jacksonian Democracy.

The success the administration gained in its fiscal policy did not extend to the proposal of a national bankruptcy law. The idea of legislating such a relief measure found a certain degree of popular approval.[16] Robert Toombs tried to guide the proposal through the Senate. He labored in the Judiciary Committee for legislation along the lines proposed by the president, and the bill he sponsored would have prohibited any bank from ever suspending specie payment. However, the committee could not fashion an enactment that met the members' economic and constitutional scruples, and so the president's recommendation came to naught.[17]

But questions over the Panic and national economic policies quickly disappeared from congressional consciousness. By January Horace Greeley wrote, with a sigh of relief, that the expected Democratic onslaught on banking institutions had faltered and died.[18] Congress

15. *Cong. Globe*, 35th Cong., 1st Sess., 106–109, 126, 130–31, 146.

16. *Cong. Globe*, 35th Cong., 1st Sess., 6, 957, 1073; F. J. Stead to James F. Simmons, February 4, 1858, J. D. Burgess to James F. Simmons, February 8, 1858, both in Simmons Papers.

17. *Cong. Globe*, 35th Cong., 1st Sess., 1858; *House Reports*, 35th Cong., 1st Sess., No. 413.

18. New York *Daily Tribune*, January 21, 1858.

easily dispatched most of Buchanan's and Cobb's recommendations in regard to the Panic. Problems created by the revulsion continued to haunt legislators, but these difficulties occupied a secondary position in comparison with other matters requiring attention—namely, Kansas.

In the brief debate over the treasury notes and the administration's explanation of the Panic, congressmen revealed their knowledge of economic theory, for positions on the Panic faithfully mirrored the free trade-protectionism controversy. Senator James F. Simmons probably demonstrated the most ardent belief in protectionist doctrines; he became the major proponent of tariff revision in the early days of the session. While dissecting and repudiating the advice of the president, Simmons revealed all the prejudices common to protectionists: that is, the beliefs that too many Americans merely lived off the efforts of the producing class; that banks needed regulation, for bankers grasped for control of industry for their own speculative ends and not for the benefit of society; and that the laborers of the country required protection. As Simmons' notoriety on economic matters grew, he received numerous letters of encouragement. One writer sent him a copy of Carey's *Letters to the President* and stated that Carey's analysis should persuade all "reasonable" men "that a tarif that would protect everything that is produced in the Country is the only thing That can be done which will give imployment to the labouring clas of the whole country [*sic*]." [19]

Moreover, the protectionist tenet that a high tariff cured unemployment found several advocates. The aged senator from Kentucky, John J. Crittenden, desired a revision of import duties because "thousands upon thousands have been and are being discharged from their means of subsistence." He told his colleagues that although currency matters needed resolution, the fate of the laborer was of more significance than banking laws: "We want the revenue which, if rightly and judiciously levied, will furnish these men employment, perhaps, and settle them again to their labor." In the House, Amos Granger of New York bitterly denounced the tariffs of 1846 and 1857 and the Democratic acceptance of free trade policies. The Democrats, Granger charged, allowed foreign goods to disrupt American industry and create unemployment: "For this *deceptive, starving, wretched* policy, the laboring man is *de-*

---

19. *Cong. Globe*, 35th Cong., 1st Sess., 68–73; James F. Simmons to Albert Gallup, December 12, 1857, Thomas Whipple to James F. Simmons, March 3, 1858, both in Simmons Papers.

coyed to vote the Democratic ticket." He warned his opponents that because so many Americans endured unemployment, a "muckle day" might be forthcoming: "1860 may be as 1840, and more abundant."[20]

In the debates over economic matters in the first few days of the congressional session, one peculiarity surfaced. Instead of economic issues penetrating the slavery agitation, the reverse proved true. When the House struggled over the treasury notes bill, N. P. Banks told the Democrats to leave financial matters to the Republicans. "We will take the negro out of the Government and allow it to give its attention to this matter," he declared. Republicans, he continued, would pay attention to the "industrial interests of the country" and legislate "for the benefit of white men." Galusha Grow told his audience that on all economic matters he stood as a staunch Democrat, "excepting as to the question who shall occupy the Territories of the Union—whether white men or black; and as to that I am not sound." Grow's declaration in the midst of the debate on treasury notes caused Virginia's William Smith to exclaim that all he ever heard was "Kansas, Kansas, Kansas. That fertile and exciting subject dances through all the mazes of metaphorical confusion in the imagination of the gentleman [Grow]."[21]

The congressional debate over financial problems and the government's looming deficits were anything but memorable or exciting. Part of the reason for this circumstance was that neither party had yet divined how the public would react to the Panic. The sectionalism that northerners and southerners invested in economic issues in the first few days of the session was typical: southerners complained that northerners sought to tax the South to death and to monopolize all the benefits of government; northerners retorted that southerners would never enact programs that would inure to the welfare of free labor because such policies usually diminished the stature of the Slave Power. Politicians, in short, used the Panic of 1857 as a cleaver in their early sectional entanglements; they awaited a distinct public movement before they honed their economic arguments into scalpels.

One state did pay attention to congressional wrangling over federal economic policy: Pennsylvania. Ever since the fateful day of suspension there had been in the state a continuous growth of high-tariff sentiment. The remnant of the American party moved surely toward the protectionist standard. At Johnstown a tariff meeting convened on

20. *Cong. Globe*, 35th Cong., 1st Sess., 203, 398–99.
21. *Ibid.*, 129, 146.

January 23, and the attendees called upon Congress to raise the tariff to alleviate the "depression and distress upon the State and the operatives engaged thereat." Democrats looked askance at these gatherings sprouting up throughout the state. "But the signs plainly are," warned the *Allegheny Mountain Echo*, "that as far as Pennsylvania is concerned, a 'Protective Tariff' will be the syren song to captivate her."[22]

The attention Congress gave to the Panic and to the problems it raised was brief and cursory. The legislators hurried to get to the matter of the Lecompton Constitution, which then consumed most of the session's time. Stephen A. Douglas split with the administration over the matter, for he believed the Kansas document was fraudulent and inexpressive of the will of the majority of settlers. Southerners and northern administration followers sought to enable Kansas to enter the Union as a slave state. Republicans stood by their 1856 convention pledge to halt the expansion of slavery and refused to countenance new slave states under any condition. The battle in Congress over the Kansas question evoked the worst sectional passions, and the arguments for and against the Lecompton Constitution revolved around constitutional interpretations, evidence of corruption and fraud, and other legal matters. Republicans often claimed that the extension of slavery was a curse to the white working man, while southerners rejoined that the territories were possessions of all Americans and that the South could not be denied its share of the national domain.[23]

The Panic of 1857 intruded only tangentially upon the Kansas debate. Joshua Giddings demonstrated how little economic subjects mattered in the controversy over slavery extension when he declared at the beginning of one of his orations that "questions of mere economy, those which pertain to banks, to internal improvements, or protective tariffs, no longer occupy the public mind." Giddings' observation was valid, for explicit references to the Panic were minimal in the debates over the admission of Kansas. When legislators did bring up the finan-

22. Lancaster (Pa.) *Examiner and Herald*, December 2, 1857; *Indiana Register* quoted by *Raftsman's Journal* (Clearfield, Pa.), December 2, 1857; *Allegheny Mountain Echo* (Johnstown, Pa.), February 3, 1858; Holt, *The Political Crisis of the 1850s*, 200–201.

23. *Cong. Globe*, 35th Cong., 1st Sess., remarks of Rep. Burroughs, 813–14; Rep. Morse, 1233–34; Rep. Farnsworth, 1206; Rep. Kellogg, 1269; Rep. Blair, 1283; Sen. Green, Appendix to *Cong. Globe*, 35th Cong., 1st Sess., 211 (hereinafter cited as *APX*); Sen. Mallory, *Cong. Globe*, 35th Cong., 1st Sess., 1136–40.

cial debacle, they did so merely to lament that Congress was expending its energy over slavery in the territories and not initiating any action designed to relieve the depression.[24]

In one instance, however, the Panic of 1857 was pressed into unforgettable service in the sectional quarrel over the Lecompton Constitution. Southerners turned to the extreme proslavery labor argument and the experience of the last months of 1857 as a means of refuting the free labor taunts of Republicans. They especially focused upon the condition of northern workers in the November bread riots. Tennessee's John Atkins, for example, warned northerners against tampering with the labor system that produced cotton: "Strike down at one blow the immense profits of slave-labor, which to-day enriches the North, and, sir, instead of the teeming millions of operatives who now fill your workshops—your mills of various kinds, not a hammer scarcely will be heard to beat, and not a spindle will charm the ear with its musical hum; grass will spring up in your streets, and plenty will desert your land. The cry will truly be 'blood or bread!'"[25]

The phrase, "Bread or blood!", so frequently raised during the Panic, also found favor with Jabez L. M. Curry of Alabama. Noting that of all the regions in the Union only the South safeguarded responsible and conservative ideals, Curry warned northerners that the "socialism and agrarianism and Fanny-Wrightism" festering in the North would finally result in the "destruction of private property." The oppressions of northern white labor had become visible during the Panic when the workers, "suffering from the terrible pecuniary crisis," had taken to the streets and "with hungry mouths [had cried] out, with startling and terrific emphasis, 'Bread or Blood!'" But at the same time southern slaves were hardly "aware of any financial pressure, because labor and capital are there [in the South] harmonized, and there is no conflict between them."[26]

Other southerners used the proslavery labor argument in the Lecompton debates as well, but national attention focused almost exclusively upon the March 4, 1858, speech of James H. Hammond.[27] His

24. *Ibid.*, for Giddings, APX, 65; see also Sen. Douglas, Bigler, Fitch, Stuart, and Broderick, 14–18, 113–17, 137–39, 158–63; remarks of Rep. Elijah Ward, APX, 302–305.

25. *Ibid.*, 750.

26. *Ibid.*, 819.

27. *Ibid.*, comments of Rep. Garnett, 1245; Sen. Clay, APX, 146–48; Rep. Gatrell, 393.

was a performance that elicited more comment than any other single speech in that session of Congress, and the phrases he uttered stalked the political world for the next three years.

Born in 1807, Hammond rose to political prominence in South Carolina by his advocacy of the rights of the South and his crusade to justify slavery. A former governor of South Carolina, Hammond had retired from politics in 1851 to devote time to his extensive cotton plantations, which he obtained through a fortuitous courtship. By the mid-1850s his interest in politics rose again, and he was more than ready to accept in 1857 a seat in the United States Senate offered him by the South Carolina legislature. Although Hammond seemed to many to be of the advance guard of states' rights men, he was a prudent, conservative individual when it came to action. While the new senator had no misgivings that secession was a legal remedy to the afflictions that the South suffered, he counseled his more fiery brethren to restrain their secessionist impulses until the entire South could act together.[28]

Hammond interpreted political movements on the basis of the economic interests involved. He was therefore eager to incorporate the effects of the Panic into the general scheme of sectional relations. He also considered government in terms of economic policy, and he noted with satisfaction that except for the Kansas imbrogolio the Democratic policy—or, more pointedly, the southern policy—ruled the nation; the National Bank was dead, internal improvement schemes blocked, and free trade "virtually installed." The extent to which Hammond believed men acted from economic motives was revealed in a letter he sent to William Porcher Miles in late 1858: "My dear Miles, the books will teach us that revolutions are [not] effected on abstractions. There must be a *pinch* of some sort, & with cotton at 10¢ & negroes at $1000 the South will know no *pinch*."[29]

Because of his preoccupation with the effect the world of commerce

---

28. Merritt, *James Henry Hammond*, 19–21, 103–12; Clement Eaton, *The Mind of the Old South* (Rev. ed.; Baton Rouge, 1969), 44–56. The best biography of Hammond is Drew Gilpin Faust, *James Henry Hammond and the Old South: A Design for Mastery* (Baton Rouge, 1982).

29. James H. Hammond to Benjamin F. Perry, December 31, 1857, in Benjamin Franklin Perry, *Reminiscences of Public Men* (Philadelphia, 1883), 108; James H. Hammond to William Porcher Miles, November 23, 1858, quoted in Lillian Adele Kibler, *Benjamin F. Perry: South Carolina Unionist* (Durham, N.C., 1946), 291.

had upon men, Hammond quickly grasped the significance of the Panic of 1857. His literary friend William Gilmore Simms excitedly wrote him about the effects the Panic had wrought: "Public opinion, at the North, is beginning to see that slavery is their profit!" According to Simms, northerners now understood the importance of slavery-produced cotton to the American economy. From a company operating cotton mills in the South, Hammond learned that the company's mills were running "continuously and profitably when Eastern mills are closed in such numbers."[30]

One other source of information probably aided Hammond in his understanding of the economic relations governing the Union and the world. During the second session of the Thirty-fourth Congress, southerners pushed a bill through both houses that allowed a representative of the United States government to travel abroad and assess the European consumption of cotton. For this exploration Franklin Pierce chose John Claiborne, a Mississippi states' rights leader and later biographer of the fiery John A. Quitman. Claiborne returned in early 1857, cutting short his visit, and presented his findings. The report substantiated the southern belief that England's economy depended upon cotton, and Claiborne further hypothesized that if the cotton supply should ever be "cut off," the event "would be followed by social, commercial, and political revulsions, the effects of which can scarcely be imagined."[31]

With these sources reinforcing his view of the importance of cotton and slavery in world affairs, Hammond was well prepared to repel any disparagement of slavery on economic grounds. William Seward on March 3 delivered a long oration that dwelt upon the beneficence and inevitability of free labor economic systems. This was the topic to which Hammond responded the next day.

Hammond presented the common southern argument in favor of the Lecompton Constitution, but then quickly turned to the assertions of Seward. The South Carolinian believed the Republicans would economically plunder the South regardless of the slavery question, and southerners therefore could not "rely on your faith when you have the

30. William Gilmore Simms to James H. Hammond, January 28, 1858, in Mary C. Simms Oliphant, Alfred Taylor Odell, and T. C. Duncan Eaves (eds.), *The Letters of William Gilmore Simms* (Columbia, S.C., 1952–56), V, 19; Hamilton Smith to James H. Hammond, January 18, 1858, in James H. Hammond Papers, LC.

31. *Senate Executive Documents*, 35th Cong., 1st Sess., No. 35, pp. 93–95.

power." Having thus repudiated coexistence with the Republican party, he then defended the economic position of the South, citing its fertility, productivity, and ability to create an export surplus. Hammond declared—incorrectly—that the wealth of a region was determined by its exports. He then pointed out the preponderance of southern staples in America's annual export tables and proclaimed the dependence of the world upon cotton: "I will not stop to depict what every one can imagine [if the cotton supply were stopped], but this is certain: old England would topple headlong and carry the whole civilized world with her. No, sir, you dare not make war on cotton. No power on earth dares make war upon it. Cotton is king." To buttress his argument about cotton's supremacy, Hammond told his colleagues to look at recent events. The Panic had destroyed old commercial houses and raised the threat of social revolution. What saved the North from social disaster, Hammond asserted, was cotton; the cotton that was sold in 1857 saved "your magnificent financiers, your cotton lords, your merchant princes."[32]

There was some truth to Hammond's pronouncements. Hammond's method of measuring wealth was erroneous, but his remarks on cotton reiterated what others had said during the Panic months. Northern business journals and newspapers had all looked to the cotton crop for their economic salvation. As to the importance of cotton for the commercial world, Hammond merely rephrased the warnings of the Cotton Supply Association and the British Parliament. The South Carolinian presented an economic argument that, if anyone had desired, might have easily been substantiated wholly from Republican and even British abolition presses.

But Hammond did not close his speech with his declarations of the invincibility of cotton; instead he engaged in an analysis of the social relations between capitalists and laborers. All societies, he stated, required a "class to do the mean duties, to perform the drudgery of life." That class, which freed the intelligent portion of society to further civilization, "constitutes the very mud-sills of society and of political government." Fortunately, southerners had found Africans, a "race inferior to [themselves], but eminently qualified in temper, in vigor, in docility, in capacity to stand the climate," to become their mudsills. What constituted the North's mudsill? The white, free laboring element were the North's slaves, for the free states had abolished "the name, but not the thing" that comprised slavery; "in short, your whole

32. *Cong. Globe*, 35th Cong., 1st Sess., 961–62.

hireling class of manual laborers and operatives, as you call them, are essentially slaves."[33]

After stressing the material comforts of the slave as compared to the impoverished condition of the hireling, Hammond summoned the specter of Malthusian economics. In the North dwelt an increasing army of the unemployed, but whereas the slaves of the South had no political power, those in the North did. "If they knew the tremendous secret, that the ballot-box is stronger than an army with bayonets, and could combine, where would you be?" Foolishly the northern slaves met in New York City parks to demand change; all they needed to do was to utilize the vote. When Hammond threatened to send labor agitators to the North, Henry Wilson and other Republicans shouted, "Send them along." Hammond skillfully ignored the bravado of his opposition, saying, "There is no need of that. They are coming here." He painted a vision of future "vigilance committees" and radical incendiaries in northern cities; the only reason they had escaped this fate, he claimed, was that the "great West" had attracted the masses and so had kept wages high in the East. The South Carolinian concluded by glorifying the conservative influence the South had stamped for decades upon the nation's governmental affairs.[34]

The "mudsill" or "cotton is king" speech of Hammond, as it became popularly known, was a product of advanced proslavery thought and wholly representative of the southern response to the northern bread riots following the Panic of 1857. Throughout the speech, Hammond utilized proslavery ideas about racial inferiority, the proper adjustment of labor and capital, the degraded condition of the free laborer, the role of the West and population pressure, and the preeminent conservatism of the South. Others touched on some of the same themes in this session of Congress, but Hammond's fame evidently stemmed from the use of the word *mudsill* to describe the northern free worker. For Hammond, *mudsill* meant a base or foundation; in the North the term implied dirt, filth, and refuse.[35]

Reaction to Hammond's oration was swift and predictable. Southerners praised his effort and especially his position on northern labor

33. *Ibid.*
34. *Ibid.*
35. This is the claim of Merritt, *James Henry Hammond,* 118–19. See also Faust, *James Henry Hammond and the Old South,* 350–51; Mark H. Stegmaier, "Intensifying the Sectional Conflict: William Seward versus James Hammond in the Lecompton Debate of 1858," *CWH,* XXXI (1985), 197–221.

conditions. The northern Democratic press, however, was largely silent and embarrassed; Hammond had just given their opponents one more slogan with which to browbeat the party. Republicans usually accepted the verdict of Horace Greeley. Hammond's attitudes, wrote Greeley, "are the sentiments of all aristocracies, and simply assert the old proposition that the few were made to rule, and the many to be governed." Yet in all the commentary about Hammond's speech, the pivotal concern, the main point of contention, was whether the laborer was most rewarded by a system of free labor or slave labor. This was the common theme shared by both the Lecompton Constitution struggle and the debate over the Panic of 1857.[36]

The Lecompton controversy came to a climax in late March. The Democratic Senate passed the bill to admit Kansas to the Union under the Lecompton Constitution, but in the House a coalition of Republicans and anti-Lecompton Democrats defeated it. To avert political disaster, both houses agreed in April upon a compromise fashioned by William English of Indiana. With the passage of the compromise measure, the story of the Lecompton Constitution had nearly drawn to a close; unfortunately, so had the first session of the Thirty-fifth Congress.

Although the heated discussion of the admission of Kansas consumed a disproportionate share of the congressmen's time, the legislators still had to contend with proposals that had become constant factors in national affairs since the beginning of the decade. Economic programs such as the continuation of river and harbor improvements, the establishment of agricultural colleges, the inauguration of a free public land policy, federal aid in the construction of a Pacific railroad, and the termination of fishing bounties absorbed a fair amount of Congress' time. Virtually all attempts to legislate new policies ran into an insuperable obstacle: the empty coffers of the federal treasury. Those who advocated new programs commonly met with some version of the argument Senator Thompson of Kentucky used against the homestead measure: "I do not think the public granary is full enough to be giving out wine

36. For Democrats, see Charleston *Daily Courier*, March 9, 1858; *Southern Recorder* (Milledgeville, Ga.), March 16, 1858; *Pennsylvania Argus* quoted by *Potter Journal* (Coudersport, Pa.), June 17, 1858. For Republicans, see *Miner's Journal* (Pottsville, Pa.), March 20, 1858; quote from New York *Daily Tribune*, March 8, 11, 1858; Herman Schlüter, *Lincoln, Labor and Slavery: A Chapter from the Social History of America* (New York, 1913), 116–17.

and oil, as they may be called for at any time."[37] Although hopes for agricultural colleges, a Pacific railroad, river and harbor improvements, and free land in the West became victims of the treasury's problems, the arguments for and against these measures fully exhibited the debate between protectionists and free traders over the economic role of the government and the fate of the laborer.

In questions over government economic policy, southern Democrats—and to a lesser extent, the southern opposition—revealed the paradox in their economic thought. When arguing on sectional matters pertaining to the Lecompton Constitution, they used advanced proslavery doctrines. But when they considered the more mundane economic activities in which the government should engage, they bared their extreme free trade views. Southern Democrats demanded a neutral federal government with respect to the economy because they feared that their section would be deprived of benefits from national legislation. Thus they worried that the route of the Pacific railroad would be situated for the advantage of northerners. Moreover, they guarded against any expansion of federal powers. W. R. W. Cobb, head of the House Committee on Public Lands, cautioned against implementing a scheme to set aside public lands to foster agricultural colleges because if "the general government possessed the power to make grants for local purposes, without a consideration, within the States, its action, in that respect, would have no limitation but such as policy or necessity might impose." In the case of river and harbor improvements, Robert Toombs complained of the "unjust system" that gave the poor man's tax dollar to the wharf owner. Alabama's Clement C. Clay, fighting to end fishing bounties, argued that such gifts to private industry encouraged "a sentiment already too pervading in the country, of dependence on the Government for support."[38]

Republicans, on the other hand, labored to convince their peers that an active federal government could end unemployment and create national conditions beneficial to all regions. Tennessee's Andrew Johnson, a Democrat who sponsored homestead legislation in the Senate but who reflected the opinions of many Republicans on the subject,

37. *Cong. Globe*, 35th Cong., 1st Sess., 2424. See also remarks of Sen. Crittenden, *ibid.*, 2426, and remarks of Sen. Benjamin on railroad legislation, *ibid.*, 1641.

38. For remarks of Sen. Johnson of Ark. and Sen. Iverson on the Pacific railroad, *ibid.*, 1641, 1643; remarks of Rep. Cobb in *House Reports*, 35th Cong., 1st Sess., No. 261, p. 2; remarks of Sen. Toombs, *Cong. Globe*, 35th Cong., 1st Sess., 2352; remarks of Sen. Clay, *ibid.*, 1934–35.

told his listeners that free land in the West would give the unemployed in the East a chance for advancement. Representative Morrill, the chief proponent of agricultural college legislation, said that the only way to return to prosperity was by improving the state of agriculture, and to do that the nation's farmers needed more education. Senator Lafayette S. Foster of Connecticut tried to ward off the threat to terminate fishing bounties to New England because "every branch of industry is now in an exceedingly depressed state," and such retrenchment could only further add to the number of jobless.[39]

The Panic of 1857 manufactured some special problems for the government. By disrupting the flow of imports into the country, the Panic had diminished tariff receipts. The lack of tariff revenue meant that for the administration to be able to balance the budget, it had to preserve every means of revenue, including land sales. This presented a dangerous political situation for the president. The Republicans under the leadership of Galusha Grow backed a resolution to suspend public land sales for ten years; the depression in the West had undermined the ability of settlers to pay the preemption fee. Under the preemption statute, a settler had the opportunity to buy the land he had improved after a certain number of years. If the farmer could not pay for the land at the appropriate time, however, it was auctioned off to the highest bidder. Buchanan sidestepped the dilemma momentarily by halting land sales for the rest of the year. But he warned that because of the exigencies of the treasury, the government's generosity would not last forever.[40]

The task of finding a way out of the financial morass fell upon the small shoulders of Howell Cobb. The secretary of the treasury understood that the Panic would reduce receipts, and as best he could, he estimated how much money the government would probably collect. Hoping that the government could escape further debt or a revision of

39. Remarks of Sen. Johnson of Tenn., *Cong. Globe*, 35th Cong., 1st Sess., 2267–69; remarks of Rep. Morrill, *ibid.*, 1693–94; remarks of Sen. Foster, *ibid.*, 2073. On economic legislation during the first session of the Thirty-fifth Congress, see Robert R. Russel, *Improvement of Communication with the Pacific Coast as an Issue in American Politics, 1783–1864* (Cedar Rapids, Iowa, 1948), 226–27; Benjamin Horace Hibbard, *A History of the Public Land Policies* (Madison, Wisc., 1965), 328–29; Madison Alexander Kuhn, "Economic Issues and the Rise of the Republican Party in the Northwest" (Ph.D. dissertation, University of Chicago, 1940), 140–41.

40. *Cong. Globe*, 35th Cong., 1st Sess., 1915; Robbins, *Our Landed Heritage*, 199; Verne E. Chatelain, "The Federal Land Policy and Minnesota Politics, 1854–1860," *Minnesota History*, XXII (1941), 233–40.

the revenue laws, Cobb began a policy of retrenchment. The Georgian urged the Congress not to consider petitions for the erection of new lighthouses, customhouses, or post offices. Aiding Cobb in his attempt to trim government expenses was J. Glancy Jones. In a series of letters to department heads, Jones asked the bureau chiefs to recommend ways to curb expenditures.[41]

The cost-conscious secretary of the treasury and the chairman of the Ways and Means Committee stumbled over an insuperable obstacle: the receipts from imports fell far short of expectations. Cobb hoped to obtain thirty-three million dollars from customs between September 30, 1857, and June 30, 1858, plus three million from the sale of lands. He also believed it possible to hold congressional appropriations to seventy-five million dollars for fiscal year 1858 and seventy-four million in fiscal year 1859. Unfortunately, customs receipts only amounted to slightly over six million dollars in the second quarter of fiscal year 1858, and the next quarter produced only seven million. Land sales added only one million dollars in these two quarters.[42] Cobb admitted that he had made a miscalculation.

On May 1, 1858, both Buchanan and Cobb sent urgent letters to Congress warning of impending fiscal disaster. Appropriations had amounted to almost ten million dollars more than Cobb had foreseen. In his explanation of the growing problems of the treasury, Cobb pointed to extraordinary expenses that no one could have predicted, especially the costly Utah expedition that had been sent to tame the Mormons. Furthermore, the nation had indulged in an unwise program of public construction under the influence of an overflowing treasury. The cure for these evils was retrenchment. Financial resources had diminished, "attributable to the fact that the trade and business of the country have not recovered as rapidly from the effects of the late revulsion as was then anticipated." Cobb believed that commerce would soon return to its normal levels and that the next fiscal year would see an end to the difficulty. But Cobb insisted on reducing expenditures to balance the budget and argued against revising the tariff, which had yet to be tested under normal conditions. The secretary of

41. *House Reports*, 35th Cong., 1st Sess., Nos. 254, 255, 257; *House Miscellaneous Documents*, 35th Cong., 1st Sess., Nos. 33, 34, 35.

42. *Senate Executive Documents*, 35th Cong., 1st Sess., No. 1, pp. 3–5; *House Executive Documents*, 35th Cong., 2nd Sess., No. 3, p. 3.

the treasury requested a new fifteen million dollar loan at 6 percent interest to be paid in ten years.[43]

The economic issues that the Panic of 1857 had raised, which had at first occupied Congress and then faded away in the Lecompton controversy, now rose again to prominence. In the Senate, Hunter tried to steer the loan through the fiery barrage leveled at it by the Republicans. Giving the explanation of the president and Secretary Cobb, Hunter declared that upon passing the loan Congress' true mission was retrenchment until governmental expenses were lowered to sixty million dollars per year. Then, Hunter continued, the "existing tariff" plus the "proceeds of the public lands" would provide ample income.[44] For the last month of the session the legislators wrangled over the loan bill. Moreover, the financial exigency affected all the remaining measures that required congressional attention.

Republicans quickly challenged the economic reasoning of the Democrats and charged that the administration's party was responsible for bloated expenditures. They especially demeaned the Utah expedition and the funds allocated for new sloops of war. Republicans felt that the motivation behind these appropriations was to expand slavery by military force into the West and Central America. John Sherman revealed one other line of thought, a favorite of all Republicans: excessive expenditures were caused by administration efforts to increase the patronage in order to buy the votes of the people. Sherman looked at the appropriation bills and declared, "In this vast mausoleum are buried your secret contracts, your jobs, your custom-houses, your marine hospitals, your Post Office deficiency and post offices, your coast survey, your courthouses—a vast catalogue of jobs to partisan favorites."[45]

Rumblings from the opposition about decreasing expenditures failed to impress the Democrats. Their party adhered to the Jeffersonian-Jacksonian tradition of free trade that called for frugal government and low taxes; the opposition had ever been the offenders of fiscal integrity. Therefore, the cry of retrenchment from the Republicans sounded

43. Message of Cobb in *Senate Executive Documents*, 35th Cong., 1st Sess., No. 60, pp. 1–3; message of the president in *Senate Executive Documents*, 35th Cong., 1st Sess., No. 68, pp. 1–3.
44. *Cong. Globe*, 35th Cong., 1st Sess, APX, 380–83.
45. *Ibid.*, quote of Rep. Sherman, 2432; see remarks of Rep. Lovejoy, 2864; Rep. Grow, 2412.

more like the "note of political contest" than conversion to sound economics. Democrats also accused the Republicans of hypocrisy, for the opposition was quite liberal when river and harbor legislation came before the Congress. Republicans raised a storm when a favorite project of Senator Zachariah Chandler, funds for improving the St. Clair flats, was dropped from the civil appropriations bill. But the Democrats failed to produce any coherent plan to reduce expenses. They instead nibbled away at small items in the appropriation bills, for example, furniture supplies, seeds delivered by the patent office, and the number of clerks in the land office.[46]

There were various ways the growing treasury deficit could be erased, but the Republicans immediately seized upon increasing the tariff. The announcement of Cobb and Buchanan that a loan would be required, after a treasury notes bill had already been passed in the first part of the session, brought irate Republicans to their feet. Leading the Republican disparagement of administration economic policies was Senator Simmons. He lashed out not only at low tariff rates but also at the warehouse system and the *ad valorem* means of calculating duties. Proponents of a tariff revision also pressed the matter into debates other than the loan bill. American party members from border states and northern Republicans interrupted discussions on internal improvements, fishing bounties, and the various appropriation bills to plead for an upward revision of the tariff.[47]

An important element in Republican and border state opposition speeches concerning the problems of the treasury was the emphasis placed on aiding the unemployed by instituting the policy of protection. When Simmons tried to change the method of evaluating foreign imports for taxation, he argued that any legislation that would entail some degree of protection would be "a great blessing to the laboring men of this country." Crittenden also believed a high tariff would reduce the number of jobless, while Tennessee's John Bell affirmed that the policy of free trade had hurt the poor in both England and America. John Covode, a Pennsylvania representative, explicitly brought together the tariff and the fate of the unemployed. Noting that the treasury was in peril and that the nation's industries were "prostrate," Covode charged the administration with "indifference" toward the

---

46. *Ibid.*, remarks of Rep. Clemens, 2811; remarks of Rep. Smith of Va., 2213, 2244; Rep. McQueen, 2390–92; on the St. Clair Flats bill, see 2575–81, 2645, 2674.

47. *Ibid.*, comments of Sen. Simmons APX, 438–39, 441–42; Sen. Bell, APX, 540.

economy and the laborer: "Hundreds, who a year ago were profitably employed, are now idle, and their families suffering," a circumstance brought about by denying to manufacturers "the incidental protection that a sufficient revenue duty would afford."[48]

Protectionism had virtually no defenders in the Democratic ranks North or South, but when southern Democrats rebutted tariff proposals they paid special attention to the question of relief and demonstrated their allegiance to the free trade explanation of economic issues. Once again, southerners enunciated doctrines that were incongruous with slaveholding. Alabama Senator Clement Clay heard some of his colleagues claim that "the labor of the country requires protection at this time." Clay stated that he had been taught to believe that protection was "simply securing to each man the fruits of his own labor." Hunter, upset by the cries for tariff revision "in order to protect the operatives who were suffering," responded by saying, "I do not think it fair to tax all other laborers in order to promote and to support another class." Tennessee's Andrew Johnson objected to the incessant Republican and old-line Whig cry that the government had to aid the people. For Johnson the idea of the government giving employment to the people was "the most dangerous doctrine that ever was sustained in any government."[49]

The arguments used in the Senate and House over the loan bill mirrored each other. The position of the House Democracy was ably outlined by J. Glancy Jones. He disavowed any intention on the part of the administration to establish a protective tariff; the Democracy would adhere to their honored tradition of a tariff for revenue only. What the administration hoped to achieve was the reduction of expenditures to fifty-five million dollars by 1860. Retrenchment and reform, not a modification of the tariff, was the policy the Democracy intended to pursue. The loan bill finally passed, only to be changed a few days later at the very end of the session. Buchanan and Cobb decided they needed more leeway and asked Congress to raise the loan from fifteen to twenty million dollars. After much grumbling, Congress acted favorably upon the recommendation.[50]

During the appropriation debates, Senator Cameron stood up to introduce a petition from Pennsylvania's ironworkers requesting a higher

48. *Ibid.*, quotes of Simmons, APX, 444, 531; remarks of Sen. Crittenden, APX, 449–50; Sen. Bell, APX, 529–33; quote of Covode, 2864–65.
49. *Ibid.*, remarks of Sen. Clay, 2079; Sen. Hunter, APX, 467; Sen. Johnson, 2589.
50. *Ibid.*, remarks of J. G. Jones, 3018–20; fate of loan bill, 2981, 3009.

tariff. He remarked that he could not recall a time in which there was "so much real distress among the laboring men of my State." In a reference obviously geared for the coming congressional elections, Cameron added that he expected no action from this particular Congress. He had told Pennsylvania workers that before they could get proper protection "they must change the majority in this Senate, they must change the majority in the other House of Congress, and above all they must change the occupant of the White House, who is the dispenser of the power which controls the legislation of this country."[51]

Cameron referred to developments occurring in the Keystone State that were visible to others as well. George W. Scranton, an iron manufacturer from Luzerne County, warned Bigler of the political consequences of inaction on the tariff. He told Bigler that changed conditions in Pennsylvania were bringing new faces into politics: "The business men, the farmers, & laboring men of our Country do not trouble themselves much with politics, or care so much who manages the affairs of Government, so long as they are profitably employed, but when the Opposite is the case, as it is now, they have nothing else to do but to aid and assist in planning schemes for the overthrow of parties in power with the hope of building up on their downfall." Republican newspapers were highly critical of Buchanan's loan policy. Cobb's estimates were too low, and hopes of curbing the government's spending habits were political illusions. In Pennsylvania the question of the tariff became thunderous. The principal journal touting protectionism, the *North American and United States Gazette*, related that in the coal and iron counties the depression had touched too many lives to be ignored. No longer was protectionism a "remote abstraction"; now it was a question of "whether the mills and furnaces shall remain closed, or whether they shall go on and give the country its needed supply of goods, and themselves support."[52]

By the middle of 1858 it was clear that the Panic had created an economic issue that was gathering political force. Pennsylvania newspapers revealed how deeply the ideas of protectionism had sunk into the state's collective economic consciousness. Editors also showed how easily they could fashion a sectional component to their tariff advocacy.

51. *Ibid.*, 2563.
52. George W. Scranton to William Bigler, May 18, 1858, in William Bigler Papers, HSP; *North American and United States Gazette* (Philadelphia), May 14, June 15, 25, 1858, hereinafter cited as Philadelphia *North American*; Eiselen, *The Rise of Pennsylvania Protectionism*, 246–47.

They blamed southerners for the state of the economy. The Philadelphia *Evening Bulletin* intimated that no longer would the North yield on economic policy, because "when it comes to a question of life and death . . . we must be excused from carrying our docility and humility to the [southern] gentlemen much further." One correspondent of John Sherman remarked, "I do not see how ever we can protect our manufacturing industry as long as we are one with the South." To add to Pennsylvania suspicions that southerners desired a complete revocation of all tariff duties, Congress published a report by William Boyce that called for the abolition of all tariffs and the imposition of direct taxes to raise revenue.[53]

The protectionist appeal increasingly tied the fates of the slave and the white worker to the tariff. "This question of protection, like that of slavery," noted the *Raftsman's Journal*, "has too long been moulded into shape and power by southern interests, to the great injury of northern mechanics and laborers." Morton·McMichael of the Philadelphia *North American* was one of the most conservative men in the state, yet even he linked slavery and the tariff together. When a reform paper demurred against the rising tariff issue, McMichael replied that those who gave all their energies to antislavery should not be so narrow as to forget the business life of the nation. There was "a very direct connection" between the questions of slave labor, free labor, and the tariff: "Protected industry elevates the laborer, while that which, like southern slave agriculture, with its markets all abroad, makes the laborer dependent on one resource alone, naturally and inevitably degrades him."[54] As the protectionists sought to elevate the free laborer, the doctrine of protectionism slowly became antislavery because slavery was the ultimate degradation of the working class.

The various economic and sectional strands inherent in protectionism were woven together into one political garment at Philadelphia on June 15, 1858, where a "Rally for Protection to American Labor" was held. Presiding was the high priest of protectionism, Henry C. Carey; his lieutenant, Morton McMichael, inaugurated the proceedings. Supposedly the assemblage was the product of an appeal of the "operatives" of the city to obtain succor from depression. The crowd

53. Philadelphia *Evening Bulletin*, June 17, 1858; John McKee to John Sherman, March 13, 1858, in Sherman Papers; *House Reports*, 35th Cong., 1st Sess., No. 407, pp. 1–6.

54. *Raftsfman's Journal* (Clearfield, Pa.), May 10, 1858; Philadelphia *North American*, April 9, June 26, 1858.

listened to the speeches of Richard W. Thompson, Humphrey Marshall, Jacob Collamer, John Covode, Simon Cameron, E. Joy Morris, and James F. Simmons. Cameron, Morris, Simmons, and Collamer were Republicans; Thompson of Indiana and Marshall of Kentucky were American party spokesmen. Most of the speeches followed the usual protectionist pattern of domestic markets, national economic independence, and concern for the laborer; the speeches by Collamer and Simmons, however, contained more important points.

Collamer stressed that the United States was still an experiment in self-government, and self-government ultimately would depend upon the material well-being of the mass of Americans. "The people are our voters; the laborers our voters; it is they that guide the destinies of this country; they should guide it; and if they cannot guide it in enlightenment it will go down in darkness." Given that the laborers truly decided the fate of the nation, the country therefore needed the policy that most elevated them. Protection offered the best policy to guard the welfare of the laborer; it was the means to escape the doom that Malthus and Ricardo had foreseen. But Collamer, alone among the protectionist speakers at the rally, hammered away at the sectional obstacle that blocked the salvation of the worker. The people of the "extreme Southern portion of the United States, who have their peculiar institutions, and their peculiar notions, consider that this whole subject of a protective tariff is a matter of no consequence."[55]

Simmons also told the audience to be wary of Democratic rhetoric, but he emphasized the economic benefits that laborers could expect from a high tariff. Admitting that he was a manufacturer, Simmons agreed with the free traders that he attempted to procure cheap labor and that the laborer tried to obtain high wages. Thus there was a conflict. "That is the nature of all. But there is a great doctrine in regard to which our interests are alike, and that is, to have the market price high. . . . In a free country we have the right to have the market price of labor high, and the only way in which this can be obtained, is to have the market price of the products of labor high." And so the formulations of Henry C. Carey became translated into political rhetoric for popular consumption. Simmons put into a simpler form the ideal of Americans in a special marketplace in which competition did

55. Details of this meeting may be found in several sources. The quote here is from the Philadelphia *Evening Bulletin*, June 16, 1858.

not reduce the worker to subsistence. Competition remained, but not the competition of the free traders; cheapness was not the ultimate goal of the economy.[56]

Pennsylvania was thus developing a particular economic argument that well suited the political goals of the Republicans. Protectionists established an economic program that could attract voters seeking an escape from recession. But Republicans could use the southern disdain for protectionism to prove that the Slave Power cared only for its own interests, not those of the nation. In particular, the Republicans charged that the Slave Power ignored the welfare of, and indeed was hostile to, free northern workers. This claim was no longer theoretical. It was offered at a time when Pennsylvanians suffered severe unemployment, making the Republican claim all the more potent.

Meanwhile other problems plagued the administration. The final tally for government appropriations was nearly eighty-two million dollars.[57] The loan bill that was intended to see the government through its difficult fiscal period had some trouble in New York's financial circles. Cobb borrowed only half of the twenty million dollar loan, and the bankers wanted to know when the treasury would offer the rest. Also, questions were raised as to whether the financiers got better terms than usual because of Cobb's inexperience.[58] The secretary hoped that the financial burden would soon ease. He told Robert Hunter that customs receipts had risen nicely in the last fiscal quarter, but there was a great falling off from the sales of public lands. Nonetheless, he estimated that he would only need to borrow ten million dollars to see the government through. His hope for solvency rested upon reducing the national budget to sixty-four million dollars. Only two shadows darkened Cobb's view: deficiencies in the Post Office and the War Department. To James Buchanan he reported the same hopes: "*Save us from deficiencies* & the Treasury will walk through the fiscal year 'like a thing of life.'"[59]

By late July the congressional elections absorbed the attention of

56. Smith, *Henry C. Carey and American Sectional Conflict*, 70–72.

57. *House Miscellaneous Documents*, 35th Cong., 1st Sess., No. 137, p. 76.

58. New York *Herald*, June 17, August 11, 1858; *Harper's Weekly*, July 17, 1858, p. 450.

59. Howell Cobb to Robert M. T. Hunter, July 26, 1858, in Charles Henry Ambler (ed.), *Correspondence of Robert M. T. Hunter, 1826–1876* (Washington, D.C., 1918), 261; Howell Cobb to James Buchanan, August 2, 1858, in Buchanan Papers.

Buchanan and Cobb. Both men knew that the Democracy was politically vulnerable in some of the northern states. "The greatest trouble will be in Illinois produced by Douglass' course," Cobb wrote Hunter, "and in Pennsylvania on account of the tariff."[60] Cobb was correct as to the areas in which the party would experience difficulty, but like his estimates of government income, he erred with regard to its magnitude.

60. Howell Cobb to Robert M. T. Hunter, July 26, 1858, in Ambler (ed.), *Correspondence of Hunter*, 261.

SIX / The Elections of 1858

It was during the elections of 1858 that Panic-related economic issues finally emerged and began to influence the course of sectional controversy. The rise of protectionist sentiment in Pennsylvania not only added an economic dimension to the debate over the expansion of slavery but also reinforced an essential point of contention between the North and the South: the different attitudes and goals that a slaveholding society and a free labor society fostered. When it became obvious that the tariff had become important to the crucial state of Pennsylvania, both the Republicans and the Democrats tried to sway the Keystone State's electorate by altering their political platforms. During the campaign of 1858, it soon became apparent that the Republicans possessed a flexibility the Democrats lacked.

In most of the states, there were few doubts as to what the results of the congressional contests of 1858 would be. Southerners and New Englanders were expected to cling to their normal party affiliations. Other states were less predictable but were of vital importance to the administration. The party renegade, Stephen A. Douglas, sought reelection in Illinois, and his fate would reveal, or so it was supposed, the extent of revolt in the Northwest. Political observers were especially interested in the results of congressional races in New York, New Jersey, and Pennsylvania because Democrats held a significant number of seats in these states. Pennsylvania and New Jersey were essential to the Democracy; they had enabled Buchanan to win the presidency in 1856. Indeed, the importance of the elections of 1858 lay in the fact that the policies of the administration were on trial in the northern states that voted Democratic in 1856; these same states were no less a requirement for Democratic victory in 1860.

Buchanan anxiously and fearfully awaited the outcome of the congressional elections. His anxiety arose from the unexpected economic problems, and his fear from the split in the party. Buchanan and his advisers knew the struggle over the Lecompton Constitution would be a prominent issue in the campaign, but they believed its effect on voting results would be minimal. Therefore the administration actively sought the defeat of Douglas and those congressmen who adhered to his principles. The policy of retribution toward Douglas dismayed many Democrats, for they felt that the Northwest would follow Douglas and that the actions of the administration would only alienate the region from the rest of the party.[1]

There were other issues that the Democrats knew the Republicans intended to press upon the public. The most disconcerting of these other matters was the economic recession and the cry for a higher tariff. In early May, Buchanan was shocked to learn that municipal elections in Philadelphia resulted in an opposition victory. Buchanan's correspondents stressed that "*national politics had nothing to do with this business.*" The ousted Democratic Mayor, Richard Vaux, pointed out that the opposition had constructed a coalition that had formerly been fragmented into separate entities. The single issue that drew the disparate elements into a fusion was the tariff: "Thus the old line whigs were seduced on the tariff issue. The men out of work, were told this was the cause and cure for their idleness." Many Pennsylvanians warned that the tariff would act as a lightning rod for the economically dispossessed. One adviser to Senator Bigler wrote that "I do not think the Lecompton question will hurt us one way or the other, but I am sure that the present State of things, actual suffering among the people of the Coal region and Iron works will operate desperately against us."[2]

The Democracy also faced a multitude of problems involving party unity. Jealousies among state Democratic leaders were rife. Besides the schism caused by the desertion of Douglas and the popular sovereignty Democrats, a number of states were divided into factions that

1. George H. Mayer, *The Republican Party, 1854–1966* (2nd ed.; New York, 1967), 53–54; James M. Mason to John Y. Mason, August 6, 1858, in Mason Family Papers, Virginia Historical Society, Richmond, Va., hereinafter cited as VHS; Howell Cobb to Alexander H. Stephens, September 8, 1858, in Ulrich Bonnell Phillips (ed.), *The Correspondence of Robert Toombs, Alexander H. Stephens, and Howell Cobb* (Washington, D.C., 1911), 442–43.

2. Robert Tyler to James Buchanan, May 5, 1858, quoted in Philip Gerald Auchampaugh, *Robert Tyler: Southern Rights Champion, 1847–1866* (Duluth, Minn., 1934), 238; Richard Vaux to James Buchanan, May 16, 1858, in Buchanan Papers; Lewis Ruser [?] to William Bigler, May 10, 1858, in Bigler Papers.

vied for the favor of the national administration. These groups sought aid and patronage, and invariably those who received little attention lost faith in the president. Buchanan realized that these internal dissensions placed the party at a disadvantage.[3]

Many of the problems facing the Democrats also confronted the Republicans. The party was still very much a coalition among the Whigs, former Democrats, nativists, and free soilers. Often these groups fought each other for supremacy on the state level. Even the title "Republican" had not become the dominant nomenclature for the opposition in many northern states. In Pennsylvania, Indiana, New Jersey, Rhode Island, and in some localities in Massachusetts, the anti-Democratic forces referred to themselves as the "People's party" or the "American-Republicans." Republicans thus entered the campaign of 1858 with a considerable amount of hope but not without an awareness of their very obvious weaknesses.[4]

The highlight of the political campaign in the Old Northwest was a series of debates between Senator Stephen A. Douglas and the Republican challenger, Abraham Lincoln. Although the seven debates consumed only a slight portion of the candidates' campaign efforts, they received national coverage because of Douglas' prominence. In the confrontations, Lincoln labored to tie Douglas to the alleged proslavery designs of the Kansas-Nebraska Act, insisted that the Dred Scott decision had vitiated Douglas' principle of allowing settlers to determine the status of slavery in the territories without federal interference, and demanded that the morality of slavery be seen as the crucial difference between Republicans and Democrats. Douglas countered by accusing Lincoln and the Republicans of harboring sectional animosity, desiring racial equality, and coercing all the states into a conformity in their constitutional practices. Douglas' main theme in the debates, however, was to defend his doctrine of popular sovereignty.[5]

3. Roy F. Nichols, *The Disruption of American Democracy* (New York, 1948), 203, 208–209; William Dusinberre, *Civil War Issues in Philadelphia, 1856–1865* (Philadelphia, 1965), 70–72; John F. Coleman, *The Disruption of the Pennsylvania Democracy, 1848–1860* (Harrisburg, Pa., 1975), 103–105.

4. Foner, *Free Soil, Free Labor, Free Men*, 167–68, 204–205.

5. The Lincoln-Douglas debates are collected in Robert W. Johannsen (ed.), *The Lincoln-Douglas Debates of 1858* (New York, 1965). Analysis and interpretation of the debates is extensive. See Don E. Fehrenbacher, *Prelude to Greatness: Lincoln in the 1850's* (Stanford, Calif., 1962), 96–142; Benjamin P. Thomas, *Abraham Lincoln: A Biography* (New York, 1952), 182–92; Johannsen, *Stephen A. Douglas*, 668–75.

Throughout the Northwest the themes enunciated by Lincoln and Douglas dominated party battles. In all the oratory that party leaders used to woo the citizenry, the preeminent topics were Kansas, race, the Slave Power, and sectionalism. There were references to immigrants and to local issues, but those seeking election in the Northwest clung tenaciously to the question of slavery in the territories. One element in the political debates of 1858 in the Northwest was conspicuous by its absence: economic issues. The financial chaos of 1857 was followed by a sharp depression, and the Northwest was adversely affected by poor business conditions. Yet discussion of national economic policy by either party in the Northwest fell into insignificance compared to the debate over slavery extension.

Republicans and Democrats did offer occasional remarks about economic matters. In Milwaukee, Republicans referred to the neglect of rivers and harbors by the national government, and the Wisconsin State Republican Convention complained that "the great commercial and industrial interests [of free labor] have been unscrupulously sacrificed to the dictation of the Slaveholding aristocracy." Ohio Democratic Senator George E. Pugh stressed that the Republicans "care not for the people nor the laborers, only for the capitalist, the banker and the employer." In the iron regions of Ohio there was some debate over the question of the tariff.[6]

But the economic issues were not explicitly connected to the Panic or to the depression. Republicans linked the lack of an adequate economic policy to the power of the slave masters in Congress, not to new demands that the economic collapse had forced upon them. In Lincoln's voluminous correspondence in 1858, there was but one mention of the tariff and a few minor references to homestead legislation. Those who offered advice to Lincoln either tried to indicate better ways of undermining the Little Giant's doctrine of popular sovereignty or, more commonly, warned him of the race question.[7] Economic issues were a distant second to the matter of slavery.

6. Resolution of Wisconsin Republicans in Milwaukee *Daily Free Democrat*, October 11, 1858; speech of George E. Pugh in Cincinnati *Daily Enquirer*, September 22, 1858; debate over tariff found in Cincinnati *Daily Gazette*, September 4, 6, October 1, 1858; Kuhn, "Economic Issues and the Rise of the Republican Party in the Northwest," 154–56.

7. For example, see Hiram M. Trimble to Abraham Lincoln, August 4, 1858, in Abraham Lincoln Papers, LC.

What was true for the Northwest also proved true for the campaigns in New England and New York. In these two regions Democrats stressed banking institutions, state extravagance, corruption, and white supremacy; they generally ignored national questions concerning the tariff, internal improvements, and public land policy. Republicans, especially in New England, were less reticent about espousing the need for new national policies, such as an upward revision of the tariff. Even though the East coast witnessed a greater discussion of economic issues than the Northwest, the topic of Kansas and slavery extension reigned supreme. Local matters appeared and questions of extravagance were raised, but, as in the Northwest, the fight over slavery simply dwarfed the attention given to national economic policies.[8]

Nor did the contests in the South produce any significant variation from the course of debate in the North. The enfeebled opposition in the South, Whigs and Americans, offered little competition to the Democracy. Regardless of their opponents' strength, southern Democrats explicitly made the question of slavery's existence the main topic of the canvass. Democrats usually refused to be deflected into debates on other matters and repeated to voters that the principal issue, in the words of Mississippi congressman John J. McRae, was "the great question growing out of the difference in the social systems of the two sections of our country relating to what is termed free and slave labor."[9]

Most of the 1858 congressional campaigns either ignored or sparingly mentioned the need for national economic policies to mitigate the effects of the Panic of 1857. Politicians throughout the nation instead concentrated on some variation of the slavery issue. There were two exceptions to the rule. In the industrial, iron-mongering states of Pennsylvania and New Jersey the results of the depression were crucial to political debates. Unlike the rest of the Union, political rhetoric in Pennsylvania and New Jersey focused primarily upon the tariff and not upon slavery in the territories. The Panic of 1857 thus had its first detectable political impact in 1858. Because of the importance of Pennsylvania in presidential elections, the influence of the Panic upon na-

8. Boston *Post,* January 30, March 5, 31, 1858; Hartford *Daily Times,* March 4, 30, 1858; Lynn (Mass.) *News,* September 14, 1858; New York *Daily Tribune,* September 11, 15, 29, October 4, 1858. For local issues, see Collins, "The Politics of Particularism," 39–40, 77–85, 170–228.

9. Letter of J. J. McRae in *Mississippian* (Jackson), September 17, 1858.

tional affairs was not as limited as might at first seem; Pennsylvania was the battleground between Republicans and Democrats for national political supremacy.

Democrats knew that in the president's home state they faced a desperate struggle. Internal dissension wracked the Keystone State Democracy. The editor of the Philadelphia *Press*, John W. Forney, had once been a favorite of Buchanan and had been considered for a cabinet post. Southern wariness toward Forney killed, momentarily, his chances of ascending to political honor. Forney, perhaps angered over southern refusal to recognize his contributions in the election of 1856, and perhaps out of conviction, turned against the administration on the Lecompton issue. Forney's editorials and speeches against Buchanan were widely reprinted. Joining Forney were a group of important anti-Lecompton Democrats headed by Governor William F. Packer. The split in the ranks of the Pennsylvania Democracy boded ill for the party.[10]

The disorder in the Democratic camp did not extend to the opposition's. Although anti-Democratic groups had problems in certain districts, no great defections took place. The nomination of Thaddeus Stevens in the Ninth Congressional District and the opposition fusion behind anti-Lecompton Democrat William Montgomery in the Twentieth angered some Republicans, Americans, and old-line Whigs, but generally the opposition in the state coalesced quite frictionlessly into one massive anti-Buchanan organization. Fusion with anti-Lecompton Democrats was often the rule and not the exception. Because of the coalition nature of the opposition in the Keystone State, the anti-administration forces referred to themselves as the "People's Party." And as surely as the People's party invited all who opposed Buchanan's Kansas policy to join them, just as surely they promoted the tariff as the major issue.[11]

When conventions of the People's party met around the state to select their congressional nominees, protection became the primary concern. Thaddeus Stevens in his acceptance speech spoke of "the languishing factories, the cold and almost idle furnaces, and the silent work-shops" that resulted from Democratic policy. A meeting in Lewistown referred to the tariff as "the only safe guard to the laboring man

10. Nichols, *The Disruption of American Democracy*, 200–206; Dusinberre, *Civil War Issues in Philadelphia*, 72–79.
11. Lancaster (Pa.) *Examiner and Herald*, September 8, October 6, 1858; Washington (Pa.) *Reporter*, June 16, July 7, 14, August 18, September 1, 1858.

for future prosperity." In the important iron county of Cambria, the People's party constructed a resolution that emphasized the importance of the tariff to wages: "We hold it to be a self-evident fact, that, if American Manufacturers must compete with those of Europe *without* Protection, we, the people, must work for European wages." Pennsylvania'a satellite, New Jersey, experienced the same phenomenon. At a New Jersey ratification meeting for the nomination of William Pennington, one speaker asserted that "the man that labors, that gains his livelihood by the sweat of his brow, is entitled to the guardian care of the Government under which he lives." [12]

Tariff proponents used the same arguments upon the Pennsylvania citizenry in late 1858 that representatives and senators had used in the last session of Congress, that Henry C. Carey had propagandized in his writings, and that editors had referred to when the Panic had struck down the banks in October, 1857. The opposition leaders stressed the domestic market, the harmony of interests, and national economic independence. Nor did the People's party ignore the labor appeal that protectionist theorists had fashioned over the decade. They insisted that reducing foreign imports would stimulate the domestic economy and thus put the jobless back to work. The tariff, in short, became the policy to end unemployment. [13]

There was a special quality to the opposition's attempt to sway laborers to the high-tariff standard. After the first shock of the Panic of 1857 rolled over Pennsylvania, the dire straits of laborers in the iron and coal mining districts resulted in a rash of strikes during the spring and summer months. Editors who favored a harmonious relationship between capital and labor wanted to defuse the riotous sentiments of the strikers. The means of doing so was to replace the employer as the villain in the laborers' eyes with Buchanan's free trade policy: "We sympathize, deeply sympathize with the condition of our workmen. It is our object to alleviate their condition, as much as in our power. The best counsel that can be tendered them under the circumstances is, to bear their heavy burden patiently, and at the Fall election to strike one united blow for 'Protection' to their industry." One editor inserted a

12. Thaddeus Stevens quoted in New York *Daily Tribune*, September 11, 1858; Lewistown (Pa.) *Gazette*, August 5, 1858; *Cambria Tribune* (Johnstown, Pa.), August 14, 1858; remarks of David C. Dodd, in Newark (N.J.) *Daily Advertiser*, September 28, 1858.

13. For example, *Raftsman's Journal* (Clearfield, Pa.), June 23, 1858; Philadelphia *North American*, August 9, 1858; Altoona (Pa.) *Tribune*, August 26, 1858.

protectionist appeal at the same time he reported a strike. After explaining the reason for the walkout, he belittled the Democratic policy of low tariffs that had wrecked the economy: protection, he wrote, had relieved the country in 1842 "and PROTECTION would relieve the country now."[14]

While protectionists sought to gain popular acceptance by appealing to the public's material interests, they did not hesitate to try to attract adherents by stressing the antislavery nature of the high-tariff program. Hammond's mudsill speech was used frequently by opposition editors to demonstrate how southern free traders disregarded the interests of northern workingmen. The opposition constructed a bridge that intimately connected the Lecompton issue with the tariff policy of the administration. In a public letter, G. Rush Petriken, an old-line Whig who hoped to become a candidate for Congress, combined the issues of Lecompton and protectionism. "Lecompton and the abrogation of all protective discrimination," he wrote, "are events that came together; oppression and wrong; popular rights disregarded in Kansas; free industry destroyed in the States." Petriken found the binding tie between slavery and low tariffs an economic one, because goods "come in FREE of duty, in direct competition with our FREE LABOR, [so] that the products of SLAVE LABOR, cotton, rice, and tobacco, may have free market in *her* [British] dominions on this continent." One protectionist editor offered the motto: "*Free Labor, Protection to American Industry, and death to the Free Trade, Pro Slavery, Sham Democratic Party!*"[15]

Into this massive onslaught on the tariff policies of the Democratic party came help from an unexpected source. In late July, news reporters discovered that the iron pipes to be used in the construction of the Washington Aqueduct were to be imported from Scotland. A contract had been made by Captain Meigs of the engineering corps to a Lawrence Myers of Philadelphia to construct the aqueduct; Myers decided to purchase Scottish iron because of it cheapness. The opposition could not have scripted a more fortuitous revelation. Here was a Pennsylvania president, informed of all the conditions in the iron districts, al-

14. *Miner's Journal* (Pottsville, Pa.), May 29, 1858; *Hollidaysburg Register* quoted by *Cambria Tribune* (Johnstown, Pa.), April 24, 1858.

15. Philadelphia *North American*, August 9, 1858; Harrisburg *Daily Telegraph*, September 14, 1858; *Daily Evening Express* (Lancaster, Pa.), August 11, 1858; B. Rush Petriken to J. M. Hancock, Dushore, *et al.*, in *Potter Journal* (Coudersport, Pa.), August 12, 1858; *Miner's Journal* (Pottsville, Pa.), June 12, 1858.

lowing his administration to purchase foreign iron while Pennsylvania endured depression. The Scotch iron pipes episode was, for the People's party, a superb example of the policy of cheapness over human welfare, of free trade over protection. Opposition journals seized the issue with all the energy they could command. At one mass meeting at Minersville several banners appeared with the slogans, "American Iron before Scotch Iron" and "No more Scotch Water Pipes." [16]

Issues other than the tariff were brought before the Pennsylvania citizenry. Extravagance, railroad construction, the tonnage tax, and the sale of the mainline canal all received due notice. These matters, however, paled before the tariff, except for one other subject: the Lecompton policy of James Buchanan. The tariff did not crowd out the question of the extension of slavery. The long speeches of John Forney made their way into print, and they dwelt solely on the fraud of the Lecompton Constitution. The editor of the Erie *Gazette* wrote, "The Issue in this State has been placed on a fair footing—the Lecompton Democracy on the one hand, and those holding directly opposed views on the other." [17] Lecompton provided the basis for fusion in several districts with Democratic congressmen who opposed Buchanan. The People's party did not abandon the slavery issue.

But what did occur in the Keystone State was the development of an opposition argument in which the tariff and slavery issues complemented each other. Both were ultimately anchored to the ideal of free labor, and it took only a modest imagination to link low tariffs, which produced low wages, to slavery extension, which threatened free labor's reward in tilling the soil. In both cases southerners stood in the way of the advancement of free labor. Neither argument was slighted by the People's party as they reached out for voters, because both were parts of the central question that the Panic of 1857 had elevated: that is, what was to be the fate of the free laborer.

In New Jersey, one Democratic editor complained that the Republicans "persisted in making this [protection] an issue in the present campaign, upon the plea that the present tariff is ruinous to home industry." Democrats, of course, knew the tariff was going to be an important

16. Descriptions of the Scotch water pipes episode may be found in *Miner's Journal* (Pottsville, Pa.), August 28, September 23, October 9. The quotes are from *Miner's Journal*, September 18, 1858.

17. Erie (Pa.) *Gazette*, September 30, 1858. Speeches of Forney in *Jeffersonian* (Stroudsburg, Pa.), October 7, 1858; *Raftsman's Journal* (Coudersport, Pa.), September 29, 1858; Bedford (Pa.) *Inquirer and Chronicle*, September 17, 1858.

issue in Pennsylvania and New Jersey. Their surprise came only from the extent to which the tariff had become the central topic of debate.[18]

Pennsylvania Democrats, whether Lecompton or anti-Lecompton, swiftly took positions favoring an increase of tariff duties, especially on coal and iron. Democrats accepted the "two questions, which our opponents have made *the* questions of the canvass; namely, those of Slavery and the Tariff." In the Fourth Congressional District in New Jersey, the administration nominee for Congress, John Huyler, announced, "I have never agreed with the free trade notions entertained by him [anti-Lecompton candidate Adrain], for I have always been in favor of adjusting the tariff for the protection of our industry." Nor did the Democrats ignore the appeal the tariff had for the laborer. When discussing the merits of Andrew Burke, the Democratic candidate for Congress in Pennsylvania's Twenty-second Congressional District, the Pittsburgh *Morning Post* added that Burke "advocates such a tariff as will result in putting every furnace in Pennsylvania, in blast, and give well paid employment to every mechanic in the State."[19]

Although the Democrats adopted a platform calling for a higher tariff, they did not forsake the hallowed ground of Jacksonian economics. Keystone State Democrats obstinately held to their belief that paper money and banks had caused the Panic and the ensuing unemployment. Senator Bigler told a Philadelphia audience that the revulsion had really been the result of an "unguarded expansion of business and credit." Another Philadelphia Democratic meeting produced two resolutions on the depressed business conditions. One called for a slight revision of duties; the other firmly stated that "to a pernicious banking system, and not to tariff acts, are we indebted for the wide-spread distress with which we have been surrounded during the past twelve months."[20]

Democrats also warned of the excesses to which protectionism might lead. Although the nation needed a greater measure of protection than was currently afforded by the tariff, New Jersey Democrats wanted no tariff that placed "unjust burthens upon the workingmen."

18. *Daily True American* (Trenton, N.J.), October 18, 1858.

19. Luzerne County Democratic meeting in *Luzerne Union* (Wilkes-Barre), September 22, 1858; quote from Johnstown Democratic meeting in *Allegheny Mountain Echo* (Johnstown, Pa.), October 6, 1858; remarks of Huyler in Newark (N.J.) *Daily Advertiser*, October 12, 1858; Pittsburgh *Morning Post*, October 6, 1858.

20. Speech of Bigler in Erie (Pa.) *Weekly Observer*, July 17, 1858; meeting of Philadelphia Democrats in Philadelphia *Evening Bulletin*, October 11, 1858.

Others argued that in their haste to procure better business conditions, Pennsylvania could not forget "the great agricultural interests of the country." A resolution at one county convention argued against the kind of tariff legislation "which makes one class of men richer and another class of men poorer." Thus Pennsylvania Democrats in 1858 did not abandon the national party interpretation of protectionism.[21]

Such peculiarities as there were in the Pennsylvania Democratic position on the tariff were easily encompassed by the latitude of the national party's standards. The cry of the Democrats was always "a tariff for revenue, with incidental protection to our own industry," and not, as the Republicans charged, free trade. In both New Jersey and Pennsylvania the Democrats repeated their hostility to a thoroughly protectionist standard and so stayed within the general ideological confines of their party.[22] Although the Pennsylvania Democracy was probably more susceptible to tariff appeals than their compatriots in other states, their general position of a revenue tariff with incidental protection was the practical party policy—not necessarily the idealistic one—to which all Democrats adhered whenever in power.

To counter opposition cries of "Free Trade Democracy," the Democrats chipped away at the soft spots in the recently acquired Republican protectionist armor. Invariably the Democrats praised the tariff of 1846 as the most judicious and equitable tariff the country ever had experienced, under which "work was plenty, . . . wages were good, and prosperity was all over the country." But the Republicans, so the Democrats charged, replaced the tariff of 1846 with the free trade tariff of 1857; a Republican congressman from Ohio, Lewis D. Campbell, proposed it and a Republican majority in Congress passed it. Democrats additionally claimed that free traders infested the Republican ranks: William Cullen Bryant, David Wilmot, the editors of the Chicago *Daily Tribune*, and the wool manufacturers of Massachusetts. Democrats argued that only their party was capable of obtaining adequate tariffs that would deal justly with all the varied interests of the nation.[23]

Of course the Democrats refused to acknowledge that the admin-

21. Democratic convention at Burlington, N.J., in *Daily True American* (Trenton, N.J.), September 15, 1858, Easton (Pa.) *Argus*, October 7, 1858; Easton county meeting in Easton (Pa.) *Argus*, August 19, 1858.

22. Pittsburgh *Morning Post*, July 22, August 18, 1858; *Compiler* (Gettysburg), September 27, 1858; *Genius of Liberty* (Uniontown, Pa.), August 26, 1858.

23. *Democratic Watchman* (Bellefonte, Pa.), October 7, 1858; *Compiler* (Gettys-

istration had any complicity in allowing Lawrence Myers to purchase Scotch water pipes for the Washington Aqueduct. The report was "a falsehood upon its face." Opposition leaders blamed the incident upon Buchanan, but actually the administration could do nothing. Contracts with the federal government were open to all companies; the lowest bidder won. When Myers found the price of Pennsylvania pipes too high he went abroad. To preclude a repetition of this incident Democrats proposed a law that would prohibit the purchase of foreign goods in the construction of American public works.[24]

Protection absorbed a great deal of the Democrats' campaign efforts, but the issue did not eradicate all other topics. In certain localities peculiar issues cropped up, such as a huge furor that erupted in Allegheny and Washington counties over a taxation question. In other counties Democrats campaigned on the issues of the sale of the Mainline Canal, the tonnage tax, and liquor laws.[25] The party of Jackson also tried to warn immigrants of nativist sentiments in the People's party. The most reiterated claim of the Keystone State Democracy was that the Republicans intended to legislate Negro equality.[26]

William Bigler inspected the health of the Democratic party in late July and wrote to Buchanan that "it is not half so bad as represented by the opposition Press nor even as believed to be by some of our own party." However, Bigler had to agree that the odds favored an opposition victory. Throughout the campaign, administration supporters worried about the raids of the Douglas men. Democrats even feared losing Berks County, a party stronghold that was the residence of J. Glancy Jones. Anti-Lecompton sentiment and Jones's statement at the

burg), July 19, September 6, 13, 27, 1858; Bedford (Pa.) *Gazette*, July 16, August 13, 20, 27, 1858; *Democratic Press* (York, Pa.), September 28, 1858.

24. Erie (Pa.) *Weekly Observer*, September 11, 1858; *Allegheny Mountain Echo* (Johnstown, Pa.), August 25, 1858; *Democratic Press* (York, Pa.), September 21, 1858.

25. Michael F. Holt, *Forging a Majority: The Formation of the Republican Party in Pittsburgh, 1848–1860* (New Haven, Conn., 1969), 244–59, emphasizes the importance of repudiation sentiment in Allegheny County. No evidence that I have seen indicates that the railroad question in Allegheny County extended much further than that area of the state. No newspaper I researched touted a local issue to the extent that repudiation was touted in Pittsburgh. The singularity of the proceedings in Allegheny County was appreciated by newspapers in New York and Philadelphia, which commented on the efforts to repudiate debts in that area. But no other county ever wormed into the columns of the major daily presses because of a similar local circumstance.

26. Easton (Pa.) *Argus*, July 8, August 5, 19, 26, 1858; *Compiler* (Gettysburg), June 21, September 7, 1858; Pittsburgh *Morning Post*, October 8, 11, 12, 1858.

end of the last session of Congress that no revision of the tariff was required worked visibly against his reelection.[27]

The organ for the Buchanan administration, the Washington *Union*, put forward the best face possible. Lecompton was "sunk out of sight and thought" and no longer troubled the Democracy, the editors asserted; the "opposition, on the contrary, are demoralized, paralyzed and divided." Nonetheless, just prior to voting day, one friend of Buchanan indicated that he believed "we will lose our state ticket, and our own county ticket, and a majority of our state representatives." He added, somewhat bewilderedly, that there seemed to be an "undercurrent at work, that we cannot check."[28] This was not quite correct; what was at work was not an undercurrent but a deluge.

Early reports seemed auspicious for the administration. The South was securely in Democratic hands, Missouri had gone solidly Democratic, and Maine's Democrats reduced the Republicans' majority. In late September news of Democratic victory in California arrived.[29] Then came the great October contests in the crucial states of Ohio, Indiana, and Pennsylvania. The results were not to the liking of the Democrats. In Pennsylvania the Democrats' congressional delegation was virtually eradicated, and anti-Lecompton Democrats won reelection in Indiana and Ohio. The news did not brighten in November. Illinois returned the renegade Douglas to the Senate and reelected the Illinois contingent of anti-Lecompton House Democrats. The administration, it seemed, had been thoroughly routed.

The Panic of 1857 indeed had an impact upon the northern congressional elections of 1858, although its electoral influence was perhaps more limited than one might expect in light of the general recession in the northern economy. As the overwhelming literary evidence suggests, the state of Pennsylvania exhibited the most emphatic political response to the business conditions wrought by the financial collapse. This response can be demonstrated quantitatively, and by extending the analysis some insight can be offered as to the operation of economic issues in mid-nineteenth-century American politics.

27. William Bigler to James Buchanan, July 30, 1858, Henry M. Phillips to James Buchanan, August 5, 1858, both in Buchanan Papers; Lebanon (Pa.) *Courier*, June 25, 1858; New York *Daily Tribune*, September 27, 28, 1858.
28. Washington (D.C.) *Union*, September 23, 1858; Charles W. Carrigan to James Buchanan, October 10, 1858, in Buchanan Papers.
29. Washington (D.C.) *Union*, September 30, 1858.

Two criteria were established to determine which states reacted politically to the Panic of 1857. First, if groups in a state voted in response to economic conditions, then there had to be a public discussion of those conditions. If the Panic of 1857 created serious dislocations in a state's economy that persisted over many months, it seems safe to assume that contemporaries would have vented their discontent publicly and that political leaders would have tried to capture disaffected voters by the articulation of an economic program. An absence of controversy over business conditions probably indicates that economic concerns were not significant factors in shaping voters' party preferences. Second, if voters did respond to an issue, economic or otherwise, then that response should appear in electoral results. Because the elections of 1858 were congressional elections (usually combined with a variety of state elections), one expects that an issue important to those voters would have produced alterations in the percentage of votes obtained by the parties and a change in the political composition of the state's congressional delegation. Even though economic issues might have been widely discussed, if no shifts can be found in popular support for the parties, then it becomes difficult to argue that the issues elevated by the Panic of 1857 had any appreciable effect on the election's outcome.

Most northern states did not exhibit any marked swing in party preferences. A comparison between the congressional elections of 1856 and 1858 fails to show any startling congressional conquests by the Republicans, although in Ohio and Indiana the party did add several new congressmen to the ranks. In Wisconsin and Michigan the Republicans actually fared worse in 1858 than they had in 1856, and most northern states did not generate any sustained discussion of economic programs except for Pennsylvania and New Jersey. Yet in New Jersey the Republicans gained only one extra seat; the Democracy, anti-Lecompton or otherwise, retained its popularity (see Appendix A for a listing of party winners in selected northern congressional districts in 1856 and 1858).

Two states, Pennsylvania and New York, did experience an upheaval in the party composition of their congressional delegations. In New York's case, however, the main factor at work seems to have been Democratic party divisions, stemming from the Lecompton issue, and from internal feuds among local party chieftains. The Democrats had won twelve congressional districts out of a total of thirty-three in 1856; in 1858 they captured only four. Yet most of these losses came in New York City where party factionalism was greatest. The squabbling party elements produced their own candidates and thus divided the total Democratic vote. Republicans successfully captured a number of congressional seats in New York by pluralities, but the polls did not reveal any sudden upsurge in popular support for Republican nominees.[30]

Pennsylvania, however, was the center of the furor over the sinking fortunes of the administration. Unlike other northern states, Pennsylvania had been generally secure Democratic territory in the 1850s and had not been beholden to Stephen Douglas or to any other national party leader. In 1856 the people of the state sent fourteen Democrats to Congress while the opposition elected eleven. In 1858 the People's party took twenty-one congressional districts; of the four Democrats who were elected, one (John Hickman) soon converted to Republicanism and another (William Montgomery) gained reelection because opposition leaders fused behind his anti-Lecompton views. The crushing failure of the administration in the campaign of 1858 was truly the failure of Pennsylvania voters to conform to expectations (see Appendix A).[31]

The cause of the Democratic debacle in Pennsylvania has aroused the interest of historians because the reversal of party control was so complete and abrupt; Republicans acquired ten more congressional districts by absolute or near-absolute majorities. Scholars have usually offered three interpretations to explain this change in party fortunes. The older view was that the tariff issue pulled wavering Democrats into the Republican camp. Others have stressed the effects of party dissension within the Democracy and the impact of Buchanan's Lecompton policy. More recent investigations about the opposition victory point to the Republicans' ability to coalesce with the great number of Know-Nothings.[32]

Many of Pennsylvania's sixty-five counties exhibited strong political

30. See Appendix A; *Tribune Almanac*, 1859, 45–46; Collins, "The Politics of Particularism," 80–85; David E. Meerse, "The Northern Democratic Party and the Congressional Elections of 1858," *CWH*, XIX (1973), 129–31.

31. *Tribune Almanac*, 1859, 52–53; Washington (Pa.) *Reporter*, July 7, 14, August 11, September 1, 1858.

32. One historian who stresses the role of the tariff in producing the Pennsylvania results of 1858 is Eiselen, *The Rise of Pennsylvania Protectionism*, 246–48. Those who stress Democratic divisions because of Lecompton include Nichols, *The Disruption of American Democracy*, 203–206; and Nevins, *The Emergence of Lincoln*, I, 401–403. Those who believe that the ability of the Republicans to capture the nativist voters best explains the Pennsylvania election returns include Holt, *Forging a Majority*, 250–54; Collins, "The Democrats' Electoral Fortunes During the Lecompton Crisis," 328–29;

affiliations to only one party. Thus in the election of 1858 several counties maintained their usual party preference; seventeen counties continued voting for the Republicans in somewhat accustomed numbers, while seventeen other counties held to the Democratic standard.[33] There were counties, however, in which a considerable political variation was evident. One group of Pennsylvania counties (Blair, Chester, Dauphin, Delaware, Huntingdon, Jefferson, Lancaster, Snyder, Somerset, and Washington) had large numbers of nativists and old-line Whigs who represented a floating element in search of a political haven. In 1858 the Republican (or People's) party became their sanctuary.[34] Another collection of Pennsylvania counties displayed more startling political behavior. These counties switched from a Democratic majority to a Republican majority (Adams, Berks, Bucks, Carbon, Centre, Clinton, Columbia, Franklin, Juniata, Lehigh, Luzerne, Lycoming, Mifflin, Montgomery, Montour, Perry, Philadelphia, Schuylkill, Venango, and Wyoming.) The magnitude of party reversals in many of these counties was impressive. For example, the Democratic percentage of the total vote in Berks County fell from an 1856 congressional election figure of 71.6 to 49.9 percent in 1858; in Carbon County, from 63.2 to 42.3 percent; in Columbia, from 76.4 to 43.1 percent; in Luzerne, from 54.1 to 34.5 percent. This group of counties proved most significant because they not only included most of Pennsylvania's coal and iron regions but also accounted for most of the congressional districts lost by the Democrats.[35]

---

and Meerse, "The Northern Democratic Party and the Congressional Elections of 1858," 121, 129–33, 135–38.

33. Counties securely in the Republican camp were Allegheny, Armstrong, Beaver, Bradford, Butler, Crawford, Erie, Forest, Indiana, Lawrence, Lebanon, McKean, Mercer, Potter, Susquehanna, Tioga, Union, and Warren. The Democratic counties were Bedford, Cambria, Clarion, Clearfield, Cumberland, Elk, Fayette, Fulton, Greene, Monroe, Northampton, Northumberland, Pike, Sullivan, Wayne, Westmoreland, and York. Conclusions are based on calculations made from the *Tribune Almanac*, 1857, 1858, 1859, 1860, and 1861.

34. Based on calculations made from the *Tribune Almanac*, 1857, 1858, 1859, 1860, and 1861.

35. The Democrats lost districts 3, 4, 5, 7, 8, 11, 12, 15, 16, 17, and 24. The counties that switched political preferences, and the districts to which they belonged, given in parentheses, are: Philadelphia (3, 4, 5); Montgomery (5); Bucks (7); Lehigh (7); Berks (8); Schuylkill (11); Columbia (12); Luzerne (12); Montour (12); Wyoming (12); Centre (15); Clinton (15); Lycoming (15); Mifflin (15); Perry (16); Adams (17); Franklin (17); Juniata (17); Venango (24); Carbon (13).

The Pennsylvania opposition's victory in 1858 was largely the result of a political fusion between Americans and Republicans. In 1856 the American party tallied over 80,000 votes; in 1857 the American gubernatorial candidate Isaac Hazelhurst garnered nearly 28,000. But in 1858 the American party as a separate entity ceased to exist. Inspection of the vote totals in those counties in which Americans wielded the balance of power reveals that cooperation between Americans and Republicans in 1858 led to victory. Although the opposition went by several names—most commonly the People's party and at times the American-Republican party—it was the Americans who sacrificed their organizational identity; with much difficulty, the American party members were being metamorphosed into Republicans.

A number of circumstances enhanced the possibilities of a coalition between Pennsylvania Republicans and Americans in 1858. Americans had been losing popular support for the past few years, and it was only by fusing with some other party that they could hope to influence political direction. Also, the furor over Lecompton and the question of slavery extension may have sufficiently aroused nativists to forgo whatever reservations they had about the Republican party and join them in an anti-administration movement. But the most plausible explanation for the behavior of Pennsylvania nativists in 1858 appears to be their reaction to the Panic of 1857 and their support for a protective tariff. Whigs dominated the American party, and the love of Pennsylvania Whigs for the American System of Henry Clay was undiminished. During the Panic of 1857, Isaac Hazelhurst made it a point to campaign on the resurrection of the tariff of 1842.[36]

Protectionist doctrines were in many instances surprisingly similar to American party principles. Know-Nothing leaders advocated more stringent requirements for naturalization, a curb on foreign religious influences in American politics (especially Catholicism), a restoration of revolutionary ideals and values, an end to the spoils system and corrupt government, and an elevation of the principle of nationality. The anti-Catholic, anti-immigrant, and anti-corruption emphasis of the

---

36. Holt, *Forging a Majority*, 154–55; Philadelphia *Evening Bulletin*, October 12, 1857; Lancaster *Examiner and Herald*, December 2, 1857; *Miner's Journal* (Pottsville, Pa.), September 26, November 14, 1857; Roger Dewey Petersen, "The Reaction to a Heterogeneous Society: A Behavioral and Quantitative Analysis of Northern Voting Behavior 1845–1870, Pennsylvania a Test Case" (Ph.D. dissertation, University of Pittsburgh, 1970), 33.

Americans appeared in various county conventions and opposition appeals in 1858, but in many ways the tariff subsumed much of the nativist argument.[37] The nationalism inherent in the home market ideal, as in "PROTECTION TO AMERICAN INTERESTS AND AMERICAN LABOR" was attractive to former Know-Nothings.[38] There was also an implied antiforeign element in the protectionist appeal, for tariff supporters stressed that free trade allowed "foreign labor" to compete with American labor and that a high tariff would eliminate this competition.[39] The tariff therefore became in 1858 an adequate vehicle for the nativist sentiments of American party members. And because of the depression in Pennsylvania, the tariff issue had enough weight to permit Americans to overlook the feared radicalism and sectionalism of the Republicans so that cooperation between the two organizations could be achieved.

Quantitative analysis of the Pennsylvania elections of 1858 lends support to the hypothesis that the recession in 1858 played a major role in the Republican victory. The investigation was guided by a certain premise. It was assumed that the essential coalition of the Democrats had already been constructed and that it made little difference whether that coalition was based on ethnocultural or economic factors.

37. On the principles of the Know-Nothings, see Holt, *Forging a Majority*, 131–41; Jean H. Baker, *Ambivalent Americans: The Know-Nothing Party in Maryland* (Baltimore, 1977), 25–40; Ronald P. Formisano, *The Birth of Mass Political Parties: Michigan, 1827–1861* (Princeton, N.J., 1971), 219–39, 246–49. For Know Nothing influence in the Pennsylvania elections of 1858 see *Cambria Tribune* (Johnstown, Pa.), July 24, 1858; Lewistown (Pa.) *Gazette*, September 2, 1858; Lebanon (Pa.) *Courier*, September 17, 1858.

38. Harrisburg *Daily Telegraph*, October 8, 1858; see also Philadelphia *North American*, May 8, 1858. It is certain that the Know-Nothings coalesced with the Republicans in Pennsylvania, but in other states that circumstance is the subject of some controversy. Those stressing the coalition of Know-Nothings and Republicans include Holt, *The Political Crisis of the 1850s*, 208–11; Thomas B. Alexander, "The Dimensions of Voter Partisan Constancy in Presidential Elections from 1840 to 1860," in Stephen E. Maizlish and John J. Kushma (eds.), *Essays on American Antebellum Politics, 1840–1860* (College Station, Tex., 1982), 70–121. For those insisting upon the minimal fusion of Americans and Republicans—or who at least emphasize the Republican refusal to accede to American party programs—see Dale Baum, *The Civil War Party System: The Case of Massachusetts, 1848–1876* (Chapel Hill, 1984), 42–53; Stephen L. Hansen, *The Making of the Third Party System: Voters and Parties in Illinois, 1850–1876* (Ann Arbor, Mich., 1980), 59–74, 82–89.

39. Lewistown (Pa.) *Gazette*, October 14, 1858; *Cambria Tribune* (Johnstown, Pa.), August 14, 1858. The role of the tariff in bringing the Republicans and Americans together can be seen in the speech of Isaac Hazelhurst to a People's Club in Philadelphia *Evening Bulletin*, November 1, 1859.

Because the Panic of 1857 was probably not an event of sufficient magnitude to realign political affiliations, the most it could have accomplished was the shearing of some groups or individuals away from the existing Democratic coalition. Hence the discussion that follows involves the characteristics of groups who left the Democracy or who joined the Republicans; it does not seek to elucidate the groups who composed the core of the party.[40]

In 1858 the Democrats suffered a reduction in their percentage vote totals in almost all counties, and this reduction was distinctly tied to the degree to which a region had iron and coal interests. Correlation coefficients (Pearson's r) were computed for several alternative circumstances in the 1858 Pennsylvania congressional election. The first set of calculations were based upon regressing a Democratic vote loss, ignoring anti-Lecompton confusions, upon the percentage of workers engaged in iron and coal enterprises in each county and upon the percentage of those in the county involved in all types of manufacturing pursuits. The resulting coefficients were -.68 and -.71 respectively. These rather strong negative correlations indicate that the more a county's work force was employed in iron and coal operations (or manufacturing), the greater was the Democratic loss. When the uncertainty of the anti-Lecompton fusions are thrown into the calculations of the Democratic vote losses, the results are far less emphatic; the Democratic vote loss regressed on the percentage of male iron and coal workers yields a weak -.33, and on percentage of all manufacturing operatives, a -.30.[41] The anti-Lecompton figures require careful handling.

40. A caution is necessary with regard to regressions involving percentage gains or losses from one election to another. If a group is highly associated with an increase or decrease in percentage of votes gained, that only means that this particular variable is contributing to additions or defections of one of the parties. It does not mean that the entire group has necessarily become part of the coalition. In some instances, a group correlating highly with a gain in one party's totals does not correlate at all with the party's percentage of total votes cast.

41. The results were computed on an SPSSX program. The Democratic loss was calculated by subtracting the average Democratic vote in the 1856 presidential, congressional, and canal commissioner elections from the Democratic percentage vote in 1858. Democratic vote losses were recorded as negative numbers; hence a significant negative correlation means that Democratic vote losses increased (became more negative) as the value of the independent variable increased. The regression equation of Democratic loss on iron and coal workers is: intercept -3.992, slope $-.395$, $r = -.683$, $R^2 = .466$, $N = 61$. The regression equation of Democratic loss on the ratio of all manufacturing employed males to adult white male population is: intercept $= -.651$, slope $-.372$, $r = -.713$, $R^2 = .508$, $N = 61$. The regression equation for Democratic vote loss in-

Often the situation was confounded by a fusion of Republicans and others with anti-Lecompton Democrats, and therefore it is not certain exactly what such vote totals say about the normal numerical support for the Democratic party. Multiple regressions confirmed the potency of the manufacturing/iron and coal worker variables in explaining the variation of Democratic percentage vote losses (exclusive of anti-Lecompton balloting).[42]

Democratic voters in the iron and coal regions indicated that they were responding to more than local stimulae by the way they cast their ballots. In state contests they offered more support for the party's nominees than in congressional races. Indeed, in several instances, given the minor fluctuations of the total vote, it seems an almost inescapable conclusion that some Democrats split their tickets (see Table 2). The comparison between congressional and state races demonstrates that local issues were probably not responsible for the variation in Democratic vote totals.

---

cluding the anti-Lecompton vote on iron and coal workers is: intercept -2.752, slope $-.219$, $r = -.322$, $R^2 = .104$, $N = 63$. The regression equation for Democratic loss including the anti-Lecompton vote on ratio of males in manufacturing is: intercept -1.336, slope $-.182$, $r = -.305$, $R^2 = .093$, $N = 63$. If one changes the standard for the Democratic vote to the county presidential percentage vote in 1856 or the gubernatorial percentage vote in 1857, the correlation coefficients are still strongly negative.

42. The multiple regressions were performed with independent variables measuring church organization (by available seating), age groups, farm capital, industrial capital, foreign born, farm size, crop production, distance from the southern border, and distance from the eastern border. These were winnowed down on the basis of best bivariate correlation with the Democratic loss variable and multicollinearity (independent variables related at .600 or higher were not permitted). The F-significance of an independent variable's contribution to R^2 had to be .15 or better for the variable to enter the equation. A multiple regression using straight Democratic vote losses as the dependent variable (excluding anti-Lecompton totals) and the iron and coal employees as one of the independent variables yielded a result of multiple $r = .807$, adjusted $R^2 = .63$. The independent variables were iron and coal employees (b $= -.319$, beta $= -.551$, F-significance $= .000$), distance of county seat from the eastern border, in miles (b $= .039$, beta $= .428$, F-significance $= .000$), and the production of hay per white adult male (b $= .756$, beta $= .164$, F-significance $= .072$). When the straight Democratic loss was used with the male manufacturing ratio, the multiple regression yielded a multiple r of .791 and an adjusted R^2 of .605. The independent variables that entered the equation were: male manufacturing employees (b $= -.353$, beta $= -.674$, F-significance $= .000$); distance East (b $= .034$, beta $= .375$, F-significance $= .000$), and percent Episcopal in 1860 (b $= .351$, beta $= .159$, F-significance $= .093$). However, the Episcopal variable is evidently a suppressor variable. Neither the iron and coal nor the male manufacturing variable contributed to explaining the variance of Democratic losses when anti-Lecompton votes were factored in.

Table 2

Comparison Between Pennsylvania Iron and Coal County Democratic Returns in the 1858 Congressional Election and the Concurrent 1858 State Supreme Court Election

County	Dem Vote, Cong (%)	Dem Vote, Sup Ct (%)	Change in Dem Vote (Col. 2 − Col. 1)	Change in Total Vote Cast (%)
Schuylkill	22.98 [a]	49.07	26.09	0.44
Monteur	38.07	48.64	10.57	3.10
Carbon	42.83	46.56	3.73	2.42
Luzerne	34.50	48.64	14.14	−2.29
Cambria	57.21	55.69	−1.52	−5.36
Armstrong	45.21	45.64	0.43	−0.84
Northumberland	44.17 [a]	59.99	15.82	−2.67
Allegheny	34.98	39.29	4.31	12.04
Lehigh	48.88	51.54	2.66	−0.40
Columbia	43.05	56.60	13.55	0.33
Blair	35.90	38.22	2.32	0.64
Clarion	56.38	61.53	5.15	−0.59
Chester	33.11	39.15	6.04	−0.26
Centre	42.83	46.56	3.73	−0.86
Berks	49.94	65.77	15.83	0.37

SOURCE: Computations made from *Tribune Almanac*, 1859
[a] Figures reflect straight Democratic ticket only; with the Democratic splinter groups added in, the Schuylkill total would be 50.20 and the Northumberland total would be 57.78.
Legend: Dem = Democratic; Cong = congressional election 1858; Sup Ct = Supreme Court election 1858

Republican gains (in percentage of the vote cast) were, however, of a slightly different character than those of Democratic losses. Republican gains in 1858 would have mirrored Democratic losses in 1858 if the opposition had been unified in 1856, for the standard used to calculate Democratic losses was based on elections in 1856. But in 1856 the opposition was not united; instead, the Republicans and Americans vied against each other for the privilege of being the North's other major party. The consequence is that Republicans obtained voters from groups dissimilar, at times, from those who defected from the Democracy. The most outstanding feature of the additions to Republican county percentage voting strength is that they were highly associated with the American party vote for Fillmore in 1856. The correlation between increases in Republican percentage of total vote, 1856–1858, and the American percentage of total vote in 1856 is .852. This high correlation reinforces the interpretation that the Americans moved solidly into the Republican (or People's party) camp in the 1858 congressional races.[43]

In terms of social attributes, the groups joining the Republicans were not especially connected with the iron and coal counties when the computation is made with 1856 as the base year. But when Republican gains are calculated using 1857 as the base year, a moderate association between Republican voting increases and industrial undertakings is visible. However, bivariate regressions also indicate that Republican gains matched well with other social factors: age categories, farm size, and, of special interest, the two German Protestant sects of German Reformed and German Lutheran (see Table 3). It appears, therefore, that Republican increases in 1858 not only came from nativist sources but also had an ethnocultural dimension.[44] Multiple regression for Republican advances, using 1856 as the base year, indicates that the most important variables contributing to Republican county increments were German Lutheran adherents (positive), middle-sized farms (negative), and youth (positive).[45] When the base year of 1857 is

43. The regression equation (1856–1858 Republican gains on percent voting for Fillmore 1856) is: intercept 2.39, slope 1.09, $r = .852$, $R^2 = .726$, $N = 64$. Republican gains thus powerfully correlate with American party voting in 1856, but it should be noted that the percentage of total vote for Republicans in 1858 does not correlate with previous American party performances. Republican total vote percentage in 1858 correlated with the American party vote in the 1854 state supreme court race yields, $r = .058$; with the 1856 Fillmore vote, $r = -.088$; with the 1857 Hazelhurst vote, $r = -.046$. Thus the overall coalition of the Republicans in 1858 does not bear a resemblance to the voting patterns of nativists 1854–1857, but the additions to the Republicans in 1858 clearly came from the nativist camp, or at least are associated with high American party vote totals in 1856.

44. See William A. Gudelunas, Jr., and William G. Shade, *Before the Molly Maguires: The Emergence of the Ethno-Religious Factor in the Politics of the Lower Anthracite Region, 1844–1872* (New York, 1976), 71–77. Gudelunas and Shade indicate that the swing group in Schuylkill County was urban German Protestants. Note that the negative correlation in Table 3 is between Republican gains and pietism, not Republican total vote and pietism.

45. The statistics of the equation are: dependent variable is Republican gains 1856–1858; independent variables are German Lutheran attendance (b = .653, beta = .402, F-significance = .000), farms 20–99 acres, divided by white male population (b =

Table 3

Bivariate Correlations of Republican Gains, 1856–1858 and
1857–1858, with Selected Socioeconomic Factors

Independent Variable	Republican Gain[a] 1856–1858 (r)	Republican Gain[b] 1857–1858 (r)
% county iron and coal employees	.205	.356*
% county manufacturing employees	.243	.445*
Industrial capital per white adult male	.327*	.530*
Farms 20–99 acres per white adult male	−.562*	−.424*
German Reformed attendance	.481*	.345*
Lutheran attendance	.570*	.331*
Presbyterian attendance	−.337*	−.251
Pietist attendance	−.471*	−.400*
Distance from southern border	−.325*	.032
Distance from eastern border	−.308	−.385*
% Age 20–29	.314*	.186
% Age 30–39	.101	.457*
% Age 50 plus	−.311*	−.540*
N = 64		

*p < .01

[a] Percentage Republican congressional vote 1858 minus percentage Republican presidential vote 1856

[b] Percentage Republican congressional vote 1858 minus percentage Republican gubernatorial vote 1857

employed, multiple regression reveals that a variable indicating manufacturing endeavor (industrial capital per white adult male) becomes a

---

−.682, beta = −.346, F-significance = .002), and age 20–29, divided by white adult males (b = 1.397, beta = .151, F-significance = .131); multiple r = .686, adjusted R^2 = .445.

significant and positive contributing factor in explaining the pattern of 1858 Republican advances between 1857 and 1858.[46]

Several forces operated in the Pennsylvania congressional elections of 1858 that make interpretation of the results somewhat uncertain, yet the statistical and literary evidence tends to confirm the view that the recession spawned by the Panic of 1857 was the predominant factor in the opposition's success. Certainly the anti-Lecompton movement hurt the Democracy, but the revolt, except in a few localities, did not assume major proportions. Although the reelection of anti-Lecompton candidates could rightfully be seen as a repudiation of the administration's policies, there is little in the returns to indicate that rank-and-file Democrats in Pennsylvania (or in other northern states) were actually deserting the party because of Lecompton. And in Pennsylvania, at least, the Panic of 1857 unquestionably worked to propel those who voted for Fillmore in 1856 into coalition with the Republicans (or People's party). Although this process was probably at work as soon as the presidential contest of 1856 ended, the hard times of 1858 only made the shortcomings of the Democracy more obvious to nativists and provided an additional and pertinent justification for them to join the Republicans. The People's party in 1858 made a plea that the reestablishment of a protective tariff would elevate wages and cure unemployment; given the hard times in the state, this issue seems to have been attractive to a small number of Democrats and the majority of those who voted for Fillmore in 1856. The Panic of 1857 was largely responsible for the opposition's success.[47]

That Pennsylvania's congressional election in 1858 probably hinged

46. The procedure eliminated the economic variable of farm size because of multicollinearity. The equation obtained, entered in hierarchical fashion, is: industrial capital (b = .023, beta = .252, F-significance = .056), pietism (b = −.146, beta = −.246, F-significance = .022), and age, fifty years and older (b = −1.263, beta = −.327, F-significance = .012), multiple r = .639, adjusted R^2 = .378.

47. The counties with splinter anti-Lecompton movements were Philadelphia (the First Congressional District), Chester, Delaware, Northumberland, and Schuylkill. There is great difficulty in distinguishing between the effects of the anti-Lecompton movement and reaction to the depression in the 1858 electoral results. Most of the time the two factors simply reinforced each other, and there is no obvious way to design a quantitative test for measuring the impact of dissident Democrats as there is for reaction to depression. A recent article by Bruce Collins on the Pennsylvania congressional election of 1858 reaches many of the same conclusions presented here, although Collins is less emphatic on the role of the tariff issue than I am. See Bruce Collins, "The Democrats' Loss of Pennsylvania in 1858," *Pennsylvaania Magazine of History and Biography*, CIX (1985), 499–536.

on economic issues and conditions does not reveal whether economic forces, rather than ethnocultural ones, were pivotal in the destruction of the second party system.[48] By focusing on Democratic voting losses over time, however, it may be possible to make some generalizations about the impact of economic affairs upon the Democratic coalition. Extending the regression of Democratic vote losses between 1857 and 1860 upon a number of selected economic variables reveals that the correlation coefficients become strong only in 1858 (see Table 4). The continued statistical significance of the correlations between manufacturing counties and Democratic vote losses after 1858, although weak, may be indicative of a lingering disposition of the iron and coal counties to vote for the opposition after 1858, but certainly not with the same strength as in that earlier year.

Using another standard for Democratic vote losses, it is possible to see the impact of an economic issue in Pennsylvania's politics from a broader perspective. The Democratic percentages of the total vote in the presidential elections of 1836, 1840, 1844, and 1848 were averaged; this became the Jacksonian standard for Pennsylvania counties in the second party system (in cases of new counties or third parties, gubernatorial and congressional elections were substituted). The difference between the Democratic vote percentages in elections from 1854 to 1860 and the Jacksonian standard were then calculated and regressed upon variables indicating economic endeavors. The resulting correlations are presented in Table 5. These coefficients demonstrate that economic factors, especially the state's industrial pursuits, did not usually affect the Democrats' ability to maintain their coalition; most of the coefficients reveal insignificant relationships between Democratic vote losses (based on the Jacksonian system) and the extent of manufacturing in the counties. However, the coefficients in Table 5 do indicate that at times economic factors could upset normal voting patterns.[49]

48. On the ethnocultural interpretation of political realignment in the 1850s consult Paul Kleppner, *The Third Electoral System, 1853–1892: Parties, Voters, and Political Cultures* (Chapel Hill, 1979), 58–72; Joel H. Silbey, "The Surge of Republican Power: Partisan Antipathy, American Social Conflict, and the Coming of the Civil War," in Maizlish and Kushma (eds.), *Essays on American Antebellum Politics, 1840–1860*, 199–229. For a questioning of the stress on ethnocultural factors see Dale Baum, "Know-Nothingism and the Republican Majority in Massachusetts: The Political Realignment of the 1850s," *JAH*, LXIV (1978), 959–86; Hansen, *The Making of the Third Party System*, xv, 37–39.

49. Multiple regressions were performed on the Democratic loss variables. Virtually without exception the variable carrying most weight was the distance of the county seat

Table 4

Bivariate Correlations of Democratic Vote Loss with Economic Variables: Pennsylvania Elections, 1857–1860

Independent Variable	Gov 1857	Cong 1858	Sup Ct 1858	Canal Cmr 1859	Pres 1860	Cong 1860	Gov 1860
Democratic Vote Loss in Election of:							
% county iron and coal employees	+.12	−.68*	−.46*	−.23	−.41*	−.38*	−.36*
N = ( )	(62)	(59)	(62)	(62)	(62)	(59)	(62)
% county manufacturing employees	+.03	−.71*	−.51*	−.31*	−.38*	−.46*	−.38*
N = ( )	(62)	(59)	(62)	(62)	(62)	(59)	(62)
Industrial capital per white adult male	−.09	−.62*	−.57*	−.36*	−.34*	−.52*	−.41*
N = ( )	(62)	(59)	(62)	(62)	(62)	(59)	(62)
Farms, 20–99 acres per white adult male	.13	.45*	.47*	.49*	.28	.44*	.38*
N = ( )	(62)	(59)	(62)	(62)	(62)	(59)	(62)

*p < .01

NOTE: Standard for Democratic vote loss is based on the presidential, congressional, and canal commissioner elections of 1856. The counties of Forest, Snyder, and Sullivan were excluded from analysis. The lower number of cases for the congressional election of 1858 is the result of anti-Lecompton fusions in several counties.

LEGEND: Gov = gubernatorial election; Cong = congressional election; Sup Ct = Supreme Court election; Canal Cmr = canal commissioner election; Pres = presidential election

---

from the southern border of the state. For example, the multiple regression for 1856 Democratic losses yielded independent variables of: distance from southern border (b = −.158, beta = −.628, F-significance = .000), pietism (combination of evangelical groups) (b = −.145, beta = −.246, F-significance = .007), and production of rye (b = .203, beta = .172, F-significance = .042), multiple r = .796, adjusted R^2 = .615. The strength of the variable measuring distance from the southern border indicates that Democrats suffered greater losses the further north the county. This finding lends credence to the idea that the parties reflected different cultures, that distance from the South and southern influences was an important element in the erosion of the Second Party System. See Kleppner, *The Third Electoral System*, 58–59.

Table 5

Bivariate Correlations of Democratic Vote Loss (Jacksonian Standard) with Selected Economic Variables: Pennsylvania Elections, 1854–1860

| | | | Democratic Vote Loss in Election of: | | | | | | | | | | |
Independent Variable	Cong 1854	Sup Ct 1854	Canal Cmr 1855	Pres 1856	Cong 1856	Gov 1857	Cong 1858	Sup Ct 1858	Canal Cmr 1859	Pres 1860	Cong 1860	Gov 1860
% county iron and coal employees	−.17	−.04	+.28*	+.12	+.07	+.16	−.31**	−.10	−.01	−.19	−.06	.00
N = ( )	(62)	(62)	(62)	(62)	(62)	(62)	(59)	(62)	(62)	(62)	(60)	(62)
% county manufacturing employees	−.13	+.07	+.34**	+.16	+.13	+.18	−.29*	−.07	−.04	−.22*	−.08	+.03
N = ( )	(62)	(62)	(62)	(62)	(62)	(62)	(59)	(62)	(62)	(62)	(60)	(62)
Industrial capital per white adult male	−.15	+.12	+.32**	+.19	+.22	+.20	−.19	−.05	−.04	−.21	−.08	+.07
N = ( )	(62)	(62)	(62)	(62)	(62)	(62)	(59)	(62)	(62)	(62)	(60)	(62)
Farms, 20–99 acres per white adult male	+.15	−.23	−.47**	−.47**	−.43**	−.43**	−.13	−.25*	−.17	−.08	−.16	−.33**
N = ( )	(62)	(62)	(62)	(62)	(62)	(62)	(59)	(62)	(62)	(62)	(60)	(62)

*p < .05   **p < .01

LEGEND: Canal Cmr = canal commissioner election; Cong = congressional election; Gov = gubernatorial election; Pres = presidential election; Sup Ct = Supreme Court election

The analysis of the Pennsylvania congressional elections of 1858 presented herein does not challenge the validity of the ethnocultural interpretation of the political realignment of the 1850s. But the results do not show economic factors to be insignificant. It would seem that in the mid-nineteenth-century United States a moderately severe economic recession could generate a short-term disruption of voting habits, but this disruption would not be likely to endure. Thus social and cultural factors may well generally describe the genesis and longevity of a realignment, but it is still possible for momentary voting gyrations to arise from other influences.[50] In particular, economic circumstances may well have determined the speed at which a realignment took place. Certainly economic events could shatter temporary political coalitions and forge new ones. In the case of Pennsylvania in 1858, the Panic momentarily gave the opposition overwhelming strength in the congressional districts and, in the longer run, speeded the absorption of Whigs and Americans into the Republican party.

The Pennsylvania election returns of October 12, 1858, dumbfounded the nation. "Never, never has any public man encountered so stern and withering a rebuke as has Mr. Buchanan in the result of the election in Pennsylvania on Tuesday," wrote the Richmond *Whig*. The election was a "rout," a "revolution," a "complete repudiation" of the administration. The victory even exceeded the most sanguine expectations of Pennsylvania's Republican and opposition leaders. In Rhode Island the Republican editor of the Providence *Daily Tribune* told his readers that the results in Pennsylvania's election "are too astounding to be passed over in silence." Another Providence paper printed a typical comment: "There is something in the Pennsylvania election that is difficult to stop writing about."[51]

James Buchanan was flattened by the blow Pennsylvania delivered to his presidency. The results, he wrote, "I have anticipated for three months. Yesterday . . . we had a merry time of it, laughing among other things over our crushing defeat. It is so great that it is absurd."

50. The view that momentary economic disturbances could generate short-term political movements has been elaborated by Paul Kleppner, *The Third Electoral System*, 361–66.

51. Quoted from Richmond (Va.) *Whig*, October 15, 1858; Lebanon (Pa.) *Courier*, October 22, 1858; Evansville (Ind.) *Daily Journal*, October 15, 20, 1858; *Raftsman's Journal* (Clearfield, Pa.), October 20, 1858; Providence *Daily Tribune*, October 16, 1858; Providence *Daily Journal*, October 16, 1858.

Laughter perhaps soothed the pain temporarily, but the president required an explanation for the defeat. A few of his Pennsylvania associates determined that the problem of party division was the central element that destroyed the Pennsylvania Democracy, not any specific issue. The debacle occurred because of "the rebellion of our own men." The party broke into factions that warred against each other and demoralized the rank and file.[52]

But most of his friends pointed to the tariff as the factor most damaging to the party. "The fatal blow," emphasized a Harrisburg correspondent, "was received in the manufacturing districts, viz. Phillips', Landy's, O. Jones', J. G. Jones—in Northampton, Lehigh, Schuylkill, and worst of all in Landy's district, made up as it is throughout with Iron and Coal interests." Buchanan generally accepted the analysis of his friends. In the city of Philadelphia the president believed the Lecompton controversy generated the party turmoil that resulted in Republican victory, but in the hinterland he pointed to the economic distress as the culprit. Writing to George M. Wharton, Buchanan offered his opinion on the party's dismal performance:

> In the past three months I had anticipated a defeat in Pennsylvania; but not one of such a Waterloo character. This was caused by a suspension of nearly all the Iron Works in the State & the great number of laborers thus cast out of employment. This has often before occurred. If the Tariff on Iron had been a hundred percent the same distress would have existed. The administration are as justly responsible for the motions of the Comet as for the low price of Iron. In the natural course of events business will revive before the next election & then with similar justice we shall enjoy the benefits of producing a return of "good times." So the world goes & we cannot prevent it.[53]

Democratic journalists in Pennsylvania readily concurred with the president's assessment. Above all other issues, they pointed to the economic recession as the agent of their electoral demise. The editor of the Allentown *Democrat* stated that the "prime cause" for the debacle was "*hard times.*" He continued, "Political theories, partizan [*sic*] machinery, and party drill, are as nothing when men are interested for their daily bread." One paper, which earlier had blamed Buchanan's

---

52. James Buchanan to Harriet Lane, October 15, 1858, in John Bassett Moore (ed.), *The Works of James Buchanan* (Philadelphia, 1908–11), X, 229; Benjamin H. Brewster to James Buchanan, October 16, 1858, in Buchanan Papers.

53. David R. Porter to James Buchanan, October 14, 1858, James Buchanan to George M. Wharton, October 16, 1858, both in Buchanan Papers.

Lecompton policy for the reversal, complained that Republicans disguised themselves as the "peculiar friends of protection to American Industry" and made the Democrats look like the party of free trade; "How much these base falsehoods contributed to their success let the returns in Luzerne, Columbia, Montour, Berks, Lehigh, Carbon and every Coal and Iron region in Pennsylvania answer."[54]

Pennsylvania Democrats from the president to party managers to newspaper editors often explicitly stated that laborers voted for the opposition in order to receive relief from the depression. While they did not portray a mass exodus of workingmen from the Democratic party, these observers evidently believed a sufficient number of laborers switched parties to create the massive Democratic defeat. The course of the Pennsylvania Democracy on this issue became clear. Democrats would not abandon their ancient and hallowed economic tenets on the tariff, would not admit the theory of protectionism to be true, and would not shift blame for the Panic of 1857 from the banks to the tariff, but they did agree that the tariff was too low and that the only remedy was "the re-establishment of the Democratic Tariff of 1846."[55]

Opposition leaders in Pennsylvania were, of course, jubilant. A significant number of the People's party saw the welcome election results originating from popular disgust at Buchanan's Lecompton policy. Generally, however, they used both the Lecompton and tariff issues to explain Republican ascendancy; they were the twin pillars of Republican victory in Pennsylvania. "The tyranny and despotism of the slave-led powers at Washington have been emphatically condemned, and their Kansas policy repudiated," affirmed the editor of the Harrisburg *Daily Telegraph*, "and with equal emphasis has the American policy of Protection to Home Industry been sustained and vindicated." The political action of the laborers was explicit in Republican journals: "The laboring classes, who saw our furances and ore banks idle, and themselves without employment, while foreign labor was furnishing us with iron," accounted for the reversal in party fortunes.[56] The Lecompton

54. Quotes in Allentown (Pa.) *Democrat* quoted by *Luzerne Union* (Wilkes-Barre), October 27, 1858, and the *Democratic Watchman* (Bellefonte, Pa.), October 28, 1858; Easton (Pa.) *Argus*, November 4, 1858. Editors did list other reasons for the defeat, such as internal party divisions and Republican trickery.

55. Bedford (Pa.) *Gazette*, November 5, 1858.

56. *Agitator* (Wellsboro, Pa.), November 4, 1858; *Bradford Reporter* (Towanda, Pa.), October 21, 1858; Harrisburg *Daily Telegraph*, October 13, 1858; Lewistown (Pa.) *Gazette*, October 14, 1858.

opposition therefore knew precisely what they had to do to keep the voters in their camp: raise the tariff and stop the expansion of slavery.

Pennsylvanians of both parties concluded that the tariff was the supreme issue in the state's congressional elections of 1858. This interpretation was not a secret confined to Pennsylvania; it was vitally important that the rest of the nation understand the reasons for the demise of the Keystone State Democracy. The analysis by Pennsylvanians of their political upheaval filtered rapidly to the other states. By December, at the latest, no politically aware person could not have understood the primacy of the tariff question in Pennsylvania.[57]

But recognition of the novel situation in Pennsylvania did not immediately lead the political parties to make an accommodation with protectionism. Former Democrats in the Republican party chastised the old-line Whig element that welcomed the return of the tariff issue. Other Republicans worried that the new emphasis on economic matters might displace the central question of slavery expansion. The New York *Evening Post* spoke for many Republicans when it declared that the "true policy of the country is not to increase, but to diminish the taxes on goods brought from abroad." The northern Democracy also did not indicate much willingness to compromise their low tariff principles. James Sheahan of the Chicago *Daily Times* offered to aid manufacturers by lowering tariff rates on raw products used by industrialists, but this direction was the opposite of that which Pennsylvanians favored. John A. Dix, a prominent New York Democrat who knew the strength of Pennsylvania's tariff sentiments, dismissed any change in policy: "Nothing could be more irrational. The spirit of the age is against commercial restriction."[58]

More important for the future of the Democracy was the response of southerners to the resurrected tariff issue, for southerners dominated the party's congressional membership and hence effectively controlled party politics. Although southern Democrats were utterly aghast at the demise of their northern brethren, and interpreted the debacle as a sign of the northern public's conversion to abolitionism, they knew

57. For Republican journals, see New York *Times*, October 13, 1858; Providence *Daily Tribune*, October 21, 1858; Cincinnati *Daily Gazette*, October 20, 1858. For Democratic analysis of the Pennsylvania elections, see *Atlas & Argus* (Albany, N.Y.), November 20, 1858; Cleveland *Daily Plain Dealer*, October 29, 1858; *Daily True American* (Trenton, N.J.), October 18, 1858.

58. New York *Evening Post*, October 8, 1858; Chicago *Daily Times*, November 23, 1858; speech of John A. Dix in New York *Times*, October 26, 1858.

that the tariff had played a major role in the Pennsylvania campaign. That fact did not soften the southern heart toward a revision of the tariff. Not long after the elections, Representative Thomas L. Clingman delivered an address to the North Carolina State Agricultural Society. In his oration Clingman lashed out at tariffs that subsidized the industrialist at the expense of the farmer. "The excuse for this is, that American labor must be protected," Clingman protested, but farmers were also laborers, so "why should they be taxed for the benefit of manufacturers?"[59]

One of the most strident southern proclamations in favor of free trade came from South Carolina Senator James H. Hammond, the author of the most publicized proslavery oration in the last session of Congress. By demonstrating his allegiance to extreme free trade concepts, he exhibited that incongruity in southern thought in which free trade economic ideas coexisted so easily with proslavery tenets. The senator gave a long speech in which he indicated that the South should virtually capitulate on the issue of slavery expansion. Hammond argued that because of the strength of cotton the South was secure within the Union. But, Hammond warned, the power of the government had to remain in southern hands, particularly on economic matters. Hammond indicated that a revision of the tariff would not be allowed: "Free trade is the test, the touchstone of free government, as monopoly is of despotism. I have no hesitation in saying that the plantation States should discard any government that made a protective tariff its policy."[60]

Hammond's view of tariff revision, while perhaps more extreme than most, reflected quite accurately the southern Democratic position. Southern Democrats would bitterly protest any retrogression from free trade tariffs. This clearly erupted in an exchange of views on the Pennsylvania election between the administration organ, the Washington *Union,* and another Washington newspaper, the *States.* John P. Heiss, a Douglas supporter, edited the *States* and denounced Buchanan's policy of proscription against Democrats who did not follow the administration's instructions on Lecompton. In late 1858 Roger A. Pryor, rep-

59. Address of Thomas L. Clingman, October 21, 1858, in Thomas L. Clingman, *Selections from the Speeches and Writings of Hon. Thomas L. Clingman, of North Carolina* (2nd ed.; Raleigh, N.C., 1878), 101–109, quotes on pp. 103, 106; Charleston *Mercury,* October 18, 1858; speech of M. L. Bonham in Charleston *Mercury,* September 10, 1858; *Daily Constitutionalist* (Augusta, Ga.), October 17, 1858.

60. Speech of Hammond in New York *Times,* November 6, 1858.

resentative from Virginia, joined Heiss and added his free trade, states' rights views.

While the *States* blamed the Pennsylvania election debacle upon Buchanan's policy of punishing Democratic dissidents, the *Union* began to agree with the majority of Pennsylvania Democrats that the issue of protectionism was the party's downfall.[61] Instantly, and very incorrectly, the *States* strongly reprimanded the *Union* for even suggesting that Democrats or the people of the United States countenanced any protectionist sentiment in their breasts: "This is the shallowest and most stupid of all their shallow and stupid dodges. Is it not a great historical fact that the Democracy is the father as well as the child of Free Trade? And is it not equally patent, that if the question at the election was a question of tariff, the Democracy, as a great party, would have swept everything before them; and the men who have been kicked out for their participation in endorsing the proscription test of Lecomptonism, would have been re-elected, if the Tariff was the test?"[62] Unfortunately, Heiss and Pryor blinded themselves to the fact that the tariff really had been a major issue in Pennsylvania. Those who had suffered from the tremendous political upheaval in the Keystone State had few illusions as to what the citizens of their state demanded from the national government.

No one understood the situation more clearly than James Buchanan. A Philadelphia Jacksonian war-horse, Duff Green, wrote to the president and promised that he would personally swing Pennsylvania back to the Democracy with a series of articles upon national issues. Explaining that his first work would deal with Kansas, Green said his following missives would outline the true policy on the tariff, because "Forney has created an impression that you are so much under *Southern* influence that you will not stand by Pennsylvania on the Tariff." Green wrote Buchanan that he had to raise the tariff in order to disprove the Republican charge of southern domination over his administration; the president had to risk the free trade flags of the South or else Pennsylvania was forever lost.[63] Another administration friend

61. *States* (Washington, D.C.), October 13, 1858; Washington (D.C.) *Union*, October 6, 1858; Washington (D.C.) *Union* quoted by *Daily National Intelligencer* (Washington, D.C.), October 15, 1858.

62. *States* (Washington, D.C.), October 14, 1858.

63. Quote from Duff Green to James Buchanan, October 14, 1858, in Buchanan Papers. See also Duff Green to James Buchanan October 29, 30, 1858, both in Buchanan Papers.

wrote to Buchanan on the need of a higher tariff and the possibility of southern reactions:

> If the democracy of the South would come up in solid column at this coming Session, and give us a Tariff—a reasonable one; with specific duties, or a home valuation (in our own ports) and so framed as to give some assurance that it would remain stable, we could right up Penna. again before the end of another year. Let it not be forgotten that there are thousands of democrats in Penna. who have stood out braving this storm, but feel that the support of their neighbors and friends are being rapidly withdrawn from them on this very issue.[64]

It was not forgotten that administration Democrats endured the wrath of the northern public over Lecompton; now the Pennsylvania Democrats requested a slight sacrifice from their southern brethren. Only a month and one-half after the Pennsylvania elections Congress would meet for its short session. Then the Pennsylvania Democracy and James Buchanan would find just how far the southern Democracy would sacrifice their positions for them. The history of that short session of Congress could have been written before it met.

64. David R. Porter to James Buchanan, October 14, 1858, in Buchanan Papers.

SEVEN / A Retrenchment Congress

Three political circumstances contributed to sectional tensions at the beginning of 1859 that were the distinct legacies of the Panic of 1857. Pennsylvania Democrats experienced the first in the congressional elections of 1858 when so many voters in the state accepted the opposition premise that a high tariff was a cure for economic depression. The second was a result of the presence of concrete economic issues whose resolution seemed urgent to large numbers of northerners. Republicans increasingly manipulated these pressing questions of federal economic policy to argue that the slaveholding interest would never countenance the passage of laws vital to the welfare of northern free workers. The third involved federal finances. The United States government relied upon two sources of revenue: the sale of public lands and taxes on imports. The Panic had diminished the revenue obtained from both sources and put the government in a difficult position. The actions of congressional leaders regarding the deficit and the wishes of Pennsylvanians indicated that the Republicans would in the end become the beneficiaries of the problems created by the Panic.

The Democratic politicians who gathered in Washington in December, 1858, for the opening of the second session of the Thirty-fifth Congress were momentarily less concerned about finances than they were about the fissures in their party and the damaging losses suffered in the elections of 1858. They knew the troubles of the party had to be solved quickly or they would be in danger of losing the presidential contest in 1860. In particular, northern Democrats longed to end party divisions over the issue of popular sovereignty. Another related matter was to recall, somehow, the voters of Pennsylvania to the party of Jackson.

Solutions to the Democracy's dilemmas over slavery and Pennsylvania proved difficult to find. A group of southern senators harbored a supreme contempt for Stephen Douglas because of his recalcitrance over Lecompton. By cajoling a Democratic caucus, Jefferson Davis, John Slidell, and the Hoosier Jesse D. Bright forced Douglas' removal from the chairmanship of the committee on territories. Many southerners did not approve of the ouster, and had not Douglas been absent perhaps this vindictive act would never have been consummated.[1] But the result was that the Democracy remained sundered because of Lecompton. The response of national party leaders to the special needs of the Pennsylvania Democrats took slightly more time to develop, but the outcome proved to be as unfortunate for the party's political health as the Kansas controversy.

President James Buchanan also weighed these matters. He tried to effect some type of peace with the popular sovereignty Democrats, but hot-headed southerners and Douglas' own intractability thwarted his goals. Buchanan encountered similar difficulties in effecting a policy that would woo back Pennsylvania's citizens. Pennsylvanians, rightly or wrongly, wanted a higher tariff, and Buchanan, believing a tariff to be economically of little help, bowed to the pressure of the October elections. Here Buchanan ran into his first obstacle. His secretary of the treasury adamantly refused to recommend any revision of the tariff.[2]

The private dispute between the president and his secretary flared into the public's eye when Buchanan's annual message and the reports of the department heads came before Congress. Buchanan wrote upon many topics in his message. He was heartened, he said, to see that Kansas was no longer a subject for further debate and that sectional acrimony over slavery in the territories had no more outlets for expression. Declaring that the Utah expedition had been necessary and had

1. Johannsen, *Stephen A. Douglas*, 681–87; Nichols, *The Disruption of American Democracy*, 224–27.

2. Elbert B. Smith, *The Presidency of James Buchanan* (Lawrence, Kans., 1975), 87–88; "Sigma" in *Daily Picayune* (New Orleans), December 9, 1858; "Independent" in Philadelphia *North American*, November 4, 22, 1858; New York *Courier* quoted in *Adams Sentinel* (Gettysburg), November 8, 1858; New York *Daily Tribune*, November 16, 1858. Editorials appeared on the question of the tariff and the president's policy but much of the information that came to the public originated from a corps of reporters in Washington. It is not known who all these reporters were; they signed their articles with such names as "Sigma," "Leo," and other cryptic pseudonyms. Whenever information from these sources are used in this chapter, the name the correspondent used—if he used one—will be included in the footnote.

ended without war, the president then advocated the acquisition of Cuba from Spain.

He next considered finances and the tariff. Explaining that the government was in no way responsible for the Panic of 1857, Buchanan maintained his earlier belief that banks and paper money had created the revulsion: "The tariff of 1857 had no agency in the result." He reiterated his fear of inflation and argued that unless inflation were controlled, all attempts to protect American industry would be useless. Buchanan nonetheless departed from free trade nostrums because the country needed more revenue and could not continue its policy of borrowing. A higher tariff that would produce more revenue would "to some extent, increase the confidence of the manufacturing interests, and give a fresh impulse to our reviving business." Buchanan argued in favor of specific duties instead of *ad valorem* taxation in order to procure for American manufacturers an incidental protection. To complement his program of increasing the revenue, Buchanan also advocated a "rigid economy" in all departments of government.[3]

Howell Cobb did not support his superior. Cobb estimated a deficit of nearly four million dollars by June 30, 1859, but nonetheless told Congress that the remainder of the loan passed in the last session of Congress would be sufficient to ensure the smooth functioning of the government. His predictions for the future rested on a retrenchment program. The first quarter of the fiscal year 1858–1859 had seen an expenditure of some twenty-one million dollars; Cobb hoped to reduce this rate to seventeen million dollars per quarter for the remainder of the fiscal year. For the next fiscal year, 1859–1860, Cobb planned to hold spending to fifty-two million dollars. Even at this sharp rate of contraction, the administration still fought deficiencies incurred during the past two years—primarily involving debts from the Utah expedition and growing problems in the postal service.[4]

Cobb could not resist the temptation to lecture the Congress, the American people, and the president on true economic principles. The secretary did not want a revision of the tariff of 1857 or an alteration of the *ad valorem* means of evaluation. He argued that protectionism harmed more industries than it helped, stimulated investment in un-

3. *Senate Executive Documents*, 35th Cong., 2nd Sess., No. 1, pp. 3–30, quotes on pp. 24, 25, 28; the financial portion of the message is on pp. 25–28.

4. *House Executive Documents*, 35th Cong., 2nd Sess., No. 3, pp. 3–5.

productive enterprises, and taxed the farmer to support the industrialist. He then defended the tariff of 1857 and insisted that it be given more time to prove its merits. Whether Cobb purposefully struck at the demands urged by the Pennsylvania Democracy is unknown, but the secretary of the treasury in one swift blow removed hopes of reinstituting the tariff of 1846: "I am well satisfied that the wants of the government do not require a permanent increase of the taxes to the extent of reviving the tariff of 1846. The duties of forty and one hundred per cent. imposed by that act are, in the present condition of trade and commerce, wholly indefensible. The public mind of the country will scarcely be brought again to acquiesce in any higher schedule than thirty per cent., the maximum of the present law."[5]

Although the administration presented conflicting proposals on the tariff, it achieved total unanimity on the need for retrenchment. The cabinet heads reported that they intended to cut their annual budget requests. John B. Floyd figured on a large savings in the War Department, but he worried about the deterioration of the improvements that had been made on the Great Lakes. Likewise, the Navy Department exhibited a paring down of estimates. Postmaster General Aaron V. Brown tried to trim expenses as well, but he also faced the task of explaining the continuous deficits incurred by his department. Blaming the indebtedness of the post office upon the Pacific mail routes that Congress demanded the nation maintain for military reasons, Brown advocated eliminating steamer mail subsidies, raising postal rates, and abolishing the congressional privilege of sending mail to constitutents free of charge, the "franking privilege." The difficulties in the Interior Department were of a different sort. Land sales were a source of revenue but the administration had foregone pressing for more funds from that source because of the depression in the West. Now, the secretary of the interior warned, national finances required action, and he hoped "to bring into the open market several millions of acres during the ensuing year."[6]

The Panic of 1857 thus began to affect public policy, but in a manner inimical to the political welfare of the Democrats. To right the budget, the administration disclosed its determination to cut expenditures. But within the cabinet reports were the seeds of much controversy because

5. *Ibid.*, 3–5, 7, 8–12, 15.
6. *Senate Executive Documents*, 35th Cong., 2nd Sess., No. 1, pp. 17, 18, 1100, 1167–77, 1183–87, 723–27, 733–35, 75.

the department heads indicated a plan of retrenchment that would impinge upon northern economic interests—postage rates, mail steamer subsidies, fishing bounties, internal improvements, and various public land schemes. The administration could escape the expected northern retribution for the cancellation of these projects if Congress raised the tariff and spared the government the task of cutting expenses elsewhere. But to advocate tariff revision risked alienating the southern Democracy. Thus the administration did not occupy an auspicious vantage point from which they could heal party wounds.

Although Buchanan received the usual compliments on his message, trouble was brewing over the part which dealt with finances. One of his Philadelphia correspondents disapproved of Cobb's report: "Although I am theoretically in favour of free trade I do not think there should have been from your cabinet opinions expressed so directly in the teeth of your message." Also disturbed was the editor of the Pittsburgh *Morning Post*, who chastised Cobb for opposing the President. Other northern Democrats, however, dissented against the proposal to institute specific duties, while some party officials praised Cobb's report as "one of the ablest that has ever issued from that Department." Indeed, the rabid free trader Roger A. Pryor mounted a crusade against the president's program.[7]

Republicans, of course, found little in Buchanan's annual message worthy of laudation. Only the tariff segment of the message evoked their praise. To the free trade organ the New York *Evening Post*, the tariff advocacy was "an attempt to conciliate the iron-masters of Pennsylvania"; to other editors Buchanan's change in policy reflected a recognition of economic reality. Old-line Whig editors found Buchanan's conversion to protectionism "unusual," and they greeted warmly the return to "the old Whig ground" of specific duties.[8]

Quite early in the congressional session, attention turned to the president's recommendation to purchase Cuba. Probably Buchanan intended to rally his divided party around territorial expansion, and his proposals received blessings from most Democrats, although some commented that only if Cuba could be obtained by honorable means

7. James C. Van Dyke to James Buchanan, December 18, 1858, in Buchanan Papers; Pittsburgh *Morning Post*, December 10, 16, 1858; Detroit *Daily Free Press*, December 10, 1858; *Daily Illinois State Register* (Springfield), December 10, 1858; Louisville *Daily Courier*, December 11, 1858; *States* (Washington, D.C.), December 7, 8, 1858.

8. New York *Evening Post*, December 7, 1858; quotes in Indianapolis *Daily Journal*, December 10, 1858; and Providence *Daily Tribune*, December 9, 1858.

would they support the measure. A Senate Democratic caucus concurred that one of the goals of the Congress should be the acquisition of the Caribbean island.[9]

The plans went awry rather quickly. The Democrats wanted to place unguarded funds in the hands of the president to enable him to purchase the island by the best means available. The proposal immediately elicited Republican objections. But the greatest obstacle the Cuba bill faced, and the one that finally thwarted the project, was the Republican charge that the scheme arose solely out of the slaveholders' desire to extend the domain of slavery. Later in the session the matter became embroiled in proposed homestead legislation and came to naught[10]

Democrats relied upon many arguments to rationalize their longings for more territory. They resurrected the theories of Manifest Destiny and expressed a hope to rescue the Cuban people from an oppressive colonial master. While some southerners openly affirmed that they wanted Cuba as a new slave state, the northern wing of the party advocated bringing Cuba under United States domination for a different reason. "WE WANT CHEAP SUGAR," declared the editor of the Albany *Atlas and Argus*. The same writer later used a common illustration of the economic importance of Cuba to the United States. The Caribbean island imported from the United States goods totaling only nine million dollars while exporting products worth forty-five million. By taking possession of Cuba, the American North would receive "in every fibre of its frame, the solid and lasting industrial and commercial benefits it would confer."[11]

The economic ramifications that would follow the acquisition of Cuba had an important political aspect for the Democrats. The Cincinnati *Enquirer* emphasized that Cuba imported little American flour, but if the Cuban tariff were removed and free trade installed, that nation's purchases would rise to a "million of barrels for their use a year."

9. *Tri-Weekly Standard* (Raleigh, N.C.), January 29, 1859; *Daily Illinois State Register* (Springfield), December 10, 1858; report of caucus in Louisville *Daily Courier*, January 18, 1859.

10. Lyman Trumbull to Abraham Lincoln, January 29, 1859, in Lincoln Papers; *Cong. Globe*, 35th Cong., 2nd Sess., remarks of Seward and Wade, 1352–54. Robert E. May, *The Southern Dream of a Caribbean Empire, 1854–1861* (Baton Rouge, 1973), 163–89, details the Cuba bill, although he does not tie the Cuba project with the recession or the controversy over the tariff.

11. *Atlas & Argus* (Albany, N.Y.), January 24, 25, 1859.

Later the *Enquirer* added that obtaining Cuba would also redound to the benefit of New England industrialists by "having the Cuban markets open to their manufacturers." Northern Democrats understood the poor business conditions that prevailed in the agricultural West, and hence they touted territorial market expansion as an appropriate solution to economic stagnation.[12]

Protectionists and free trade Democrats thus offered a clear choice between remedies for the depression; one advocated decreasing foreign trade, and the other proposed the creation of greater markets by territorial annexation. James Gordon Bennett of the New York *Herald* was one of many who recognized that the tariff and Cuban questions were competing political solutions for the economic recession brought about by the Panic of 1857. Bennett conceded that *ad valorem* taxation had failed and that the administration should inaugurate a program of specific duties. However, he said, the tariff was no cure for a revulsion. Acquisition of new territories would spur business back to prosperity because new land "opens new employments for labor, constructs new ways for the conveyance of man and his products everywhere, and by extending the field of its usefulness gives a greater value to every man's labor and every man's wealth."[13] Bennett would again find occasion during this session of Congress to remark upon the intimate connections between the tariff and Cuba.

Slowly the tottering financial condition of the government pushed aside the furor over Cuba. The House Ways and Means Committee met throughout January, 1859, to find some financial scheme upon which all the members of the committee might agree. Because J. Glancy Jones had been appointed minister to Austria, the duties of the chairmanship fell to John S. Phelps of Missouri. Phelps, a believer in low tariffs, was a pragmatic man, but his committee divided over the question of raising more revenue. Phelps wanted to raise some tariff rates but not alter the *ad valorem* system; in this he found support from Henry M. Phillips of Pennsylvania. Opposing any increase in duties and favoring the continued expedient of borrowing were three south-

12. Cincinnati *Daily Enquirer*, January 21, March 5, 1859; *Allegheny Mountain Echo* (Johnstown, Pa.), January 26, 1859; Easton (Pa.) *Argus*, February 3, 1859; *Pennsylvanian* quoted by Erie (Pa.) *Weekly Observer*, October 23, 1858.

13. New York *Herald*, October 23, 1858. See also comments of John A. Dix, who said in October, 1858, that the best tariff Pennsylvania "could possibly have is to be found in the annexation of Cuba and Mexico," New York *Times*, October 26, 1858.

ern representatives: John Letcher of Virginia, James F. Dowdell of Alabama, and Martin J. Crawford of Georgia. Those who recommended a higher tariff and a change to specific duties were the Republicans Justin Morrill of Vermont, William A. Howard of Michigan, and American party representative Henry Winter Davis of Maryland. The committee reached stalemate after stalemate; John Phelps and Howell Cobb met often to find a compromise solution. Cobb bent his scruples far enough to suggest that some schedules in the tariff act of 1857 could be raised a few percentage points, but he still denigrated any attempt to revise the tariff in its entirety. He bitterly opposed the president's suggestion that specific duties should be substituted for *ad valorem* duties.[14]

The political ramifications of the tariff issue were quickly revealed. Republicans caucused and announced their approval of a modification of the tariff. Pennsylvania Democrats had gathered earlier and resolved to act as a unit in favor of the tariff proposals in the president's message. Members of the Pennsylvania Democracy also told Phelps that unless he obtained an alteration in the tariff, he could not depend upon the votes of Pennsylvanians on other appropriation measures. The Democratic journals of the Keystone State generally followed the tariff situation and relayed the news from Washington to their readers. Editors praised the efforts of the state's Democrats regarding the tariff and raised expectations that the party would honor Pennsylvania's requests.[15]

Pennsylvania's motivation for a higher tariff was not a secret. When Pennsylvania ironmasters gathered for a convention in Philadelphia in early January, James Gordon Bennett counted the numbers which iron commanded and decided that the tariff question could be the "turning point in the reconstruction of parties, or the balance of power in the next Presidential election." He was further impressed about the potential of the tariff question by the resolutions of the Pennsylvania legislature that petitioned Congress for an upward revision of import duties. Realizing that Pennsylvania was the decisive state in presidential

14. New York *Daily Tribune*, January 27, 1859; Philadelphia *North American*, January 17, 28, 1859; *Harper's Weekly*, February 5, 1859, p. 86.

15. Indianapolis *Daily Journal*, January 28, 1859; Pittsburgh *Morning Post*, January 13, 1859; "Cleveland" in Cincinnati *Daily Enquirer*, January 27, 1859; Pittsburgh *Morning Post*, January 14, 28, 1859; *Democratic Watchman* (Bellefonte, Pa.), February 3, 1859; Bedford (Pa.) *Gazette*, January 28, 1859.

campaigns, Bennett felt that the Democracy either had to steal the tariff issue or consummate the purchase of Cuba.[16]

The Pennsylvania situation was not unknown to the other members of the Democratic party, particularly the southerners. Roger A. Pryor castigated the Pennsylvanians for their espousal of protectionism. As far as the South was concerned, protectionism was just another form of abolitionism. "The imposition of intolerable burdens upon the productions of slave-labor is but another though more insidious expedient for the prostration of the South," Pryor said. He did not mean that the president or the Pennsylvania Democracy intended such a result; rather, he said, "we only argue upon the inevitable effect of the policy." Throughout January, Pryor applied a stinging whip to Democratic backsliders.[17]

While Pennsylvania Democrats scampered about the Capitol telling all party members of their political problems in the Keystone State, John Phelps reported that the House Ways and Means Committee had failed to make progress on a tariff compromise. The Democratic leadership determined that a party caucus was necessary to plot a unified strategy on the issue. But, as one correspondent warned Buchanan, a caucus could produce a humiliating rebuke by rejecting his proposals.[18]

On Saturday, January 29, Democratic senators met to map out a plan for rescuing the government's finances. William Bigler attempted to gain approval of the president's program. Oddly enough, he received a measure of southern support. Both Robert Toombs of Georgia and Judah P. Benjamin of Louisiana indicated their willingness to allow specific duties on the great staples. One of the leading states' rights advocates in the Senate, Alfred Iverson of Georgia, explained he was not averse to a moderate increase in duties as long as all the tariff schedules were equally affected.

All hopes of some compromise measure were dashed by the imposing figure of Robert Hunter. Hunter immediately disposed of any idea that the tariff might be revised or specific duties imposed. Illinois' Stephen Douglas, remembering his denunciation in the caucus that defined the party stand on Lecompton, questioned Hunter about the mode of levying duties and asked if the caucus assumed a position to

---

16. New York *Herald,* January 5, 21, 1859.
17. *States* (Washington, D.C.), December 9, 1858.
18. William L. Hirst to James Buchanan, February 1, 1859, in Buchanan Papers.

which all Democrats had to adhere or else be ousted from the party. Hunter, irritated at Douglas' attempt to compare the issue of the tariff with the issue of Lecompton, curtly replied that all Democrats believed the "tariff should be revenue, but that the mode of assessing the duties was not a party test."[19] Finally the caucus concurred in retrenching expenses to save the government from bankruptcy.

The president was "reported to be much annoyed" by the action of the Senate caucus. He was not alone. James Gordon Bennett exploded at the attitude of Hunter and the states' rights Democracy. Hunter had called a new tariff "inexpedient," to which Bennett queried, "How 'inexpedient,' Mr. Hunter? Why?—Where? The only inexpediency in this matter, we apprehend, is between the protective democrats of Pennsylvania and the free trade democracy of the South." For Bennett, the only "remaining chance for the demoralized democracy" was the Cuba bill, and the opportunity for its passage was slight. The editor of the Cleveland *Daily Plain Dealer* also remarked on the disharmony of the Democracy. He took Douglas' position and pondered over the fact that on the tariff, which encompassed "the interests of twenty-five millions of people," Democrats of the North "are allowed to think as they please," but on "the temporary question and the peculiar form of application of a State for admission" to the Union, the party leaders "crammed down the party's throat" the only allowable response.[20]

But few editors matched the raw anger of the proprietor of the Pittsburgh *Morning Post* who had already led his readers to believe that the national Democracy would respond to Pennsylvania's needs. Senator Slidell's offer to cut expenditures instead of revising the tariff "is certainly cool from a man who proposes $30,000,000 for the purchase of Cuba," the *Morning Post*'s editor exclaimed. He also stated that Democratic senators were neglecting the welfare of the nation to pursue impractical, idealistic visions and reported a common Pennsylvania Democratic fear: "A President is to be made in 1860, and the great wants of the people are of little account in the game which the politicians at Washington are playing."[21]

The Senate Democrats' action was not the only chilling blast that shriveled Pennsylvania plans for a modification of the tariff. Democrats

19. The Senate Democratic caucus can be found in any number of newspapers. The quote herein used is from Charleston *Mercury*, February 2, 1859.

20. New York *Herald*, January 30, 31, 1859; Cleveland *Daily Plain Dealer*, February 1, 1859.

21. Pittsburgh *Morning Post*, February 1, 1859.

in the House also started a series of caucuses to plot their strategy. On February 1, Phelps explained the dilemma that deadlocked the Ways and Means Committee; the audience to which he spoke was primarily composed of southern representatives. The outcome was never in doubt. They accepted the resolutions proffered by Georgia's Martin Crawford, which called for no change in the tariff, the establishment of a retrenchment committee, and the passage of legislation allowing the treasury to reissue treasury notes to meet government obligations.[22]

The next caucus occurred on February 5, but in the meantime Cobb had written to Phelps that an alteration of some tariff duties would be necessary if the government were to remain solvent. This assembly did not move so easily to a solution. The committee on retrenchment estimated that the government could save ten million dollars by slashing expenditures for printing, the coastal survey, and the military. Phelps, however, contended that the nation had to return to the tariff of 1846, and Daniel Sickles of New York questioned whether Congress should dismiss so readily the estimates of department administrators. When Crawford tried to force through a resolution adopting the reissuance of treasury notes, the meeting broke up. The next caucus left the question open. Crawford's hope of killing proposed tariff changes failed, but no other action obtained approval either; the only agreement was to adopt Sickles' expedient resolution of conferring with Senate Democrats.[23]

Caucus action on the tariff left bitterness throughout the Democratic party, particularly among the Pennsylvanians. They seceded from the regular Democratic meetings and set up their own, resolving to support the president's recommendations on finances and to refuse any new loan legislation. One hostile Washington correspondent recorded the reaction of one of the "most noted gas-bags in the House," Philadelphia's Thomas Florence. Upon hearing the decision of other Pennsylvania Democrats, Florence exclaimed, "This will never do—I can't attend such a caucus—here's another split in the Democratic party!" A reporter at the Capitol remarked, "You can scarcely imagine how bitter the Pennsylvania Democrats are against Senator Hunter. They curse him savagely and vehemently." Hardly less mortifying was the way Secretary of the Treasury Cobb was "permitted to assail every position

22. New York *Herald*, February 2, 1859; New York *Daily Tribune*, February 3, 1859.
23. *House Executive Documents*, 35th Cong., 2nd Sess., No. 83, pp. 1–4; New York *Times*, February 4, 5, 7, 1859; New York *Herald*, February 6, 10, 1859.

and principle of his [Buchanan's] Message on this subject." While Buchanan was "indignant" over the caucuses, the rumor spread that Cobb, when asked what differences existed between him and the president, supposedly replied, "The President is opposing the Administration."[24]

Both the president and Senator Bigler understood the effect the recalcitrance of the southern members would have upon the Pennsylvania Democracy's future. The Panic of 1857 had produced a depression in Pennsylvania that left numerous citizens of the state pleading for a higher tariff. The southern Democrats in caucus had decisively vetoed any attempt of the party to readjust the tariff. Pennsylvania voters would therefore continue to look unfavorably upon the Democratic party. Bigler was told by one correspondent that "something must be done or we, as a party, will be hopelessly in a minority in this State for years." But in his letters Bigler must have detected a troublesome note, for his confidants blamed the South for the troubles in Pennsylvania—and their attitudes became not unlike those of the Republicans: "We are willing to stand by the South and carry their Niggers for them; more than this we cannot do and upon this Tariff question I hope no northern man will yield to the South."[25]

An agonized Democratic press in Pennsylvania tried to present the party in its best light. Editors generally printed the tariff speeches of Bigler or other Pennsylvania Democrats and then pointed an accusing finger at the inactivity—and therefore the insincerity—of the opposition on tariff revision. Many papers simply printed the proceedings of the caucuses without comment. Only the Pittsburgh *Morning Post* publicly lashed out at the Democrats who had once found opposition to the president's Lecompton policy a crime, but who "are now warring upon and defying the same President upon a question of national policy, more important than any other before the country." But the *Morning Post* was singular in this instance; whatever thoughts burned in the minds of other Democratic editors stayed hidden and unprinted.[26]

24. New York *Herald*, February 6, 1859; "Sigma" in *Daily Picayune* (New Orleans), February 8, 1859; "CYD" in *Daily Ohio State Journal* (Columbus), February 10, 1859; "Cleveland" in Cincinnati *Daily Enquirer*, February 9, 1859; Erie (Pa.) *Gazette*, February 10, 1859; Milwaukee *Daily Free Democrat*, February 3, 1859, evidently taken from New York *Daily Tribune*.

25. Justin [?] Clymer to William Bigler, February 9, 1859, Edward M. Clymer to William Bigler, February 8, 1859, both in Bigler Papers.

26. Pittsburgh *Morning Post*, February 7, 1859.

Just as upset about the sudden magnitude of the tariff issue and the divisions over it were the southern Democrats. Southern newspaper reporters wrote of the "heretical Democracy" of Pennsylvania that threatened to aid the opposition if a new tariff was not adopted "and the States Rights Democracy are amazed at the effrontery of the demand, since so much has been yielded already to her solicitation." Southerners brought out their theories of states' rights and complained of the injustice perpetrated by high tariffs upon their section. The standard rejection of protectionist claims did not mean that southerners misunderstood the motivations of Pennsylvanians. Caucus meetings received wide coverage in the southern press, and the actions of the Pennsylvania representatives were known to all. Moreover, reports sufficiently explained why Pennsylvania so desperately wanted a higher tariff: "The iron interest of Pennsylvania and New Jersey controls the party politics of those States. At the President's election in 1856, that interest was with Mr. Buchanan. In the last fall elections it was against him. It will be against the Democratic candidate in 1860, unless it now be conciliated by a specific duty on iron."[27]

The Washington *States* provided disturbing answers to the question of how the southern Democrats intended to treat Pennsylvania and its electoral votes. The columns were undoubtedly the product of Pryor. He praised the decision of the senate caucus and applauded the retrenchment resolutions of the House Democrats. Fearlessly he lowered his editorial wrath on anyone who strayed from the states' rights ranks, and when Cobb agreed to a minor alteration in the tariff, Pryor called for his resignation. He heaped scorn upon the fear that Pennsylvania might be lost to the Democracy in 1860. The action of the Pennsylvanians was disgraceful; they now threatened the party by declaring that "no man shall be nominated at Charleston who refused to acquiesce in their demand; and unless the Democracy agree to give them protection, Pennsylvania will apostatize to the Opposition in 1860." Pryor wrote heatedly that the states' rights Democracy would "repel" this threat "with contempt." Admitting that Pennsylvania had been of

27. "Tau" in Charleston *Daily Courier*, February 7, 1859; "R" in *Tri-Weekly Standard* (Raleigh, N.C.), February 26, 1859; "Veritas" in Richmond (Va.) *Enquirer*, February 4, 1859; Charleston *Mercury*, February 8, 26, 1859; *Mississippian* (Jackson), February 15, 22, 1859; *Daily Constitutionalist* (Augusta, Ga.), February 5, 1859; "Malou" in New Orleans *Daily Crescent*, February 11, 1859; "Leo" in Charleston *Daily Courier*, February 3, 1859.

service to the Democracy in the past, he insisted that the principle meant too much. For years Democrats allowed Pennsylvanians to profess openly their "heresy," but now the "demand is unsufferable."[28]

The southern animosity toward Pennsylvania's pro-tariff sentiment concealed one important fact: the rest of the northern Democracy tended to agree with their southern brethren. Most northern Democrats did not favor readjusting the tariff and were especially adamant against inaugurating specific duties. Editors often praised Senator Hunter's defense of the tariff of 1857. One journalist printed Hunter's rebuttal of the protectionist doctrines of Rhode Island's James F. Simmons and concluded the column with the words, "Three Cheers for Senator Hunter."[29]

Republicans enjoyed immensely the spectacle of bickering Democrats. In Pennsylvania the opposition newspapers gleefully reported that their predictions had proven correct: the southern wing of the Democracy would never allow a revision of the tariff.[30] Outside of Pennsylvania Republican editors loved to play upon the theme of the so-called harmonious Democracy. One writer adroitly summed up the troubles within the Democratic ranks: "The picture is a rich one! Forney and Douglas against the Administration on the Kansas question; Forney and the Administration against Douglas and the *States* on the Tariff question; and Forney against the Washington *Union*, Mr. Buchanan, and Mr. Douglas on the Thirty Million [Cuba] project."[31]

Republicans quickly offered their explanation of southern resistance to Buchanan's tariff proposals. Greeley's Washington correspondent, James Shepherd Pike, spoke for many when he penned an analysis of the Democrats' tariff dilemma. "Nothing can be done with the great body of the Democratic party," he asserted, because it was "a Southern Planters' and Slavery party, devoted to Free-Trade and against anything and everything that favors Northern or Free State interests." Republicans also knew what this tariff fight meant for their organization. The *Illinois State Journal* questioned Pryor about calling the loss of Pennsylvania a "trifling 'defection.'" Pennsylvania, the editor assured

28. *States* (Washington, D.C.), February 1, 2, 3, 5, 7, 9, 1859.

29. Quote from Cleveland *Daily Plain Dealer*, February 17, 1859; Cincinnati *Daily Enquirer*, February 20, 1859; *Atlas & Argus* (Albany, N.Y.), January 31, 1859.

30. For example, *Cambria Tribune* (Johnstown, Pa.), February 5, March 12, 1859.

31. Chicago *Press and Tribune*, February 3, 1859; Evansville (Ind.) *Daily Journal*, February 15, 1859.

the Democrats, was not "a state which the Democracy could afford, at any time, to spare," and even less now, for "with the help of the 'Keystone,' Democratic success at a presidential election is difficult; without it, impossible."[32]

As the tariff grew in importance, some Republicans began to recant their earlier free trade economic ideas. During the Panic of 1857 the editors of the Chicago *Press and Tribune* were quite sure that banks and paper money caused the revulsion and they scoffed at tariff theories. The editors still wished to maintain slavery as the principal issue of politics, but now they saw more clearly—presumably from the Pennsylvania opposition election tallies in 1858 rather than from Divine guidance—that a better tariff was required to "revivify our iron, lead and manufacturing interests." Connecting the matter of "white industry and commerce" with the sectional controversy, they also made the leap that tied the fate of the tariff to the "Slave Power's" control of national legislation.[33]

E. Peshine Smith wrote to Henry Carey that Pryor was doing the protectionists the greatest service possible by identifying protectionism with antislavery: "I think the 'States' is doing for us what it could be hard work for us to do ourselves—by the declaration that 'Protection is Freesoilism in disguise.' This is what is wanted to make a protective party *en block* of the Republicans. Our brethren of democratic antecedents were tender footed on this subject & had to be handled very carefully. Their faith is too new to bear the imposition of new articles of the old Whig creed directly tendered at our hands." Carey himself enjoyed the sight of a bankrupt administration refusing to find the means to pull itself out of insolvency. And in Illinois, Lincoln's law partner, William Herndon, also saw the political result of Democratic mismanagement of the revenue question. "The Tariff is killed," he wrote Lyman Trumbull, and "Pennsylvania is justly paid."[34]

But Republicans proved to be slower learners than Smith expected. Free soil papers refused to give the tariff ascendancy over the slavery issue. A Columbus, Ohio, editor incorrectly stated that a return to the tariff of 1846 would be sufficient for even "the most zealous protec-

---

32. "J.S.P." in New York *Tribune*, February 4, 1859; *Daily Illinois State Journal* (Springfield), February 15, 1859.

33. Chicago *Press and Tribune*, December 10, 1858.

34. E. Peshine Smith to Henry C. Carey, February 6, 1859, in Gardiner Collection; William H. Herndon to Lyman Trumbull, February 5, 1859, in Trumbull Papers.

tionist." In Chicago, "Long John" Wentworth took pains to demonstrate that American manufacturing was not depressed and that free trade benefited both Great Britain and the United States. New York City editor Henry J. Raymond had grave doubts about altering the tariff, for constantly tinkering with the tariff was "vexatious" to the stability of commerce. Moreover, he wrote, "the days of Protection, as a national policy, are numbered." And, of course, the New York *Evening Post* refused to budge from its free trade economic principles.[35] The Republican embrace of protectionism thus took a considerable amount of time and effort to achieve, for party members were well aware of the treacherous nature of their coalition and so proceeded with extreme caution on the issue.

During the week that the Democratic caucuses tried to solve the government's financial woes, the Congress commenced debates upon whether they should or should not revise import duties. Largely the debates rehashed positions taken since Henry Clay first proposed the American System. Proponents of high tariffs used the home market ideal, whereas free traders stressed allowing people to purchase from whomever they wished. The one focal point dominating discussion, however, was that the national coffers were empty. Protectionists unceasingly argued that the Panic of 1857 and the depression that followed it proved that the tariff of 1857 could never generate sufficient income to meet the needs of the government. Those who endorsed low tariffs typically responded by saying that the tariff of 1857 produced enough funds for an economical government but not an extravagant one; therefore, expenses had to be slashed.[36]

Retrenchment became the common cry of all those who favored purity in government. The Democrats adopted the retrenchment program because it offered an escape from a tariff alteration. The Republicans also scurried to hoist the retrenchment banner, for they hoped to seize the extravagance issue and to part the president from some of his patronage powers. Newspapers of both parties favored the paring down of the "bloated" bureaucracy. Early in February, Senator Andrew Johnson of Tennessee sponsored a resolution calling for a budget that lim-

35. *Daily Ohio State Journal* (Columbus), February 14, 1859; Chicago *Weekly Democrat*, February 5, March 5, 1859; New York *Times*, December 8, 1858, February 1, 1859; New York *Evening Post*, February 1, 2, 3, 7, 9, 1859.
36. *Cong. Globe*, 35th Cong., 2nd Sess., remarks of Sen. Toombs, 897–98; Sen.

ited federal expenditures to fifty million dollars.[37] Until the end of the session senators and representatives vied with each other in reducing federal spending.

Appropriation bills for the government offered every member of the Congress a chance to strut his determination to exorcise the spirit of wastefulness. Republicans tended to insist upon economizing in those areas where government patronage was greatest: naval yards, the military services, customhouses, federal buildings, and the post office. When considering an outlay of funds for a Charleston customhouse, Nehemiah Abbott of Maine said the project existed solely to "feed hungry, and clothe naked Democratic politicians, who rely on Government patronage, and government contracts, for subsistence." Republicans aimed specifically at these areas of federal expenditures out of a conviction that the administration had corruptly used contracts and employment opportunities to ensure Democratic victories in recent elections. Democrats, though professing their desire to diminish outlays for the military and the post office, indicated that they sought reductions that would not harm the party's capabilities to reward the faithful. The Democrats usually explained the "extravagance" of the Pierce and Buchanan administrations by claiming that inflated appropriations were the work of an earlier Congress under control of the Republicans.[38]

Each item in the appropriation list came under severe scrutiny, but usually some congressman found ample reasons for not cutting a particular project. When the navy appropriation bill came before the Senate, the Republicans pointed to abuses in the naval yards. James Hammond and Jefferson Davis denied that wrongdoing was prevalent and argued that the nation required a strong navy for commercial reasons. Georgia's James Seward proposed to strike out all monies given to the armories at Springfield, Massachusetts, and Harpers Ferry, Virginia, which immediately brought a rebuke from Calvin Chaffee of Massachusetts. When the Senate Committee on Military Affairs tried to enforce a reduction of pay for officers, the former secretary of war, Jefferson

---

Bigler, 878–79; Sen. Clingman, 923; Sen. Simmons, 928; Sen. Hunter, 1014–16; Rep. Morris of Pa., 757.

37. Andrew Johnson's resolution in *Cong. Globe*, 35th Cong. 2nd Sess., 991.

38. *Ibid*, remarks of Abbott, APX, 191, remarks of Sen. Hunter, 1016–17; remarks of Sen. Toombs, APX, 186–87. On the corruption issue, see David E. Meerse, "Buchanan, Corruption, and the Election of 1860," *CWH*, XII (1966), 117–20.

Davis, denounced the "wild hand of retrenchment" that was injuring national defense.[39]

The end results amounted to little more than quibbling about a few minor items. As New Hampshire's A. H. Cragin said, congressmen "have been valiant in their attacks on sundry small items of appropriation." He especially pointed to the "bold and successful fight . . . made against a few pine boxes, which cost $2 50 a piece." The objects upon which congressmen exercised their parsimony did not escape public notice. One Washington correspondent complained of the "harping at great length upon mileage and other small potato expenditures."[40]

The rush to slash expenditures inevitably stirred sectional animosities whenever congressmen threatened to curtail funds for local projects. To cure the post office of its perennial deficiency, Republicans moved to cut unremunerative postal routes in the South; southerners for their part hoped to raise the postage rates, much to the anger of the northern press. Southerners claimed that the Yankees were attempting to deprive their region of all benefits of national largesse by voting against appropriations for southern post offices, lighthouses, and customhouses. Northern congressmen, however, were furious that the administration had halted mail subsidies for transoceanic steamship companies and that the Postmaster General had decided upon a mail line to California that utilized a southern route. Yet much of the discussion over appropriations was confined to party considerations. Squabbles over specific appropriations usually produced a debate between members from the affected locales rather than a general battle pitting the sections against each other.[41]

The government's financial troubles killed other projects dear to the hearts of many politicians. The Pacific railroad received a fair amount of attention but the old quarrel over the designated route was coupled with the empty treasury, a combination that proved to be an insurmountable obstacle to any hopes that Congress might look favorably

39. *Cong. Globe*, 35th Cong., 2nd Sess., on naval appropriation bill, 1522–31; remarks of Rep. James Seward of Ga., 1162–69; remarks of Sen. Davis, 1034.

40. *Ibid.*, remarks of Rep. Cragin, APX, 176; "Malou" in New Orleans *Daily Crescent*, February 11, 1859; "J.S.P." in New York *Daily Tribune*, February 11, 1859.

41. *House Miscellaneous Documents*, 35th Cong., 1st Sess., No. 108, pp. 8–9; *Senate Executive Documents*, 35th Cong., 2nd Sess., No. 1, pp. 732–34; *Cong. Globe*, 35th Cong., 2nd Sess., debates on pp. 1152–55, 1230–32, 1276–81; Russel, *Improvement of Communication with the Pacific Coast as an Issue in American Politics*, 222–26; Royal Meeker, *History of Shipping Subsidies* (New York, 1905), 150–57.

upon the enterprise. Congress did finally pass Zachariah Chandler's pet project of improving the St. Clair Flats, but Buchanan then vetoed the measure for financial as well as constitutional reasons.[42]

Several other legislative proposals ran into the retrenchment mentality. The homestead and agricultural college acts depended upon Congress' willingness to manipulate public lands for nonrevenue purposes. Plans utilizing the public domain immediately encountered the budget dilemma, for the estimates of Cobb hinged on securing several million dollars from land sales. In the Senate, Toombs and Hunter protected the designs of Cobb from alteration. Not only did they hope to thwart any new program that might make use of public lands, but they also declared that western settlers were to receive no more leniency from the administration. Hunter, when commenting upon Andrew Johnson's retrenchment resolutions, pointed to the proceeds that Cobb had expected from sales of public lands. Yet the sales had been postponed. "I know and I appreciate the excuse," Hunter said; for reasons of humanity the administration had allowed preemptioners more time to acquire funds to pay for their lands. But now the treasury needed the money and the lands would go on the market.[43]

Toombs demonstrated less sympathy than Hunter. "This is an ordinary source of revenue," he stated, "and it was the duty of the Government, when it called upon us to appropriate money to survey new public lands, to bring those public lands into market as soon as it could be conveniently done." Westerners, Toombs charged, strove to obtain a homestead measure so they would not have to pay for the land. James F. Simmons challenged the policies advocated by Toombs. He correctly pointed out that land sales would only dispossess the preemptioners and asked, "Is that the way to help the poor?" Southerners knew the political consequences of forced land sales in Kansas, Minnesota, Iowa, and other western states and territories. Yet, in their zeal to add to the revenue, and thereby protect the tariff of 1857, southerners invited political defeat in that region.[44]

42. For the Pacific railroad see *Cong. Globe,* 35th Cong., 2nd Sess., debate on 157, 260–65, 305–11, 352–59, 577–85, 629; APX, 250–51, 278, 294; Russel, *Improvement of Communication with the Pacific Coast as an Issue in American Politics,* 226–30. For the St. Clair Flats veto, see Chicago *Press and Tribune,* March 8, 1859; Milwaukee *Daily Free Democrat,* March 9, 1859; Kuhn, "Economic Issues and the Rise of the Republican Party in the Northwest," 144–48.

43. *Cong. Globe,* 35th Cong., 2nd Sess., 1016.

44. *Ibid.,* remarks of Sen. Toombs, 898; remarks of Sen. Simmons, 931; remarks of

Surprisingly, Justin Morrill's agricultural colleges bill managed to pass both houses of Congress. This was particularly unexpected, for in the Democratic Senate southerners wielded significant influence, and they generally disapproved of the measure. The bill escaped their wrath because northerners banded together with a few border state Whigs to enable the legislation to succeed. The one insuperable obstacle for the agricultural colleges proposal, however, was President Buchanan. He promptly vetoed the measure as an unconstitutional enactment further depleting the treasury. The Republican press screamed. Many Republicans saw the act as a beneficent measure designed "to advance and elevate the pursuits of Agriculture and Mechanics," and they labeled Buchanan's action an example of the Slave Power's hostility to measures that would improve the lot of the free laborer.[45]

Congress spared Buchanan the onus of vetoing a homestead measure, for the legislation did not get out of the Senate. Republicans, of course, affirmed that the bill was needed to assist the northern wage earner, although a few disputed the idea of giving the public domain away free of charge. The Democrats were not unified on the issue. Most southerners disliked the proposal, believing it to be unfair to the older states and inimical to slavery expansion, while the northern Democratic press generally praised the idea of providing free land for the actual settler.[46] Fortunately, the inability of the homestead bill to get to the president's desk saved the northern wing of the party from the humiliation of justifying Buchanan's undoubted veto.

The last ten days of Congress were a whirlwind attempt to finish the government's business by March 4, the day of adjournment. Finances dominated the attention of Congress and the administration. Debates over appropriation bills reached their bitterest point, but still no action was taken to provide extra funds for the expected deficiencies. Pennsylvania Democrats refused to cooperate with the party and

Rep. Letcher and Rep. Phelps, 1487; Chatelain, "The Federal Land Policy and Minnesota Politics, 1854–1860," 233–42; Paul Wallace Gates, *Fifty Million Acres: Conflicts over Kansas Land Policy, 1854–1890* (Ithaca, N.Y., 1954), 77–80.

45. *Cong. Globe*, 35th Cong., 2nd Sess., 857, 1412–13; quote from Chicago *Press and Tribune*, March 1, 1859; Hibbard, *A History of the Public Land Policies*, 328–30; Paul Wallace Gates, "Western Opposition to the Agricultural College Act," *Indiana Magazine of History*, XXXVII (1941), 107–22.

46. Reinhard H. Luthin, *The First Lincoln Campaign* (Cambridge, Mass., 1944), 13; Washington (D.C.) *Union*, October 6, 1858; Washington (Pa.) *Examiner*, February 10, 1859; Cleveland *Daily Plain Dealer*, February 11, 1859.

turned down all requests for a loan or a reissuance of treasury notes unless the tariff was revised. Together with the Republicans, the Pennsylvania Democrats created a huge logjam in Congress.

Phelps, the chairman of the Ways and Means Committee, finally determined that the best he could manage was to request Congress to readopt the tariff of 1846 with the free list of 1857 (the list of imported goods exempted from duties). Attempts to reach a compromise in committee had failed, so he requested a suspension of the rules in the House to take up his proposal. A majority decided to debate a new tariff, but not the two-thirds needed to suspend the rules. The tariff failed.[47]

Buchanan and Cobb anxiously watched the proceedings in Congress as the days slipped away. The treasury needed money or it could not pay its debts. Still the Pennsylvania Democrats refused to countenance any loan or treasury note bill until the Congress raised the tariff. On March 2, the Senate finally secured an amendment to the civil appropriations bill allowing a twenty million dollar reissuance of treasury notes.[48]

But the Pennsylvania Democratic delegation held firm. Buchanan sent an urgent notice to both houses of Congress on March 3, requesting that Congress provide for the solvency of the government. He feared that last year's issue of treasury notes would become due and the government would be unable to redeem them. The Pennsylvania House Democrats did not budge, but neither would the House entertain a motion to reconsider the tariff. Congress continued to legislate through the night, until at 7:00 A.M. on March 4, the Pennsylvania Democracy caved in to the personal pleas of Howell Cobb. The treasury note reissuance became law. Only Owen Jones, William Dewart, and Wilson Reilly kept their pledge not to vote for any aid to the government unless the tariff was revised.[49]

The inability of the administration to obtain a revision of the tariff was not the only political failure of this session of Congress. The agitation over the slavery question had not abated, nor had the breach between the Douglas Democracy and the rest of the party been healed. Republican legislation constantly fell before the threat of Buchanan's

47. New York *Times*, February 21, 1859; New York *Daily Tribune*, February 22, 28, 1859; *Cong. Globe*, 35th Cong., 2nd Sess., 1412.

48. *Cong. Globe*, 35th Cong., 2nd Sess., 1571.

49. *Senate Executive Documents*, 35th Cong., 2nd Sess., No. 44, p. 1; New York *Daily Tribune*, March 4, 1859; John Eddins Simpson, *Howell Cobb: The Politics of Ambition* (Chicago, 1973), 129–130.

veto and the fiscal emergency. Oregon became a new state, but not without another struggle over the volatile question of slavery in the territories. Almost everyone connected with this Congress left with bitterness and disgust.

Voting patterns in the Senate and House in the third session of the Thirty-fourth, the two sessions of the Thirty-fifth, and the first session of the Thirty-sixth Congresses reveal the successes and the difficulties the parties encountered with economic issues. Both the Republicans and the lower South—the cotton South—acted as unified blocs on almost all policy questions. But the national Democratic party splintered. Northern Democrats were more susceptible to regional economic pressures, and on certain subjects they clashed significantly with the desires of the southern Democracy. The border slave state opposition, however, occupied something of a middle ground. On some economic topics they sided with the Republicans, while on others they took Democratic stands. Yet on most matters, including to some extent slavery, the southern opposition was markedly different from its Democratic counterpart.

Tables 6 and 7 present voting tabulations for a number of Senate and House roll-call votes divided into categories of regional party affiliation. The figures represent the percentage of individuals in each category voting "aye" for the motion under consideration; an explanation of each roll-call is provided in the notes to the tables. Because in many instances the number of legislators voting in certain categories was so small, the actual tally of "ayes" is given in parentheses. Only those individuals who voted were counted; pairings as well as affirmations of how some legislators would have voted were ignored. The states of the far West (California and Oregon) were excluded because interest centered principally on the North-South division.[50]

Democratic voting, particularly in the House, establishes the fact that the party suffered important internal splits based on region. Except for the well-known difficulties involving Lecompton, the Democrats hung together on most slavery-related subjects. It was on economic issues that the party fragmented. Southern Democrats generally took a

50. From these figures one can construct indices of dissimilarity as designed by Holt, *The Political Crisis of the 1850s*, 26–27. For a detailed investigation of voting patterns based on Guttman scaling, see Thomas B. Alexander, *Sectional Stress and Party Strength: A Study of Roll-Call Voting Patterns in the United States House of Representatives, 1836–1860* (Nashville, 1967), 91–109.

united stand regarding most roll-calls on tariffs, internal improvements, and the financial condition of the treasury, and the most solid bloc of all was that of the Deep South (South Carolina, Georgia, Florida, Alabama, Mississippi, Louisiana, Texas, and Arkansas). Northern Democrats, however, followed regional self-interest. Democrats in the Mid-Atlantic region (New York, New Jersey, and Pennsylvania) and those from the New England area—a vanishing breed—often sided with the Republicans. These individuals, as one might suspect, supported tariff revision, the homestead policy, and internal improvements. On the other hand, Democrats from the Great Lakes states (Ohio, Indiana, Michigan, Illinois, Wisconsin, Iowa, and Minnesota) more often than not mirrored southern opinion on economic concerns except for two subjects: improvements on the Great Lakes (the St. Clair Flats bill) and, especially, federal disposition of western lands. While Great Lakes Democrats agreed that the West should not be used to promote agricultural colleges, they showed total disagreement with their southern compatriots on homestead legislation and the suspension of land sales. On the question of the tariff, however, the Great Lakes and the southern Democrats had but one voice: no revision.

Although economic issues produced a separation between northern and southern Democrats, it would probably be an error to assume that northern Democrats were acting like Republicans on subjects of economic policy. Northern Democrats were responding to perceived regional interests on specific topics; they did not share with the Republicans a comprehensive ideal of economic progress fostered by governmental activity. Nonetheless, there were sufficient northern Democratic defections from a pure Jacksonian standard of economic propriety to enable southerners to fret that northern legislators, irrespective of party affiliation, had a growing tendency to act in concert on all matters of economic policy. And, of course, southerners interpreted this tendency to mean that northerners sought to advance the welfare of their free labor society regardless of the consequences for the slaveholding South.[51]

The behavior of the southern opposition—principally Whigs and Americans—partially belies the idea that southerners were of one mind in matters of federal policy. On economic questions, southern opposition legislators favored tariff revision, approved of agricultural

---

51. Note that from the data in Tables 6 and 7 it would appear that the Democracy had difficulty in achieving unity on subjects dealing with the West.

Table 6

Senate Affirmative Votes by Party and Section for Selected Roll-Call Votes, 1857–1860 (Percentages)

Roll-Call Vote	Democrats									Sou Opp	Republicans			
	AD	S	SB	SO	SW	N	NE	NM	NL	S	AR	NE	NM	NL
Slavery-Related														
1. Lecompton	88 (29)	100 (22)	100 (8)	100 (8)	100 (6)	64 (7)	50 (1)	100 (3)	50 (3)	60 (3)	00 (0)	00 (0)	00 (0)	00 (0)
2. English Bill	91 (28)	100 (21)	100 (7)	100 (8)	100 (6)	70 (7)	50 (1)	100 (3)	60 (3)	67 (2)	00 (0)	00 (0)	00 (0)	00 (0)
3. Ore Adm	73 (21)	60 (12)	71 (5)	33 (2)	71 (5)	100 (9)	100 (2)	100 (2)	100 (5)	25 (1)	60 (10)	57 (4)	100 (3)	50 (3)
4. Kan Adm	91 (28)	100 (24)	100 (9)	100 (7)	100 (8)	67 (4)	00 (0)	100 (1)	75 (3)	100 (1)	00 (0)	00 (0)	00 (0)	00 (0)
Expansion														
5. Cuba	00 (0)	00 (0)	00 (0)	00 (0)	00 (0)	00 (0)	00 (0)	00 (0)	00 (0)	100 (1)	100 (16)	100 (8)	100 (3)	100 (5)
Far West														
6. Cal Tel	60 (20)	35 (7)	38 (3)	00 (0)	67 (4)	87 (13)	100 (4)	100 (3)	75 (6)	100 (3)	100 (10)	100 (5)	100 (2)	100 (3)
7. Pac RR	61 (19)	84 (16)	75 (6)	100 (5)	83 (5)	27 (3)	50 (1)	33 (1)	17 (1)	50 (2)	43 (6)	71 (5)	00 (0)	20 (1)
8. Pac Tel	59 (13)	47 (10)	56 (5)	43 (3)	40 (2)	100 (3)	100 (1)	100 (1)	100 (1)	—	93 (15)	100 (6)	100 (3)	86 (6)
Economic														
9. Tariff 1857	84 (25)	95 (18)	83 (5)	100 (8)	100 (5)	64 (7)	50 (2)	33 (1)	100 (4)	100 (2)	75 (6)	75 (3)	100 (2)	50 (1)

10. Treas Notes	83 (24)	90 (17)	89 (8)	100 (5)	80 (4)	70 (7)	50 (1)	100 (3)	60 (3)	67 (3)	25 (4)	38 (3)	50 (1)	00 (0)
11. Homestead	73 (22)	95 (18)	100 (8)	83 (5)	100 (5)	36 (4)	100 (1)	100 (3)	00 (0)	80 (4)	29 (4)	57 (4)	00 (0)	00 (0)
12. Govt Loan	93 (25)	94 (16)	83 (5)	100 (7)	100 (4)	90 (9)	100 (1)	100 (3)	83 (5)	50 (2)	00 (0)	00 (0)	00 (0)	00 (0)
13. Fish Bount	91 (29)	100 (21)	100 (7)	100 (7)	100 (7)	73 (8)	00 (0)	100 (3)	83 (5)	100 (3)	00 (0)	00 (0)	100 (3)	00 (0)
14. Ag Coll	13 (3)	00 (0)	00 (0)	00 (0)	00 (0)	50 (3)	100 (1)	100 (1)	33 (1)	80 (4)	100 (17)	100 (8)	100 (3)	100 (6)
15. Treas Notes	100 (22)	100 (15)	100 (8)	100 (3)	100 (4)	100 (7)	100 (1)	100 (1)	100 (5)	100 (1)	89 (8)	100 (6)	00 (0)	100 (2)
16. Homestead	77 (25)	96 (22)	89 (8)	100 (7)	100 (7)	33 (3)	50 (1)	100 (1)	17 (1)	33 (1)	00 (0)	00 (0)	00 (0)	00 (0)
17. St Clair	26 (8)	11 (2)	25 (2)	00 (0)	00 (0)	63 (6)	100 (2)	67 (2)	33 (2)	50 (2)	100 (17)	100 (9)	100 (3)	100 (6)
18. Tariff	10 (4)	04 (1)	00 (0)	13 (1)	00 (0)	50 (3)	100 (2)	100 (1)	00 (0)	100 (4)	100 (17)	100 (8)	100 (3)	100 (6)
19. Tariff	10 (3)	00 (0)	00 (0)	00 (0)	00 (0)	50 (3)	100 (2)	100 (1)	00 (0)	75 (3)	100 (17)	100 (8)	100 (3)	100 (6)
20. Govt/Loan	94 (26)	100 (21)	100 (5)	100 (6)	100 (6)	71 (5)	00 (0)	50 (1)	100 (4)	—	00 (0)	00 (0)	100 (3)	00 (0)
21. Tariff	93 (23)	100 (21)	100 (5)	100 (6)	100 (6)	67 (2)	—	00 (0)	100 (2)	—	00 (0)	00 (0)	100 (3)	00 (0)
22. Homestead	77 (21)	68 (15)	40 (4)	83 (5)	100 (6)	100 (6)	100 (1)	100 (1)	100 (4)	—	95 (19)	88 (7)	100 (3)	100 (9)

NOTE: % is percentage of individuals in the category who voted "aye"; ( ) is the actual number of individuals in the category who voted "aye."

LEGEND: AD = All Democrats; S = All Southern Democrats; SB = Border State (Del., Md., Va., N.C., Ky., Tenn., Mo.); SO = Old South (S.C., Ga., Fla., Ala.); SW = Southwest (Ark., Miss., La., Tex.); N = All Northern Democrats; NE = New England (Maine, N.H., Vt., Conn., Mass., R.I.); NM = Northern Mid-Atlantic (N.Y., Pa., N.J.); NL = Great Lakes (Ohio, Ind., Ill., Wisc., Mich., Iowa, Minn.); Sou Opp = Southern Opposition; AR = All Republicans.

SOURCES AND EXPLANATION OF ROLL-CALLS:

1. Lecompton. Passage of Lecompton enabling act, March 23, 1858, *Cong. Globe*, 35th Cong., 1st Sess., 1264–65.

2. English bill. Passage of the English Compromise bill on Kansas administration, April 30, 1858, *ibid.*, 1899.

3. Ore Adm. Admission of Oregon enabling act, May 18, 1858, *ibid.*, 2209.

4. Kan Adm. Vote to postpone consideration of admission of Kansas, June 5, 1860, *Cong. Globe*, 36th Cong., 1st Sess., 2625.

5. Cuba. Vote to lay purchase of Cuba bill on the table, February 25, 1859, *Cong. Globe*, 35th Cong., 2nd Sess., 1363.

6. Cal Tel. Bill to construct a telegraph to California, February 26, 1857, *Cong. Globe*, 34th Cong., 3rd Sess., 298.

7. Pac RR. Motion to lay proposed Pacific Railroad bill on the table, April 17, 1858, *Cong. Globe*, 35th Cong., 1st Sess., 1647.

8. Pac Tel. Bill to construct telegraph to Pacific Coast, March 26, 1860, *Cong. Globe*, 36th Cong., 1st Sess., 1345.

9. Tariff 1857. Vote to concur in report of joint committee on tariff bill, March 2, 1857, *Cong. Globe*, 34th Cong., 3rd Sess., 1062.

10. Treas Notes. Vote on treasury notes bill, December 19, 1857, *Cong. Globe*, 35th Cong., 1st Sess., 103.

11. Homestead. Vote to postpone consideration of homestead bill, May 27, 1858, *ibid.*, p. 2426.

12. Govt Loan. Vote on permitting the government to obtain $15 million in loans, May 26, 1858, *ibid.*, 2405.

13. Fish Bount. Vote on discontinuation of fishing bounties bill, May 19, 1858, *ibid.*, 2239.

14. Ag Coll. Vote on agricultural college bill, February 7, 1859, *Cong. Globe*, 35th Cong., 2nd Sess., 857.

15. Treas Note. Vote on reissuing treasury notes, March 3, 1859, *ibid.*, 1571.

16. Homestead. Motion to postpone consideration of the homestead bill, February 17, 1859, *ibid.*, 1076.

17. St Clair. Vote on bill to improve the St. Clair Flats, December 21, 1858, *ibid.*, 155.

18. Tariff. Vote on amendment to appropriation measure establishing specific duties, March 2, 1859, *ibid.*, 1564.

19. Tariff. Vote on proposition by Sen. Simmons to institute specific duties, March 3, 1859, *ibid.*, 1632.

20. Govt. Loan. Amendment to legislative appropriation bill enabling the government to borrow $20 million, June 13, 1860, *Cong. Globe*, 36th Cong., 1st Sess., 2930.

21. Tariff. Vote to postpone House tariff bill until next session, June 15, 1860, *ibid.*, 3027.

22. Homestead. Vote on homestead bill, May 10, 1860, *ibid.*, 2043.

Table 7

House Affirmative Votes by Party and Section for Selected Roll-Call Votes, 1857–1860 (Percentages)

Roll-Call Vote	Democrats									Sou Opp	Republicans			
	AD	S	SB	SO	SW	N	NE	NM	NL	SB	AR	NE	NM	NL
Slavery-Related														
1. Lecompton	14 (24)	01 (1)	00 (0)	05 (1)	00 (0)	43 (23)	33 (1)	28 (9)	68 (13)	50 (6)	98 (85)	100 (25)	100 (29)	100 (31)
2. English Bill	84 (101)	96 (65)	100 (39)	90 (18)	89 (8)	72 (36)	50 (1)	76 (22)	68 (13)	50 (6)	04 (3)	04 (1)	04 (1)	03 (1)
3. Ore Adm	82 (97)	74 (48)	89 (31)	35 (7)	100 (10)	91 (49)	100 (2)	83 (25)	100 (22)	00 (0)	18 (15)	17 (4)	03 (1)	36 (10)
4. Kan Adm	35 (27)	02 (1)	04 (1)	00 (0)	00 (0)	93 (26)	—	92 (11)	94 (15)	19 (4)	99 (96)	100 (24)	98 (41)	100 (31)
5. N Mex	03 (2)	00 (0)	00 (0)	00 (0)	00 (0)	08 (2)	—	18 (2)	00 (0)	09 (1)	98 (93)	96 (25)	97 (36)	100 (32)
Far West														
6. Pac RR	83 (87)	89 (57)	88 (30)	89 (16)	92 (11)	79 (30)	33 (1)	95 (18)	68 (11)	50 (6)	04 (1)	04 (1)	04 (1)	03 (1)
7. Pac Tel	27 (17)	17 (8)	26 (6)	00 (0)	29 (2)	43 (9)	—	46 (5)	40 (4)	28 (5)	90 (77)	100 (26)	78 (29)	96 (22)
Economic														
8. Tariff 1857	94 (65)	98 (47)	96 (24)	100 (15)	100 (8)	86 (18)	100 (2)	78 (7)	90 (9)	60 (9)	40 (36)	80 (20)	32 (10)	18 (6)
9. Treas Notes	93 (92)	92 (49)	97 (24)	100 (17)	67 (8)	96 (43)	100 (3)	96 (23)	94 (17)	58 (7)	07 (5)	13 (3)	04 (1)	04 (1)
10. Ag Coll	23 (21)	11 (6)	11 (3)	18 (3)	00 (0)	36 (15)	100 (2)	52 (13)	00 (0)	82 (9)	88 (59)	100 (20)	100 (18)	78 (21)

	AD	S	SO	SB	SW	N	NE	NM	NL	Sou Opp	AR	NE	NM	NL
11. Treas Notes	85 (86)	100 (58)	100 (34)	100 (14)	100 (10)	66 (28)	50 (1)	50 (13)	94 (14)	56 (5)	06 (4)	09 (2)	05 (1)	05 (1)
12. Land Sales	23 (21)	13 (7)	23 (7)	00 (0)	00 (0)	38 (14)	50 (1)	47 (8)	28 (5)	11 (1)	100 (75)	100 (23)	100 (23)	100 (29)
13. St Clair	41 (33)	07 (3)	04 (1)	00 (0)	29 (2)	76 (30)	100 (2)	83 (20)	60 (8)	44 (4)	100 (74)	100 (20)	100 (28)	100 (26)
14. Tariff	28 (29)	04 (2)	07 (2)	00 (0)	00 (0)	59 (27)	100 (1)	86 (24)	12 (2)	100 (8)	94 (60)	100 (21)	91 (21)	90 (18)
15. Tariff	32 (37)	09 (6)	17 (6)	00 (0)	00 (0)	61 (31)	67 (2)	90 (26)	16 (3)	85 (11)	96 (77)	100 (25)	96 (26)	93 (26)
16. Tariff	27 (30)	02 (1)	03 (1)	00 (0)	00 (0)	58 (29)	100 (3)	89 (25)	06 (1)	83 (10)	95 (77)	100 (24)	96 (27)	90 (26)
17. Fish Bount	78 (89)	98 (62)	97 (35)	100 (18)	100 (9)	55 (27)	33 (1)	31 (9)	100 (17)	67 (8)	06 (5)	00 (0)	00 (0)	18 (5)
18. Govt Loan	94 (57)	98 (45)	100 (19)	95 (18)	100 (8)	80 (12)	—	67 (4)	89 (8)	58 (11)	21 (17)	41 (9)	03 (1)	25 (7)
19. Tariff	13 (9)	02 (1)	05 (1)	00 (0)	00 (0)	42 (8)	—	89 (8)	00 (0)	67 (8)	96 (86)	100 (26)	94 (34)	93 (26)
20. Homestead	33 (19)	03 (1)	04 (1)	00 (0)	00 (0)	100 (18)	—	100 (8)	100 (10)	05 (1)	100 (83)	100 (24)	100 (32)	100 (27)

NOTE: % is percentage of individuals in the category who voted "aye"; ( ) is the actual number of individuals in the category who voted "aye."

LEGEND: AD = All Democrats; S = All Southern Democrats; SB = Border States (Del., Md., Va., N.C., Ky., Tenn., Mo.); SO = Old South (S.C., Ga., Fla., Ala.); SW = Southwest (Miss., Ark., La., Tex.); N = All Northern Democrats; NE = New England (Maine, N.H., Vt., Conn., Mass., R.I.); NM = Northern Mid-Atlantic (N.Y., Pa., N.J.); NL = Great Lakes (Ohio, Ind., Ill., Wisc., Mich., Iowa, Minn.); Sou Opp = Southern Opposition; AR = All Republicans.

SOURCES AND EXPLANATIONS OF ROLL-CALLS:

1. Lecompton. Vote on bill to resubmit Kansas Constitution to people of Kansas (*i.e.*, defeat of the enabling bill), April 1, 1858, *Cong. Globe*, 35th Cong., 1st Sess., 1437–38.

2. English Bill. Passage of compromise on Kansas Constitution, April 30, 1858, *ibid.*, 1905–1906.

3. Ore Adm. Admission of Oregon enabling legislation, February 12, 1859, *Cong. Globe*, 35th Cong., 2nd Sess., 1011.

4. Kan Adm. Admission of Kansas enabling legislation, April 11, 1860, *Cong. Globe*, 36th Cong., 1st Sess., 1672.

5. N Mex. Bill to nullify slave laws in Territory of New Mexico, May 10, 1860, *ibid.*, 2046.

6. Pac RR. Motion to lay bill on Pacific Railroad on the table, December 19, 1857, *Cong. Globe*, 35th Cong., 1st Sess., 105.

7. Pac Tel. Bill to construct telegraph to Pacific, May 24, 1860, *Cong. Globe*, 36th Cong., 1st Sess., 2329.

8. Tariff 1857. House concurs with Senate amendments to tariff of 1857, March 2, 1857, *Cong. Globe*, 34th Cong., 3rd Sess., 971.

9. Treas Notes. Treasury note bill, December 22, 1857, *Cong. Globe*, 35th Cong., 1st Sess., 154.

10. Ag Coll. Agricultural college bill, April 22, 1858, *ibid.*, 1742.

11. Treas Notes. Treasury note reissue legislation, March 3, 1859, *Cong. Globe*, 35th Cong., 2nd Sess., 1681.

12. Land Sales. Amendment to suspend land sales, January 20, 1859, *ibid.*, 493.

13. St Clair. Bill to improve St. Clair Flats, March 2, 1859, *ibid.*, 1598.

14. Tariff. Motion to suspend rules to consider the tariff, March 3, 1859, *ibid.*, 1788.

15. Tariff. Motion to suspend rules to consider the tariff, February 20, 1859, *ibid.*, 1411–12.

16. Tariff. Motion to suspend rules to consider the tariff, February 21, 1859, *ibid.*, 1197.

17. Fish Bount. Motion to suspend rules to consider a bill repealing fishing bounties, February 21, 1859, *ibid.*, 1197.

18. Govt Loan. Bill to enable the government to contract loans, June 22, 1860, *Cong. Globe*, 36th Cong., 1st Sess., 3254–55.

19. Tariff. Tariff bill of 1860 (Morrill), May 10, 1860, *ibid.*, 2056.

20. Homestead. Homestead bill (Senate version), May 21, 1860, *ibid.*, 2221–22.

colleges, and divided over internal improvements and Buchanan's financial measures. But their voting record varied considerably from the Democrats. What is more striking is that on the major questions of Lecompton and the English compromise bill, the two principal slavery-related measures, the opposition still maintained its distance from the southern Democratic stance. This feature of southern opposition voting lends credence to the claim of Michael F. Holt and Marc Kruman that the existence of a viable two-party system led the parties to espouse different views on all subjects of public controversy.[52] Yet it must be remembered that outside of the border slave states the southern opposition was virtually nonexistent—at least in its capacity to elect federal officials. And the reasons for which the southern opposition quarreled with southern Democrats over slavery extension were certainly different from those of the Republicans.[53]

In contrast to the Democrats, the Republicans acted as a party unit on virtually every roll-call vote listed in Tables 6 and 7, whether the issue was slavery expansion, communication with California, Buchanan's financial schemes, or economic issues. The one exception was the tariff of 1857; on that bill Republicans followed regional self-interest. But after the Panic of 1857, Republicans were nearly unanimous that the tariff required an upward adjustment. The one topic that especially elicited a unified party stand was federal disposition of public lands. There were virtually no defections from the Republican position on agricultural colleges, suspension of western land sales, and the adoption of a homestead policy. It may be surmised, therefore, that a central feature of the Republican party was its concern over the fate of the West. Finally, the disparity between Republican and cotton-South Democratic voting should be noted: on almost every issue they were at polar opposites.

The virtually monolithic stand of Republican congressmen on economic and slavery-related issues indicates that by the Thirty-fifth and Thirty-sixth Congresses past party affiliations were not influencing the way party members were casting their votes. Yet tensions among the

52. Holt, *The Political Crisis of the 1850s*, 3–5, 235–36; Marc W. Kruman, *Parties and Politics in North Carolina, 1836–1865* (Baton Rouge, 1983), 140–42. Holt uses this explanation in a slightly different context, arguing that the second party system confined the slavery controversy, and only when political realignment occurred in the 1850s and weakened the national parties did the slavery issue emerge in full fury.

53. See, for example, Dwight Lowell Dumond, *The Secession Movement, 1860–1861* (New York, 1931), 94–98, 105–106; and Kruman, *Parties and Politics in North Carolina*, 104–107, 172–78.

different groups composing the Republican coalition did exist, especially between former Democrats and Whigs. Republican unanimity on congressional policy questions before the war was probably a result of an intense desire to defeat the supposed machinations of the Slave Power, the sense of crisis among Democrat-Republicans overcoming their normal Jacksonian proclivities. When the problem with the Slave Power ceased after the Civil War, and after the first stages of Reconstruction had been completed, the party experienced considerable internal turmoil because of dissension between ex-Democrats and ex-Whigs over economic issues.[54]

The second session of the Thirty-fifth Congress was more important than many historians have indicated. Scholarly attention has usually focused upon the first session of this Congress, when the Lecompton controversy shook the political firmament, and the first session of the Thirty-sixth Congress, when both parties readied themselves for the 1860 presidential contest.[55] In 1859, however, the Democratic party had the opportunity to remove or at least to limit the damage that vexatious economic issues were inflicting upon its appeal in the North. The condition of the treasury afforded the Democracy a chance to solve the federal government's fiscal dilemmas and at the same time to meet some of the economic wishes of the Pennsylvania and Great Lakes Democracy regarding the tariff and western land policy. In this session of Congress, the matter of slavery's expansion into the territories was much less a distraction than in other sessions. But the Democracy utterly failed to come to grips with the problem of federal finances. By their inability to arrange a satisfactory solution to fiscal affairs, the party sacrificed the initiative in policy making and allowed the Republicans to win the battle over economic programs.

The tariff was the most important issue in the 1859 congressional session. Because of the condition of the treasury, the Democrats had every justification to combine tariff revision with a retrenchment program. Instead the Democracy did not effect a change in the tariff, and

54. A table of Republican congressional roll-call voting, 1857–1860, broken into categories of past party affiliations, has been omitted because the unanimity of the Republicans precludes finding significant deviations among Republicans based on previous political attachments. For Republican coalition problems after the war, see Michael E. McGerr, "The Meaning of Liberal Republicanism: The Case of Ohio," *CWH*, XXVIII (1982), 307–23.

55. For example, compare the treatment of these sessions of Congress by Nevins, *The Emergence of Lincoln*, I, 250–304, 440–59, and II, 112–31, 171–202.

financial necessity then compelled them to pursue policies that further weakened the party in the North. No longer could Democrats allow a leakage of funds to river and harbor improvements. Perhaps more importantly, the Democrats took one of the worst positions imaginable on the question of the public lands. The Northwest had suffered severely because of the crop damage of 1858 and the falling off of European demand, and the settlers in the West, the preemptioners, could not pay for their land if public land auctions took place. However, Buchanan, Hunter, and Toombs demanded that auctions be held. This was indeed a tragic reversal of the party's former platform of aiding and encouraging the western settler. Because the budget was so tightly constructed, because Cobb had cut so many corners to keep inviolate the tariff of 1857, and because he had estimated expenses so closely, the Democrats had to preserve every possible revenue source. Thus in March, 1859, the party turned its back on the settler and, in another reversal of Jacksonian economics, allowed the national debt to swell.

While the Democracy alienated northerners who desired particular commercial projects and angered westerners who longed for favorable land policies, it also infuriated Pennsylvanians on the tariff question. It was no secret to anyone in politics that Pennsylvania was a crucial state in national politics. Pennsylvania was the battlefield of presidential elections; whichever party captured Pennsylvania also captured the presidency. The elections of 1858 had presented one portentous and undeniable fact: the opposition had gained an absolute majority in the Keystone State. And they had done so by using the tariff issue. Congressional Democrats outside of the Middle Atlantic states recklessly ignored the Pennsylvanians' cry for aid and actually substantiated the contention of the opposition that the Democracy would not listen to the groans of free white labor and effect needed policy changes. The proceedings of Congress proved the Republicans correct in their assertion that the Slave Power wielded the sinews of government in slavery's behalf and cast aside the interests of the free states. A more convincing demonstration of the Slave Power, from a Republican viewpoint, could not have been arranged.

A revision of the tariff failed, in the final analysis, because the southern Democracy refused to alter the tariff of 1857. This obstinate position is not easily explained. In a political sense, the Democracy in all parts of the nation knew the issues involved in the Pennsylvania election of 1858, and during the congressional session the demands of the Pennsylvania Democracy received wide notice. Besides the newspaper sources, Pennsylvania Democrats undoubtedly told other representatives of their dilemma and how necessary an upward revision of the tariff was to the party's future in the Keystone State.

What emerges as the gravest error of judgment by southern Democrats was the labeling of their Pennsylvania cohorts as protectionists and renegades to the true faith, for the Pennsylvanians actually stayed within the broad outlines of the general party stance on the tariff. Except possibly for the editor of the Pittsburgh *Morning Post*, no Pennsylvania Democrat ever approved of the doctrine of protectionism as defined by Henry Carey or Henry Clay. In the heat of the election of 1858, the Pennsylvania Democracy stuck faithfully to the creed of a revenue tariff with incidental protection. The tariff of 1846 was constantly hailed as the best one in the nation's history; the opposition lashed out at that tariff and demanded a return to the distinctly protective tariff of 1842. Throughout the campaign of 1858 Pennsylvania Democrats upheld the ideals of commercial exchanges and low taxation. This was all within the general framework of free trade. When the southerners tarnished the Pennsylvania Democrats with the title of "protectionists," they libeled their party compatriots who braved the horrendous protectionist onslaught and denigrated the Pennsylvania party's faithful stand on the issue of low and equitable tariffs.

Southern Democrats were not, however, monolithic in their attitudes toward the tariff. Certainly party ideologues on free trade—for example, William Boyce, John Letcher, and Roger A. Pryor—wavered not an inch from their doctrines. But this was not true of all southerners. Senator Alfred Iverson was as staunch a proslavery and southern rights man as existed in this particular Congress, and at one point he practically advocated secession. Yet Iverson still recognized political realities, and in a letter he counseled others to revise the tariff before Congress was overwhelmed with protectionists. He also feared that if the tariff were not removed from debate "the subject would form one of the exciting elements of the next presidential election, and would sweep the democratic party from Congress in every tariff State, and probably in every free State in the Union." But if the Democrats acted when they still had a congressional majority, they could "remodel the tariff to suit our own policy." Iverson demonstrated that he was thinking distinctly of Pennsylvania, for he wrote that he was not averse to changing the duty to 30 percent "on iron, coal, and other similar articles." [56]

56. *Cong. Globe*, 35th Cong., 2nd Sess., 242; letter of Iverson in Washington (D.C.) *Union*, February 26, 1859.

There were recurring reports about southerners who would agree to a substitution of the tariff of 1846 for that of 1857 for a few years. John S. Phelps attempted to persuade Congress to accept the idea, and John Savage of Tennessee and even Senator Hunter warmed to the plan as a fair compromise. The editors of the Washington *Union* argued that "what was democratic for ten years previously to 1857 would certainly not be anti-democratic after that period," a sentiment that the Richmond *Examiner* echoed.[57] The point was well taken. Pennsylvania Democrats asked for little more than the tariff of 1846—they had, after all, lauded that tariff incessantly in the 1858 elections—and the party could have justifiably ignored the other demands of the Pennsylvanians. By enacting the tariff of 1846 Democrats could reasonably have argued that they had stayed within the bounds of free trade doctrines, had responsibly met the requirements of the treasury, and had shown a flexibility toward the various elements that composed the party. Moreover, they would have escaped the harsh policies that financial stringency dictated they follow toward the western settler. A higher tariff would have allowed enough small river and harbor appropriations to pass so as not to wholly incense the northern states. Indeed, if the southern Democrats had thought in national rather than sectional terms, they could have gutted the Republican charge of the Slave Power conspiracy by using the tariff to demonstrate their willingness to sacrifice a little for the benefit of northern white workingmen, while all the time maintaining traditional Democratic economic policies. None of this occurred. Instead the southern Democrats allowed the Republicans to picture southerners as men whose only concern was to guard the economic and social welfare of the peculiar institution.

Yet the southerners' stance was neither economically irrational nor out of character with their constitutional scruples. Southerners, particularly Democrats, had long felt that high tariffs gave the federal government too much power, and a powerful federal government was always a threat to local control over slavery.[58] In pressing for the lowest possible tariff, southern legislators were only representing their sec-

57. "Independent" in Philadelphia *North American*, January 5, 15, 1859; New York *Herald*, February 12, 1859; Washington (D.C.) *Union*, February 25, 1859; Richmond (Va.) *Examiner* quoted in Charleston *Mercury*, February 25, 1859.

58. The southern apprehension over high tariffs possibly creating a stronger, and therefore possibly meddling, national government is a theme developed by William W. Freehling, *Prelude to Civil War: The Nullification Controversy in South Carolina, 1816–1836* (New York, 1965), 126–27, 138–39; Kaufman, *Capitalism, Slavery, and Republican Values*, 83–84, 86, 104.

tion's obvious economic interests, which presumably was one of the reasons the southern people elected them. A high tariff could potentially harm their prosperity. In the nineteenth century, the tariff was *the* taxing power of the government. Southerners had responded angrily to the tariffs of 1828 and 1842; their experiences reinforced their belief that a high tariff rendered slavery less profitable. For southerners, then, a high tariff resulted in distinct economic disadvantages that they, as all persons, strove to avoid.

The mismanagement of the tariff issue was not solely the fault of the southern Democracy. Northern Democrats, particularly in the Great Lakes region, evinced no desire to aid the Pennsylvanians in raising tariff rates. Except in Pennsylvania and New Jersey, the Democracy simply did not favor tariff revision. But southerners took the lead in battling the legions of protectionism and thus earned the ill will of the Keystone State. They did not emerge from the congressional session as statesmen.

Beyond their economic fears and trepidations of a more potent federal government, southern Democrats probably felt the tariff had a symbolic meaning. After losing the race for Kansas, the word *compromise* came into even greater disrepute than previously. If, as Hammond had argued in late 1858, the South could no longer expand, then the section needed to buttress its position in the Union by assuming control over the nation's economic policies. Having this effective power over national legislation, the South need not fear the onslaught of Republicans and abolitionists. But to acquiesce in a compromise on such matters as the tariff only further indicated the erosion of southern strength in the councils of government. Southerners needed a compensation for their loss of Kansas; this compensation became the nation's economic policy. Nonetheless, practical statesmanship offered a better means for southerners to maintain their political hegemony. Out of pride of their past and fear for their future, southerners pursued a course of pettiness and narrow sectionalism in the halls of Congress.[59]

59. One development in political affairs in 1859 has not been particularly well noted by other historians. In 1859 a number of states held congressional races. Most of these contests were unremarkable, but in the border slave states a virtual revolution occurred. In 1857, Kentucky, Tennessee, North Carolina, and Virginia elected 35 Democrats and 6 opposition candidates to Congress; in 1859 these numbers were 19 Democrats and 22 opposition members. This election in the border states represents as great an upheaval, if not more so, as the northern 1858 congressional returns. Perhaps historians have overlooked this fascinating turn of events because soon after came John Brown's raid on Harpers Ferry, and in Virginia the gubernatorial race between Letcher and Goggin over-

shadowed the congressional elections. There may have been some connection between the Panic of 1857 and the Democratic reverses in these states, but an investigation of some newspaper sources fails to locate any sustained mention of economic policies or anything directly linked to the Panic. Instead, opposition victories in the border states seem to have arisen from a resurgent Whiggery that was thoroughly repulsed by the Buchanan administration's financial doings, Democratic party corruption, and the imbroglio in Kansas. It is doubtful that federal deficits caused such an upheaval in the border states, especially since in an economic sense those deficits had a minimal impact on business conditions. The reinvigoration of Whiggery perhaps arose out of a sense that the Democratic party was endangering the nation and betraying the true interests of the South, at least in the eyes of former Whigs. See Raleigh (N.C.) *Weekly Register; Semi-Weekly Standard* (Raleigh, N.C.); Richmond (Va.) *Whig,* Richmond (Va.) *Enquirer,* Louisville *Daily Courier,* and the Knoxville *Whig* between April and August, 1859. See also Nevins, *The Emergence of Lincoln,* II, 61–67; Arthur Charles Cole, *The Whig Party in the South* (Washington, D.C., 1913), 331–35; William S. Hitchcock, "The Limits of Southern Unionism: Virginia Conservatives and the Gubernatorial Election of 1859," *JSH,* XLVII (1981), 57–72; Thomas E. Jeffrey, "National Issues, Local Interests, and the Transformation of Antebellum North Carolina Politics," *JSH,* L (1984), 68–69.

EIGHT / Economic Resurrection and the Rights of Labor

The functioning of the economy in 1859 and 1860 buttressed many of the sectional arguments that the financial crash of 1857 had evoked. Southerners found much evidence in the slow recovery of northern businesses to confirm their opinion that the welfare of the North depended upon trade with the South; they believed that this circumstance could be used with telling force in the political battle over slavery. The outbreak of northern labor unrest in 1859 and 1860 also proved useful to southerners; they again employed proslavery labor doctrines to explain the sudden occurrence of northern strikes and to tout the superiority of slavery as a means of adjusting the relations between capital and labor. The increasing tempo of worker dissatisfaction, however, raised in an emphatic manner for northerners the interrelated questions of the material well-being of the laborer and the stability of American social institutions.

The American economy exhibited signs of revival in 1859. The nadir of the depression associated with the financial collapse came at the close of 1857, and poor economic conditions persisted throughout 1858. In 1859 there emerged a substantial though halting return to prosperity, as not all regions fared equally well. The South continued to enjoy business success while the North Atlantic states were able to achieve pre-Panic levels of industrial output. A business depression, however, continued to plague the western agricultural states in 1859. Westerners still lacked an adequate market for their breadstuffs. Only in the middle of 1860 did demand for western staples increase and end the region's peculiar market difficulties, and it was at that time that the economic effects of the Panic finally disappeared.

Although business conditions were improving, financial leaders followed prudent policies in 1859 and 1860. Call loans and short-term paper were available, but bankers refused long-term credit. The editors of *Bankers' Magazine* and *Hunt's Merchants' Magazine* commented on the steady increase in specie holdings and deposits.[1] One principal variation in the money market occurred in the spring of 1859 when investors paid heed to the rumor that France and Austria would soon be at war. European investments in the Northwest were liquidated, which created an additional flow of specie out of that hard-pressed area. The war scare also created a financial stringency in the East. However, European conditions were not grave enough or of sufficient duration to alter significantly the American money market, and after June, 1859, the financial system resumed its normal functioning.[2]

Easterners noted a slow improvement in manufacturing in the spring months of 1859. Iron, coal, and textile production increased in 1859, although the true surge in industrial activity was to come in 1860 (see Table 8). Other difficulties besides the general recession hampered recovery in certain industries. Shipbuilders still constructed obsolescent wooden vessels, and textile manufacturers suffered excessive competition from marginal producers. New England shoe manufacturers continued to endure hard times because the West, one of the shoe industry's principal markets, had not yet recovered.[3]

As the northeastern manufacturers worked themselves out of recession, the cotton-growing South bounded to higher levels of prosperity. The Panic had only temporarily affected southern staples, and in the next three years the slaveholding states enjoyed continuous expansion, which astonished economic writers. The primary reason for southern well-being was, of course, the seemingly insatiable European demand for cotton. The years from 1857 to 1860 witnessed an incredible output of the fiber; cotton bales exported from the South numbered 2,266,000

1. "Notes on the Money Market" section in *Bankers' Magazine*, XIII (January-June, 1859), XIV (July-December, 1859); "Commercial Chronicle and Review" section in *Hunt's*, XL (January-June, 1859), XLI (July-December, 1859), XLII (January-June, 1860).

2. *Hunt's*, XL (June, 1859), 710, XLI (July, 1859), 76–81, XLI (August, 1859), 196–97; Boston Board of Trade, *Seventh Annual Report* (Boston, 1861), 61.

3. For textile and iron production, see New York *Daily Tribune*, February 5, April 1, May 3, June 2, 11, July 1, 1859; *Hunt's*, XL (February, 1859), 199, XL (March, 1859), 327–28. For shipbuilding see *Hunt's*, XL (May, 1859), 581; New York *Times*, November 28, 1859. For shoe manufacturing consult Lynn (Mass.) *Weekly Reporter*, February 12, 1859, January 21, 28, 1860; Blanche Evans Hazard, *The Organization of the Boot and Shoe Industry in Massachusetts Before 1875* (Cambridge, Mass., 1921), 106–107.

Table 8

Selected Industrial Output, 1856–1860

Year	Pig Iron[a] (000 tons)	Coal[b] (000 tons)	New England Textiles[c] (000 yards)	Vessels Built[d] (tons)
1856	883	7858	775,000	469,000
1857	798	7693	661,000	379,000
1858	705	7772	766,000	242,000
1859	840	8589	856,000	157,000
1860	920	9578	850,000	213,000

[a] All types of pig iron; compiled from James M. Swank, *History of the Manufacture of Iron in All Ages,* 376.

[b] All types of coal recorded in the Schuylkill, Lehigh, and Wyoming regions; compiled from *Miner's Journal* (Pottsville, Pa.), January 12, 1861.

[c] Estimates of New England textile output taken from Lance E. Davis and H. Louis Stettler, "The New England Textile Industry, 1825–1860: Trends and Fluctuations," in *Output, Employment, and Productivity in the United States After 1800* (New York, 1966), 221. Vol. XXX of Conference on Research in Income and Wealth, *Studies in Income and Wealth.*

[d] For years ending on June 30. Compiled from *Hunt's Merchants' Magazine,* XLV (August, 1861), 179.

in 1857; 2,452,000 in 1858; 3,006,000 in 1859; and 3,812,000 in 1860. Tobacco, the other major southern export crop, had a more troublesome time. Southerners gained only $17,010,000 from the tobacco export trade in fiscal year 1858. They obtained a decade high of $21,070,000 the next fiscal year, but in 1860 the proceeds from foreign tobacco sales slipped to $15,907,000. Tobacco growers faced declining prices in the last two years of the decade, but this occurred partially because of their abundant crops. Evidently tobacco farmers still trusted the profitability of the staple because they continued to harvest record amounts.[4]

Although the Northeast and the Middle Atlantic states rebounded from depression and the South entered into the glory years of King Cotton, the Great Lakes region was still in an economic quagmire. The grain growing states of Ohio, Illinois, Indiana, Wisconsin, Michigan,

4. *House Executive Documents,* 36th Cong., 2nd Sess., No. 2, pp. 401, 471; Robert, *The Tobacco Kingdom,* 155–57; Wright, *The Political Economy of the Cotton South,* 90–97.

and Iowa encountered severe problems in marketing their staples. European demand for wheat and corn fell to an extremely low level in 1859. England had purchased 8,560,000 bushels of wheat and 4,184,000 bushels of corn in the fiscal year ending June 30, 1857; in the fiscal year ending June 30, 1859, the respective totals were a paltry 984,000 and 332,000 bushels. Flour fared no better.[5]

Some of the West's agricultural problems were the product of drought and pests. But the damage done to western cereals by weather conditions and insects was less significant for the welfare of the region than its inability to market the crops it did raise. When rumors of an impending European war obtained some credence in the spring of 1859, prices on the Chicago exchange rose in anticipation of a large European demand for foodstuffs. The demand never materialized and prices drooped once again, the farmers "experiencing a heavy disappointment."[6]

The fall trade of 1859 did not alleviate the debt problems of the West. Financial editors noted with resignation that only a home demand for breadstuffs existed, not a foreign one. Only one favorable item appeared in the market columns: Europeans had a poor fall harvest and this led to a rise in exports of American cereals at the end of the year. There were further expectations that the difficulties of foreign agriculture might bring a return to European demand in 1860.[7]

The salvation of the West did indeed come in 1860. Throughout the spring reports circulated that European farmers were experiencing grave troubles. In the summer the rumors received verification as the call for American foodstuffs went out. The rejoicing began in the middle of August. "The good time has come," announced the Chicago *Press and Tribune*, while the New York *Daily Tribune* called the huge shipment of grains "THE RESURRECTION OF THE WEST." By October 1860

5. Unnumbered reports entitled, "Commerce and Navigation of the United States," *Senate Executive Documents*, 35th Cong., 2nd Sess., pp. 24–25, 48–49; *Senate Executive Documents*, 36th Cong., 1st Sess., pp. 24–25, 48–49; *House Executive Documents*, 36th Cong., 2nd Sess., No. 2, p. 401. The total value of breadstuff exports for fiscal years 1856 to 1860 were: 1856–57, $75,723,000; 1857–58, $53,236,000; 1858–59, $40,401,000; 1859–60, $48,452,000.

6. Bidwell and Falconer, *History of Agriculture in the Northern United States*, 336; Chicago *Press and Tribune*, June 15, 20, July 19, September 28, 1859; quote from New York *Times*, August 8, 1859; James E. Boyle, *Chicago Wheat Prices for Eighty-One Years: Daily, Monthly, and Yearly Fluctuations and Their Causes* (Ithaca, N.Y., 1922), 7.

7. Chicago *Press and Tribune*, August 4, 1859; Indianapolis *Daily Journal*, August 5, 26, October 6, November 9, 1859; *Bankers' Magazine*, XIV (December, 1859), 494; *Hunt's*, XLI (December, 1859), 716–19.

the Cleveland *Daily Plain Dealer* exulted over the economic turn-about: "The foreign demand for cereals continues brisk, and every steamer from over the big waters puts prices up, up, up." In the fiscal year ending June 30, 1859, the United States exported 3,002,000 bushels of wheat; in fiscal year 1860 the total was 4,155,000; but in the fiscal year ending June 30, 1861, the amount grew to 31,238,000.[8]

One other economic endeavor revived due to the increased commerce in foodstuffs—the western railroads. In 1857 Americans had generally lashed out at the poor management of railroads, the stock devices used to entice investors, and the unwarranted expansion of facilities into the West. Not the least of the incidents arousing public disapproval were the railroad freight wars that developed among the great trunk lines, especially the New York Central and the New York and Erie. Aside from the cannibalistic trunk lines, however, eastern railroads did not fare poorly in 1859. A rise in local traffic had produced ample revenue. Southern roads had also prospered. But the western railroads did not share in the success of the eastern and southern lines. In 1858 the roads of the Old Northwest had "suffered severely in diminished gross earnings." Financial and business journalists hoped 1859 would be different, and they pointed to the agricultural crops as the only means "to give business to our railroads and to relieve the commercial embarrassment that presses so hardly [*sic*] upon the new States."[9]

The railroads at last found salvation in the tremendous outpouring of cereals to the east coast during 1860. Railroad shares responded well during the summer and fall months of 1860 (see Table 9). The improved position of railroad stock and bonds came from the increase in European orders for American breadstuffs, for these orders provided the railroads with freight, which greatly enhanced their earnings. By the

8. *Bankers' Magazine*, XV (September, 1860), 255; *Hunt's*, XLII (April, 1860), 456, XLIII (August, 1860), 208, XLIII (September, 1860), 326–27; Chicago *Press and Tribune*, August 15, 1860; New York *Daily Tribune*, August 31, 1860; Cleveland *Daily Plain Dealer*, October 12, 1860; wheat figures from *Eighth Census* (Washington, D.C., 1864), II, p. cxl; *House Executive Documents*, 36th Cong., 2nd Sess., No. 2, p. 417.

9. *American Railroad Journal*, March 12, 1859, p. 169, March 26, 1859, p. 200, May 7, 1859, p. 296, June 11, 1859, p. 376; New York *Daily Tribune*, March 21, 1859; *Harper's Weekly*, April 23, 1859, p. 258, August 27, 1859, p. 546; *American Railway Times*, March 12, 1859, January 21, 1860; *American Railroad Journal*, July 23, 1859, p. 472.

Table 9

Selected Biweekly Railroad Quotations, March–September, 1860

	Railroad Stock Quotation													
	March		April		May		June		July		August		September	
Railroad	2	16	8	20	4	18	1	15	6	20	3	17	27	21
NY Central	70	73	78	80	79	81	82	81	82	83	84	87	85	88
NY Erie	8	10	12	16	17	21	20	17	19	22	23	27	29	37
Mich. Sou.	8	8	10	13	12	12	11	13	13	17	18	21	22	23
Mich. Cent.	36	40	46	49	48	48	52	49	48	53	61	66	71	70
Ill. Cent.	67	60	62	60	59	61	63	61	63	70	76	86	86	87
Cleveland & Toledo	19	20	26	30	28	30	29	29	31	36	39	47	45	48
Rock Island	63	65	64	64	66	70	75	72	71	74	80	83	79	78

SOURCE: *Bankers' Magazine* XIV (June, 1860), 973, XV (August, 1860), 166, XV (October, 1860), 335.

summer of 1860 market reporters jubilantly trumpeted the return of the western railroads to prosperity.[10]

With the revival of the West in the summer of 1860 the Panic of 1857 may be said to have ended, for the economy had returned to its pre-1857 condition. Although the South had experienced only minor business difficulties at the close of 1857 and the beginning of 1858, and the Northeast and Middle Atlantic states had regained much of their prosperity by the middle of 1859, it was not until the West recovered in 1860 that the nation entered a new round of the business cycle.[11] But the new-found prosperity of 1860 was not destined to last. Just as the economy appeared on the brink of another expansionary period, political factors intervened. The election of Abraham Lincoln in November, 1860, led the Deep South to secede from the political Union, and this entailed a secession from the economic Union as well. As a result the North was prematurely plunged back into a depression. The poor business conditions that plagued the first two years of the Lincoln administration, however, were not a continuation of the problems that had begun in late 1857. The odd fluctuation of the economy in 1860— prosperity in the summer and fall, and depression in the winter— would have an interesting effect upon the appeal of Democrats and Republicans in the presidential campaign of that year.

The regional peculiarities of the economy's recovery from the Panic of 1857 permitted southerners to extend their claim that the country's economic health depended upon cotton. The major factor giving credence to this boast was the continued depression in the West, which momentarily darkened the attitudes of capitalists and manufacturers about the prospects of that section. Instead, financiers and industrialists turned to the booming market of the South as the place to sell merchandise and invest funds. The extent to which the South offered more opportunities for increased trade and investment can be seen in a comparison of railroad construction between the South and the North (see Table 10).[12]

10. *Hunt's*, XLIII (September, 1860), 327, XLIII (October, 1860), 454, 456–57, XLIII (November, 1860), 587–89; *Bankers' Magazine*, XV (August, 1860), 168, XV (November, 1860), 414–15; *American Railroad Journal*, March 10, 1860, pp. 212–13; Huston, "Western Grains and the Panic of 1857," 14–32.

11. Most historians who have charted the Panic of 1857 have usually referred to the spring of 1859 as the turning point of the depression. See Van Vleck, *The Panic of 1857*, 73–94; Taylor, *The Transportation Revolution*, 350.

12. According to E. R. Wicker, Poor's figures are highly inaccurate. See Wicker,

Table 10

Northern and Southern Mileage Added to Railroads, 1856–1860

| | Ringwalt's Estimates | | Poor's Estimates | |
Year	Total Slave States	Total Free States	Total Slave States	Total Free States
1856	542.51	961.41	1065	1210
1857	839.71	1297.47	916	1473
1858	878.58	996.29	1068	833
1859	1047.63	672.39	1004	726
1860	956.73	409.80	130	531

SOURCE: J. L. Ringwalt, *Development of Transportation Systems in the United States* (1888; rpr. New York, 1966), 142–45, 174–77; Henry V. Poor, *Manual of the Railroads of the United States for 1875–'76* (New York, 1875), xvi.

The difference in business conditions between the West and the South received due weight in newspapers and journals. During the spring trade of 1859, the New York *Daily Tribune's* weekly review of the dry goods market constantly referred to the enormity of the southern trade and at the same time lamented the reduction in traffic between the East and the West. *Hunt's Merchants' Magazine* reported that textile manufacturers were evincing "a disposition to recognize the high credit of the southern section of the country, where the large crops have sold at such remunerative prices." The journal of southern economic progress, *De Bow's Review,* also noted that the West was failing to provide the hoped-for outlet for eastern manufacturing surpluses and that the South was making up for the western deficiency. One Philadelphia correspondent reported to the New York *Daily Tribune* in late 1859 that businesses in the North now advertised heavily in the South and have spared "no cost to make themselves and their wares known through the cotton and tobacco regions, which seem to have escaped the exigencies of the great crash two years ago, and are now flush with money from sales of heavy crops at maximum prices." An Indiana editor, reflecting upon the economic changes the Panic had wrought, simply

"Railroad Investment Before the Civil War," in *Trends in the American Economy in the Nineteenth Century* (Princeton, N.J., 1960), 506. Vol. XXIV of Conference on Research in Income and Wealth, *Studies in Income and Wealth.* Ringwalt's figures are more in accord with Wicker's findings, and for this reason both sets of figures are offered.

stated, "at present the South is, beyond question, outstripping the North and East in the accumulation of wealth, if not in the increase of population."[13]

Many northern industrialists rallied to try to win over the southern market. James Reid Anderson, principal owner of the Tredegar Iron Works in Richmond, found a new and vigorous competition from the North for southern railroad equipment sales. The shoe manufacturers of Lynn, Massachusetts, appeared reticent to extend credit to westerners but not to southerners.[14]

As a new economic axis between the Northeast and the South materialized, some northern businessmen altered their positions on political issues. Because the economy had not returned to the degree of prosperity for which so many longed, many businessmen shrank back from a sectionalism that could further hinder trade. Northeastern merchants and industrialists needed the southern market; they were not about to indulge in any activity that could destroy the only commerce which brought profits.[15]

Southerners well understood the economic patterns that existed between the sections of the Union in 1859 and 1860. William Gilmore Simms wrote Senator Hammond about the prospects of a new conservative party emerging in the Union, although he felt that the belated arrival of such an organization could not halt the Republican party's growth. He doubted whether a truly conservative party could ever succeed unless the nation fell into desperate political straits. However, he said, "The really working & business world, when urged by despair, will always conquer. And one thing rather favors the organization of this party now. It is that the trade of the country has *not* recovered from the revulsion of 1856 [*sic*]! This is *felt* and, no doubt, this feeling works to a considerable extent in the Northern mind." Hammond probably agreed with Simms's assessment of the effect of the Panic upon the northern business community. In the spring of 1860 he re-

13. New York *Daily Tribune*, February 12, 28, March 11, April 8, June 3, 1859; *Hunt's*, XL (April, 1859), 462; *De Bow's Review*, XXVII (July, 1859), 106–107; New York *Daily Tribune*, September 2, 1859; Evansville (Ind.) *Daily Journal*, February 24, 1859.

14. Charles B. Dew, *Ironmaker to the Confederacy: Joseph R. Anderson and the Tredegar Iron Works* (New Haven, Conn., 1966), 34–37; New York *Daily Tribune*, January 30, 1860; Lynn (Mass.) *Weekly Reporter*, February 12, 1859.

15. Philip S. Foner, *Business & Slavery: The New York Merchants & the Irrepressible Conflict* (1941; rpr. New York, 1968), 143, 145, 149–53; Thomas H. O'Connor, *Lords of the Loom: The Cotton Whigs and the Coming of the Civil War* (New York, 1968), 125–33.

stated to Francis Lieber his belief that cotton was king: "I firmly believe that the slaveholding South is now the controlling *power* of the world—that no other power would face us in hostility." [16]

Other southerners also held dear the idea of unconquerable cotton. *De Bow's Review* commented that cotton had become even "more indispensable to the commercial world." High prices for slaves, Virginia agricultural reformer Edmund Ruffin claimed, were a result of the large demand for cotton that caused a labor shortage in the South. There was no question among southerners that slavery provided the means by which cotton was raised and their well-being secured. "The bondage of the African at the South," wrote one newspaper editor, "is as necessary to her agricultural prosperity, as fresh air is to the healthy condition of the body." [17]

The South's dominant position in the economy was not the only subject southerners discussed in 1859. Politicians continued to denounce northerners for their position on the expansion of slavery into the territories, and fire-eaters openly avowed secession. At the southern commercial convention held in Vicksburg in May, 1859, the participants debated almost exclusively the topic of reopening the Atlantic slave trade. [18] Despite the fact that most southerners addressed the issue of slavery expansion in 1859, however, the knowledge they had of current economic affairs grew to be a most important element in their justification of slavery's value to the Republic. Events in late 1859 and early 1860 would demonstrate that short of secession southerners would depend more upon economic weapons to prod northerners into appropriate constitutional behavior than upon any other means.

As southerners gloried in the economy's revelation of their section's commercial power, northerners grappled with a problem that the Panic of 1857 had so forcefully brought to public awareness: the fate of the

16. William Gilmore Simms to James H. Hammond, January 10, 1859, in Oliphant, Odell, and Eaves (eds.), *The Letters of William Gilmore Simms*, IV, 105; James H. Hammond to Francis Lieber, April 19, 1858, in Thomas Sergeant Perry (ed.), *The Life and Letters of Francis Lieber* (Boston, 1882), 311.

17. *De Bow's Review*, XXVII (July, 1859), 106–107; Edmund Ruffin, "The Effects of High Prices of Slaves," *De Bow's Review*, XXVI (June, 1859), 647–48; A Florida Farmer, "Southern Prosperity," *De Bow's Review*, XXVII (July, 1859), 36–38; quote from *Mississippian* (Jackson), September 3, 1858.

18. Herbert Wender, *Southern Commercial Conventions, 1837–1859* (Baltimore, 1930), 228–31; John G. Van Deusen, *The Ante-Bellum Southern Commercial Conventions* (Durham, N.C., 1926), 56–70, 75–78.

free laborer. In 1859 the question of the well-being of the wage earner became a matter of some concern in the North because of the resurgence of the trade union movement. The Panic had wrecked many infant labor organizations and left in its wake a scattered, demoralized, and disgruntled working class. But when the economy revived in early 1859 so did the organizational aims of the workers. By the fall of 1859, labor turnouts had become so commonplace that the future of the American worker had again become a central topic of discussion.[19]

The North's bout with labor restlessness began at the very outset of 1859 when a short-lived strike at Bloomington, Illinois, occurred among employees of the Chicago, Alton, and St. Louis Railroad. In the succeeding months, newspapers recorded strikes among Newark cordwainers, New Jersey tunnel gangs, Philadelphia hatters, New York piano makers, Albany and Troy iron molders, and Schuylkill county coal miners, among others. The New York *Herald* exclaimed that the operatives of New Jersey "seem to be almost on a general strike." Many of the turnouts arose from the inability of numerous firms, especially the railroads, to pay their men for past services; in the East, efforts were made to regain pre-Panic wage scales. There were also constant attempts by workers to secure employer recognition of trade unions that would act as the agents to protect "the rights of labor."[20]

Northerners reacted to the workers' unrest with wariness. Most commentators objected to strikes because they were often accompanied by violence. They also felt that strikes usually were incapable of producing the desired results. Editors and other observers, both Democratic and Republican, doubted the wisdom of conducting walkouts during depressed times. They also maintained that strikes were violations of economic laws and thus could only end in disaster. In early 1860, northerners would obtain the opportunity to write upon the labor problem at greater length, but even in the fall of 1859 there was the

19. For the economic status of the wage earner in 1860, see Harold G. Vatter, *The Drive to Industrial Maturity: The U.S. Economy, 1860–1914* (Westport, Conn., 1975), 115–18; and Stanley Lebergott, *Manpower in Economic Growth: The American Record Since 1800* (New York, 1964), 150–53.

20. Bloomington, Ill., strike in Chicago *Press and Tribune*, January 15, 18, 19, 1859; quote of New York *Herald*, April 14, 1859; other strikes in James C. Sylvis, *The Life, Speeches, Labors and Essays of William H. Sylvis* (Philadelphia, 1872), 31–32; *Atlas & Argus* (Albany, N.Y.), September 8, 1859; New York *Times*, April 2, August 16, September 6, 12, 21, 1859; New York *Daily Tribune*, March 1, 10, October 15, 1859; *Miner's Journal* (Pottsville, Pa.), May 7, 1859; Pittsburgh *Morning Post*, April 7, September 3, 24, 1859; Detroit *Daily Free Press*, September 3, 4, 6, 1859.

recognition that, in the words of the *Scientific American,* "the labor question appears to be assuming greater importance than it has done for a great number of years past."[21]

At the same time that the North confronted a new wave of labor unrest, John Brown and his followers invaded the federal arsenal at Harpers Ferry and unleashed the South's most violent sectional passions. Southerners looked with horror on Brown's attempt to foment an insurrection in an established slave state. They immediately blamed the Republicans for the episode and characterized Brown's attack as a practical manifestation of Republican antislavery pronouncements. Republicans, of course, denied any complicity in Brown's actions and denounced the raid, but they also refused to alter their position on slavery.[22]

The deeds of John Brown begged for some remonstrance on the part of southerners to show northerners how tense relations between the sections were. Certain agitators called for extreme action: immediate secession or a conference of the slave states to list demands northerners would have to meet in order to keep the Union intact. These and other similar proposals failed to generate much support as most southerners still wanted to preserve the Union if at all possible. One suggestion, however, did obtain a wide hearing and elicited a favorable response. The Panic of 1857 and its aftermath had given southerners concrete evidence that their region's market was the pivotal one in the nation's economy. If southerners closed their market to northern wares, the Yankees would receive an adequate warning of both the height of feeling in the South and the commercial might of southern staples. Thus numerous newspaper contributors called for a nonintercourse movement in which southerners would boycott northern products.[23]

One of the common hopes of those who advocated nonintercourse with the North was the possible establishment of southern commercial independence. The proponents of nonintercourse forwarded a plan first devised by Edmund Ruffin in 1857 that called for state taxation on northern products by using the license laws. Many southerners main-

21. *Scientific American,* n.s., September 3, 1859, p. 153; Pittsburgh *Morning Post,* March 26, September 28, 1859; New York *Times,* April 2, September 6, 1859; *Atlas & Argus* (Albany, N.Y.), September 8, 1859; New York *Herald,* May 29, 1859.

22. On the southern reaction to John Brown's raid, see especially Channing, *Crisis of Fear,* 17–56.

23. Richmond (Va.) *Enquirer,* January 3, 17, 20, 31, February 3, 1860; Channing, *Crisis of Fear,* 100–102, 112–17; New Orleans *Daily Crescent,* January 3, 1860.

tained that by taxing foreign goods out of the market, the South would be forced to develop its own industrial, financial, and commercial facilities. Although numerous nonintercourse rallies were held and resolutions supporting a boycott of northern wares were passed, the movement never did produce legislation establishing a licensing system in any of the slave states. Southern radicals found that there was considerable opposition to a nonintercourse policy that might result in harming the South's economy more than the North's. And the movement also encountered an insuperable legal obstacle: the licensing system was obviously in violation of the U.S. Constitution's provisions on interstate commerce. Consequently, the only nonintercourse movement that emerged out of the mass of proposals was one that relied upon a voluntary abstension from the purchase of northern goods.[24]

There was an oddity to the licensing system, and indeed to the whole nonintercourse movement, that did not go unnoticed. Calls for legislation that would reduce imports to build up an internal market had a name: Henry Clay's American System. A licensing system was just a euphemism for a tariff. Southern radicals, who almost to a man supported free trade dogmas, suddenly found the reasoning of protectionists to be highly logical, useful, and even imperative. Mark A. Cooper, one of the more quoted writers on the subject of nonintercourse, employed, consciously or unconsciously, the reasoning of high tariff advocates: let the South purchase "what is made at home, even at a higher price, since in that, the cheaper article made abroad, is not economy for them. If brought abroad, it enriches others, and keeps us poor and dependent." Edmund Ruffin clearly understood the conflict between nonintercourse and free trade, but he never resolved the inconsistency. Although he reiterated his faith in free trade and his abhorrence of tariffs, he nonetheless admitted that Henry C. Carey— Ruffin named him specifically—was "perfectly correct" about the advantages of a domestic market.[25]

The central hope behind the nonintercourse movement was that the

24. Edmund Ruffin, "The True Policy for the Southern States," nos. 1, 2, 5, 1857, in Edmund Ruffin Papers, VHS; Mark A. Cooper in *Daily Constitutionalist* (Augusta, Ga.), January 10, 19, 1860; "Domestic Industry" in Charleston *Daily Courier*, January 17, February 8, 1860; Richmond (Va.) *Enquirer*, December 2, 9, 1859, January 13, 1860. There was southern opposition to the nonintercourse movement; for example, *Daily Picayune* (New Orleans), December 10, 11, 1859.

25. Mark A. Cooper in *Daily Constitutionalist* (Augusta, Ga.), January 19, 1860; Ruffin, "The True Policy for the Southern States," nos. 2, 3, 4, 1857, in Ruffin papers.

South could influence northern behavior and opinions by demonstrating the dependence of Yankee prosperity upon the southern market. In late 1859 and early 1860, the faith southerners placed in the power of their economy was a product of the experience of the Panic of 1857 and the recovery that occurred afterwards. Northern Democrats also paid attention to the economic patterns that the Panic of 1857 had exposed, and they quickly adopted the southern argument that the linchpin of national economic success was southern agriculture. When northerners met in a number of Union meetings after the Harpers Ferry raid to assure southerners that they thoroughly repudiated the extremism of John Brown, Democrats hammered away at the necessity of placating southerners for economic reasons. Many Democrats stated that the Panic of 1857 was the proof that without the southern market the North would be plunged into depression. Democratic orators, like Robert Tyler of Philadelphia, made a concerted effort to persuade "the great mass of the business men of the country" to reject Republican doctrines because of the damage antislavery pronouncements inflicted upon intersectional trade.[26]

Republicans, of course, dismissed the notion that an effective stoppage of southern purchases of northern goods could be accomplished. The New York *Times* conducted a survey of mercantile firms to find out what effect the alleged voluntary boycott was having. Merchants uniformly indicated that trade had never been better. For the most part, Republicans doubted whether human attempts to alter trading patterns could ever be successful. Like the editor of the Newark *Daily Advertiser,* most Republicans believed that "*profit,* not *politics,* governs their [merchants'] operations." Moreover, added the New York *Times,* southerners would continue to buy goods where prices most suited them because "the South is not one whit behind the North in its worship of the almighty dollar."[27]

Two interesting facets of the southern nonintercourse movement developed in late 1859 and early 1860. The first derived from the economic arguments southerners employed and the goals they hoped to achieve. Southerners used the experience of the Panic of 1857 to show northerners how dependent the free states were upon the southern

26. Quote of Robert Tyler in Philadelphia *Evening Bulletin*, December 8, 1859; New York *Times*, December 9, 20, 24, 1859; Detroit *Daily Free Press*, January 7, 1860; O'Connor, *Lords of the Loom*, 136–38.

27. New York *Times*, January 16, 18, 19, 1860; Newark *Daily Advertiser*, January 23, 1860.

economy; they attempted to persuade the Yankee monied class that its continued prosperity was contingent upon the health of southern cotton. This was a considerable reversal of the way southerners had used the Panic in late 1857 and early 1858. At that time firebrands and publicists called for southern independence because, it was alleged, the Panic unmasked the colonial status of the South. By 1859, because the southern economy was doing so well while the North's was mired in depression, the Panic of 1857 became an argument favoring the Union. The 1857 collapse seemingly disclosed the fact that northern prosperity required southern cotton. And if northerners could be tamed by economic threats, there was no need for disunion. Northern Democrats accepted this line of argument, and this appeal made a prominent appearance in the election of 1860.

A second feature of the nonintercourse movement involved southern predictions as to the effect of the removal of the southern trade on the northern laborer. Many nonintercourse propagandists stated that a cessation of southern trade would incite bread riots like those witnessed during the Panic of 1857. Republicans sneered at the suggestion that the South could so influence the North, but this was a premature boast, for events turned against the Republicans.[28] In the first few months of 1860, the question of the fate of the worker rose to haunt the free labor ideals of the Republican party.

An interesting conjunction of the several themes connected with the Panic of 1857 occurred on February 22, 1860: the shoemakers of Lynn, Massachusetts, inaugurated a strike which eventually became the greatest labor outburst in pre–Civil War American history. But although the strike involved the practical questions of union organization, wages, and craft standards, it also took place at a moment when sectional rancor was at a fever pitch and when southerners were stressing the power of southern agricultural staples and the susceptibility of northern society to labor turmoil. For northerners, however, the Lynn strike and the southern taunts that accompanied it, evoked, as had the bread riots in 1857, a searching discussion about the fate of the free laborer.

The cordwainers of Lynn had many grievances against their employ-

---

28. Raleigh (N.C.) *Weekly Register*, December 21, 1859; *Mississippian* (Jackson), January 19, 1860; New York *Daily Tribune*, January 17, 1860; Chicago *Press and Tribune*, February 9, 1860.

ers. For years the workers had believed that the owners were grinding them down by extracting more work for less pay and by lowering craft standards by sending jobs into the countryside for novices to perform. The Panic of 1857 brought the artisans' resentment to a head. Under the depressed business conditions, employers slashed wages and reduced employment. In response to the hard times, the shoemakers formed a secret union and started a strike fund. In early February, 1860, they presented their demands to the manufacturers. When they were rebuffed, the cordwainers walked off their jobs.

From its center in Lynn, the strike spread outward. Shoemaking employed more Massachusetts citizens than any other enterprise—fifty thousand men and twenty thousand women—and by the middle of March nearly one-half of these individuals had joined the walkout. The workers' protest did not stop at the Massachusetts border; it soon involved cordwainers throughout New England. But the manufacturers held firm and refused to accede to the artisans' demand. By mid-April, because of improved business conditions, they offered higher wages but refused to recognize the shoemakers' union. By this time many of the artisans were in desperate straits and went back to work; the great strike simply dissolved. Although the shoemakers obtained more adequate remuneration, they failed to establish a union and the right to collective bargaining.[29]

Southerners immediately interpreted the Lynn strike in the same manner that they had interpreted the bread riots of 1857: the strike was a manifestation of the poor treatment of free labor in the North and a portent of eventual class war. They repeatedly compared the material well-being of the slave to the impoverished condition of the shoemaker. Robert Barnwell Rhett told his small readership that such strikes were "the natural results of the natural conflict between Capital and Labor," because the cardinal economic dictum by which manufacturers lived was to "keep their laborers as near the starvation point as circumstances and the efficient operation of their factories will allow." John P. Heiss's *States and Union* believed the industrialists of the nation were the backbone of the Republican party. "We really think, sometimes," Heiss wrote, that capitalists "desire to divert the attention of the free laborers from the exactions to which they are subjected, and

29. For a fuller description of the Lynn strike, see Faler, "Workingmen, Mechanics and Social Change," 328–42, 354–70, 414–15, 462–67; Alan Dawley, *Class and Community: The Industrialist Revolution in Lynn* (Cambridge, Mass., 1976), 74–76.

therefore hire orators, and editors, and lecturers, to disfigure African slavery as much as possible." Southerners were also quick to point out that the New England strike was directly traceable to the nonintercourse movement and that now the workers began to understand how slavery benefited them.[30]

Northern Democrats seldom referred to the proslavery labor doctrines of their southern brethren, but they did find the South's market explanation well suited to their needs. Democrats above the Mason-Dixon Line argued that the Lynn strike was the product of the southern withdrawal of orders for northern goods. They then used the strike as an example of the South's economic power and warned their constituents that if Republicanism was not overthrown, the South would secede and bring about a disastrous depression in the North. One Democratic journal printed the letter of a Boston merchant that explained the causes of the shoe strike: "Our great market, the South, is for the present nearly lost to us. Our former large customers there now either decline to make any purchases, or buy very sparingly. The reason is, the state of feeling there, caused by recent events, towards the North."[31]

The Lynn strike confronted Republicans with a challenge to the sincerity of their free labor appeal. Republicans campaigned on the general theme that only the free labor system guaranteed progress and economic advancement. A corollary was that the free labor system amply rewarded the individual for his efforts. A general uprising of artisans in the stronghold of Republicanism did not fit well with Republican assertions as to the superior condition of the free laborer.

A typical response of Republicans to the shoemakers' strike came from Abraham Lincoln. Visiting his son who was attending school in the East, Lincoln spoke on the issues of the strike, although he professed ignorance about the particular labor problems in the region. Lincoln told audiences in Hartford and New Haven that he rejected the Democratic assertion that southern nonintercourse was responsible for New England's depressed economic condition. Most of his re-

30. *States and Union* (Washington, D.C.), March 2, 1860; *Semi-Weekly Mississippian* (Jackson), March 23, 1860; Charleston *Mercury*, March 21, 1860; *States and Union* (Washington, D.C.), March 2, 22, 1860; *Southern Confederacy* quoted by Charleston *Daily Courier*, March 13, 1860.

31. Quote in *New Hampshire Patriot & State Gazette* (Concord), February 22, 1860; New York *Herald*, March 7, 1860; Chicago *Daily Times*, March 2, 1860; Boston *Post*, February 21, 22, 1860.

marks, however, illustrated the benefits of the system of free labor as opposed to that of slave labor. *"I am glad to see that a system of labor prevails in New England under which laborers CAN strike when they want to,"* Lincoln argued. He further stated that the free laborer was always able to better his condition and climb up the social ladder. Then Lincoln turned to the topic of slavery and compared the relative merits of each system, emphasizing that under slavery the laborer was deprived of all avenues of advancement. He warned that if the spread of slavery were not halted, sooner or later slave labor would compete directly with free labor and drive wages down to the subsistence level. Sentiments similar to those of Lincoln were repeated numerous times in the Republican press.[32]

Politicians and sectional partisans were interested in the Lynn strike primarily for its usefulness in validating one side or the other's arguments in the controversy over slavery, but the debate over the walkout also elicited comments upon one topic that the Panic of 1857 had thrust to the forefront of the public's consciousness, that of the fate of the worker in free society. In the barrage of observations made about the Lynn strike, Americans demonstrated that they desired the worker to have adequate remuneration for his toil and every opportunity for advancement. To insure that the worker would obtain material rewards, Americans during the Lynn strike indicated their willingness to implement the labor program fashioned by economic theorists and politicians: free land, high tariffs, and education. But the public also made it plain that they would not tolerate any fundamental change in the country's economic or social institutions, that they were not going to support any program that included more than free land, high tariffs, and education.

The shoemakers of Lynn had a fairly coherent idea of the economic institutions they wished to see established. The subject of a redistribution of wealth or the eradication of property rights was never raised by the organizers of the strike, nor did any newspaper account ever re-

32. Speech of Abraham Lincoln at Hartford in Roy P. Basler, Dolores Marion Pratt, and Lloyd A. Dunlop (eds.), *The Collected Works of Abraham Lincoln,* (New Brunswick, N.J., 1953), IV, 7–9; Lincoln's speech at New Haven in *ibid.,* IV, 24–25; Bernard Mandel, *Labor Free and Slave: Workingmen and the Anti-Slavery Movement in the United States* (New York, 1955), 156–59; Gabor S. Borit, *Lincoln and the Economics of the American Dream* (Memphis, 1978), 181–85; Springfield (Mass.) *Daily Republican,* February 21, 1860; New York *Daily Tribune,* March 16, 28, 1860; Pittsburgh *Dispatch,* February 29, 1860; Boston *Daily Advertiser,* February 24, 1860.

cord such sentiments among the cordwainers. Instead, the workers stated that they believed labor and capital had equal rights and that a harmony of interests ought to prevail. They felt, however, as evidenced by their actions, that the capitalists had destroyed the harmony in order to obtain greater profits. To secure the "rights of labor," to ensure that capital did not enslave labor, the Lynn shoemakers demanded a trade union.[33]

The Lynn shoe manufacturers rigidly opposed the objectives of the operatives and refused to acknowledge the union as the shoemakers' bargaining agent. Just as importantly, the owners blamed the economic miseries of the workers on economic conditions over which they had no control. A group of Haverhill bosses stated that they had no desire to grind down their operatives and that they actually were "anxious that labor should be suitably paid." However, the manufacturers warned that higher wages could not be achieved by strikes; wages could only be raised "whenever the condition of the trade shall justify it." The bosses argued that the problem with current wages in shoe manufacturing was "an overplus of workmen and manufactures." In other words, supply and demand, rather than human needs, fixed the remuneration of the operative.[34]

In the final analysis, both Republicans and Democrats agreed with the bosses rather than with the laborers. Democrats appeared to castigate the power of capital more than the Republicans, whereas the Republicans seemed more skeptical of the designs of the workers than the Democrats. But their conclusions were ultimately mirror images of each other. Republican and Democratic commentators reluctantly agreed that under certain conditions a strike, in Horace Greeley's words, was "not only justifiable but praiseworthy" but then quickly added that those conditions almost never appeared. Generally, Democrats and Republicans said that strikes usually produced unconscionable violence and destroyed the harmonious attitude that should characterize the relations between capital and labor.[35]

Neither Republicans nor Democrats believed that trade unions

33. New York *Herald* quoted by Boston *Post*, March 9, 1860; Lynn (Mass.) *Weekly Reporter*, February 11, 1860; Boston *Traveller* quoted by New York *Daily Tribune*, February 18, 1860.

34. *Bay State* (Lynn, Mass.), March 22, 1860; quotes from Haverhill (Mass.) *Gazette*, March 9, 1860.

35. Quotes from New York *Daily Tribune*, September 2, 1859; Boston *Evening Transcript*, February 27, 1860; Springfield (Mass.) *Daily Republican*, February 21, 1860; Cin-

were valid economic institutions, whatever social value they might possess. They did not accept the shoemakers' claim that a trade union was required to offset the increasing power of capital. In fact, both parties agreed with the manufacturers that the reason for the depressed wage rate was not the avarice of the bosses but rather market conditions and the oversupply of labor. And Democrats and Republicans could not sanction trade unions even in the abstract because the institutions were a violation of economic laws. According to the Lynn operatives, the reason for a union was to protect the economic rights of the laborers—that is, to ensure that wages never fell below a certain standard. Democrats and Republicans rejected the idea that human beings could manipulate wages; wages, said William Cullen Bryant, were not set "by the will of the employer or the employed, but by the great natural causes under which both are bound." The Democratic editor of the Pittsburgh *Morning Post* had enunciated the same principle in 1859, stating that "no arbitrary rules can compel capital to pay for labor when the product is not in demand in the market." And both parties agreed with the *Post's* final comment as to how wages were determined: "Labor, like any other commodity, is subject to the inevitable laws of supply and demand."[36]

Despite the negative response most middle-class Americans gave to the Lynn strikers' demands for a union, they were nonetheless concerned about the extent of northern labor unrest. The Lynn strike was singular only in the size of the turnout; it was not unique in its revelation of general labor disquietude. To combat the rise of unionist sentiment among the working class, journalists and politicians turned ever more readily to the program of high tariffs, free land, and education. During the Lynn strike, many believed an adequate solution to the shoemakers' difficulties was to send men to the West. Horace Greeley wrote, "Let us have the Homestead bill passed, and a few hundreds of thousands thus attracted from shoemaking and other trades to agriculture" would increase eastern wages. Lynn's congressional representative, John B. Alley, also told the shoe operatives to look to the home-

---

cinnati *Daily Enquirer,* April 7, 1860; Pittsburgh *Morning Post,* March 16, 1860; Boston *Post,* February 21, 1860; *Atlas & Argus* (Albany, N.Y.), September 8, 1859.

36. Haverhill (Mass.) *Gazette,* March 9, 1860; Boston *Evening Transcript,* February 24, 1860; *Bay State* (Lynn, Mass.), March 8, April 19, 1860; Cincinnati *Daily Enquirer,* April 7, 1860; New York *Evening Post,* March 8, 1860; Pittsburgh *Morning Post,* March 26, 1859.

stead measure as a means of removing the labor surplus: "I hope to see our manufactories less crowded than they now are, and the dawn of a brighter day for the American mechanic."[37]

The Panic of 1857 had raised with considerable emphasis the question of the fate of the free laborer in a capitalistic society, and the state of the economy between 1857 and 1860 incited further labor unrest that constantly reminded the public of the issue. The Lynn strike was just one of many walkouts that elicited a debate in 1859 and 1860 on the future of the American wage earner. This debate easily lent itself to the sectional struggle over the existence and extension of slavery. Southerners, of course, quickly used the situation to demonstrate slavery's superiority in caring for the worker. The other manner in which the problem of the free laborer invaded the sectional dispute, however, may have been of more significance. Northerners, realizing that they needed to make some provision for the welfare of their industrial workers, gradually came to adopt the program of high tariffs, free land, and education—a program that would not entail a restructuring of the social edifice. These policies aroused the anger of southerners, however, because they saw tariffs, free western land for settlers, and federal aid to education as inimical to their section's material interests. Thus the labor program of the North became antislavery. During the election of 1860 the Republicans adopted this agenda as one suiting their oft-stated purpose: to elevate the free laborer of the North by circumscribing the slave labor of the South.

37. New York *Herald*, April 24, 1860; Chicago *Press and Tribune*, May 14, 1860; *Public Ledger and Daily Transcript* (Philadelphia), March 9, 10, 12, 1860; Cincinnati *Daily Enquirer*, March 11, 17, 1860; Pittsburgh *Dispatch*, May 16, 1860; New York *Daily Tribune*, March 13, 28, May 1, 1860; letter of John B. Alley to strikers, March 13, 1860, in Lynn (Mass.) *News*, March 21, 1860. For an elaboration upon the sectional aspects of the Lynn strike, see Huston, "Facing an Angry Labor," 197–212.

NINE / The Election of 1860

The Panic of 1857 shaped the presidential campaign of 1860 in a number of ways. The Panic's most obvious effect was the injection of specific economic policy questions into the controversy between North and South. For most of the 1850s sectional agitators had used economic arguments for and against slavery, but the onslaught of depression in late 1857 transformed the subject of federal policy from a debate over sectional favoritism into a controversy over the preservation of the free labor system. Republicans seized upon this aspect of the Panic of 1857—the need to protect northern free labor society by appropriate federal enactments—and quickly sharpened it into a deadly sectional argument: that is, that southerners not only cared little about northern free workers but also actively sought their degradation. Thus Republicans easily placed the experiences of the Panic of 1857 within the conceptual framework of the Slave Power conspiracy, adding to it a more urgent fear that southern political domination could destroy the viability of the North's free enterprise economy. Democrats, however, could also manipulate the Panic of 1857 to their advantage. By focusing attention upon the economic conditions between the sections in 1857 and 1858, Democrats illustrated the extent to which northern prosperity and social harmony depended upon a sure access to the southern market. This became the principal weapon Democrats used to thwart the Republican courtship of the northern business community.

Aside from the rhetorical stand of the parties, the Panic of 1857 played a major role in shaping party campaign strategy. Most politicians understood that the uncertain states, especially Pennsylvania, would have a determining influence upon the outcome of the presidential election, and they also realized that, because of the recession,

Pennsylvania was susceptible to an appeal for a high tariff. But there were further political complications. Throughout the uncertain states of the North and the border states were conservatives of Whig and nativist ancestry who disliked the extremism of both the Republicans and the Democrats. The Panic of 1857 had produced the economic issues that allowed northern conservatives to fuse with Republicans in the congressional elections of 1858. John Brown's raid and the possibility of a radical being nominated by the Republicans had loosened the tenuous bonds between the two groups. In terms of political maneuvering by the parties, therefore, the central questions were how to obtain votes in the doubtful states, particularly Pennsylvania, and how to conciliate the large floating bloc of disgruntled conservative voters.

Party leaders since late 1859 had been debating over the best presidential nominees for their organizations. Although Democratic and Republican officials certainly desired individuals who would uphold appropriate positions on the question of slavery expansion, they also viewed the matter of nominations in practical terms. Virtually all political leaders recognized that the election of 1860 would depend upon the voting results in the uncertain states of Illinois, Indiana, Pennsylvania, and New Jersey. In 1856 these states had voted Democratic and placed James Buchanan in the presidency; party managers expected these states to wield the same influence in 1860.

Equally apparent to party managers was the critical role that Pennsylvania assumed in presidential elections. In 1859 the Kentucky Whig John J. Crittenden announced to a Philadelphia gathering that "in this great contest which is impending, Pennsylvania is, perhaps, more than any other State of the Union the arbiter of our country's politics." Stephen A. Douglas concurred; he told a Pittsburgh crowd that "never in the history of this country had the Democratic party ever elected a President without the vote of Pennsylvania." A Republican newspaper editor in Harrisburg reiterated the same sentiment, reminding the Republicans that if they swept the entire North except for Pennsylvania and New Jersey, "they will lack two votes of an election."[1]

Aspirants for the Republican presidential nomination quickly demonstrated their understanding of Pennsylvania's electoral importance,

1. Crittenden speech in Philadelphia *Evening Bulletin*, January 16, 1859; Douglas speech in Pittsburgh *Morning Post*, September 6, 1859; *Pennsylvania Telegraph* (Harrisburg), December 5, 1859.

and they also disclosed that they knew the significance of the tariff issue to the voters of that state. Thus Salmon P. Chase, overeager candidate for the Republican nomination, found it convenient to bend his free trade scruples. In late 1859 he penned a public letter in which he stated that the tariff should be adjusted so as to "secure and promote the interests of labor—of our own labor—and the general well-being of our own people." Joseph Medill, an Illinois editor who was promoting Abraham Lincoln's candidacy, also recognized the necessity of winning Pennsylvania's favor. He wrote to Lincoln that Pennsylvania would support the Springfield attorney because he was "right on the tariff" and "exactly right on all other issues." Medill then asked, "Is there any man who could suit Pennsylvania better?"[2]

Regardless of the divisions rending the Democracy, northern and southern party leaders acknowledged the indispensability of Pennsylvania's twenty-seven electoral votes. Prior to the convention, Stephen Douglas tried to defuse the explosiveness of the tariff question. He told an interviewer that protectionism "has ceased to be a political issue, there being men in both parties, and in all parts of the country, who take different views and stand upon both sides." Robert Toombs, representing southern Democratic opinion, also acknowledged the weight of Pennsylvania in the nomination process. He knew that "Penn. wants a tariff man," and he realized that Pennsylvania's protectionist desires dimmed the chances for any southerner to obtain the nomination.[3]

An additional factor complicated national politics in 1860. Old-line Whigs and nativists formed a new party to challenge the sectionalism they believed to be animating the Democrats and Republicans. In 1858 and early 1859 conservatives found the financial and economic programs of the Buchanan administration reprehensible; but John Brown's raid and the new southern threat of secession in late 1859 eroded the frail alliance they had constructed with the Republicans. Thus by early 1860 many Unionists sought an adequate political organization that faithfully reflected their national outlook. Led by such old-line Whig

2. Salmon P. Chase to T. R. Stanley, October 25, 1859, in New York *Daily Tribune*, January 18, 1860; Joseph Medill to Abraham Lincoln, 1859, quoted from Reinhard H. Luthin, *The Real Abraham Lincoln* (Englewood Cliffs, N.J., 1960), 206–207.

3. J. Madison Cutts, *A Brief Treatise Upon Constitutional and Party Questions, and the History of Political Parties, as I Received it Orally from the Late Senator Stephen A. Douglas, of Illinois* (New York, 1866), 32, 158–59, quote on p. 160; Robert Toombs to Alexander H. Stephens, March 16, 1860, in Phillips (ed.), *The Correspondence of Robert Toombs, Alexander H. Stephens, and Howell Cobb*, 465.

luminaries as former New York Governor Washington Hunt, Kentucky Senator John J. Crittenden, and Virginia Congressman Alexander H. Boteler, the conservatives created a new organization, the Constitutional Union party.[4]

The leaders of the Constitutional Union party saw themselves as a serious threat to the hegemony of the Republicans and the Democrats. The Unionists feared that the radicals were ascendent among the Republicans; the verification of that idea, at least in the Unionist mind, was the likelihood that the alleged radical William H. Seward would become the Republican presidential nominee. They further believed that a Seward candidacy would send Republican conservatives to their organization. A partial confirmation of Unionist conjecture occurred in early 1860 when Rhode Island Whigs and nativists broke ranks with the free soil, former Democratic portion of the party. The Rhode Island conservatives demonstrated their numerical power by electing their candidate, William Sprague, and defeating the regular Republican nominee, Seth Padelford.[5] In addition to the Rhode Island victory, there were ample signs that the Constitutional Union party would do well in the uncertain states. The organizational head of the party, Alexander H. Boteler, learned from a New Jersey conservative "that the New Jersey Americans were both sick and ashamed of their associates [the Republicans]." One Pennsylvanian wrote Boteler that nativists had joined in an alliance with the Republicans not out of any common principles between the two camps, but because nativists would do "anything to beat the Democrats."[6]

The importance of the new party was that its appeal was to the group that Republicans desperately needed for victory. Nor was this by accident. The Unionists expected the Republicans to nominate a radical, like Seward, and thereby alienate conservatives in the doubtful states. Washington Hunt virtually conceded that the hope of the Union-

4. Edm. C. Pechin to Alexander R. Boteler, November 19, 1859, in Alexander R. Boteler Papers, DU; Washington Hunt to John J. Crittenden, April 9, 1860, in Coleman, *The Life of John J. Crittenden*, II, 189–90; F. Granger to John J. Crittenden, January 28, 1860, in John J. Crittenden Papers, DU; Holt, *The Political Crisis of the 1850s*, 207–11.

5. See James L. Huston, "The Threat of Radicalism: Seward's Candidacy and the Rhode Island Gubernatorial Election of 1860," *Rhode Island History*, XLI (1982), 86–99; Mario H. DiNunzio and Jan T. Galkowski, "Political Loyalty in Rhode Island—A Computer Study of the 1850s," *Rhode Island History*, XXXVI (1977), 93–95.

6. J. W. Bryce to Alexander R. Boteler, December 2, 1859, Jacob Devries to Alexander R. Boteler, February 10, 1860, both in Boteler Papers.

ists was to thwart the Republican bid for presidential victory. He did not believe the conservatives could actually sweep the nation, but, he said, "in several states the conservative men have sufficient strength to turn the scale."[7] The Constitutional Union party had as its unstated goal the defeat of the Republicans in uncertain states.

The Democrats, the first of the parties to hold a nominating convention, encountered so many internal problems that they could not react to the political conditions that the Panic of 1857 had created. Instead the Democrats were locked in a struggle over the party position on slavery expansion. In the Senate, Jefferson Davis pressed for adoption of a code that would provide for federal protection of slavery in the territories, and this became the standard for the southern states' rights Democracy. Northern Democrats by and large remained faithful to Stephen A. Douglas' vision of popular sovereignty. The dispute between the two wings of the party became even more ominous because of the position taken by the delegation from Alabama. At their state convention, the Alabama Democrats resolved that neither the federal nor a territorial government could ban slavery in the public lands. They further declared that their propositions were "*cardinal principles*" and that if the national convention failed to agree to their deliberations on the slavery issue, the state's delegates would abandon the meeting.[8]

When the Democrats finally congregated in hot and humid Charleston on April 23, the fissures between the northern and southern wings had grown too great to be closed. The platform committee divided over the slavery extension issue and finally produced two reports, one favoring popular sovereignty, the other supporting a territorial slave code. By virtue of their numbers the Douglas delegates carried the popular sovereignty report. At this juncture the Alabama delegation revolted and was soon joined by the members who represented the Deep South. Those who remained, individuals from the North and the border South, attempted to name a presidential candidate. Although the northerners had a majority and cast their votes for Douglas, the Little Giant did not

7. Washington Hunt to John J. Crittenden, April 9, 1860, in Coleman, *The Life of John J. Crittenden,* II, 189–90.

8. *Southern Advocate* (Huntsville, Ala.), January 25, 1860; Alexander S. Danbridge to Robert M. T. Hunter, January 16, 1860, in Robert M. T. Hunter Papers (#8753-d), Manuscripts Department, University of Virginia Library, Charlottesville, Va.

obtain the two-thirds majority the rules required. After several days of fruitless attempts to make Douglas the candidate, the angry, frustrated, and weary delegates postponed the proceedings until June, when they would reconvene in Baltimore. When the Democrats did gather in Baltimore to complete the unfinished business of Charleston, the break between the two wings was made final. Douglas became the candidate of one faction of the Democracy, and, after a short "bolters'" convention, John C. Breckinridge became the nominee of the other.[9]

Before the Democratic party finally split into two camps at Baltimore, Horace Greely mocked the Democrats for concentrating solely upon the slavery issue: "Why not tell us what is the Democratic doctrine with regard to the Homestead policy? Ditto the Tariff bill now pending in the Senate?" Greeley had his partisan purposes, of course, but his comments pointed out a singular failure of the Democrats in 1860: neither wing of the party offered an economic program, save for the token gestures of approving a transcontinental railroad and the acquisition of Cuba. At Charleston one brave Pennsylvanian submitted a resolution favoring a higher tariff, but the proposition was laughed out of the hall.[10] So absorbed were the Democrats over the issue of slavery expansion that they paid no heed to the economic issues or to the new political alignments that the Panic of 1857 had produced. Not only did both wings of the Democracy fail to handle the concrete matters of tariff, homestead, and rivers and harbors legislation, but they also neglected to respond in some visible manner to the political wishes of the nation's conservatives.

One week after the Charleston convention, the "fossils and fogies" of American politics assembled at Baltimore to nominate their candidate for the presidency. The old-line Whigs and Fillmore men behaved in a perfectly gentlemanly and businesslike way. They had no problem with the issue of slavery because they simply avoided the subject—at least in public. For their platform they adopted a single statement declaring rigid adherence to the Constitution and to the continued existence of the Union. They chose John Bell of Tennessee and the famed

9. Dumond, *The Secession Movement*, 65–91; Johannsen, *Stephen A. Douglas*, 746–70; M[urat] Halstead, *Caucuses of 1860: A History of the National Political Conventions of the Current Presidential Campaign* (Columbus, Ohio, 1860), 36–77.

10. New York *Daily Tribune*, June 15, 1860; Bedford (Pa.) *Inquirer and Chronicle*, May 11, 1860; Charleston Democratic Convention Papers, DU.

but ancient Massachusetts Whig orator Edward Everett for their presidential and vice-presidential candidates.[11]

Although the Constitutional Union party sought to elevate the ideals of Union and nationalism above all other matters, there were some unwritten planks in the platform. While the convention preferred to leave the volatile topic of slavery alone, the southern conservatives had in actuality adopted a position on the extension of slavery that was very similar to that of the southern states' rights Democracy. The conservatives, moreover, had a hidden economic plank. One old-line Whig informed the *National Intelligencer* just prior to the convention that the mission of the conservatives was the education of the northern public to the economics of slavery and federal relations. Northerners had to understand how important slavery was to their prosperity.[12]

Unlike the Democrats and the Constitutional Union party, the Republicans seized every opportunity for political advancement that the Panic of 1857 had afforded. This was particularly true in the two most important tasks of the convention: the construction of a platform and the nomination of a presidential candidate. Republicans grasped the economic issues the Panic had resurrected and embedded them in their resolutions and nominees. By so doing, Republicans hoped to convince Pennsylvanians that their party was the best political vehicle available for fulfillment of the Keystone State's economic aspirations and to persuade conservatives that the Republican party adhered to prudent, constitutional principles.

One of the delegates at the Chicago Republican convention was Horace Greeley. The cherubic newspaperman, who was chosen to represent Oregon, had distinct ideas about what issues could bring success to the party. As he wrote to one individual prior to the convention, an "Anti-Slavery man *per se* cannot be elected; but a Tariff, River-and-Harbor, Pacific Railroad, Free-Homestead man, *may* succeed *although* he is Anti-Slavery." Greeley understood the changes that the Panic of 1857 had wrought, and as a member of the platform committee he was in a position to implement his views. Greeley, however, wanted to sac-

11. Halstead, *Caucuses of 1860*, 112–18; New York *Daily Tribune*, May 10, 11, 1860.

12. Donald Walter Curl, "The Baltimore Convention of the Constitutional Union Party," *Maryland Historical Magazine*, LXVII (1972), 263–66; Dumond, *The Secession Movement*, 93–94; "T. J. B." in *Daily National Intelligencer* (Washington, D.C.), April 17, 1860.

rifice too many of the party's antislavery goals to suit the other commit-teemen, and consequently the economic planks of the platform were not as strong as Greeley would have preferred. The editor of the New York *Tribune* desired a strong tariff statement to attract Pennsylvanians, but according to Gustav Koerner, another committee member and a former Democrat, the stand the Chicago convention took on the tariff "did not differ essentially from former Democratic declarations on the subject."[13]

The Republican platform of 1860 exhibited some marked changes from the platform of 1856. Republicans still maintained the supremacy of the slavery issue and insisted that freedom was the "normal condi-tion" of the territories. Unlike the 1856 declaration of principles, how-ever, Republicans in 1860 devoted considerable space to economic issues. They favored a homestead act, river and harbors legislation, a moderately protective tariff, and the construction of a Pacific railroad. The party fashioned the economic planks to bring conservatives into the party and to capture those areas of the nation with particular eco-nomic interests, especially Pennsylvania. On another level, however, the Republicans were responding to the question of the fate of the la-borer. A portion of the tariff plank read: "We commend that policy of national exchanges which secures to the working men liberal wages, to agriculture remunerating prices, to mechanics and manufacturers an adequate reward for their skill, labor, and enterprise."[14] The Republi-cans in 1860 grasped the labor solution that economic theorists and popular writers had developed for the last two decades and that they

13. Horace Greeley to Mrs. R. M. Whipple, April [?], 1860, quoted from Jeter Allen Isely, *Horace Greeley and the Republican Party, 1853–1861: A Study of the "New York Tribune"* (1947; rpr. New York, 1965), 266, see also pp. 289–92; Thomas J. McCormack (ed.), *Memoirs of Gustave Koerner, 1809–1896* (Cedar Rapids, Iowa, 1909), II, 87.

14. Horace Greeley and John F. Cleveland, *A Political Text-Book for 1860* (New York, 1860), 27. The Republican party in general looked favorably upon upward tariff revision, federal aid to internal improvements and education, and the establishment of a free public land policy. These programs generated some dissent within the leadership, however, especially in the case of the tariff, for the Chicago platform was not a forthright call for protection and was purposely left ambiguous. Certain elements of the party, such as the New York Barnburners, protested any move toward protectionism. Nonetheless, most Republicans saw the political wisdom of appearing to favor upward tariff revision in order to win Pennsylvania, and thus many were willing to momentarily bend their eco-nomic principles. See the discussion of this point above, in Chaps. 6 and 7. For an ex-ample of Republican opposition to interpreting the Chicago platform as favoring protec-tionism, see New York *Evening Post*, May 18, 30, 1860.

had stressed during the Panic of 1857: a high tariff to obtain wage protection from foreign pauper labor, a homestead act to keep the supply of labor limited, and an agricultural colleges act to provide the worker with educational facilities so that he might progress to better paying occupations.[15]

The second chore of the convention was to determine the party's standard-bearer. Republicans knew that the sundering of the Democratic party was no guarantee of victory in November, and they did not take the Constitutional Union party lightly. The party leaders moved steadily and surely toward the goal of nominating an individual who would keep the party coalition together but who would also attract northern conservatives.

Horace Greeley was one of several Republicans who had quite early called for fusion with old-line Whigs and nativists. Influenced by the role the conservatives had played in the Pennsylvania elections of 1858, Greeley tried to persuade his party cohorts that the path to the presidency was paved with economic issues and a tightening of the immigration laws, not with antislavery slogans. In advocating that the Republican program needed to jettison some of its radical sentiments, Greeley was not abandoning his own personal desire to eradicate slavery. Rather, he believed that the country desperately needed a victory over the Slave Power, but as he often said, he lacked "faith that the anti-slavery men of this country have either the numbers or the sagacity required to make a President." Greeley did not accept the idea that the only worthwhile victory was one that manifested a total devotion to the highest free soil standards; he was willing to compromise Republican idealism to achieve a measure of political success because he assumed that in the course of time all the principles of antislavery would be accepted.[16]

---

15. The existence of economic planks in the Republican platform has led some historians to declare that the Republicans moderated their antislavery views and entered upon a path of conservatism; see, for example, Luthin, *The First Lincoln Campaign*, 148–49. Other historians have questioned the alleged Republican turn to conservatism; see, for example, Foner, *Free Soil, Free Labor, Free Men*, 214; Fehrenbacher, *Prelude to Greatness*, 156–59. Regardless of how Whiggish the planks seemed, Republicans advocated the solutions to economic depression that had the greatest popularity. Most of the historians of the antebellum period do not see the Republican platform of 1860 as a platform to benefit labor, although there are strong reasons to believe the Republicans earnestly believed their policies would do so.

16. Horace Greeley to George E. Baker, April 28, 1859, quoted in Thurlow Weed

Greeley's advice—and particularly the nominees he offered as wise choices for the Republican nomination—did not incite enthusiasm from other Republicans. In response to Greeley's cry of fusion with the nativists, the Chicago *Press and Tribune* announced that the Republican standard was not to be lowered "one jot or tittle." A correspondent of Israel Washburn wrote, "How utterly futile it is to think of standing on the ticket and rotten platform of Horace Greeley and Co." Even E. Peshine Smith, who loved the old Whig doctrines, declared to Henry C. Carey that the New York *Evening Post* "has got to be a much more reliable representative of the Republicans of this state—notwithstanding its heresy of free trade—than the Tribune."[17]

Greeley's persistence in promoting fusion with the conservatives stemmed from one conviction: that the frontrunner for the nomination, William H. Seward, could not win the election. Seward had two inadequacies that many besides Greeley feared would result in a Republican defeat at the polls. His enunciation of the phrase the "irrepressible conflict" in 1858 was linked to John Brown's raid on Harpers Ferry, and he was thus tabbed a radical. Whether Seward deserved such a classification was beside the point; in 1860 he appeared to be radical to a large number of voters. His other drawback arose from his tenure as governor of New York when he proposed state aid to parochial schools. Seward's open dislike of nativism jeopardized his standing with the one group the Republicans desperately needed to achieve victory, the remnant of the American party.[18]

Although Seward had many staunch supporters, his liabilities became more obvious the more closely the Republicans scrutinized his credentials. Republicans counted on winning the uncertain states and

---

Barnes (ed.), *Memoir of Thurlow Weed* (Boston, 1884), I, 225; Elbridge G. Keith, "The National Republican Convention of 1860," *University of Illinois Bulletin*, I (May 15, 1904), 11; Glyndon G. Van Deusen, *Horace Greeley: Nineteenth Century Crusader* (New York, 1953), 218–28, 238–42; Van Deusen, *Thurlow Weed: Wizard of the Lobby* (Boston, 1947), 235–51.

17. Chicago *Press and Tribune*, April 22, 1859; Rev. Amory Battles to Israel Washburn, February 8, 1859, quoted in Gaillard Hunt, *Israel, Elihu and Cadwallader Washburn: A Chapter in American Biography* (New York, 1925), 63–64; E. Peshine Smith to Henry C. Carey, February 21, 1860, in Gardiner Collection.

18. Horace Greeley to George E. Baker, April 28, 1859, quoted in Barnes (ed.), *Memoir of Thurlow Weed*, I, 255; Van Deusen, *William Henry Seward*, 214–21, 225–26; Charles Granville Hamilton, *Lincoln and the Know Nothing Movement* (Washington, D.C., 1954), 8–9.

had weighed presidential candidates according to their ability to attract the voters in those states. But in the doubtful states of Indiana, Illinois, Pennsylvania, and New Jersey the group of voters to be won were the conservatives who deprecated sectionalism and despised radicalism. Seward's name, as was revealed in the Rhode Island gubernatorial election, had become associated with all those attitudes the conservatives feared. More than one commentator stated that Seward would lose the presidential election.[19]

The principal difficulty with Greeley's plan of fusing with conservatives was that such an action would only drive off the free soil, former Democrat element. Extreme care in the selection of candidates had to be exercised to pacify the different groups that composed the party. Seward had the unenjoyable distinction of being disliked by two sets of Republicans. Besides the nativists and conservatives, former Democrats in New York were leery of Seward. They felt that if Seward were elected president, corruption would soon follow because of the presence of Seward's manager, Thurlow Weed. As William Cullen Bryant wrote to his coeditor John Bigelow, "There are bitter execrations of Weed and his friends passing mouth to mouth among the old radical democrats of the Republican party here."[20]

The coalition nature of the Republican party, plus the desire on the part of most leaders to nominate an individual attractive to the Whigs and nativists, began eliminating other Republican presidential hopefuls. Salmon P. Chase longed for the nomination, but he was far more radical than Seward on the slavery issue and thus alienated the conservatives. Edward Bates of Missouri, on the other hand, was too conservative. A leader of Missouri's Know-Nothings, Bates had a poor reputation among the former Democrats in the Republican camp, and he also repelled German immigrants, who constituted an important part of the organization in the Midwest. Simon Cameron of Pennsylvania also mounted an effort to win the nomination. He had some strong points— he led an important portion of the Pennsylvania party, his appeal in the Keystone State was undisputed, and his political ancestry was Demo-

19. E. J. Nightingale to James F. Simmons, January 19, February 15, 1860, in Simmons Papers; Charles A. Dana to James S. Pike, March 10, 1860, quoted in Jellison, *Fessenden of Maine*, 123; Huston, "The Threat of Radicalism," 96–99.

20. William C. Bryant to John Bigelow, February 20, 1860, quoted in John Bigelow, *Retrospections of An Active Life* (New York, 1909), I, 253; Van Deusen, *William Henry Seward*, 225–26; Sewell, *Ballots for Freedom*, 361.

cratic. But the Andrew Curtin-Henry C. Carey clique of the state's Republican (People's) party undermined Cameron's bid. Besides the state rivalry between the two groups, Cameron's reputation for honesty was low. The government corruption that seemed to follow his steps hampered his attractiveness.[21]

As the requirement for unifying the Republican coalition began narrowing the field of possible nominees, the less-acclaimed leaders of the party became more serious contenders. This was the case of Abraham Lincoln. Despite his 1858 debates with Douglas and a speaking tour in the East in January, 1860, Lincoln lacked a national following. His chief deficiency was his inexperience in national affairs, for his total firsthand knowledge of congressional business came from one stint as an Illinois representative from 1846 to 1848.

But whatever Lincoln lacked in national qualifications, he more than made up for in party credentials. Lincoln fitted the coalition requirements of the Republicans perfectly. He hailed from one of the doubtful states, and he was able to unite all the wings of Illinois Republicanism behind his candidacy, as evidenced in his two campaign managers: David Davis, a former Whig, and Norman B. Judd, an ex-Democrat. Moreover, Lincoln appealed to both conservatives and antislavery zealots. As a former admirer of Henry Clay and a strong believer in constitutional government, Lincoln attracted conservatives. For his refusal to lower the antislavery standards of the party in his struggle against Douglas, however, Lincoln obtained the gratitude of former Democrats. This special quality of Lincoln was succinctly pointed out by the Chicago *Press and Tribune:* Lincoln had "that radicalism which a keen insight into the meaning of the anti-slavery conflict, is sure to give," yet he also embodied "constitutional conservatism."[22]

Despite his liabilities, Seward was clearly the front-runner for the Republican nomination. But the other candidates preyed upon Seward's weaknesses in intense lobbying efforts at Chicago. Particularly

21. Bradley, *Simon Cameron,* 136, 146–47; F. I. Herriott, "The Conference in the Deutsches Haus Chicago, May 14–15, 1860: A Study of Some of the Preliminaries of the National Republican Convention of 1860," *Transactions of the Illinois State Historical Society for the Year 1928* (Springfield, Ill., 1928), 145–91; Marvin R. Cain, *Lincoln's Attorney General: Edward Bates of Missouri* (Columbia, Mo., 1965), 108–14; Donnal V. Smith, "Salmon P. Chase and the Election of 1860," *Ohio Archaeological and Historical Publications,* XXXIX (1930), 518–23; Hans L. Trefousse, *Benjamin Franklin Wade: Radical Republican from Ohio* (New York, 1963), 121–27.

22. Chicago *Press and Tribune,* February 16, 1860.

astute were Lincoln's managers, Judd and Davis. They concentrated their efforts upon the uncertain states of Indiana and Pennsylvania where Republican leaders had already determined that Seward could not carry the election. Thus on May 18, when delegates voted for the party's standard-bearer, the coalition nature of the Republican organization eroded the support for Seward. The convention chose Lincoln on the third ballot after some Ohio delegates switched their votes. But the choice of the vice-presidential candidate was just as revealing about the nature of the Republican coalition as was the selection of the presidential nominee: Hannibal Hamlin of Maine, a former Democrat.[23]

Certain factors thus accounted for Lincoln's nomination. The first was that Lincoln suited the internal needs of the party more adequately than any other candidate, because he was satisfactory to both the organization's conservative and radical factions. Lincoln additionally provided the Republicans with a candidate who could appeal to the northern old-line Whigs and nativists who had aided the Republican cause in 1858, but whose ties to the organization had loosened under the impact of John Brown's raid and Seward's alleged radicalism. One of the essential considerations of delegates to the Chicago convention was to undercut the threat of losing conservative Republicans to the Constitutional Union party. Lincoln appeared to be the superior of the other candidates for that purpose.

The strategy of foiling the Constitutional Union party's appeal to conservatives by nominating Lincoln achieved magnificent results. James F. Simmons found that the renegade Americans of Rhode Island expressed pleasure in Lincoln's candidacy, and one Indiana editor stated that the Bell movement would be "an utter failure" in his state. Correspondents informed Lincoln that his nomination removed the threat of a bolt by the Fillmore men in Pennsylvania. Washington Hunt pondered over the defection of the editor of the Buffalo *Commercial* to Lincoln's campaign on the basis that Lincoln was an honest and conservative man. "This view, unsound and fallacious as it is," wrote Hunt, "operates upon many persons who are disposed to follow the current

---

23. Thomas, *Abraham Lincoln*, 207–11; Willard L. King, *Lincoln's Manager: David Davis* (Cambridge, Mass., 1960), 134–41; Hunt, *Hannibal Hamlin of Maine*, 114–20; Van Deusen, *William Henry Seward*, 225–26; Greeley and Cleveland, *A Political Text-Book for 1860*, 27–28. Kenneth M. Stampp, *The Imperiled Union: Essays on the Background of the Civil War* (New York, 1980), 155–60, stresses the role of Lincoln's managers in obtaining the nomination, but the conservative surge in electoral strength had more to do with the decision of the convention.

and take refuge in what they consider a strong and prosperous party." Lincoln, in other words, undermined the conservative appeal of the Unionists without forgoing the radicalism inherent in Republican doctrines.[24]

The Republicans therefore responded appropriately to the political conditions of 1860, some of which the Panic of 1857 had helped to produce. They adopted the necessary and popular economic proposals that northerners desired, and they sought to placate the uneasy old-line Whigs and Fillmore men. Yet there was an oddity about Lincoln's nomination. Many historians have interpreted Lincoln's triumph at Chicago as a sign of growing conservatism in the Republican party.[25] Unquestionably the delegates at Chicago purposefully selected Lincoln on the basis that he could appeal to conservatives without losing the support of the antislavery element of the party. It is not certain, however, that in his personal beliefs Lincoln represented a decline of antislavery conviction.

One of the peculiarities of Lincoln's quest for the Republican nomination was his reticence to court the Pennsylvania delegation with a public declaration in favor of protectionism. Certainly other candidates for the Republican nomination—Chase and Cameron, for example—sought to capture Pennsylvania's delegates by advocating tariff revision. As a former Whig, Lincoln had campaigned on and believed in the benefits of protection. Yet as an aspirant for the Republican nomination he played down the tariff issue in 1859 and 1860. To the pertinent inquiries of Edward Wallace of Reading, Pennsylvania, Lincoln wrote that although he "was an old Henry Clay tariff Whig," and that the passage of time had not altered his views, yet "it is my opinion, that, just now, the revival of that question will not advance the cause itself, or the man who revives it." Lincoln knew the electoral importance of Pennsylvania, but he nonetheless refused to endorse publicly a higher tariff.[26]

24. G. W. Jackson to James F. Simmons, June 1, 1860, in Simmons Papers; James E. Harvey to Abraham Lincoln, May 21, June 5, 1860, both in Lincoln papers; David Davis, *et al.*, to Orville H. Browning, May 21, 1860, in Orville Hickman Browning Papers, Illinois Historical Survey, Urbana, Ill.; quote from Washington Hunt to John Bell, May 24, 1860, in John Bell Papers, LC.

25. For example, Randall and Donald, *The Civil War and Reconstruction*, 131; Luthin, *The Real Abraham Lincoln*, 215; Stampp, *The Imperiled Union*, 150.

26. Lincoln's earlier remarks on tariffs may be found in Basler, Pratt, and Dunlop (eds.), *The Collected Works of Abraham Lincoln*, I, 287, 334, 381–82, 407–16, II, 158;

By the early months of 1860 the northern Fillmore nativists and old-line Whigs had produced a definition of conservatism. As one Rhode Islander phrased it, "I think it is time something was done for the white folks & for the business of the country & not be forever quarrelling about Slavery." By that criterion Lincoln was not a conservative. When Lincoln journeyed into New England in early 1860, even as the Rhode Island Republicans split into free soil and American camps, he stated his understanding of the true political issue: "For, whether we will or not, the question of Slavery is *the* question, the all absorbing topic of the day." Lincoln's refusal to dilute the antislavery sentiment of the party placed him in company with the radicals.[27] Although Lincoln did not adhere to a great number of radical antislavery doctrines, he certainly disagreed with many, if not most, of the proposals of the conservatives. Thus there was, and unintentionally so, a deceptive quality to Lincoln's candidacy. Conservatives could and would support Lincoln because of his past affiliation with the Whig party, but the Lincoln of 1860 was not the same as the Lincoln of 1844. In 1860 Lincoln's ideas about the crucial issues of the day bore more common ground with the radicals than with the conservatives.

While the nominating conventions were selecting their presidential candidates and elaborating party platforms, the nation's legislators were, somewhat distractedly, conducting the federal government's business. The first session of the Thirty-sixth Congress had a considerable number of chores to attend to, especially financial ones. Many of the projects the Congress considered were politically motivated. Republicans, sensing their electoral possibilities, promoted the economic issues the Panic had resurrected. At the same time they stressed economic matters, they tried to discredit the administration by investigating charges of corruption in the printing office, the naval yards, and the War Department. Republicans lambasted the unwillingness of the administration to institute necessary economic programs because of the govern-

---

letters of Lincoln to Edward Wallace, *ibid.*, III, 487, IV, 49; Gabor S. Borit, "Old Wine into New Bottles: Abraham Lincoln and the Tariff Reconsidered," *Historian*, XXVIII (1966), 290–313; Schlüter, *Lincoln, Labor and Slavery*, 181–85; Reinhard H. Luthin, "Abraham Lincoln and the Tariff," *AHR*, XLIX (1944), 613–24.

27. E. J. Nightingale to James F. Simmons, January 19, 1860, in Simmons Papers; Lincoln's speech at New Haven, Conn., March 6, 1860, in Basler, Pratt, and Dunlop (eds.), *The Collected Works of Abraham Lincoln*, IV, 14.

ment's financial problems; yet, they claimed, Buchanan and his cabinet officers refused to trim those government expenditures that existed only to service the patronage needs of the Democratic party. In short, the health of the Democratic party, obtained through place and plunder, came before salutary economic policies.[28]

After the House elected a Speaker, which involved a bitter and acrimonious struggle that lasted for two months, the Republicans, by virtue of their increased numbers from the congressional elections of 1858, organized the House. The congressmen then moved quickly to the financial problems of the government, for the president's message again reiterated the woeful condition of the treasury. Justin Morrill, with considerable aid from the skilled parliamentarian John Sherman, fashioned a tariff bill that essentially reestablished the rates of the Walker tariff of 1846, with modifications in the mode of valuation and the customhouse system. Sherman claimed that the bill was designed to provide the government with adequate income and that there was "no reason why this bill should be considered a party measure." The House, under Republican control, approved the tariff revision.[29]

In the Senate, the House's tariff proposals fell into the hands of Robert M. T. Hunter. Hunter knew of the legislation's importance to Pennsylvania Democrats. He acknowledged that Pennsylvanians had ruined his presidential aspirations "because of my Tariff opinions," and he received communications from Democrats in Pennsylvania begging him to support Morrill's work. Such efforts proved fruitless. Hunter moved to scuttle the work of the House and he led a successful fight to postpone consideration of the tariff until the next session. The factor making Hunter's course so aggravating to Pennsylvanians, however, was that while he worked against a new tariff, he introduced an amendment to the legislative appropriation bill to allow the government to borrow twenty-one million dollars. Once again the federal government

28. Klein, *President James Buchanan*, 338–39; Meerse, "Buchanan, Corruption, and the Election of 1860," 116–31.

29. On the speakership fight, consult Potter, *The Impending Crisis*, 386–89. On government finances see *Senate Executive Documents*, 36th Cong., 2nd Sess., No. 2, p. 22; *Senate Executive Documents*, 36th Cong., 1st Sess., No. 3, pp. 6–10. On the tariff, see *Cong. Globe*, 36th Cong., 1st Sess., 903, 1394, 1757–70, 1827–92, 1950–58, 1972–81, 2012–56, 2049–56, Sherman quote on p. 1950; John Sherman, *Recollections of Forty Years in the House, Senate and Cabinet: An Autobiography* (Chicago, 1895), I, 185–86, 191; Pitkin, "The Tariff and the Early Republican Party," 154–59; Edward Stanwood, *American Tariff Controversies in the Nineteenth Century* (New York, 1903), II, 120–21.

failed to garner sufficient income from the tariff and public lands to pay its debts. And, once again, the Senate Democratic leadership failed to seize an opportunity afforded by the nation's finances to quell discontents within their party.[30]

Republicans also promoted one other major piece of legislation: a homestead bill. In this endeavor the Republicans obtained help from Senator Andrew Johnson, who also favored granting free land to the actual settler. Johnson recognized that the Senate would not sanction a true homestead measure, such as the one Galusha A. Grow submitted to the House, so he framed a proposal that amounted to little more than the lowering of the price of land and instituting more specific restrictions on eligibility. Eventually the Republicans accepted Johnson's bill as a temporary measure. Southern senators, who previously had harbored reservations about the homestead legislation, now supported Johnson's version. Thus an earlier opponent of the measure, Senator James S. Green of Missouri, pronounced his blessings on Johnson's project because "instead of being a homestead bill . . . it has dwindled down and become simply a measure proposing to reduce the price of the public lands on certain conditions." Johnson's proposal passed both Houses and awaited President Buchanan's determination of its merits.[31]

Buchanan, much to the amazement of the Republicans and to the annoyance of the Northwest Democracy, vetoed the homestead act. He justified his action by claiming that the treasury could not afford to give up the revenue it obtained from land sales and that the Constitution did not favor such schemes. But Buchanan had reasons for vetoing the bill that he did not commit to paper: he feared the reaction of southerners and he also worried that the lure of free land in the West might produce a new bleeding Kansas.[32]

One aspect of the homestead veto highlighted the growing concern Americans had over the plight of the laborer. Republicans, perhaps

30. Quote from Robert M. T. Hunter to George Booker, April 16, 1860, in George Booker Papers, DU; Henry S. Acker to Robert M. T. Hunter, June 8, 1860, in Ambler (ed.), *Correspondence of Hunter*, 333–34. For the course of the Morrill tariff in the Senate, see *Cong. Globe*, 36th Cong., 1st Sess., 3009–17, 3027, 3187–91; for the loan, pp. 2916, 3010, 3089–94, 3221, 3231; Pitkin, "The Tariff and the Early Republican Party," 174–79.

31. Quote of Green in *Cong. Globe*, 36th Cong., 1st Sess., 1991; Nevins, *The Emergence of Lincoln*, II, 188–90; DuBois and Mathews, *Galusha A. Grow*, 83–84.

32. Buchanan's veto message in *Cong. Globe*, 36th Cong., 1st Sess., 3263–64. See the interpretations of Buchanan's veto offered by Gates, *The Farmer's Age*, 76; Klein, *President James Buchanan*, 346–47; Nevins, *The Emergence of Lincoln*, II, 191.

practicing their oratory for the forthcoming campaign, argued in favor of both the Morrill tariff and the homestead bill by stating that the two measures would benefit the working man. Buchanan responded to that rationalization in his veto of the homestead bill:

> The honest poor man, by frugality and industry, can, in any part of our country, acquire a competence for himself and his family, and in doing this he feels that he eats the bread of independence. He desires no charity, either from the Government or from his neighbors. This bill, which proposes to give him land at an almost nominal price, out of the property of the Government, will go far to demoralize the people, and repress this noble spirit of independence. It may introduce among us those pernicious social theories which have proved so disastrous in other countries.[33]

The president's reference to the labor theory that lay behind the bill was a tacit recognition that the Republicans were in earnest when they claimed that the homestead proposal would elevate the laborer.

In late June the congressional session ended and Buchanan lost his last opportunity to influence the election of 1860 by allowing the Democratic party to point to legislative triumphs. Of course, events often circumscribed the president's ability to obtain the policies he desired. Nonetheless, Buchanan failed to provide the leadership the Democracy required; instead, his decisions acted against the welfare of the Democracy. Leaving aside the highly significant question of his role in the Lecompton Constitution debacle, the president managed to alienate the North on virtually every economic issue that arose during his tenure of office. Buchanan cracked the party whip on recalcitrant anti-Lecompton Democrats but failed to push administration Democrats into the readoption of the tariff of 1846. In 1859 he angered northerners over his vetoes of legislation concerning river and harbor improvements and agricultural colleges. In 1860 he killed the northern Democracy's hopes for a homestead bill. (This is a list of only the major pieces of legislation Buchanan scotched; there were other minor issues in which the administration voted against northern economic interests.) Although congressional Democrats deserve much of the blame for their reluctance to act intelligently upon economic issues, Buchanan did not provide the nonsectional leadership the party so desperately needed. The most galling aspect of the Democrats' and Buchanan's handling of the economic issues was that they were aware of the possible price of their obstinacy: the loss of Pennsylvania, New Jersey, and the

33. *Cong. Globe*, 36th Cong., 1st Sess., 1508–12, 1826–83, 3264.

Old Northwest. While positive actions on these matters might not have guaranteed these states to the Democracy, the party's refusal to yield to any material demands of the citizens there revealed how insensitive party leaders had become to political possibilities. The party chieftains, and Buchanan perhaps more so than others, acted without political wisdom or vision.

The Panic of 1857 greatly shaped the substance of political oratory in the campaign of 1860. The political parties made a concerted effort to win Pennsylvania, and they recognized the new importance economic policies had in the sectional debate. Republicans were more successful than the others in appearing to be the organization that stood for the new, popular economic proposals; moreover, they skillfully blended the program of free western land, high tariffs, and government aid for internal improvements with their general emphasis during the election upon the glory of a free society and the necessity of elevating the laborer. The Panic of 1857 also afforded the Democrats a special opportunity to use to their advantage. Toward the end of the campaign, Democrats would refer to the 1857 crash as an example of the economic chaos that would visit the North if the South should secede. By this tactic the Democrats hoped to frighten the business community into a rejection of the Republican party.

The common factor in the strategic thinking of all the parties in 1860 was the necessity of achieving victory in Pennsylvania. Lincoln watched political developments in the Keystone State closely, particularly the rivalry between the Carey-Curtin and Cameron factions. That Lincoln understood the crucial electoral significance of Pennsylvania was demonstrated by a letter he wrote to Hannibal Hamlin. Explaining that rumors had reached him that claimed that Hamlin had told others that the Democrats would do well in Maine's September state races, Lincoln requested an explanation and added that such a close result "would, I fear, put us on the down-hill track, lose us the [October] State elections in Pennsylvania and Indiana, and probably ruin us on the main turn in November."[34]

Republican leaders acknowledged the vital necessity of obtaining the Keystone State's twenty-seven electoral votes and understood the primacy of the tariff issue there. In Lincoln's correspondence from indi-

34. Abraham Lincoln to Hannibal Hamlin, September 4, 1860, in Basler, Pratt, and Dunlop (eds.), *The Collected Works of Abraham Lincoln*, IV, 110.

viduals in other states, there were reports on the movements of Whigs, Constitutional Union men, Democrats, Fillmore nativists, and others, but there were few references to economic matters. But in Lincoln's mail from Pennsylvania, the correspondents hammered away at the importance of the tariff. State Republican Committee Chairman Alexander McClure explained that all orators whom the national committee intended to send to Pennsylvania "should be thoroughly familiar with the Tariff question—a question I believe, that has not been nearly so prominent in your struggles in Illinois as it has been here."[35]

The Republicans were not alone in their emphasis upon Pennsylvania's pivotal role in the election. Upon his nomination by the Constitutional Union party, John Bell in a letter to Alexander H. Boteler laid out his ideas as to how the organization should conduct the campaign. Bell realized that the defeat of Lincoln was one of the primary goals of the Unionists; this required a Unionist victory in one of the northern states. Bell immediately pointed to Pennsylvania as the state that would have a determining influence on the outcome of the November poll. He also indicated that conservatives had a fair chance of electoral success there because of the large number of old-line Whigs and nativists. He furthermore understood the appeal of the tariff: "Pennsylvania must be made to see, if possible, that if she goes for 'Lincoln' she dooms her interests to long years of neglect, if not to comparative ruin."[36]

The Breckinridge Democrats also testified to the electoral power of Pennsylvania. Howell Cobb penned a letter to his fellow Georgians informing them that northerners did support southern rights: "This was particularly the case in Pennsylvania and other States to whose votes . . . we look with the greatest confidence for the election of our candidates." John Slidell stated in a speech that the "whole contest, in my opinion, turns on the vote of Pennsylvania." The great irony in such pronouncements by Breckinridge Democrats was that for the past two years they had completely repudiated the expressed wishes of the Keystone State's citizenry. An example of the fallacious thinking of Breckinridge Democrats in regard to Pennsylvania was a letter Isaac I. Stevens, chairman of the National Democratic Committee, sent to R. M. T. Hunter. Stevens asked Hunter to stump Pennsylvania and New Jersey, "the battle ground in the present contest." But Pennsylvania, as Hunter

35. A. K. McClure to Abraham Lincoln, June 16, 1860, in Lincoln Papers.
36. John Bell to Alexander R. Boteler, typescript letters of July 2, and July 30, 1860, in Boteler Papers; Joseph Howard Parks, *John Bell of Tennessee* (Baton Rouge, 1950), 354–55, 361–62.

well knew, did not wish to see the principal congressional leader who had thwarted the passage of a tariff revision that nearly everyone in the state had wanted.[37]

Stephen A. Douglas hoped to emerge victorious in 1860 by garnering the Northwest and certain southern states; he also counted upon the Bell ticket to take away voting strength from both the Breckinridge Democracy and the Republicans. He also understood the critical position of Pennsylvania in the election and the importance of the tariff to Pennsylvanians. Douglas usually campaigned on his popular sovereignty views, but in Pennsylvania even Douglas, free trader though he was, bowed to the pro-tariff sentiment. At a speech in Harrisburg, Douglas lambasted the sectionalism that interfered with the creation of a solution for the nation's finances. He then interjected, "The only remedy is a proper tariff."[38]

The election of 1860 was a complicated one. In every part of the country slavery-related issues dwarfed all other topics. Douglas campaigned almost exclusively upon his doctrine of popular sovereignty, which contained minimal references to economic subjects. In the South the Breckinridge Democracy stressed southern rights in the territories, while the southern Bell supporters claimed that the Breckinridge people were secessionists who plotted to destroy the Union. They also insisted that the Democracy had failed in its attempt to protect the peculiar institution. In the North the Republicans relied upon public approval of their desire to halt the spread of slavery and to limit the power of slaveholders in national affairs. Part of the complexity of the election of 1860 involved the infighting between the Douglas, Breckinridge, and Bell forces, as all groups sought legitimacy in the eyes of the voters.[39]

Throughout the North Republicans emphasized the various eco-

37. Howell Cobb to Robert Collins, *et al.*, May 9, 1860, in Phillips (ed.), *The Correspondence of Robert Toombs, Alexander H. Stephens, and Howell Cobb*, 473; speech of John Slidell in New Orleans, quoted in Springfield (Mass.) *Daily Republican*, September 28, 1860; Isaac I. Stevens to Robert M. T. Hunter, July 18, 1860, in Hunter Papers.

38. Stephen A. Douglas to Charles H. Lanphier, July 5, 1860, in Robert W. Johannsen (ed.), *The Letters of Stephen A. Douglas* (Urbana, Ill., 1961), 498; speech of Douglas at Harrisburg in New York *Times*, September 8, 1860.

39. On the general issues of the campaign, see Ollinger Crenshaw, *The Slave States in the Presidential Election of 1860* (Baltimore, 1945), *passim;* John V. Mering, "The Constitutional Union Campaign of 1860: An Example of the Paranoid Style," *Mid-America*, LX (1978), 95–106; Luthin, *The First Lincoln Campaign, passim;* John T. Hubbell, "The Douglas Democrats and the Election of 1860," *Mid-America*, LV (1973), 109–21.

nomic programs they hoped to enact. In the West they touted the homestead, in the Great Lakes region they promised federal aid for improvement of river and harbor facilities, and in New England they raised the banner of a protective tariff and a continuation of fishing bounties. In very few localities, however, did an economic question arise that challenged the supremacy of the slavery issue. The Republicans generally used economic policies to demonstrate the undue influence of slavery upon national legislation. Most economic appeals simply did not exist outside of the slavery context. The one exception to this rule was, of course, Pennsylvania. As one editor there wrote, "The question of the tariff is the great question in the election of tomorrow. As to the question of slavery, it is of far less immediate importance."[40]

Republicans readily used their economic proposals in the election of 1860 as a means to demonstrate even further their concern for the welfare of the free laborer. One of the Republicans' primary arguments against the expansion of slavery was that it brought the slave and the free worker into direct wage competition. By their espousal of tariffs, homesteads, and internal improvements, Republicans claimed that they would directly benefit the mechanic by eliminating unfair labor competition and by opening up other avenues of advancement. Moreover, the Republicans tried to tar the Democracy with aristocratic slogans. They commonly reprinted portions of Hammond's mudsill speech, and they made good use of a talk that Douglas' running mate, Herschel V. Johnson, had given in Philadelphia in 1856. Johnson had explained to a mass meeting that in the special case of the Negro, capital should own labor. Republicans leaped upon the indiscretion and trumpeted it before the nation as "THE DOUGLAS-JOHNSON DOCTRINE: 'CAPITAL SHOULD OWN ITS LABOR.'" Enticing workingmen into the Republican party by stressing their independence from capital and their right to fair wages was a common and frequent tactic of Lincoln's supporters.[41]

40. Luthin, *The First Lincoln Campaign,* 178–82, 186–87, 196; Foner, *Free Soil, Free Labor, Free Men,* 304; Philadelphia *Evening Bulletin,* October 8, 1860. For the importance of the tariff, see Eiselen, *The Rise of Pennsylvania Protectionism,* 259–60; Robert L. Bloom, "Newspaper Opinion in the State Election of 1860," *Pennsylvania History,* XXVIII (1961), 351–64.

41. Speech of Richard Oglesby in Chicago *Press and Tribune,* August 1, 1860; *Daily Illinois State Journal* (Springfield), August 29, September 7, October 2, 1860; Evansville (Ind.) *Daily Journal,* October 11, 1860; Richmond (Ind.) *Palladium,* September 6,

Democrats utilized one economic argument that generated some nervousness on the part of Republicans. New York Democrats warned that a Republican victory would lead to a dissolution of the Union and plunge the country into an economic chaos like the one experienced in 1857. James Gordon Bennett called upon the "conservatives," the "leading and influential citizens," and the "respectable classes" to denounce Lincoln and embrace nationalism. The one-time scourge of Wall Street, Fernando Wood, entreated businessmen to see that their economic prosperity depended upon the defeat of Lincoln: "A free intercommunication and free exchange of commodities between the several parts of the Confederacy, now so greatly jeoparded [sic], are indispensable to continued prosperity." In Ohio the Cincinnati *Enquirer* reminded industrialists "that since the crisis of 1857 manufacturers of machinery, in the free States, have been obliged to rely almost entirely upon the South for the sale of their goods."[42]

Democratic attempts to influence businessmen to abandon the Republican party worried the partisans of Lincoln. Several individuals indicated that the April reversal in Rhode Island and the near disaster in Connecticut resulted to some extent from the desertion of businessmen who feared the Republicans' radicalism.[43] By the fall whatever hearing the Democrats might have obtained for their market argument was lost in the growing prosperity of the nation; the European call for grains went out and a record shipment of western breadstuffs moved East throughout the autumn. Reports from agents in New York and Philadelphia revealed to the Republicans not only that merchants and manufacturers were adhering to their principles but that the Democrats were failing in their quest to raise campaign funds. Perhaps if the conditions of October, 1859, had prevailed, the Republican grip on the business community would have been significantly lessened. But, as one correspondent stated, improved economic conditions destroyed

1860; Philadelphia *North American,* October 5, 1860; Pittsburgh *Dispatch,* September 28, 1860.

42. New York *Herald,* July 24, 25, 26, August 12, 1860; speech of Wood in New York *Times,* September 18, 1860; Cincinnati *Daily Enquirer,* October 19, 1860; A Merchant of Philadelphia, *The End of the Irrepressible Conflict* (Philadelphia, 1860), 7–13, 16, 27, 38–39; Thomas P. Kettell, *Southern Wealth and Northern Profits* (New York, 1860), 80–105, 133, 137–38.

43. V. E. Piollet to William Bigler, February 12, 1860, in Bigler Papers; Herman Kriesmann to "Friend Huth," April 11, 1860, enclosed in John Wentworth to Abraham Lincoln, April 21, 1860, in Lincoln papers.

the Democratic economic appeal: "The bountiful harvest with which we have been blessed, seems to me, by its proving that the welfare and wealth of the Republic are not dependent upon Cotton, and consequently, (as some hold,) on Slavery, to be the voice of the God of nations on your side."[44]

The presidential election of 1860 had three distinct phases. The first came in mid-September when, coupled with some southern states that had voted in August, Maine and Vermont registered the will of the people concerning states offices. The second period ended on October 9, when several large northern states selected their congressmen and state administrators. The October elections included Indiana, Ohio, and Pennsylvania. Lastly came the presidential election on November 6.

The first phase of the election passed with only mild surprises. Missouri elected a Douglasite as governor, and Kentuckians chose a Bell leader as their chief executive. Maine and Vermont later rolled up impressive Republican victories. The loss of Maine shattered any illusions Douglas had about cracking solid New England, and the Missouri and Kentucky polls frightened Breckinridge supporters into more frenzied campaigning.[45]

In the opinion of many political strategists the results of the October elections in Indiana and Pennsylvania would determine the presidential race. Buchanan received optimistic reports from his friends as to the likelihood of a Democratic gubernatorial victory, but the Republican camp was singing an entirely different tune. An exuberant Alexander McClure told Lincoln that *"We cant lose the State!"* McClure proved the better prognosticator, for on October 9, Andrew Curtin obtained 262,403 votes to Democrat Henry Foster's 230,239. In Indiana the Republican gubernatorial nominee had a majority of nearly 10,000 votes, and in Ohio the Republicans won a State Supreme Court judgeship by almost 13,000 ballots.[46]

44. H. M. McNeeley to Joseph Medill, September 1, 1860, in Joseph Medill to Abraham Lincoln, September 10, 1860, Alexander K. McClure to Abraham Lincoln, August 27, 1860, Thurlow Weed to Abraham Lincoln, August 13, 1860, Elliott F. Shepard to Abraham Lincoln, September 24, 1860, all in Lincoln Papers.
45. New York *Daily Tribune*, August 11, September 6, 11, 1860; Johannsen, *Stephen A. Douglas*, 792–94; Frank H. Heck, *Proud Kentuckian: John C. Breckinridge, 1821–1875* (Lexington, Ky., 1976), 87–89.
46. N. E. Paine to James Buchanan, September 27, 1860, Hiram B. Swain to James

News of the Pennsylvania tabulations shocked and dismayed Democrats and Union men. An immediate sense of defeatism filled the whole of the Democratic ranks, North and South. "The fact is, and there is no use in assuming any other," a Philadelphian wrote to Buchanan, that "the state is freesoiled and abolitionized." In South Carolina William Trescott told Senator Hammond that the "elections in Penn. have fairly settled the Presidential campaign." Alexander R. Boteler found the same forecasts of gloom in his correspondence: "The result of the elections in Indiana, Ohio, and Pennsylvania is very discouraging, and leaves but little hope of Lincoln's defeat."[47]

From the wreck of Democratic and Unionist hopes in Pennsylvania came several simultaneous movements. In the South talk of disunion became rife. Conservatives tried to dissuade their hot-blooded neighbors from precipitate action, but the states' rights journals began pronouncing the presidential election as a choice between Union and secession. Northern Democrats heard the cry and made the question of nationalism or sectionalism the major issue. Out of fear that secession sentiment in the South was gaining, and from a conviction that Lincoln had the presidency in his grasp, Stephen A. Douglas turned South to campaign for the Union and moderation.[48]

Perplexed and angered by the southern cry of disunion, Republicans held their ground and refused to retreat from their platform or their ideas. Northern Democrats, sensing an approaching crisis, tried to unite all the warring factions together in order to stop Lincoln's election. And while the northern parties were reacting to the threat of southern secession, James Gordon Bennett's New York *Herald* headlined falling stock prices and warned of an imminent financial collapse. The economic argument of the Democrats was trumpeted louder than ever. The *Herald,* for example, asserted that the "crisis of 1857" had taught "a lesson not soon to be forgotten," for if the cotton crop

---

Buchanan, October 4, 1860, in Buchanan Papers; Alexander K. McClure to Abraham Lincoln, October 3, 1860, in Lincoln Papers; *Tribune Almanac,* 1861, pp. 47, 59, 63.

47. William L. Hirst to James Buchanan, October 12, 1860, in Buchanan Papers; William H. Trescott to James H. Hammond, October 14, 1860, in Hammond Papers; R. B. Brobian [?] to Alexander R. Boteler, October 15, 1860, in Boteler Papers.

48. *Daily Picayune* (New Orleans), October 10, 11, November 1, 1860; Raleigh (N.C.) *Weekly Register,* October 24, 31, 1860; *Southern Advocate* (Huntsville, Ala.), October 24, 1860; Cincinnati *Daily Enquirer,* October 25, 31, 1860; Cleveland *Daily Plain Dealer,* October 20, 26, 31, 1860; Detroit *Daily Free Press,* October 28, 30, 31, November 1–4, 1860; Johannsen, *Stephen A. Douglas,* 797–98.

did not move, New York would again hear the cry of "bread or blood!" [49]

Fusions occurred in New Jersey, Pennsylvania, and New York, but they were all imperfect. Both the Breckinridge and Douglas camps refused to cooperate. In New York the merchants played an important role in bringing the two sides together, but when they saw the possibility of a moot electoral college and an election thrown into the volatile House of Representatives, they declared that even the election of Lincoln would be better than a political stalemate. Opponents of Lincoln in New Jersey enjoyed more success as they established a workable formula to bring together the Bell and Breckinridge electors. In the crucial state of Pennsylvania, however, factional hostilities reduced the possibilities of any effective fusion. [50]

The impotence of the fusion movement was revealed on November 6 when Lincoln won New York state by a 50,000 vote majority and also conquered every free state except New Jersey. Lincoln obtained 180 electoral votes, or 27 more than necessary for election. Douglas captured almost 1,000,000 votes, but he won only one state, Missouri. Three border states were claimed by Bell—Virginia, Kentucky, and Tennessee—while Breckinridge took the remainder. Lincoln had won by clear majorities in all states except New Jersey, Oregon, and California, and these were not needed for his elevation to the presidency. With but just under 40 percent of the popular vote, Abraham Lincoln had secured the highest office in the land. [51]

The Republicans achieved their goal of electing a president but did not fare so well in the congressional races. The congressional elections of 1860 returned the Republicans to the position they had held in 1857 with the single exception of Pennsylvania. A corollary to Republican failures in congressional contests was the resurgence of the Democracy.

Republicans once again dominated Wisconsin and Michigan, and those two states no longer had Democratic congressmen. The number of Illinois Democratic representatives stayed the same. Ohio's Democrats were able to send eight members to Congress as they had done in

49. New York *Herald*, October 27, 1860; Bray Hammond, *Sovereignty and an Empty Purse: Banks and Politics in the Civil War* (Princeton, N.J., 1970), 27; Philip S. Foner, *Business & Slavery*, 198–206.

50. Luthin, *The First Lincoln Campaign*, 195–96, 215–16; Nichols, *The Disruption of American Democracy*, 350; Philip S. Foner, *Business & Slavery*, 179–206.

51. Potter, *The Impending Crisis*, 441–43; Crenshaw, *The Slave States in the Election of 1860*, 304–305.

1856. Indiana Democrats, however, still suffered the party division that had cost them two seats in 1858; in 1860 the Republicans maintained this edge. In the Atlantic seaboard states of New Jersey and New York the Democracy regained its strength. The Empire State Democrats won back the seven seats they had lost in 1858 as New York City returned to the Democratic fold. New Jersey Democrats also appeared to have rebounded from the setback of 1858; three Democrats again took their places in the state's congressional delegation.

The Democratic renaissance in state elections fell short in the one area where the Democrats needed most to recapture their popularity. Pennsylvania continued to vote Republican. Although the Democrats returned to power in some districts, they lost others. In Philadelphia victory continued to elude the Democracy, although Republicans won in several districts by pluralities instead of majorities. In 1858 the result of the congressional elections had been twenty-one Republicans to four Democrats; in 1860 the totals were almost as dismal, nineteen Republicans to six Democrats (see Appendix A).

The October and November elections presented other unwanted news for the Pennsylvania Democracy. In the gubernatorial race, where some 492,000 Pennsylvanians cast their ballots, the Democrat Foster obtained some 230,000 votes, just a few hundred shy of the number Buchanan had received in 1856. The total poll in 1856 had been 461,000, which meant nearly 30,000 more Pennsylvanians voted in 1860 than in 1856. The source of these additional voters did not matter as much as the fact that the increased turnout aided only Curtin, not Foster. It was also obvious that the Republicans had won the contest for the old-line Whig-Fillmore voters. The 82,000 ballots cast for Fillmore in 1856 could have shown up only in Curtin's totals. Democrats suffered even more in the presidential election. Not only did Lincoln acquire 6,000 more ballots than the number obtained by Curtin, but the Democratic total fell by some 20,000 suffrages, from 230,239 to 208,412.[52]

There were some peculiarities in the county tabulations for 1860. Most of the counties that traditionally had been Democratic or Republican remained so in 1860; the only exception being that the lower voter turnout in the presidential canvass allowed the Republicans to seize victory in some normally Democratic counties, such as Cambria. But the counties that had switched party allegiances in 1858 displayed

52. Figures obtained from *Tribune Almanac*, 1861, p. 47.

Table 11

Correlations of Republican Gains, 1856–1860, with American Party Voting (Fillmore), 1856

American Party Vote (Fillmore) 1856 with:	Pearson's r	N	Intercept	Slope	R^2
Republican gain 1856–58 Congress	.852	64	2.39	1.09	.726
Republican gain 1856–59 canal commissioner	.955	64	−1.51	1.20	.911
Republican gain 1856–60 president	.963	64	5.47	1.06	.927
Republican gain 1856–60 Congress	.919	64	2.19	1.13	.844
Republican gain 1856–60 governor	.980	64	2.47	1.08	.960

NOTE: Republican gain calculated by subtracting the percentage Republican presidential vote in 1856 from the percentage Republican vote in the indicated elections of 1859 and 1860.

interesting variations, particularly the iron and coal regions. Often citizens of the populous coal and iron counties reverted to Democratic candidates in the state races but then voted for Republicans in the congressional ones.[53] Moreover, the counties that had produced the election results of 1858 accounted for almost the entire falling off of Democratic votes between the October and November elections (see Appendix B).

By 1860 the influence of the Panic of 1857 upon the Keystone State's politics had waned but had not altogether disappeared. Democratic vote losses in 1860 were weakly related to industrial pursuits; the negative association, however, was statistically significant.[54] Somewhat more interesting were Republican gains. Republican additions from 1856 to 1860 correlated very strongly indeed with the 1856 Fillmore vote (see Table 11). Moreover, Republican increases continued to be

53. Based on computations made from *Tribune Almanac*, 1861.
54. These figures were reported in Chap. 6, Table 4. The bivariate correlations between iron and coal workers and Democratic losses in the presidential, congressional, and gubernatorial races were −.41, −.38, −.36, respectively; the correlations for county male manufacturing employees and Democratic losses were −.38, −.46, and −.38, respectively.

Table 12

Bivariate Correlations of Republican Gains, 1857–1859 and
1857–1860, with Socioeconomic Variables

Independent Variables	Republican Gain			
	1857–1859[a] (r)	1857–1860[b] (r)	1857–1860[c] (r)	1857–1860[d] (r)
% county iron and coal employees	.249	.379*	.315*	.326*
% county manufacturing employees	.414*	.523*	.453*	.510*
Industrial capital per white adult male	.490*	.551*	.538*	.583*
Farms, 20–99 acres per white adult male	−.558*	−.501*	−.537*	−.544*
German Reformed attendance	.391*	.281	.347*	.327*
Lutheran attendance	.402*	.290	.340*	.306*
Methodist attendance	−.502*	−.273	−.262	−.315*
Pietism attendance	−.507*	−.438*	−.445*	−.427*
Distance from southern border	−.490*	−.144	−.271	−.275
Distance from eastern border	−.241	−.253	−.402*	−.347*
% Age 30–39, males	.270	.438*	.336*	.352*
% Age 50 plus, males	−.305*	−.578*	−.424*	−.466*
N = 64				

*p < .01

[a] 1857 election is gubernatorial; 1859 is canal commissioner.

[b] 1860 election is presidential.

[c] 1860 election is congressional.

[d] 1860 election is gubernatorial.

related to certain socioeconomic phenomena, including county industrial operations, religious pietism, German Lutheran and German Reform attendance, and various age categories (see Table 12). Multiple regressions demonstrated that economic factors were important in Republican gains from 1857 to 1860. Iron and coal interests may have been less significant in the Pennsylvania elections of 1860 than they had been in 1858, but their power had not disappeared altogether. The Democracy had failed to placate the iron and coal districts.[55]

If, as the *New Hampshire Patriot* said, Pennsylvania were the "Solferino" of the election of 1860, then the Democrats were surely the Austrians and the Republicans the French.[56] The Keystone State had become the foundation of Republican victory. By winning Pennsylvania, Lincoln had entered the White House.

And by losing Pennsylvania, the Democracy suffered its greatest defeat, forcing southerners to a fateful decision. With a Republican in the White House, the South feared for the safety of its peculiar institution. As soon as Lincoln was elected, the *Semi-Weekly Mississippian* announced its opinion: "The Deed is Done—Disunion the Remedy." South Carolina moved swiftly and surely to secession. There was little doubt as to the reason for the bursting of the political ties between the North and South. Secession occurred because the South felt it had to protect the institution of slavery.[57] The immediate cause of the southerners' action was Lincoln's election; the immediate cause of Lincoln's election was the transformation of Pennsylvania from a Democratic to a Republican state. The Panic of 1857 played no small part in that transformation.

55. For the regression concerning Republican gains 1857–1860 (gubernatorial races 1857 and 1860), the results were: industrial capital (b = .018, beta = .343), pietist attendance (b = −.073, beta = −.217), and age, 50 years and older (b = −.430, beta = −.195), multiple r = .660, adjusted R^2 = .386. No other variables contributed significantly to explanation of variance.

56. *New Hampshire Patriot & State Gazette* (Concord), October 3, 1860. As it turned out, Pennsylvania was not strictly required to elect Lincoln in 1860, for if the state's electoral votes are subtracted from the total Lincoln obtained, he still had enough to win the presidency. This circumstance arose primarily because of unexpected Republican victories in California and Oregon. However, during the campaign the Republicans insisted that they needed Pennsylvania for victory, and they were probably correct. If Foster had won in the gubernatorial race, perhaps that success would have eroded Lincoln's strength along the border regions and in other doubtful states.

57. *Semi-Weekly Mississippian* (Jackson), November 9, 1860; Nichols, *The Disruption of American Democracy,* 353; Channing, *Crisis of Fear,* 288–93; William Barney, *The Road to Secession: A New Perspective on the Old South* (New York, 1972), xiii–xv, 136–37.

TEN / Conclusion

A study of the Panic of 1857 does not dislodge the primacy of slavery as the cause of the American Civil War.[1] Following the monetary collapse, the all-absorbing topic of debate continued to be slavery throughout the North and the South. The Panic of 1857 reintroduced some economic programs into political discussion, but, except in Pennsylvania and New Jersey, these economic concerns failed to generate a

---

1. The statement that slavery was ultimately the cause of the Civil War is simply my general understanding of the current historiographical trend in antebellum American scholarship. To say that slavery caused the Civil War, however, is not to say *how* slavery caused the Civil War—whether by economic confrontation, cultural antagonism, political machinations, or the like. See Eric Foner, "The Causes of the American Civil War: Recent Interpretations and New Directions," *CWH*, XX (1974), 197–214; Eric Foner, "Politics, Ideology, and the Origins of the American Civil War," in George M. Fredrickson (ed.), *A Nation Divided: Problems and Issues of the Civil War and Reconstruction* (Minneapolis, 1975), 15–34; Don E. Fehrenbacher, *The South and Three Sectional Crises* (Baton Rouge, 1980), 1–7 and *passim*. There have been recent attempts to explain the origins of the Civil War without emphasizing the slavery issue: Ronald P. Formisano, *The Birth of Mass Political Parties*, 5–8, 244, 326–29, stresses the rise of ethnocultural politics in the North, the spirit of anti-partyism, and anti-southernism; Michael F. Holt, *The Political Crisis of the 1850s*, 2–10, ingeniously and persuasively argues that the collapse of the second party system ended the ability of American politics to contain the slavery issue; and Joel H. Silbey, "The Surge of Republican Power," 199–299, theorizes that the growth of evangelism in the North drove southerners to fear that northerners sought to impose Yankee standards on the southern mode of living—a fear of cultural imperialism. There are merits in all these interpretations, but also some difficulties as well. Why northerners would be anti-South without reference to slavery begs elucidation. Although the demise of the Jacksonian party system may have indeed enabled slavery to become the dominant national issue, it still needs to be demonstrated why the elevation of that subject was so inherently dangerous that it could wreck a government. And one could quite easily explain southerners' fear of the meddling nature of northern evangelism precisely because that cultural disposition of the Yankees threatened to meddle with slavery.

response that in any sense rivaled the popularity of the slavery extension issue. Indeed, most politicians used the resurrected economic issues as a means to buttress their convictions for or against slavery; very few individuals jettisoned the subject in order to entice the public into their ranks on the basis of simple regional self-interest. Even in Pennsylvania and New Jersey, the People's party sought to merge, not separate, the ideals of protectionism and antislavery. But if the Panic did not change the basic nature of the sectional controversy, it did direct attention to one of the most salient features of that debate—the fate of the laborer.

Many of the specific effects the Panic of 1857 generated in the political realm grew out of the different experiences of the sections in adjusting to economic adversity. The crash originated in the reduction of European demand for American breadstuffs because of the end of the Crimean War, an economic circumstance that was abetted by some unsound American banking practices. Out of the recession that followed the monetary suspension came certain facts which no one disputed. The Great Lakes region was the area most severely affected by the monetary failure, and the troubles of westerners were quickly passed to those enterprises in the East that depended upon western sales. The South almost totally escaped the ravages of the Panic. Indeed, many Americans acknowledged that the South was seemingly impervious to economic fluctuations and that the prosperity of the Atlantic economy rested upon southern production of cotton. [2]

Undoubtedly the Panic of 1857 did contribute to the South's exaggerated estimation of the power of cotton in world commerce, but this development did not necessarily encourage secessionist dreams. The Panic of 1857 probably deflated the economic rationale for secession. At first various southerners manipulated the economic and social results of the monetary collapse to flaunt before the North the material richness of their unique civilization, the most flamboyant example being the "Cotton is King" oration of James H. Hammond in 1858. But by 1859 and 1860 many ardent states' rights southerners, like Hammond, perceived that the Panic had humbled northern propertied interests and had made them more amenable to southern demands. Many southerners concluded that by flexing its economic might the South could obtain the support of the northern propertied classes and thereby control the government. Hence the South could safely remain in the Union because its economic strength offset its political liabilities.

2. Nevins, *The Emergence of Lincoln*, I, 196–98.

To some extent the reaction of northern businessmen validated the hopes of southerners that Yankee merchants and industrialists could be taught to worship at the altar of southern rights. Perhaps a number of northern entrepreneurs did chafe at the alleged southern agrarian control of the federal government's economic policy, and it may well have been that the Panic of 1857 convinced these capitalists to seek the overthrow of southern influence. Yet the history of the Panic of 1857 does not reveal such motivations. Most northern business interests were more concerned with obtaining access to the southern market than with promoting new federal legislation. In the two years following the financial crash, the South's economy expanded and provided the only certain market for northern wares. This circumstance dampened any ardor for economic sectionalism on the part of northern businessmen. Ultimately they had to make a decision as to what was more important to their enterprises: the possible gains that might accrue from enactment of high tariff, internal improvement, homestead, and Pacific railroad legislation; or the remuneration actually obtained from the southern market. Between 1858 and 1860 most northerners left no doubt that they believed the tangible benefits of the southern market far outweighed the possible advantages that might result from federal programs.[3]

The irony of the Panic of 1857 was that although its sectional influence was at first much more visible in the South than in the North, it was ultimately in the North rather than in the South that the Panic had its greatest political impact. When the banks declared specie suspension in October, 1857, the Democrats exhibited near unanimity on the causes of and the remedies for the Panic; there were virtually no dissenters in the Democratic ranks over economic issues. The Republicans, however, revealed in the autumn of 1857 how incapable they momentarily were of handling economic questions. They wanted to keep political debate on the one issue that unified the numerous groups that composed their party—the extension of slavery into the territories. But the monetary stringency soon took the form of a business depres-

---

3. There is one caveat to add to this interpretation of the political desires of northern businessmen after the Panic of 1857. Owners of large firms with national contacts may have exhibited different political viewpoints than smaller businessmen who serviced a local market. Proprietors of larger enterprises were probably more conservative in their evaluation of the slavery issue because of their profitable trade with the southern states; entrepreneurs of lesser size lacked commercial intercourse with southerners, and hence the economic pressures of maintaining intersectional contacts did not so influence their political considerations.

sion in the North that lasted for several years. The hard times produced a popular demand for the federal government to institute various economic programs to stimulate the economy. Westerners desired free land for actual settlers, inhabitants of the Great Lakes area wanted expanded river and harbor improvements, Pennsylvanians insisted upon a higher tariff, and nearly everyone approved of constructing a railroad to the Pacific coast.

The strength of the new economic issues varied from state to state. In the West, the South, and Northeast, political dialogue over economic programs became more noticeable than in the past, but it most certainly did not displace the slavery question. The rise of protectionist sentiment in Pennsylvania and New Jersey was different. There the issue of the tariff equaled the issue of slavery extension. One of the peculiarities of the Panic of 1857 was that it affected the politics of Pennsylvania so strongly, rather than those of some other state. Of all the northern states the Democrats required for presidential victories, the Keystone State was foremost. The Panic had introduced an explosive economic issue in the very heart of northern Democratic strength; the Panic had created conditions that rendered the glittering political jewel of Pennsylvania susceptible to Republican thievery.

Both political parties had an equal opportunity to use the Panic to their electoral advantage. At first it seemed as though the Panic would inure to the benefit of the Democrats. The party of Jackson raised the banner of hard money and captured much of the anger the public felt toward bankers; moreover, the Democrats exhibited a cohesiveness on economic matters that augured well for their handling of any other problem created by the financial suspension. Yet, the Republicans gained politically from the Panic. When in the elections of 1858 the Republicans saw the power of the tariff over the voting habits of Pennsylvanians, they moved slowly to adopt protection as one of their programs; they did likewise with other economic schemes that attracted voters, advocating such ideas as agricultural colleges, homesteads for actual settlers, and internal improvements. Adoption of this economic program by the Republican party was not easily accomplished, for there were several factions which detested some of the proposals. But the commitment of most Republicans to destroy the Slave Power enabled them to sacrifice some of their scruples about economic policy to obtain enough extra voters to elect an antislavery president.

The Democrats failed to respond with the political astuteness of the Republicans. The Democrats faced two dilemmas; one incapacitated them, and the other embarrassed them. The Democratic unity on most economic issues originated in the party's embrace of free trade theory, which called for laissez faire government and unobstructed commercial exchanges among the peoples of the world. The policies that gained support among northerners after the Panic of 1857 were those necessitating an interventionist government and the erection of barriers to foreign trade. Democrats, moreover, confronted an emergency in the federal government's budget. Because of the commercial crisis, the government's income from customs duties and land sales fell drastically, and the Buchanan administration faced a mounting deficit. The problem was to find the appropriate means by which the government could balance income with expenditures. The Democrats had a number of options by which they could rebalance the budget—but they chose the one that most infuriated large numbers of northern voters.

In the elections of 1858 the importance of the new economic issues became apparent to everyone. Of all the states that held congressional elections, the major change occurred in Pennsylvania. Political observers quickly deduced two significant factors in that state's campaign. The first, upon which virtually everyone agreed, was the political preeminence of the tariff. The second was the ability of the Republicans to draw nativists and old-line Whigs into the party on the basis of resurrected economic concerns. Throughout the nation political leaders understood the portent of these two movements. Although the conservatives had only momentarily joined ranks with the Republicans, the combined numbers of Fillmore men and Republicans made it likely that in 1860 the opposition could sweep the entire North. The loss of Pennsylvania, moreover, indicated that the main prop of Democratic presidential victories had fallen; Pennsylvania's conversion to the opposition was taken to mean, correctly, that the doubtful states were gathering under the Republican standard.

The loss of Pennsylvania and the sudden importance of various economic issues did not doom the Democracy to inevitable defeat in the North. Democrats actually had a marvelous opportunity to undermine the Republican economic appeal and to demonstrate their concern for the material welfare of northerners. The government's financial problems might have aided the Democrats by providing an excuse to raise revenue and thereby allow certain programs to be instituted. In particular, the falling off of customs receipts gave the Democrats the chance to revert to the tariff of 1846, which would have satisfied the Pennsylvania Democracy. By thus augmenting federal revenue the

Democrats could then have permitted other legislation northerners desired—for example, a reduction in western land prices, river and harbor improvements, and steamship subsidies.

The Democrats failed to seize this opportunity. Instead they substituted a program that angered numerous northern interests. Democrats preferred to snub Pennsylvania's tariff sentiments even though the tariff of 1857 failed to generate sufficient revenue. They inaugurated a program of retrenchment that curtailed subsidies to northern companies and deprived the Great Lakes region of funds for internal improvements. They insisted that the government obtain revenue from western lands by holding public auctions. The retrenchment policy also killed such projects as agricultural colleges and free homesteads for actual settlers. Whatever may have been the economic wisdom of Democratic financial policy between 1858 and 1860, it was a political blunder. Northern Democrats in the late 1850s needed allies in order to produce victory. The only sources available to them—as in 1856—were Unionists, conservatives, and Whigs. A proper handling of the troubles the Panic of 1857 produced might have enabled these Unionists to feel comfortable under the Democratic standard. Democrats foolishly squandered this opportunity. They pressed for policies in the economic realm that were bound to anger conservatives and thus alienated the group that could have provided them the margin of victory in 1860.

Economic issues did not have to play a role in the election of 1860. By their own intransigence, Democrats allowed Republicans to take advantage of the economic questions that the Panic had reinvigorated. The failure of the Democrats to deal adequately with these economic matters arose from two distinct sources. The Democratic party, North and South, was generally hostile to an upward tariff revision. Southern Democrats, however, orchestrated the defeat of congressional tariff proposals and thus earned the enmity of northern protectionists. The southern Democrats' opposition to increasing the tariff had the same origin as the northern Democrats' except for one other factor that probably more than any other blinded southerners to the necessity of accommodating northern economic aspirations. In the Lecompton controversy, southerners, sensing that they had essentially lost the slavery extension contest, developed a siege mentality that elevated devotion to principles above expediency; above all, compromise was seen to be a sign of weakness. The denigration of compromise as an honorable means of adjusting sectional tensions came distinctly out of the battle over slavery, but it affected all other topics of debate as well. Inevitably, the new southern adherence to principles was applied to the resurgence of economic issues in the North.

Republicans, of course, finally adopted a wide array of economic programs in 1860 that enticed northerners to their standard. They were very calculating about these policies. Republicans strained their coalition only enough to permit a mild acceptance of protectionism, free homesteads, and government subsidies. And they took decided aim at conservatives and Pennsylvanians. Regardless of the party's sincerity in the espousal of these policies, the leadership embraced them for political reasons. Through economic issues Republicans hoped to capture the conservative element in the doubtful states and so achieve national political dominance.

The role the Panic of 1857 played in enabling the Republicans to seize the Presidency in 1860 must be weighed against two other considerations. First, the Republican party acquired the bulk of its membership before economic issues had obtained any vitality, and hence the strength of the organization clearly stemmed from slavery-related issues. Second, the path to the White House in 1860 was cleared for the Republicans by the division of the Democratic party into two wings, which was entirely the result of the controversy over slavery extension. Although these factors certainly increased the probability of a Republican victory in 1860, it is not apparent that by themselves they would have converted the essential doubtful state of Pennsylvania to Republicanism. The economic issue of protectionism was absolutely essential in transforming Pennsylvania from a Democratic to a Republican state. In his memoirs, James G. Blaine explained the mechanics of the Republican victory in 1860:

> To hundreds of thousands of voters who took part in that memorable contest, the tariff was not even mentioned. Indeed this is probably the fact with respect to the majority of those who cast their suffrages for Mr. Lincoln. It is none the less true that these hundreds of thousands of ballots, cast in aid of free territory and as a general defiance to the aggressions of the pro-slavery leaders of the South, would have been utterly ineffectual if the central and critical contest in Pennsylvania had not resulted in a victory for the Republicans in October. The tariff therefore had a controlling influence not only in deciding the contest for political supremacy but in that more momentous struggle which was to involve the fate of the Union.[4]

4. James G. Blaine, *Twenty Years of Congress: From Lincoln to Garfield* (Norwich, Conn., 1884–86), I, 207.

The tangible political alteration the Panic of 1857 wrought, therefore, was the resuscitation of economic issues that had been of minor importance in the sectional controversy in the early 1850s, but which proved attractive to old-line Whigs and nativists in the doubtful states in 1858 and 1860. Without question, the slavery controversy was the centerpiece of Republican ideology and was responsible for the party's growth in the North. But it is not so certain that the slavery question by itself could have immediately elevated the Republicans from the party of opposition to the party of domination. By reinvigorating economic issues, the Panic of 1857 allowed the Republicans to entice those conservatives into their organization who had previously rejected the party's strictures on slavery. The significance of this group of voters was that they proved to be the margin of victory for the Republicans in 1860.

There are several aspects of the Panic of 1857 that bear upon the historiographical dispute over the causes of the Civil War. The manner in which the Panic of 1857 affected sectional attitudes does not support the assertions of progressive historians that the monetary disturbance convinced northern businessmen that they had to wrest control of the government away from southern agrarians. In fact, the economic relations that held sway after the Panic tended to make northern propertied interests more agreeable to the South's political demands.[5] The history of the financial collapse of 1857 also fails to substantiate the findings of the revisionists, who asserted that the Civil War sprang from a generation of blundering politicians who preferred unrestrained emotionalism to calm reflection. Although the refusal of southerners to compromise on economic issues, especially the tariff, does exhibit some elements of irrationality—or at least unstatesmanlike attitudes— other circumstances cast doubts upon the revisionist analysis. In the debate over banking and economic relations during the Panic months, northerners and southerners revealed that they shared many common ideas and had no trouble at all understanding each other. Moreover,

5. The best examples of the progressive viewpoint are Louis M. Hacker, *The Triumph of American Capitalism: The Development of Forces in American History to the End of the Nineteenth Century* (New York, 1947), 328–29; and Charles A. Beard and Mary R. Beard, *The Rise of American Civilization* (New York, 1927), I, 629–45. Although the progressives sought an economic cause for the Civil War, they never produced an in-depth study of the Panic. For other refutations of the progressive interpretation see Philip S. Foner, *Business & Slavery;* O'Connor, *Lords of the Loom.*

the economic arguments northerners and southerners used were highly logical, for such expressions clearly derived from the work of economic theorists; economic thinking, in short, was unusually precise and consistent. Finally, the revisionists erred in discounting the weight and the importance of economic concerns to Americans from 1857 to 1860; the economic issues were substantive, not symbolic.[6]

The experience of the United States during the Panic of 1857 also fails to corroborate certain modern theories of Civil War causation. Since the 1950s a group of scholars have emphasized the peculiarities of antebellum southern civilization. The different values and institutions of the North and the South supposedly interfered with the creation of a workable compromise between the two sections over the issue of slavery. Yet, during the Panic of 1857 southerners revealed that, although they had a proslavery argument that was unique to that region, on most matters they espoused the middle-class virtues that northerners upheld.[7] Likewise, the events connected with the Panic do not support the neoabolitionist view that the Civil War ultimately originated in the debate over the morality of slavery. In the general discussion of business conditions following the financial crash, it became apparent that Americans of that age did not separate moral questions so easily from economic ones. An economic issue could easily be, and often was, seen as a moral issue.[8] In most instances, northerners focused on the southerners' refusal to acquiesce to the economic policies the Panic had brought back into the political arena. They ascribed the recalcitrant

6. For examples of revisionist attitudes see Randall and Donald, *The Civil War and Reconstruction;* George Fort Milton, *The Eve of Conflict: Stephen A. Douglas and the Needless War* (Boston, 1934). On the question of rationality, see Michael P. Johnson, *Toward a Patriarchal Republic: The Secession of Georgia* (Baton Rouge, 1977), xvii–xx; J. G. De Roulhac Hamilton, "Lincoln's Election an Immediate Menace to Slavery in the States?" *AHR,* XXXVII (1932), 700–11. See the excellent critique of revisionism in Kenneth M. Stampp, *The Imperiled Union,* 199–244.

7. Nevins, *Ordeal of the Union,* II, 537–54; Genovese, *The Political Economy of Slavery,* 5–9, 34–35; and McPherson, "Antebellum Southern Exceptionalism," 230–44, emphasize the unique qualities of antebellum southern culture. This interpretation has been questioned by Thomas P. Govan, "Was the Old South Different?" *JSH,* XXI (1955), 447–55; William R. Taylor, *Cavalier and Yankee: The Old South and American National Character* (New York, 1969), 15–18; Pessen, "How Different from Each Other Were the Antebellum North and South?" 1119–49.

8. Good examples of the neoabolitionist interpretation of the coming of the Civil War are Dwight Lowell Dumond, *Antislavery: The Crusade for Freedom in America* (Ann Arbor, Mich., 1961); and Dumond, *Antislavery Origins of the Civil War in the United States* (Ann Arbor, Mich., 1939), 109–14.

southern position to the operation of the Slave Power conspiracy, which northerners defined as the attempt of slaveholders to control all aspects of national life for their own aggrandizement.[9]

During the 1970s historians have developed three additional theories as to the origins of the Civil War. One of these emphasizes the ethnocultural dimensions of party politics. Historians of this persuasion argue that an evangelical (pietistic) religious outlook characterized the mentality of the Republicans, whereas Democrats evinced a more tolerant, liberal (liturgical) disposition. They postulate that Republicans finally won the political contest for the presidency because the party acquired over time the suffrages of old-line Whig and nativist adherents.[10] The caveat that a study of the Panic of 1857 places upon this interpretation is that the Republican capture of nativists and conservatives was no simple and predetermined matter. The financial crash produced a demand for economic programs that fitted nicely the economic views of conservatives; by adopting these economic programs as their own, Republicans were able to entice the nativists into their camp. But the alliance between Republicans and conservatives was always uneasy, and the Republicans had to work continuously at convincing their new recruits that they had shed dangerous radical tendencies and had accepted constitutionally sound principles. As the Rhode Island gubernatorial election demonstrated, conservatives could just as easily break away from the Republicans as join them. The final accession of conservative voting strength to the Republican party in 1860 was less a predetermined outcome than a masterful stroke of creative political strategy.

A number of scholars in the past few years have turned to an ideological explanation of the coming of the Civil War by focusing on the concept of republicanism. Both northerners and southerners, these authors contend, cherished an ideal of an independent, politically aware citizenry who valued local autonomy and who feared that outside forces sought to reduce the status of freemen to that of depen-

9. See Larry Gara, "Slavery and the Slave Power," 5–18; Thornton, *Politics and Power in a Slave Society*, 444–59; Holt, *The Political Crisis of the 1850s*, 187–89.

10. Holt, *Forging a Majority*, 8, 299–305; Formisano, *The Birth of Mass Political Parties*, 292–300; Thomas B. Alexander, "The Dimensions of Voter Partisan Constancy in Presidential Elections from 1840 to 1860," 113–120. Republican difficulties with conservatives were also pointed out in Holt, *The Political Crisis of the 1850s*, 207–11; and William E. Gienapp, "Nativism and the Creation of a Republican Majority in the North Before the Civil War," *JAH*, LXXII (1985), 541–57.

dence and servility. In both the North and the South conspiracy theories arose about the designs of the other section. Northerners came increasingly to see the actions of southern slaveholders as a plot to extinguish northern liberties, representative government, and economic well-being. In the same vein, southerners viewed the rise and advance of the northern free soil movement as an attempt to destroy southern white supremacy and prosperity by depriving southerners of their natural rights and degrading them to the level of slaves.[11] This study encounters the ideology of republicanism largely in connection with economic issues, although the thesis that both northerners and southerners acted upon the belief that their freedoms were being endangered has been frequently employed. There is, however, a distinct caution to be propounded with regard to the interpretation. When northerners and southerners justified their economic schemes, they always utilized republican rhetoric. Supposedly original republicanism had its greatest economic affinity with the doctrine of free trade, but it is clear that by the antebellum decade, if not before, protectionism had also been invested with republican virtues. In short, the concept of republicanism becomes a less discriminating analytical tool when the topics become less general and more specific. This observation therefore raises a question about the nature of republican ideology: whether it operated as an independent force, a sort of definable substance in political affairs, or whether it functioned as a rhetorical garment that covered the actual forces creating controversy. The awkwardness of republicanism as an explanatory device is that it was so pervasive. Hence one important point that needs to be addressed is which aspect of antebellum politics deserves emphasis: the republicanism by which individuals interpreted sectional tensions, or the various economic and social pressures that produced sectional tensions.

The other recent interpretation of the origins of the Civil War appears under the rubric of modernization. Advocates of the modernization thesis, which is an admittedly nebulous and imprecise concept, insist that the sectional conflict was the result of a clash of institutional structures and ideologies between a northern society which was quickly

11. On republicanism, see Thornton, *Politics and Power in a Slave Society*, xviii–xxi, 57–58, 204–27; Holt, *The Political Crisis of the 1850s*, 4–5, 151–52; Jean H. Baker, *Affairs of Party: The Political Culture of Northern Democrats in the Mid-Nineteenth Century* (Ithaca, N.Y., 1983), 114–76; John McCardell, *The Idea of a Southern Nation: Southern Nationalists and Southern Nationalism, 1830–1860* (New York, 1979), 331, 336–37; Cooper, *The South and the Politics of Slavery*, 370–71.

adapting to the processes of urbanization and industrialization, and a southern society that was struggling to retain the traditional values of a parochial, nonmarket agrarian civilization. The history of the Panic of 1857 adds evidence, with some modifications, in support of one aspect of the modernization explanation of the cause of the Civil War. Since the early 1970s, historians have used to one degree or another the idea that Republicans were the great exponents of a free labor society and that the conflict between the sections was a struggle over which labor system, free or slave, would ultimately prevail in the United States.[12] The Panic of 1857 underscores the centrality of that debate.

Historians have been perhaps so preoccupied with the coming of the sectional crisis that they have tended to underestimate the importance of the labor movement of the 1850s and what it meant to the controversy over slavery. It was in the decade of the 1850s that the first national unions were established and the principles of craft unionism fleshed out. The decade was also one of tremendous labor turmoil, not the least of which occurred between 1857 and 1860.[13] The rise of the labor movement presented numerous problems for northerners. On the one hand, they wanted the laborer to receive just compensation for his toil and to be materially comfortable, but on the other hand they

12. See Richard D. Brown, *Modernization: The Transformation of American Life, 1600–1865* (New York, 1976), 3–22, 159–76; Raimondo Luraghi, "The Civil War and the Modernization of American Society: Social Structure and Industrial Revolution in the Old South Before and During the War," *CWH*, XVIII (1972), 230–50; McPherson, *Ordeal By Fire*, 5–37; Eric Foner, *Free Soil, Free Labor, Free Men*, 11–27. A recent interpretation of the genesis of the Civil War is based on the idea that southern civilization reflected Celtic cultural values and found a natural enemy in northern civilization, a product of English cultural traditions. A good example of this literature is Grady McWhiney and Perry D. Jamieson, *Attack and Die: Civil War Military Tactics and the Southern Heritage* (University, Ala., 1982), 170–78. This study of the Panic of 1857 has nothing to propound in regard to this "Celtic fringe" theory of the American Civil War.

13. See Walter Licht, *Working for the Railroad: The Organization of Work in the Nineteenth Century* (Princeton, N.J., 1983), 245–49; Norman Ware, *The Industrial Worker, 1840–1860: The Reaction of American Industrial Society to the Advance of the Industrial Revolution* (1924; rpr. Chicago, 1964), 227–40; Daniel J. Walkowitz, *Worker City, Company Town: Iron and Cotton-Worker Protest in Troy and Cohoes, New York, 1855–84* (Urbana, Ill., 1978), 82–89; Susan E. Hirsch, *Roots of the American Working Class: The Industrialization of Crafts in Newark, 1800–1860* (Philadelphia, 1978), 117–23. The connections between labor activity during the antebellum decades and political developments have begun to receive attention from political historians; see, for example, Ronald P. Formisano, *The Transformation of Political Culture: Massachusetts Parties, 1790s–1840s* (New York, 1980), 324–43; Baker, *Affairs of Party*, 47; Baum, *The Civil War Party System*, 27–32.

disapproved of any basic change in the free enterprise economic system. One contributor to the *North American Review* rather succinctly
summarized the dilemma northerners were confronting:

> Next to the origin of wealth, the inquiry which most interests us is with
> regard to the means used to distribute, with uniform equity, among all
> classes, the wealth which labor produces, which means should be so regu-
> lated as to secure to labor such sure and liberal compensation as shall pre-
> serve its energies and satisfactorily reward its toil. Our machinery for this
> purpose is, it must be confessed, as full of defects and imperfections as
> man himself; but we cannot afford to destroy it, for the whole fabric of
> society rests upon it, and our only hope is in regulating, repairing, im-
> proving, and adjusting its various portions with judicious care.[14]

The Republicans were able to meet and respond to the sudden rise
of worker unrest in the 1850s. Their free labor ideology was more than
an amalgamation of middle class sentiments about thrift, industriousness, social mobility, and free market economics. Although Republicans often used the word *labor* in its broadest sense, to indicate any
physical or mental exertion, they also commonly endowed the word
with a more modern meaning, often using the term *laborers* to refer to
a wage-earning working class. And this definition of labor found a snug
home in the Republicans' antislavery tirades. The great organizing
theme of the Republicans in regard to the South was the Slave Power
conspiracy; an important element of this indictment of the aims of
slaveholders was the fear that the slave masters sought to reduce
northern operatives to the level of southern slaves.

Few Republicans exhibited much pessimism about the fate of the
free worker. They certainly did not believe that the northern free enterprise system would produce a society divided into the wealthy few
and the multitudinous poor. It appears, rather, that in the first bloom
of industrialism Republicans caught the sense of change that the transformation inspired and the possibilities for improvement that the machine age could bring about. Republicans assumed that they could circumvent other nations' disruptive experience with the new technology
and instead offer the worker a high standard of living and an intellectually and morally rewarding life.

Slavery endangered the Republican vision of the nation's future on
several specific points. The most obvious fear was that slaves might

14. "The Commerce and Currency of the United States," *North American Review*,
XC (January, 1860), 47.

eventually compete directly with free labor and depress the free laborer's condition to that of a slave. This was essentially the same argument Republicans made against slavery's extension into the western territories, that free white labor could not compete against black slave labor.[15] Republicans realized that if free laborers ever fell into such a miserable state as slavery they could pose a danger to the country's economic and social institutions. Due to the democratic nature of American politics, workers could vote. If their condition deteriorated into pauperism, workers could vote themselves into power, overturn the social order, and redistribute property. This possibility had to be eliminated.

To ensure the future well-being of northern free workers, Republicans proposed two courses of action. The first was to halt the expansion of slavery, to limit it to a geographical region. This would, it was hoped, forestall the dreaded competition between free and slave labor. The second was to offer a program of minimal governmental intervention in the economy to make certain that the rule of competition did not work against the economic interests of northern operatives. Thus Republicans advocated the policies of protectionism, education, internal improvements, and free homesteads for actual settlers.[16] Although Republicans were concerned over the fate of the laborer, they were generally neither labor reformers nor abolitionists. They sought, rather, to preserve their own economic and political system, and they perceived that the threat to this system originated in outside and unfair attacks on the material welfare of the northern middle and lower classes.

Southerners, of course, refused to accede to northern legislative demands and especially rejected any meddling with the health of the peculiar institution. Slaveholding constituted one of the greatest forms of

15. The theme of southern free and slave labor relations is discussed in Ira Berlin and Herbert G. Gutman, "Natives and Immigrants, Free Men and Slaves: Urban Workingmen in the Antebellum American South," *AHR*, LXXXVIII (1983), 1176–77, 1195–1200. The Republican and antislavery confrontation with the labor question is treated to some extent and placed in an international perspective by Marcus Cunliffe, *Chattel Slavery and Wage Slavery: The Anglo-American Context, 1830–1860* (Athens, Ga., 1979), 51–57, 72–75, 90.

16. Richard Hofstadter, "The Tariff Issue on the Eve of the Civil War," *AHR*, XLIV (1938), 50–55; Hacker, *The Triumph of American Capitalism*, 329, 336; Eric Foner, *Free Soil, Free Labor, Free Men*, 173–75, all stress that the demand for high tariffs arose from industrialists rather than from a concern for the plight of the worker. But see James L. Huston, "A Political Response to Industrialism," 35–55.

wealth in the South, and from that wealth came a stream of income that gave the region its prosperity. Southerners not only had an immense tangible economic interest in the preservation of the peculiar institution, they also viewed slavery as the most appropriate means of governing the relations between two dissimilar races.[17] Southerners were thus socially and economically wedded to a slave labor system, and they could have hardly considered the Republican program as anything else but a direct threat to their way of life.

In the 1850s the question of the expansion of slavery into the territories became the specific issue that generated sectional rancor, but in time another issue would have risen to take its place. Behind most of the sectional disputes over legislative action involving the western territories, diplomatic relations, and economic policy was the more general question of whether the free or slave labor system would prevail. The Panic of 1857 entered that debate and helped the Republicans to win the presidency in 1860. Because of the accession of an antislavery party to governmental authority, southerners seceded from the Union. Even if the Republicans had squandered their political opportunities in 1860, the eventual victory of an antislavery party was nearly inevitable. What kept sectionalism alive was not the political machinations of ambitious politicians but the unavoidable tensions that arose from the coexistence of a free labor and a slave labor society in one polity. The Panic of 1857 had made the tension obvious and had aided in producing a political change, but the Panic was only a moderate downswing in the business cycle. The volatile nature of the American economy ensured that other panics lay in the future, and time has proven that they were considerably more potent. Under these conditions, the debate over the fate of the free laborer, and thereby the fate of free society, could only become more pressing and eventually force northerners to opt for antislavery doctrines. Hence the inevitability of a political crisis over slavery—although not necessarily of armed conflict—resulted from the incompatible institutional demands the two labor systems placed upon the nation and the insistence of each section's political representatives that the legislation of the country be molded solely to fortify and perpetuate the economic institutions of their particular region.

17. Channing, *Crisis of Fear*, 286–93; Wright, *The Political Economy of the Cotton South*, 141–44, 147–50.

Appendix A

Party Victors in Selected Northern State Congressional Contests, 1856–1860

Maine Cong. Dist.	1856	1858	1860
1	R	R	R
2	R	R	R
3	R	R	R
4	R	R	R
5	R	R	R
6	R	R	R

Massachusetts Cong. Dist.	1856	1858	1860
1	R	R	R
2	R	R	R
3	R	R	R
4	R	R	R
5	R	R	CU
6	R	R	R
7	R	R	R
8	R	R	R
9	R	R	R
10	R	R	R
11	R	R	R

New Jersey Cong. Dist.	1856	1858	1860
1	R	R	R
2	R	R	R
3	D	ALD	D
4	D	ALD	D
5	D	R+	D

Illinois Cong. Dist.	1856	1858	1860
1	R	R	R
2	R	R	R
3	R	R	R
4	R	R	R
5	D	ALD	D
6	D	ALD	D
7	D	ALD	D
8	D	ALD	D
9	D	ALD	D

Ohio

Cong. Dist.	1856	1858	1860
1	D	D	D
2	D	R	R
3	R	D	D
4	R	D	D
5	R	R	R
6	D	D	D
7	R	R	R
8	R	R	R
9	D	R	D
10	D	R	R
11	R	D	R
12	D	D	D
13	R	R	R
14	R	R	R
15	D	R	D
16	R	R	R
17	D	R	D
18	R	R	R
19	R	R	R
20	R	R	R
21	R	R	R

Pennsylvania

Cong. Dist.	1856	1858	1860
1	D	D	D*
2	R	R	R
3	D	R	R
4	D	R	R
5	D	R	R
6	D	ALD	R
7	D	R	D
8	D	R	D
9	R	R	R
10	R	R	R

Pennsylvania

Cong. Dist.	1856	1858	1860
11	D	R	R
12	D	R	R
13	D	D	D
14	R	R	R
15	D	R	R
16	D	R	D
17	D	R	R
18	R	R	R
19	R	R	R
20	D	ALD	D
21	R	R	R
22	R	R	R
23	R	R	R
24	D	R	R
25	R	R	R

Vermont

Cong. Dist.	1856	1858	1860
1	R	R	R
2	R	R	R
3	R	R	R

Michigan

Cong. Dist.	1856	1858	1860
1	R	D	R
2	R	R	R
3	R	R	R
4	R	R	R

Wisconsin

Cong. Dist.	1856	1858	1860
1	R	R	R
2	R	R	R
3	R	D	R

Iowa Cong. Dist.	1856	1858	1860
1	R	R	R
2	R	R	R

Indiana Cong. Dist.	1856	1858	1860
1	D	D	D
2	D	D	D
3	D	R	R
4	D	D	D
5	R	R	R
6	D	R	R
7	D	ALD	D
8	R	R	R
9	R	R	R
10	R	R	R
11	R	R	R

New York Cong. Dist.	1856	1858	1860
1	D	R+	D+
2	D	R+	D+
3	D	D+	D+
4	D	ALD	IND
5	D	D+	D+
6	D	D+	R
7	D	R+	D+

New York Cong. Dist.	1856	1858	1860
8	D	R+	D+
9	D	R+	D+
10	R	R	R
11	D	R+	D
12	R	R+	R
13	R	R+	R
14	D	R+	D
15	R	R	R
16	R	R	R
17	R	R	R
18	R	R+	D
19	R	R	R
20	R	R	R
21	R	R	R
22	R	R	R
23	R	R	R
24	R	R	R
25	R	R	R
26	R	R	R
27	R	R	R
28	R	R	R
29	R	R	R
30	R	R	R
31	R	R	R
32	D	R+	R
33	R	R	R

SOURCE: Compiled from *Tribune Almanac,* 1857, 1859, 1861

LEGEND: D = Democrat; R = Republican; N = American Party; ALD = Anti-Lecompton Democrat; IND = Independent; CU = Constitutional Union; + = Union of opposition; * = Given to Democrat on basis of contested election

Appendix B

Democratic Vote Losses in the Election of 1860 in Pennsylvania Counties Changing Party Preference

County	(1) October Election Cong	(2) October Election Gov	(3) November Election Pres	(4) Difference Gov–Cong (Col. 2– Col. 1)	(5) Difference Gov–Pres (Col. 2– Col. 3)
Adams	2,767	2,849	2,680	82	169
Berks	9,993	10,318	9,260	325	1,058
Bucks	6,281	6,330	5,661	49	669
Carbon	3,638	3,652	3,499	14	153
Centre	2,834	2,824	2,449	−10	375
Clinton	1,707	1,703	1,316	−4	387
Columbia	2,476	2,586	2,452	110	134
Franklin	3,356	3,379	3,137	23	242
Juniata	1,410	1,465	1,149	55	316
Lehigh	4,481	4,556	4,239	75	317
Luzerne	6,119	6,916	6,803	797	113
Lycoming	3,128	3,034	2,589	−94	445
Mifflin	1,457	1,490	1,272	33	218
Montgomery	6,520	7,392	7,099	872	293
Montour	1,134	1,220	1,097	86	123
Perry	1,864	2,128	1,751	264	377
Philadelphia	38,101	42,119	30,893	4,018	11,226
Schuylkill	6,761	7,067	5,390	306	1,677

Venango	2,101	2,122	1,938	21	184
Wyoming	1,295	1,366	1,245	71	121
Totals	107,423	114,516	95,919	7,093	18,597

SOURCE: Computed from *Tribune Almanac*, 1861

LEGEND: Cong = congressional election; Gov = gubernatorial election; Pres = presidential election

Bibliography

Primary Sources

MANUSCRIPTS

Manuscript Department, William R. Perkins Library, Duke University, Durham, N.C.
  Bell, James Martin. Papers.
  Booker, George. Papers.
  Boteler, Alexander R. Papers.
  Campbell Family. Papers.
  Charleston Democratic Convention. Papers.
  Crittenden, John J. Papers.
Illinois Historical Survey, Urbana, Ill.
  Browning, Orville Hickman. Papers.
Manuscripts Division, Library of Congress, Washington, D.C.
  Bell, John. Papers.
  Hammond, James H. Papers.
  Lincoln, Abraham. Papers.
  Sherman, John. Papers.
  Simmons, James Fowler. Papers.
  Trumbull, Lyman. Papers.
  Van Buren, Martin. Papers.
Historical Society of Pennsylvania, Philadelphia, Pa.
  Bigler, William. Papers.
  Buchanan, James. Papers.
  Chase, Salmon Portland. Papers.
  Cooke, Jay. Papers.
  Gardiner, Edward Carey. Collection.

Manuscripts Department, University of Virginia Library, Charlottes-
ville, Va.
  Hunter, Robert M. T. Papers (#8753-d).
Virginia Historical Society, Richmond, Va.
  Mason Family. Papers.
  Ruffin, Edmund. Papers.

PERIODICALS

American Railroad Journal, 1857–60.
American Railway Times, 1857–60.
Atlantic Monthly, 1857–60.
Bankers' Magazine, 1857–61.
De Bow's Review, 1857–60.
Frank Leslie's Illustrated Newspaper, 1857–60.
Harper's New Monthly Magazine, 1857–60.
Harper's Weekly, 1857–60.
Hunt's Merchants' Magazine, 1857–60.
North American Review, 1857–60.
Russell's Magazine, 1857–60; reprinted by Ams Press, New York, 1965.
Scientific American, 1857–60.
Southern Literary Messenger, 1857–60.
Southern Planter, 1857–60.
Tribune Almanac, 1857–61.
United States Democratic Review, n.s., 1857–60.

NEWSPAPERS

Alabama
  Mobile *Daily Register*, 1857–60.
  Southern Advocate (Huntsville), 1857–60.
Connecticut
  Hartford *Daily Times*, 1857–60.
Georgia
  Daily Constitutionalist (Augusta), 1860.
  Federal Union (Milledgeville), 1857–60.
  Southern Recorder (Milledgeville), 1857–60.
Illinois
  Chicago *Daily Democrat*, 1857–58.
  Chicago *Daily Times*, 1857, 1859, 1860.
  Chicago *Daily Tribune*, 1857–58.
  Chicago *Press and Tribune*, 1858–60.

Chicago *Weekly Democrat*, 1859–60.
Daily Illinois State Journal (Springfield), 1857–60.
Daily Illinois State Register (Springfield), 1857–60.
Indiana
Evansville *Daily Journal*, 1858–60.
Indianapolis *Daily Journal*, 1857–60.
Richmond *Palladium*, 1858–60.
Kentucky
Louisville *Daily Courier*, 1857–60.
Louisiana
Daily Picayune (New Orleans), 1857–60.
New Orleans *Daily Crescent*, 1857, 1859, 1860.
Massachusetts
Bay State (Lynn), 1857–60.
Boston *Daily Advertiser*, 1860.
Boston *Evening Transcript*, 1857–60.
Boston *Herald*, 1860.
Boston *Post*, 1857–60.
Haverhill *Gazette*, 1857–60.
Liberator (Boston), 1857–60.
Lynn *News*, 1857–60.
Lynn *Weekly Reporter*, 1857–60.
Springfield *Daily Republican*, 1857–60.
Michigan
Detroit *Daily Free Press*, 1857–60.
Mississippi
Mississippian (Jackson), 1857–60.
Mississippi Free Trader (Natchez), 1857–60.
Vicksburg *Daily Whig*, 1858–60.
New Hampshire
New Hampshire Patriot & State Gazette (Concord), 1857–60.
New Jersey
Daily True American (Trenton), 1857–60.
Newark *Daily Advertiser*, 1857–60.
New York
Atlas & Argus (Albany), 1857–60.
National Anti-Slavery Standard (New York), 1857–60.
New York *Daily Tribune*, 1857–60.

New York *Evening Post*, 1857–60.
New York *Herald*, 1857–60.
New York *Times*, 1857–60.
North Carolina
    Raleigh *Weekly Register*, 1857–60.
    Semi-Weekly Standard (Raleigh), 1857–60.
Ohio
    Anti-Slavery Bugle (Salem), 1857–60.
    Cincinnati *Daily Enquirer*, 1857–60.
    Cincinnati *Daily Gazette*, 1857–60.
    Cleveland *Daily Plain Dealer*, 1857–60.
    Daily Ohio State Journal (Columbus), 1857–60.
Pennsylvania
    Adams Sentinel (Gettysburg), 1857–60.
    Agitator (Wellsboro), 1857–60.
    Allegheny Mountain Echo (Johnstown), 1857–60.
    Altoona *Tribune*, 1858–60.
    Bedford *Gazette*, 1857–60.
    Bedford *Inquirer and Chronicle*, 1857–60.
    Bradford *Reporter* (Towanda), 1857–60.
    Cambria Tribune (Johnstown), 1857–60.
    Compiler (Gettysburg), 1857–60.
    Daily Evening Express (Lancaster), 1858.
    Democratic Press (York), 1857–60.
    Democratic Watchman (Bellefonte), 1857–60.
    Easton *Argus*, 1857–60.
    Erie *Gazette*, 1857–60.
    Erie *Weekly Observer*, 1857–60.
    Genius of Liberty (Uniontown), 1858.
    Harrisburg *Daily Telegraph*, 1857.
    Jeffersonian (Stroudsburg), 1858–60.
    Lancaster *Examiner and Herald*, 1857–60.
    Lebanon *Courier*, 1857–60.
    Lewistown *Gazette*, 1857–60.
    Luzerne Union (Wilkes-Barre), 1857–60.
    Miner's Journal (Pottsville), 1857–61.
    North American and United States Gazette (Philadelphia), 1858–60.
    Pennsylvania *Daily Telegraph*, 1857–60.
    Philadelphia *Evening Bulletin*, 1857–60.
    Pittsburgh *Dispatch*, 1859–60.

Pittsburgh *Morning Post*, 1858–60.
Potter Journal (Coudersport), 1857–60.
Public Ledger and Daily Transcript (Philadelphia), 1860.
Raftsman's Journal (Clearfield), 1857–60.
Washington *Examiner*, 1857–60.
Washington *Reporter*, 1857–60.
Rhode Island
    Providence *Daily Journal*, 1859–60.
    Providence *Daily Tribune*, 1857–59.
South Carolina
    Charleston *Daily Courier*, 1857–60.
    Charleston *Mercury*, 1857–60.
Tennessee
    Knoxville *Whig*, 1857–60.
Virginia
    Richmond *Enquirer*, 1857–60.
    Richmond *Whig*, 1857–60.
Washington, D.C.
    Daily National Intelligencer, 1857–60.
    National Era, 1857–60.
    States, 1857–59.
    States and Union, 1859–60.
    Washington *Union*, 1857–59.
Wisconsin
    Milwaukee *Daily Free Democrat*, 1857–60.

GOVERNMENT PUBLICATIONS

Congressional Globe. 34th Cong., 3rd Sess., through 36th Cong., 1st Sess.
De Bow, James D. B., comp. *Statistical View of the United States . . . Being a Compendium of the Seventh Census*. Washington, D.C. 1854.
Eighth Census. 4 vols. Washington, D.C., 1864.
House Executive Documents. 35th Cong., 1st Sess., through 36th Cong., 2nd Sess.
House Miscellaneous Documents. 35th Cong., 1st Sess.
House Reports. 35th Cong., 1st Sess.
Kennedy, Joseph C. G., comp. *Preliminary Report on the Eighth Census*. Washington, D.C., 1862.

Senate Executive Documents. 35th Cong., 1st Sess., through 36th Cong., 2nd Sess.

U.S. Department of Commerce, Bureau of the Census. *Historical Statistics of the United States: Colonial Times to 1970.* Washington, D.C., 1975.

CONTEMPORARY BOOKS, PAMPHLETS, AND MEMOIRS

Bigelow, E. B. *Remarks of the Depressed Condition of Manufactures in Massachusetts.* Boston, 1858.

Bigelow, John. *Retrospections of an Active Life.* 5 vols. New York, 1909.

Blaine, James G. *Twenty Years of Congress: From Lincoln to Garfield.* 2 vols. Norwich, Conn., 1884–86.

Boston Board of Trade. *Annual Reports.* Boston, 1857–61.

Bowen, Francis. *The Principles of Political Economy.* Boston, 1856.

Carey, Henry C. *Financial Crises: Their Causes and Effects.* In Vol. I of *Miscellaneous Works of Henry C. Carey.* 2 vols. Philadelphia, 1865.

———. *Letters to the President, on the Foreign and Domestic Policy of the Union.* In Vol. I of *Miscellaneous Works of Henry C. Carey.* 2 vols. Philadelphia, 1865.

———. *Manual of Social Science: Being a Condensation of the "Principles of Social Science" by H. C. Carey.* Edited by Kate McKean. Philadelphia, 1866.

Clingman, Thomas L. *Selections from the Speeches and Writings of Hon. Thomas L. Clingman, of North Carolina.* 2nd ed. Raleigh, N.C., 1878.

Colton, Calvin. *The Rights of Labor.* 3rd ed. New York, 1847.

Colwell, Stephen. *The Claims of Labor, and Their Precedence to the Claims of Free Trade.* Philadelphia, 1861.

———. *The South: A Letter from a Friend in the North.* Philadelphia, 1856.

Cox, Samuel S. *Eight Years in Congress, from 1857–1865.* New York, 1865.

Cutts, J. Madison. *A Brief Treatise Upon Constitutional and Party Questions, and the History of Political Parties, as I Received it Orally from the Late Senator Stephen A. Douglas, of Illinois.* New York, 1866.

Dealtry, William. *The Laborer: A Remedy for His Wrongs: Or, A Disquisition on the Usages of Society.* Cincinnati, 1869.

Everett, Edward. *The Mount Vernon Papers.* New York, 1860.

Fitzhugh, George. *Cannibals All! or Slaves Without Masters.* Edited by C. Vann Woodward. Cambridge, Mass., 1960.

Fowler, Wm. Worthington. *Ten Years in Wall Street.* Hartford, Conn., 1870.

Gibbons, James S. *The Banks of New-York, Their Dealers, The Clearing House, and the Panic of 1857.* New York, 1864.

Greeley, Horace. *Essays Designed to Elucidate the Science of Political Economy.* Boston, 1870.

Greeley, Horace, and John F. Cleveland. *A Political Text-Book for 1860.* New York, 1860.

Halstead, M[urat]. *Caucuses of 1860: A History of the National Political Conventions of the Current Presidential Campaign.* Columbus, Ohio, 1860.

[Hooper, Samuel.] A Merchant of Boston. *Currency or Money: Its Nature and Uses, and the Effects of the Circulation of Bank-Notes for Currency.* Boston, 1855.

————. *An Examination of the Theory and the Effect of Laws Regulating the Amount of Specie in Banks.* Boston, 1860.

Kettell, Thomas P. *Southern Wealth and Northern Profits.* New York, 1860.

McClure, Alexander K. *Old Time Notes of Pennsylvania.* 2 vols. Philadelphia, 1905.

A Merchant of Philadelphia. *The End of the Irrepressible Conflict.* Philadelphia, 1860.

Opdyke, George. *A Treatise on Political Economy.* New York, 1851.

Perry, Benjamin Franklin. *Reminiscences of Public Men.* Philadelphia, 1883.

Pickering, John. *The Working Man's Political Economy, founded upon the Principle of Immutable Justice, and the Inalienable Rights of Man.* Cincinnati, 1847.

Rhode Island Society for the Encouragement of Domestic Industry. *Transactions for the Year 1857.* Providence, 1858.

Ruffin, Edmund. *The Political Economy of Slavery; or, The Institution Considered in regard to its Influence on Public Wealth and the General Welfare.* N.p., [1857].

Sawyer, George S. *Southern Institutes; or, An Inquiry into the Origin and Early Prevalence of Slavery and the Slave-Trade.* Philadelphia, 1859.

Sherman, John. *Recollections of Forty Years in the House, Senate and Cabinet: An Autobiography.* 2 vols. Chicago, 1895.

Smith, E. Peshine, *A Manual of Political Economy.* New York, 1853.

Tucker, George. *Political Economy for the People.* Philadelphia, 1859.

Walker, Amasa. *The Nature and Uses of Money and Mixed Currency, with a History of the Wickaboag Bank.* Boston, 1857.

―――. *The Science of Wealth: A Manual of Political Economy.* Philadelphia, 1872.

Wayland, Francis. *Elements of Political Economy.* 4th ed. Boston, 1856.

Weston, George M. *Southern Slavery Reduces Northern Wages.* Washington, D.C., 1856.

Wolfe, Samuel M. *Helper's Impending Crisis Dissected.* Philadelphia, 1860.

PUBLISHED LETTERS, SPEECHES, DIARIES, AND OTHER
CONTEMPORARY MATERIAL

Ambler, Charles Henry, ed. *Correspondence of Robert M. T. Hunter, 1826–1876.* Washington, D.C., 1918.

Ames, Mary Lesley, ed. *Life and Letters of Peter and Susan Lesley.* 2 vols. New York, 1909.

Barnes, Thurlow Weed, ed. *Memoir of Thurlow Weed.* 2 vols. Boston, 1884.

Basler, Roy P., Dolores Marion Pratt, and Lloyd A. Dunlop, eds. *The Collected Works of Abraham Lincoln.* 8 vols. New Brunswick, N.J., 1953.

Brown, Harry James, and Frederick D. Williams, eds. *The Diary of James A. Garfield.* 3 vols. East Lansing, Mich., 1967.

Johannsen, Robert W., ed. *The Letters of Stephen A. Douglas.* Urbana, Ill., 1961.

―――. *The Lincoln-Douglas Debates of 1858.* New York, 1965.

McCormack, Thomas J., ed. *Memoirs of Gustave Koerner, 1809–1896.* 2 vols. Cedar Rapids, Iowa, 1909.

Moore, John Bassett, ed. *The Works of James Buchanan.* 12 vols. Philadelphia, 1908–11.

Nevins, Allan, and Milton Halsey Thomas, eds. *The Diary of George Templeton Strong.* 4 vols. New York, 1952.

Oliphant, Mary C. Simms, Alfred Taylor Odell, and T. C. Duncan Eaves, eds. *The Letters of William Gilmore Simms.* 5 vols. Columbia, S.C., 1952–56.

Perry, Thomas Sergeant, ed. *The Life and Letters of Francis Lieber.* Boston, 1882.

Phillips, Ulrich Bonnell, ed. *The Correspondence of Robert Toombs, Alexander H. Stephens, and Howell Cobb.* Washington, D.C., 1911.

Ruchames, Louis, and Walter M. Merrill, eds. *The Letters of William Lloyd Garrison.* 6 vols. Cambridge, Mass., 1971–81.

Schafer, Joseph, trans. and ed. *Intimate Letters of Carl Schurz, 1841–1869.* 1928; rpr. New York, 1970.

Secondary Sources

MONOGRAPHS, ARTICLES, AND GENERAL WORKS

Abbott, Richard H. *Cobbler in Congress: The Life of Henry Wilson, 1812–1875.* Lexington, Ky., 1972.

Alexander, Thomas B. *Sectional Stress and Party Strength: A Study of Roll-Call Voting Patterns in the United States House of Representatives, 1836–1860.* Nashville, 1967.

———. "The Dimensions of Voter Partisan Constancy in Presidential Elections from 1840 to 1860." In *Essays on American Antebellum Politics, 1840–1860*, edited by Stephen E. Maizlish and John K. Kushma. College Station, Tex., 1982.

Auchampaugh, Philip Gerald. *Robert Tyler: Southern Rights Champion, 1847–1866.* Duluth, Minn., 1934.

Baker, Jean H. *Affairs of Party: The Political Culture of Northern Democrats in the Mid-Nineteenth Century.* Ithaca, N.Y., 1983.

———. *Ambivalent Americans: The Know-Nothing Party in Maryland.* Baltimore, 1977.

Barney, William. *The Road to Secession: A New Perspective on the Old South.* New York, 1972.

Baum, Dale. "Know-Nothingism and the Republican Majority in Massachusetts: The Political Realignment of the 1850s." *Journal of American History*, LXIV (1978), 959–86.

———. *The Civil War Party System: The Case of Massachusetts, 1848–1876.* Chapel Hill, 1984.

Beard, Charles A., and Mary R. Beard. *The Rise of American Civilization.* 2 vols. New York, 1927.

Berlin, Ira, and Herbert G. Gutman. "Natives and Immigrants, Free Men and Slaves: Urban Workingmen in the Antebellum American South." *American Historical Review*, LXXXVIII (1983), 1175–1200.

Berry, Thomas Senior. *Western Prices Before 1861: A Study of the Cincinnati Market.* Cambridge, Mass., 1943.

Bidwell, Percy Wells, and John I. Falconer. *History of Agriculture in the Northern United States, 1620–1860.* Washington, D.C., 1925.

Billington, Ray Allen. *The Protestant Crusade, 1800–1860: A Study of the Origins of American Nativism.* New York, 1952.

Bloom, Robert L. "Newspaper Opinion in the State Election of 1860." *Pennsylvania History*, XXVIII (1961), 346–64.

Bogart, Ernest Ludlow. *Financial History of Ohio.* Urbana-Champaign, Ill., 1912.

Bolino, August C. *The Development of the American Economy.* 2nd ed. Columbus, Ohio, 1966.

Boney, F. N. *John Letcher of Virginia: The Story of Virginia's Civil War Governor.* University, Ala., 1966.

Borit, Gabor S. *Lincoln and the Economics of the American Dream.* Memphis, 1978.

———. "Old Wine into New Bottles: Abraham Lincoln and the Tariff Reconsidered." *Historian*, XXVIII (1966), 289–317.

Boyle, James E. *Chicago Wheat Prices for Eighty-One Years: Daily, Monthly, and Yearly Fluctuations and Their Causes.* Ithaca, N.Y., 1922.

Bradley, Erwin Stanley. *Simon Cameron, Lincoln's Secretary of War: A Political Biography.* Philadelphia, 1966.

Broude, Henry N. "The Role of the State in American Economic Development." In *United States Economic History: Selected Readings*, edited by Harry N. Scheiber. New York, 1964.

Brown, John Crosby. *A Hundred Years of Merchant Banking: A History of Brown Brothers and Company, Brown, Shipley & Company and the Allied Firms.* New York, 1909.

Brown, Richard D. *Modernizataion: The Transformation of American Life, 1600–1865.* New York, 1976.

Bunting, W. H., comp. and annotator. *Portrait of a Port: Boston, 1852–1914.* Cambridge, Mass., 1971.

Cain, Marvin R. *Lincoln's Attorney General: Edward Bates of Missouri.* Columbia, Mo., 1965.

Caldwell, Stephen A. *A Banking History of Louisiana.* Baton Rouge, 1935.

Campbell, Claude A. *The Development of Banking in Tennessee.* Nashville, 1932.

Carsel, Wilfred. "The Slaveholders' Indictment of Northern Wage Slavery." *Journal of Southern History*, VI (1940), 504–20.

Chalmers, Leonard. "Tammany Hall, Fernando Wood, and the Struggle to Control New York City, 1857–1859." *New-York Historical Society Quarterly*, LIII (1969), 7–33.

Channing, Stephen A. *Crisis of Fear: Secession in South Carolina.* New York, 1970.

Chatelain, Verne E. "The Federal Land Policy and Minnesota Politics, 1854–1860." *Minnesota History*, XXII (1941), 227–48.

Cole, Arthur Charles. *The Whig Party in the South.* Washington, D.C., 1913.

Coleman, Mrs. Chapman [Ann Mary Butler Crittenden]. *The Life of John J. Crittenden, with Selections from his Correspondence and Speeches.* 2 vols. Philadelphia, 1871.

Coleman, John F. *The Disruption of the Pennsylvania Democracy, 1848–1860.* Harrisburg, Pa., 1975.

Collins, Bruce W. "The Democrats' Electoral Fortunes During the Lecompton Crisis." *Civil War History*, XXIV (1978), 314–31.

———. "The Democrats' Loss of Pennsylvania in 1858." *Pennsylvania Magazine of History and Biography*, CIX (1985), 499–536.

———. "Economic Issues in Ohio's Politics During the Recession of 1857–1858." *Ohio History*, LXXXIX (1980), 46–64.

Conkin, Paul K. *Prophets of Prosperity: America's First Political Economists.* Bloomington, Ind., 1980.

Cooper, William J., Jr. *The South and the Politics of Slavery, 1828–1856.* Baton Rouge, 1978.

Crenshaw, Ollinger. *The Slave States in the Presidential Election of 1860.* Baltimore, 1945.

Cunliffe, Marcus. *Chattel Slavery and Wage Slavery: The Anglo-American Context, 1830–1860.* Athens, Ga., 1979.

Curl, Donald Walter. "The Baltimore Convention of the Constitutional Union Party." *Maryland Historical Magazine*, LXVII (1972), 254–77.

Current, Richard N. *The Civil War Era, 1848–1873.* Madison, Wisc., 1976. Vol. II of William F. Thompson, ed., *The History of Wisconsin.* 6 vols. projected.

Davis, David Brion. *The Slave Power Conspiracy and the Paranoid Style.* Baton Rouge, 1969.

Davis, Lance E., and H. Louis Stettler, III. "The New England Textile Industry, 1825–60: Trends and Fluctuations." In *Output, Employment, and Productivity in the United States After 1800.* New York, 1966. Vol. XXX of Conference on Research in Income and Wealth, *Studies in Income and Wealth.*

Dawley, Alan. *Class and Community: The Industrial Revolution in Lynn.* Cambridge, Mass., 1976.

Dew, Charles B. *Ironmaker to the Confederacy: Joseph R. Anderson and the Tredegar Iron Works.* New Haven, Conn., 1966.

DiNunzio, Mario H., and Jan T. Galkowski. "Political Loyalty in Rhode Island—A Computer Study of the 1850s." *Rhode Island History,* XXXVI (1977), 93–95.

Dorfman, Joseph. *The Economic Mind in American Civilization.* 5 vols. 1946; rpr. New York, 1966.

DuBois, James T., and Gertrude S. Mathews. *Galusha A. Grow: Father of the Homestead Law.* Boston, 1917.

Dumond, Dwight Lowell. *Antislavery: The Crusade for Freedom in America.* Ann Arbor, Mich., 1961.

———. *Antislavery Origins of the Civil War in the United States.* Ann Arbor, Mich., 1939.

———. *The Secession Movement, 1860–1861.* New York, 1931.

Dusinberre, William. *Civil War Issues in Philadelphia, 1856–1865.* Philadelphia, 1965.

Eaton, Clement. *A History of the Old South.* 2nd ed. New York, 1966.

———. *The Mind of the Old South.* Rev. ed. Baton Rouge, 1969.

Eiselen, Malcolm Rogers. *The Rise of Pennsylvania Protectionism.* Philadelphia, 1932.

Faust, Drew Gilpin. *James Henry Hammond and the Old South: A Design for Mastery.* Baton Rouge, 1982.

———. *A Sacred Circle: The Dilemma of the Intellectual in the Old South, 1840–1860.* Baltimore, 1977.

Fehrenbacher, Don E. *The Dred Scott Case: Its Significance in American Law and Politics.* New York, 1978.

———. *Prelude to Greatness: Lincoln in the 1850's.* Stanford, Calif., 1962.

———. *The South and Three Sectional Crises.* Baton Rouge, 1980.

Fishlow, Albert. *American Railroads and the Transformation of the Ante-Bellum Economy.* Cambridge, Mass., 1965.

Folwell, William Watts. "The Five Million Loan." *Collections of the Minnesota Historical Society,* XV (1915), 189–214.

Foner, Eric. "The Causes of the American Civil War: Recent Interpretations and New Directions." *Civil War History*, XX (1974), 197–214.

———. *Free Soil, Free Labor, Free Men: The Ideology of the Republican Party Before the Civil War.* New York, 1970.

———. "Politics, Ideology, and the Origins of the American Civil War." In *A Nation Divided: Problems and Issues of the Civil War and Reconstruction*, edited by George M. Fredrickson. Minneapolis, 1975.

Foner, Philip S. *Business & Slavery: The New York Merchants & the Irrepressible Conflict.* 1941; rpr. New York, 1968.

Formisano, Ronald P. *The Birth of Mass Political Parties: Michigan, 1827–1861.* Princeton, N.J., 1971.

———. *The Transformation of Political Culture: Massachusetts Parties, 1790s–1840s.* New York, 1980.

Fredrickson, George M. *The Black Image in the White Mind: The Debate on Afro-American Character and Destiny, 1817–1914.* New York, 1971.

Freehling, William W. *Prelude to Civil War: The Nullification Controversy in South Carolina, 1816–1836.* New York, 1965.

Gara, Larry. "Slavery and the Slave Power: A Crucial Distinction." *Civil War History*, XV (1969), 5–18.

Gates, Paul Wallace. *The Farmer's Age: Agriculture, 1815–1860.* New York, 1960.

———. *Fifty Million Acres: Conflicts over Kansas Land Policy, 1854–1890.* Ithaca, N.Y., 1954.

———. "Western Opposition to the Agricultural College Act." *Indiana Magazine of History*, XXXVII (1941), 103–36.

Genovese, Eugene D. *The Political Economy of Slavery: Studies in the Economy & Society of the Slave South.* New York, 1965.

———. *The World the Slaveholders Made: Two Essays in Interpretation.* New York, 1969.

Gienapp, William E. "Nativism and the Creation of a Republican Majority in the North Before the Civil War." *Journal of American History*, LXXII (1985), 529–59.

Gillespie, Neal C. *The Collapse of Orthodoxy: The Intellectual Ordeal of George Frederick Holmes.* Charlottesville, Va., 1972.

Ginsberg, Judah B. "Barnburners, Free Soilers, and the New York Republican Party." *New York History*, LVII (1976), 475–500.

Going, Charles Buxton. *David Wilmot, Free-Soiler: A Biography of the Great Advocate of the Wilmot Proviso.* New York, 1924.

Goodrich, Carter. *Government Promotion of American Canals and Railroads, 1800–1890.* New York, 1960.

Govan, Thomas P. "Was the Old South Different?" *Journal of Southern History,* XXI (1955), 447–55.

Green, Arnold W. *Henry Charles Carey: Nineteenth Century Sociologist.* Philadelphia, 1951.

Green, Fletcher M. *Constitutional Development in the South Atlantic States, 1776–1860: A Study in the Evolution of Democracy.* Chapel Hill, 1930.

Green, George D. *Finance and Economic Development in the Old South: Louisiana Banking, 1804–1861.* Stanford, Calif., 1972.

Gregory, Francis W. *Nathan Appleton: Merchant and Entrepreneur, 1779–1861.* Charlottesville, Va., 1975.

Gudelunas, William A., Jr., and William G. Shade, *Before the Molly Maguires: The Emergence of the Ethno-Religious Factor in the Politics of the Lower Anthracite Region, 1844–1872.* New York, 1976.

Gunderson, Gerald. "The Origin of the American Civil War." *Journal of Economic History,* XXXIV (1974), 915–50.

Hacker, Louis M. *The Triumph of American Capitalism: The Development of Forces in American History to the End of the Nineteenth Century.* New York, 1947.

Hahn, Steven. *The Roots of Southern Populism: Yeoman Farmers and the Transformation of the Georgia Upcountry, 1850–1890.* New York, 1983.

Hamilton, Charles Granville. *Lincoln and the Know Nothing Movement.* Washington, D.C., 1954.

Hamilton, J. G. De Roulhac. "Lincoln's Election an Immediate Menace to Slavery in the States?" *American Historical Review,* XXXVII (1932), 700–11.

Hammond, Bray. *Banks and Politics in America from the Revolution to the Civil War.* Princeton, N.J., 1957.

———. *Sovereignty and an Empty Purse: Banks and Politics in the Civil War.* Princeton, N.J., 1970.

Handlin, Oscar, and Mary Flug Handlin. *Commonwealth: A Study of the Role of Government in the American Economy: Massachusetts, 1774–1861.* Rev. ed. Cambridge, Mass., 1969.

Hansen, Stephen L. *The Making of the Third Party System: Voters and Parties in Illinois, 1850–1876.* Ann Arbor, Mich., 1980.

Hartz, Louis. *Economic Policy and Democratic Thought: Pennsylvania, 1776–1860.* Cambridge, Mass., 1948.

Hazard, Blanche Evans. *The Organization of the Boot and Shoe Industry in Massachusetts Before 1875.* Cambridge, Mass., 1921.

Heath, Milton Sidney. *Constructive Liberalism: The Role of the State in Economic Development in Georgia to 1860.* Cambridge, Mass., 1954.

Heck, Frank H. *Proud Kentuckian: John C. Breckinridge, 1821–1875.* Lexington, Ky., 1976.

Heilbroner, Robert L. *The Worldly Philosophers: The Lives, Times, and Ideas of the Great Economic Thinkers.* New York, 1961.

Helderman, Leonard C. *National and State Banks: A Study of Their Origins.* Boston, 1931.

Herriott, F. I. "The Conference in the Deutsches Haus Chicago, May 14–15, 1860: A Study of Some of the Preliminaries of the National Republican Convention of 1860." In *Transactions of the Illinois State Historical Society for the Year 1928.* Springfield, Ill., 1928.

Hibbard, Benjamin Horace. *A History of the Public Land Policies.* Madison, Wisc., 1965.

Hirsch, Susan E. *Roots of the American Working Class: The Industrialization of Crafts in Newark, 1800–1860.* Philadelphia, 1978.

Hitchcock, William S. "The Limits of Southern Unionism: Virginia Conservatives and the Gubernatorial Election of 1859." *Journal of Southern History,* XLVII (1981), 57–72.

Hite, James C., and Ellen J. Hall. "The Reactionary Evolution of Economic Thought in Antebellum Virginia." *Virginia Magazine of History and Biography,* LXXX (1972), 476–88.

Hofstadter, Richard. *The American Political Tradition and the Men Who Made It.* New York, 1948.

———. "The Tariff Issue on the Eve of the Civil War." *American Historical Review,* XLIV (1938), 50–55.

Holt, Michael F. *Forging a Majority: The Formation of the Republican Party in Pittsburgh, 1848–1860.* New Haven, Conn., 1969.

———. *The Political Crisis of the 1850s.* New York, 1978.

———. "The Politics of Impatience: The Origins of Know Nothingism." *Journal of American History,* LX (1973), 309–31.

Hubbell, John T. "The Douglas Democrats and the Election of 1860." *Mid-America,* LV (1973), 108–33.

Hudson, Michael. *Economics and Technology in 19th Century Ameri-*

can Thought: The Neglected American Economists. New York, 1975.

Hunt, Gaillard. *Israel, Elihu and Cadwallader Washburn: A Chapter in American Biography.* New York, 1925.

Hunt, H. Draper. *Hannibal Hamlin of Maine: Lincoln's First Vice-President.* Syracuse, N.Y., 1969.

Huston, James L. "Abolitionists and an Errant Economy: The Panic of 1857 and Abolitionist Economic Ideas." *Mid-America,* LXV (1983), 15–27.

———. "Facing an Angry Labor: The American Public Interprets the Shoemakers' Strike of 1860." *Civil War History,* XXVIII (1982), 197–212.

———. "The Panic of 1857, Southern Economic Thought, and the Patriarchal Defense of Slavery." *Historian,* XLVI (1984), 163–86.

———. "A Political Response to Industrialism: The Republican Embrace of Protectionist Labor Doctrines." *Journal of American History,* LXX (1983), 35–57.

———. "The Threat of Radicalism: Seward's Candidacy and the Rhode Island Gubernatorial Election of 1860." *Rhode Island History,* XLI (1982), 86–99.

———. "Western Grains and the Panic of 1857." *Agricultural History,* LVII (1983), 14–32.

Isely, Jeter Allen. *Horace Greeley and the Republican Party, 1853–1861: A Study of the "New York Tribune."* 1947; rpr. New York, 1965.

James, F. Cyril. *The Growth of Chicago Banks.* 2 vols. New York, 1938.

James, John A. *Money and Capital Markets in Postbellum America.* Princeton, N.J., 1978.

Jeffrey, Thomas E. "National Issues, Local Interests, and the Transformation of Antebellum North Carolina Politics." *Journal of Southern History,* L (1984), 43–74.

Jellison, Charles A. *Fessenden of Maine: Civil War Senator.* Syracuse, N.Y., 1962.

Jenkins, William Sumner. *Pro-Slavery Thought in the Old South.* Chapel Hill, 1935.

Johannsen, Robert W. *Stephen A. Douglas.* New York, 1973.

Johnson, Michael P. *Toward a Patriarchal Republic: The Secession of Georgia.* Baton Rouge, 1977.

Kaiser, Carl William, Jr. *History of the Academic Protectionist-Free Trade Controversy in America Before 1860.* Philadelphia, 1939.

Kaplan, A. D. H. *Henry Charles Carey: A Study in American Economic Thought*. Baltimore, 1931.

Kaufman, Allen. *Capitalism, Slavery, and Republican Values: Antebellum Political Economists, 1819–1848*. Austin, Tex., 1982.

Keith, Elbridge G. "The National Republican Convention of 1860." *University of Illinois Bulletin*, I (May 15, 1904).

Kibler, Lillian Adele. *Benjamin F. Perry: South Carolina Unionist*. Durham, N.C., 1946.

King, Alvy L. *Louis T. Wigfall: Southern Fire-eater*. Baton Rouge, 1970.

King, Willard L. *Lincoln's Manager: David Davis*. Cambridge, Mass., 1960.

Kinley, David. *The History, Organization and Influence of the Independent Treasury of the United States*. New York, 1893.

Klebaner, Benjamin J. "Poor Relief and Public Works During the Depression of 1857." *Historian*, XXII (1960), 264–79.

Klein, Philip Shriver. *President James Buchanan: A Biography*. University Park, Pa., 1962.

Kleppner, Paul. *The Third Electoral System, 1853–1892: Parties, Voters, and Political Cultures*. Chapel Hill, 1979.

Knox, John Jay. *A History of Banking in the United States*. New York, 1900.

Krooss, Herman E., and Paul Studenski. *Financial History of the United States*. 2nd ed. New York, 1963.

Krug, Mark M. *Lyman Trumbull: Conservative Radical*. New York, 1965.

Kruman, Marc W. *Parties and Politics in North Carolina, 1836–1865*. Baton Rouge, 1983.

Kuhn, William E. *History of Nebraska Banking: A Centennial Retrospect*. Lincoln, Neb., 1968.

Lake, Wilfred S. "The End of the Suffolk System." *Journal of Economic History*, VII (1947), 183–207.

Lebergott, Stanley. *Manpower in Economic Growth: The American Record Since 1800*. New York, 1964.

Lesesne, J. Mauldin. *The Bank of the State of South Carolina: A General and Political History*. Columbia, S.C., 1970.

Licht, Walter. *Working for the Railroad: The Organization of Work in the Nineteenth Century*. Princeton, N.J., 1983.

Littlefield, Henry M. "Has the Safety Valve Come Back to Life?" *Agricultural History*, XXXVIII (1964), 47–49.

Luraghi, Raimondo. "The Civil War and the Modernization of American Society: Social Structure and Industrial Revolution in the Old South Before and During the War." *Civil War History,* XVIII (1972), 230–50.

Luthin, Reinhard H. "Abraham Lincoln and the Tariff." *American Historical Review,* XLIX (1944), 609–29.

———. *The First Lincoln Campaign.* Cambridge, Mass., 1944.

———. *The Real Abraham Lincoln.* Englewood Cliffs, N.J., 1960.

McCardell, John. *The Idea of a Southern Nation: Southern Nationalists and Southern Nationalism, 1830–1860.* New York, 1979.

McCoy, Drew R. *The Elusive Republic: Political Economy in Jeffersonian America.* Chapel Hill, 1980.

McGerr, Michael E. "The Meaning of Liberal Republicanism: The Case of Ohio." *Civil War History,* XXVIII (1982), 307–23.

McGouldrick, Paul F. *New England Textiles in the Nineteenth Century: Profits and Investment.* Cambridge, Mass., 1968.

McPherson, James M. "Antebellum Southern Exceptionalism: A New Look at an Old Question." *Civil War History,* XXIX (1983), 230–44.

———. *Ordeal by Fire: The Civil War and Reconstruction.* New York, 1982.

McWhiney, Grady, and Perry D. Jamieson. *Attack and Die: Civil War Military Tactics and the Southern Heritage.* University, Ala., 1982.

Magdol, Edward. *Owen Lovejoy: Abolitionist in Congress.* New Brunswick, N.J., 1967.

Mandel, Bernard. *Labor Free and Slave: Workingmen and the Anti-Slavery Movement in the United States.* New York, 1955.

Mangold, George Benjamin. *The Labor Argument in the American Protective Tariff Discussion.* 1908; rpr. New York, 1971.

May, Robert E. *The Southern Dream of a Caribbean Empire, 1854–1861.* Baton Rouge, 1973.

Mayer, George H. *The Republican Party, 1854–1966.* 2nd ed. New York, 1967.

Meeker, Royal. *History of Shipping Subsidies.* New York, 1905.

Meerse, David E. "Buchanan, Corruption, and the Election of 1860." *Civil War History,* XII (1966), 116–31.

———. "The Northern Democratic Party and the Congressional Elections of 1858." *Civil War History,* XIX (1973), 119–37.

Mering, John V. "The Constitutional Union Campaign of 1860: An Example of the Paranoid Style." *Mid-America*, LX (1978), 95–106.

Merritt, Elizabeth. *James Henry Hammond, 1807–1864*. Baltimore, 1923.

Milton, George Fort. *The Eve of Conflict: Stephen A. Douglas and the Needless War*. Boston, 1934.

Mints, Lloyd W. *A History of Banking Theory in Great Britain and the United States*. Chicago, 1945.

Mitchell, Broadus. *William Gregg: Factory Master of the Old South*. Chapel Hill, 1928.

Morton, J. Sterling, Albert Watkins, and George L. Miller. *Illustrated History of Nebraska*. 3rd ed. 3 vols. Lincoln, Neb., 1911.

Nevins, Allan. *The Emergence of Lincoln*. 2 vols. New York, 1950.

———. *Ordeal of the Union*. 2 vols. New York, 1947.

Nichols, Roy Franklin. *The Disruption of American Democracy*. New York, 1948.

Nichols, Roy Franklin, and Philip S. Klein. "The Election of 1856." In *The Coming to Power: Critical Presidential Elections in American History*, edited by Arthur M. Schlesinger, Jr., Fred L. Israel, and William P. Hansen. New York, 1972.

North, Douglass C. *The Economic Growth of the United States, 1790–1860*. Englewood Cliffs, N.J., 1961.

Nye, Russel Blaine. *Fettered Freedom: Civil Liberties and the Slavery Controversy, 1830–1860*. Urbana, Ill., 1972.

Oakes, James. *The Ruling Race: A History of American Slaveholders*. New York, 1982.

Oates, Stephen B. *With Malice Toward None: The Life of Abraham Lincoln*. New York, 1977.

O'Connor, Thomas H. *Lords of the Loom: The Cotton Whigs and the Coming of the Civil War*. New York, 1968.

Owsley, Frank Lawrence. *King Cotton Diplomacy: Foreign Relations of the Confederate States of America*. Chicago, 1931.

Parks, Joseph Howard. *John Bell of Tennessee*. Baton Rouge, 1950.

———. *Joseph E. Brown of Georgia*. Baton Rouge. 1977.

Pelling, Henry. *American Labor*. Chicago, 1960.

Pessen, Edward. "How Different from Each Other Were the Antebellum North and South?" *American Historical Review*, LXXXV (1980), 1119–49.

Pleasants, Samuel Augustus. *Fernando Wood of New York City*. New York, 1948.

Poor, Henry V. *Manual of the Railroads of the United States for 1875–'76.* New York, 1875.

Porter, Glenn, and Harold C. Livesay. *Merchants and Manufacturers: Studies in the Changing Structure of Nineteenth-Century Marketing.* Baltimore, 1971.

Potter, David M. *The Impending Crisis, 1848–1861.* Edited by Don E. Fehrenbacher. New York, 1976.

Primm, James Neal. *Economic Policy in the Development of a Western State: Missouri 1820–1860.* Cambridge, Mass., 1954.

Randall, James G., and David H. Donald. *The Civil War and Reconstruction.* Rev. ed. Boston, 1969.

Ransom, Roger L., and Richard Sutch. *One Kind of Freedom: The Economic Consequences of Emancipation.* London, 1977.

Rayback, Joseph G. *A History of American Labor.* Rev. ed. New York, 1966.

Redlich, Fritz. *The Molding of American Banking: Men and Ideas.* 2nd ed. 2 vols. 1947; rpr. New York, 1968.

Reed, Merl E. *New Orleans and the Railroads: The Struggle for Commercial Empire, 1830–1860.* Baton Rouge, 1966.

Rezneck, Samuel. "The Influence of Depression Upon American Opinion, 1857–1859." *Journal of Economic History,* II (1942), 1–23.

Riddleberger, Patrick W. *George Washington Julian: Radical Republican.* Indianapolis, 1966.

Ringwalt, J. L. *Development of Transportation Systems in the United States.* 1888; rpr. New York, 1966.

Robbins, Roy M. *Our Landed Heritage: The Public Domain, 1776–1936.* Princeton, N.J., 1942.

Robert, Joseph Clarke. *The Tobacco Kingdom: Plantation, Market, and Factory in Virginia and North Carolina, 1800–1860.* Durham, N.C., 1938.

Roper, Laura Wood. *FLO: A Biography of Frederick Law Olmstead.* Baltimore, 1973.

Russel, Robert Royal. *Economic Aspects of Southern Sectionalism, 1840–1861.* Urbana, Ill., 1923.

———. *Improvement of Communication with the Pacific Coast as an Issue in American Politics, 1783–1864.* Cedar Rapids, Iowa, 1948.

Schatz, Ronald W. "Review Essay: Labor Historians, Labor Economics, and the Question of Synthesis." *Journal of American History,* LXXI (1984), 93–100.

Schlüter, Herman. *Lincoln, Labor and Slavery: A Chapter from the Social History of America.* New York, 1913.

Sellers, Charles Grier, Jr. "Who Were the Southern Whigs?" *American Historical Review,* LIX (1954), 335–46.

Sewell, Richard H. *Ballots for Freedom: Antislavery Politics in the United States, 1837–1860.* New York, 1976.

———. *John P. Hale and the Politics of Abolition.* Cambridge, Mass., 1965.

Shade, William Gerald. *Banks or No Banks: The Money Issue in Western Politics, 1832–1865.* Detroit, 1972.

Shannon, Fred A. "A Post Mortem on the Labor-Safety-Valve Theory." *Agricultural History,* XIX (1945), 31–38.

Sharkey, Robert P. *Money, Class, and Party: An Economic Study of Civil War and Reconstruction.* Baltimore, 1959.

Silbey, Joel H. "The Surge of Republican Power: Partisan Antipathy, American Social Conflict, and the Coming of the Civil War." In *Essays on American Antebellum Politics, 1840–1860,* edited by Stephen E. Maizlish and John J. Kushma. College Station, Tex., 1982.

Simpson, John Eddins. *Howell Cobb: The Politics of Ambition.* Chicago, 1973.

Smith, Alfred Glaze, Jr. *Economic Readjustment of an Old Cotton State: South Carolina, 1820–1860.* Columbia, S.C., 1958.

Smith, Donnal V. "Salmon P. Chase and the Election of 1860." *Ohio Archaeological and Historical Publications,* XXXIX (1930), 516–607.

Smith, Elbert B. *The Presidency of James Buchanan.* Lawrence, Kans., 1975.

Smith, George Winston. *Henry C. Carey and American Sectional Conflict.* Albuquerque, 1951.

Smith, Henry Nash. *Virgin Land: The American West as Symbol and Myth.* Cambridge, Mass., 1950.

Smith, Walter Buckingham, and Arthur Harrison Cole. *Fluctuations in American Business, 1790–1860.* Cambridge, Mass., 1935.

Spengler, Joseph J. "Population Theory in the Ante-Bellum South." *Journal of Southern History,* II (1936), 360–89.

Spiegelman, Mortimer. "The Failure of the Ohio Life Insurance and Trust Company, 1857." *Ohio State Archeological and Historical Quarterly,* LVII (1948), 247–65.

Stampp, Kenneth M. *The Imperiled Union: Essays on the Background of the Civil War.* New York, 1980.

Stanwood, Edward. *American Tariff Controversies in the Nineteenth Century.* 2 vols. New York, 1903.

Stegmaier, Mark J. "Intensifying the Sectional Conflict: William Seward versus James Hammond in the Lecompton Debate of 1858." *Civil War History,* XXXI (1985), 197–221.

Stewart, James Brewer. *Holy Warriors: The Abolitionists and American Slavery.* New York, 1976.

———. *Joshua R. Giddings and the Tactics of Radical Politics.* Cleveland, 1970.

Strode, Hudson. *Jefferson Davis: American Patriot, 1808–1861.* New York, 1955.

Swank, James M. *History of the Manufacture of Iron in All Ages, and Particularly in the United States from Colonial Times to 1891.* Philadelphia, 1892.

Sylvis, James C. *The Life, Speeches, Labors and Essays of William H. Sylvis.* Philadelphia, 1872.

Taft, Philip. *Organized Labor in American History.* New York, 1964.

Takaki, Ronald T. *A Pro-Slavery Crusade: The Agitation to Reopen the African Slave Trade.* New York, 1971.

Taussig, Frank W. *The Tariff History of the United States.* 7th ed. New York, 1923.

Taylor, George Rogers. *The Transportation Revolution, 1815–1860.* New York, 1951.

Taylor, William R. *Cavalier and Yankee: The Old South and American National Character.* New York, 1969.

Temin, Peter. "The Panic of 1857." *Intermountain Economic Review,* VI (1975), 1–12.

Thomas, Benjamin P. *Abraham Lincoln: A Biography.* New York, 1952.

Thompson, William Y. *Robert Toombs of Georgia.* Baton Rouge, 1966.

Thornton, J. Mills, III. *Politics and Power in a Slave Society: Alabama, 1800–1860.* Baton Rouge, 1978.

Trefousse, Hans L. *Benjamin Franklin Wade: Radical Republican from Ohio.* New York, 1963.

Trescott, Paul B. *Financing American Enterprise: The Story of Commercial Banking.* New York, 1963.

Troy, Leo. *Organized Labor in New Jersey.* Princeton, N.J., 1965.

Unger, Irwin. *The Greenback Era: A Social and Political History of American Finance, 1865–1879.* Princeton, N.J., 1964.

Van Deusen, Glyndon G. *Horace Greeley: Nineteenth Century Crusader.* New York, 1953.

————. *Thurlow Weed: Wizard of the Lobby.* Boston, 1947.

————. *William Henry Seward.* New York, 1967.

Van Deusen, John G. *The Ante-Bellum Southern Commercial Conventions.* Durham, N.C., 1926.

Van Vleck, George Washington. *The Panic of 1857: An Analytical Study.* New York, 1943.

Vatter, Harold G. *The Drive to Industrial Maturity: The U.S. Economy, 1860–1914.* Westport, Conn., 1975.

Walkowitz, Daniel J. *Worker City, Company Town: Iron and Cotton-Worker Protest in Troy and Cohoes, New York, 1855–84.* Urbana, Ill., 1978.

Warden, Robert B. *An Account of the Private Life and Public Services of Salmon Portland Chase.* Cincinnati, 1874.

Ware, Norman. *The Industrial Worker, 1840–1860: The Reaction of American Industrial Society to the Advance of the Industrial Revolution.* 1924; rpr. Chicago, 1964.

Welter, Rush. *The Mind of America, 1820–1860.* New York, 1975.

Wender, Herbert. *Southern Commercial Conventions, 1837–1859.* Baltimore, 1930.

Wicker, E. R. "Railroad Investment Before the Civil War." In *Trends in the American Economy in the Nineteenth Century.* Princeton, N.J., 1960. Vol. XXIV of Conference on Research in Income and Wealth, *Studies in Income and Wealth.*

Williamson, Jeffrey G. *American Growth and the Balance of Payments, 1820–1913: A Study of the Long Swing.* Chapel Hill, 1964.

Wish, Harvey. *George Fitzhugh: Propagandist of the Old South.* Baton Rouge, 1943.

Woodward, C. Vann. "George Fitzhugh, *Sui Generis.*" Introduction to George Fitzhugh, *Cannibals All! or Slaves Without Masters.* Edited by C. Vann Woodward. Cambridge, Mass., 1960.

Wooster, Ralph A. *The People in Power: Courthouse and Statehouse in the Lower South, 1850–1860.* Knoxville, 1969.

Wright, Gavin. *The Political Economy of the Cotton South: Households, Markets, and Wealth in the Nineteenth Century.* New York, 1978.

DISSERTATIONS

Collins, Bruce William. "The Politics of Particularism: Economic Issues in the Major Northern States of the U.S.A., 1857–1858." Ph.D. dissertation, Cambridge University, England, 1975.

Ecke, Melvin Willard. "The Fiscal Aspects of the Panic of 1857." Ph.D. dissertation, Princeton University, 1951.

Faler, Paul Gustaf. "Workingmen, Mechanics and Social Change: Lynn, Massachusetts, 1800–1860." Ph.D. dissertation, University of Wisconsin, 1971.

Kuhn, Madison Alexander. "Economic Issues and the Rise of the Republican Party in the Northwest." Ph.D. dissertation, University of Chicago, 1940.

Petersen, Roger Dewey. "The Reaction to a Heterogeneous Society: A Behavioral and Quantitative Analysis of Northern Voting Behavior 1845–1870, Pennsylvania a Test Case." Ph.D. dissertation, University of Pittsburgh, 1970.

Pitkin, Thomas Monroe. "The Tariff and the Early Republican Party." Ph.D. dissertation, Western Reserve University, 1935.

Index